DATE DUE

DEMCO, INC. 38-2931

Cultures under Siege

Collective Violence and Trauma

edited by

Antonius C. G. M. Robben

Utrecht University

Marcelo M. Suárez-Orozco

Harvard University

 CAMBRIDGE
UNIVERSITY PRESS

PUBLISHED BY THE PRESS SYNDICATE OF THE UNIVERSITY OF CAMBRIDGE
The Pitt Building, Trumpington Street, Cambridge, United Kingdom

CAMBRIDGE UNIVERSITY PRESS
The Edinburgh Building, Cambridge CB2 2RU, UK   www.cup.cam.ac.uk
40 West 20th Street, New York, NY 10011-4211, USA   www.cup.org
10 Stamford Road, Oakleigh, Melbourne 3166, Australia
Ruiz de Alarcón 13, 28014 Madrid, Spain

First published 2000

Printed in the United Kingdom at the University Press, Cambridge

Typeface Plantin 10/12 pt   *System* 3b2   [CE]

A catalogue record for this book is available from the British Library

Library of Congress Cataloguing in Publication data
Cultures under siege: collective violence and trauma / edited by
Antonius C. G. M. Robben, Marcelo M. Suárez-Orozco.
    p.   cm. – (Publications of the Society for Psychological Anthropology)
ISBN 0 521 78026 8 (hb) – ISBN 0 521 78435 2 (pb)
1. Violence – Cross-cultural studies.
2. Collective behavior – Cross-cultural studies.
3. Violence – Psychological aspects.   4. Ethnopsychology.
5. Political violence.   6. Genocide.
I. Robben, Antonius C. G. M., 1953–
II. Suárez-Orozco, Marcelo M., 1956–   III. Series.
HM886.C85 2000
303.6–dc21   99–049062   CIP

ISBN 0 521 78026 8 hardback
ISBN 0 521 78435 2 paperback

For Robert A. LeVine

Contents

x   Contents

Preface

The unimaginable suffering and systematic devastation in Kosovo, the highly orchestrated programme of ethnic cleansing and rape in Bosnia, and the well-organized genocidal killings in Rwanda are recent examples of some of the terrible atrocities we have witnessed during the late twentieth century. Will the twenty-first century augur more horror and suffering? While no one can answer that question, even a casual survey of the last century's atrocities and its traumatic consequences suggests that we must continue to ponder such an ominous future. We hope that this volume will contribute in three ways to the understanding of future outbreaks of collective, large-scale violence and the multiple traumas they generate: first, by emphasizing that violence and trauma should be studied and analyzed in conjunction, rather than separately; secondly, by advancing an interdisciplinary approach to violence and trauma; and thirdly, by focusing on intra-psychic as well as social and cultural processes, by paying explicit attention to the effects of violence and trauma on both the individual and the social group.

The image on the frontispiece of this book captures many of its major themes. David Seymour took this photograph of a girl named Tereska in 1948 in a Polish residence for traumatised children. Tereska had grown up in a concentration camp, and her drawing on the blackboard was her representation of 'home'. We have chosen this timeless image of human suffering because the majority of the papers in this collection refer to traumatised children, their resiliency in violent contexts, and the importance of the home for them.

This collection brings together multi-level analytic approaches that cross over the traditional social science disciplinary boundaries by involving psychoanalysts, cultural psychologists, and social anthropologists. It is the result of a dialogue over half a decade among colleagues working in many different parts of the world. Their international standing and their commitment to interdisciplinary research on violence and trauma distinguish the scholars involved in this project.

We are grateful to many institutions for their support, especially critical during the earliest phases of this work. A core group was able to meet in Cambridge, Massachusetts, upon the initiative of Antonius Robben to prepare the agenda for the subsequent workshop in Europe. This meeting was made possible by a generous grant from the Innovation Fund of the Rockefeller Foundation. We are grateful to the Department of Human Development and Psychology at Harvard University for facilitating that first encounter. A grant from the Rockefeller Foundation allowed us to convene a larger group at the Foundation's Bellagio Study and Conference Center in Bellagio, Italy. The conference was entitled *Civilization and Its Enduring Discontents: Violence and Aggression in Psychoanalytic and Anthropological Perspective*, and was held on 2–6 September 1996. This volume contains one-half of the papers presented at the workshop. We want to thank Gilbert Herdt and Bonno Thoden van Velzen for co-organizing the conference. We would also like to extend our gratitude to Susan Garfield of the Bellagio Center Office in New York, and the staff of Villa Serbelloni in Italy, in particular Gianna Celli, Pasquale Pesce, and Andrea Gilerdoni, for hosting this international meeting with great hospitality and professionalism. Naomi Quinn, Editor of the Society for Psychological Anthropology Series with Cambridge University Press, did a superb job guiding this project through its various phases. Her patience, good humour, and wisdom were greatly appreciated. We thank Jessica Kuper of Cambridge University Press for bringing this project to a successful completion. Finally, we dedicate this volume to Robert A. LeVine whose life's work best captures the spirit of interdisciplinary collaboration that gave birth to this project.

ANTONIUS C. G. M. ROBBEN
MARCELO M. SUÁREZ-OROZCO

Acknowledgement

We thank International Universities Press, Inc for permission to quote a section of text from Rangell, I. & Moses-Hrushovski, R. (eds) (1996) 'The Interminable Uncanniness' by Yolanda Gampel, in *Psychoanalysis at the Political Border, Essays in Honor of Rafael Moses*, pp. 88–89 (2 pages).

Contributors

ROBERTA J. APFEL, MD, MPH, is Clinical Associate Professor of Psychiatry at the Harvard Medical School (Beth Israel-Deaconess Hospital) and on the Faculty of the Boston Psychoanalytic Society and Institute. She is co-editor of *Minefields in Their Hearts: The Mental Health of Children in War and Communal Violence.*

KATHERINE PRATT EWING is Associate Professor of Cultural Anthropology and Director of Graduate Studies in Cultural Anthropology at Duke University and Chair of Duke's South Asia Committee. She is the author of *Arguing Sainthood: Modernity, Psychoanalysis and Islam,* and editor of the volume *Shari'at and Ambiguity in South Asia Islam.*

YOLANDA GAMPEL is a Professor of Psychology in the Faculty of Social Sciences, the Department of Psychology, and in the School of Psychotherapy in the medical school at Tel Aviv University. She is a training analyst in and past president of the Israel Psychoanalytical Association.

NORMAN ITZKOWITZ is a Professor of Ottoman History in the Department of Near Eastern Studies at Princeton University. He is the author of *Ottoman Empire and Islamic Tradition* and, in addition, he has co-authored three books with Vamik Volkan, *The Immortal Atatürk*; *Richard Nixon: A Psychobiography*; and *Turks and Greeks: Neighbours in Conflict.*

DAVID J. DE LEVITA is a child psychiatrist, and a training and supervising analyst in Amsterdam. He is emeritus Professor of Transgenerational Sequelae of War at the Catholic University of Nijmegen, the Netherlands. He is the author of *The Concept of Identity,* and co-editor of *Adolescentie Vandaag* (original in Dutch). A consultant of the Johannes Wier Foundation for the Protection of Human Rights and the organization Wings of Hope, David de Levita has in recent years conducted workshops in Albania and the former Yugoslavia to train local professionals in the treatment of war traumata.

T. M. LUHRMANN is Professor of Anthropology at the University of California, San Diego. Her publications include *Persuasions of the Witch's Craft*, *The Good Parsi*, and the forthcoming *Of Two Minds: The Growing Disorder of American Psychiatry*.

ANTONIUS C. G. M. ROBBEN is Professor of Anthropology at Utrecht University, the Netherlands. He is the author of *Sons of the Sea Goddess: Economic Practice and Discursive Conflict in Brazil*, and co-editor (with Carolyn Nordstrom) of *Fieldwork under Fire: Contemporary Studies of Violence and Survival*. He is past President of the Netherlands Society of Anthropology.

BENNETT SIMON, MD, is Clinical Professor of Psychiatry at the Harvard Medical School (Cambridge Hospital), and training and supervising analyst at the Boston Psychoanalytic Society and Institute. He is co-editor of *Minefields in Their Hearts: The Mental Health of Children in War and Communal Violence*.

CAROLA SUÁREZ-OROZCO is a Lecturer and Senior Research Associate in Human Development and Psychology at the Harvard Graduate School of Education. She is the co-director of the Harvard Immigration Projects and the co-principal investigator of a five-year longitudinal study of immigrant adolescent adaptation to schools and society. Her book, co-authored with Marcelo Suárez-Orozco, entitled *Transformations: Migration, Family Life, and Achievement Motivation Among Latino Adolescents*, won the 1996 Social Policy Book Award from the Society for Research on Adolescence.

MARCELO M. SUÁREZ-OROZCO is Professor of Human Development and Psychology, co-director of the Harvard Immigration Project, chair of the Interfaculty Committee on Latino Studies, and a member of the Executive Committee of the David Rockefeller Center for Latin American Studies at Harvard University. His most recent books include *Transformations: Migration, Family Life, and Achievement Motivation Among Latino Adolescents*, co-authored with Carola Suárez-Orozco, and the edited volume *Crossings: Mexican Immigration in Interdisciplinary Perspectives*.

VAMIK D. VOLKAN, MD, is Professor of Psychiatry and director of the Center for the Study of Mind and Human Interaction, University of Virginia School of Medicine. The author of some thirty books on clinical and psychopolitical topics, his most recent publications include *Bloodlines: From Ethnic Pride to Ethnic Terrorism*, and *Das Versagen der Diplomatie: Zur Psychoanalyse nationaler, ethnischer und religiser Konflikte* (original in German).

1 Interdisciplinary perspectives on violence and trauma[1]

Marcelo M. Suárez-Orozco and Antonius C. G. M. Robben

The purpose of this volume is to broaden the dialogue between psycho-analysis and anthropology. We do so by focusing on a set of empirical and theoretical issues around the study of violence and trauma in comparative perspective. Can psychoanalysis and anthropology develop and sustain a mutually intelligible and fruitful conversation around the enduring problem of collective violence and massive trauma? How can this conversation negotiate the fact that psychoanalysts apply their craft to the intra-psychic level of analysis while anthropologists focus on the socio-cultural level? What are the necessary parameters for such conversation?

This book is based on the claim that for a variety of empirical and theoretical reasons an interdisciplinary dialogue on large-scale violence and trauma can indeed lead to the mutual enrichment of both anthro-pology and psychoanalysis. First, large-scale violence takes place in complex and over-determined socio-cultural contexts which intertwine psychic, social, political, economic, and cultural dimensions. Secondly, collective violence cannot be reduced to a single level of analysis because it targets the body, the psyche, as well as the socio-cultural order. Thirdly, the understanding of trauma cannot be restricted to the intra-psychic processes of the individual sufferer because it involves highly relevant social and cultural processes. Fourthly, the consequences of massive trauma afflict not only individuals but also social groups and cultural formations.

The twentieth century brought us some of the most barbaric episodes of large-scale violence and trauma. The Holocaust, the Cambodian killing fields, the unprecedented state terror generated by the Latin American counter-insurgency campaigns, the organized ethnic cleans-ings and sexual assaults in the former Yugoslavia, and the carefully

---

[1] We thank Carola Suárez-Orozco for her insightful comments on an earlier draft of this chapter.

1

orchestrated inter-ethnic bloodbaths in Rwanda and Burundi are recent examples. They suggest a unique and enduring human capacity for highly elaborate *collective forms of violence and destructiveness* which cannot be reduced simplistically to either 'natural' or 'cultural' causes. This book does not engage the old-fashioned binary 'nature–nurture' polemic. The tired old claim that it is the nature of our genetic blueprint to be efficient killers is as irrelevant to the present effort as the counter-claim that to unlock the secrets of our darkness we must keep our gaze on social institutions and cultural formations – such as on genocidal 'cultural models' of eliminationist racism (Goldhagen 1996).[2] The reductionism of the first variety collapses under the weight of ideology, religion, ethnicity, gender, and class – cultural formations that chisel the human capacity for destruction into seemingly endless designs. The 'culturalists' in the nature–nurture coin often face the trap of circular reasoning as well as the formidable task of having to account for the overwhelmingly diverse sets of cultures and levels of social organization managing stunningly destructive feats (see Ingham 1996:196–221; Edgerton 1992). The space worth cultivating, we claim, is somewhere between those two analytical dead-ends.

Although aggression is hardly the monopoly of the human species, humans alone have developed the higher-order neocortical capacities – the very capacities that separate us from other species in the animal kingdom – for efficient, systematized, and over-determined acts of collective violence. In the eternal words of Freud, 'Man is a wolf to man. Who in the face of all his experience of life and of history will have the courage to dispute this assertion' (Freud 1930:111). In the more technical words of psychological anthropologist John Ingham:

Organized violence has occurred, and continues to occur, at every level of social complexity. Murder and feuding were frequent among hunter-gatherers, peoples sometimes thought to be relatively peaceful. Headhunting and murderous retribution against suspected sorcerers were common among horticultural societies. Many tribal societies were warlike. Most preindustrial states were militaristic, and some even ritualized their hegemony with human sacrifice. And wars between states and, increasingly, terrorism and ethnic violence are commonplaces in the modern world (Ingham 1996:196).

This volume examines a variety of manifestations of organized vio-lence and massive trauma reflecting a commitment to interdisciplinary dialogue. How are cultural identities implicated in and reshaped by

---

[2] Goldhagen, for example, in his best selling book reduces the Holocaust to German culture. He writes 'many Germans willingly brutalized and killed Jews and did so because they grew up in a culture where a virulent form of anti-Semitism was commonplace' (1996:38).

large-scale violence? How are collective violence and mourning encoded into cultural narratives and how are such narratives psychologically implicated in the transgenerational workings of trauma? How do second-generation survivors cope with the inherent 'radioactivity' of massive trauma? How are cultural formations, including symbols, folk models, and rituals mobilized to inscribe, resist, and heal trauma? What psychocultural processes are involved in children's responses to violence? How are gender differences played out in the sequelae of violence?

There is of course a history to the relationship between psychoanalysis and anthropology – a history that is too complex to summarize here (see Suárez-Orozco 1994). Many leading psychoanalysts since Freud have had enduring interests in cultural formations and the comparative record. Freud himself, for better or worse, read with great gusto the leading social theorists – including the proto-anthropologists of his day – and articulated various theoretical constructs on a variety of ethnographic matters – including totemism, magic, and ritual.

While previous interdisciplinary conversations between anthropology and psychoanalysis proved uneven – with dismal failures (remember the 'swaddling hypothesis'?) as well as exciting developments (such as the Linton–Kardiner seminar at Columbia) – the dialogue has been rather focused on a handful of themes. Ubiquitous among them have been (1) the debate over the Oedipus complex; (2) the relationships between the cultural patterning of childrearing, personality, and social institutions; and (3) culture and mental illness. While a number of prominent psychological anthropologists have worked on issues of aggression (see, *inter alia*, Hallowell 1940; Kluckhohn 1962; Spiro 1978; and Edgerton 1997 and 1992) our objective is to expand the dialogue systematically to include issues of large-scale violence and trauma.

Why be interdisciplinary? Interdisciplinary efforts interrupt the taken-for-granted practices that can bureaucratize disciplinary work. Interdisciplinary work imposes certain mutual calibrations of theoretical models, methodological strategies, and analytic perspectives. By definition interdisciplinary work subverts the reductionistic impulses common to many disciplinary enterprises. Furthermore, the different professional practices of anthropologists and psychoanalysts have direct effects on the interdisciplinary study of violence and trauma, which should be mined for the enrichment of both disciplines.

As in other fields of inquiry in the human sciences, some observers – among them victims of massive trauma – have questioned the validity of *any* outsider's analytical perspectives – let alone interdisciplinary efforts. These observers have argued that only 'first-hand' experience can lead to authentic knowledge. While from the vantage point of the late twentieth century most social scientists are well aware of the problem of positionality in scholarship of this sort, we make a plea for the complementary significance that is a *sine qua non* of interdisciplinary work. We therefore reject mono-causal explanations and advocate the use of processual, multi-levelled approaches grounded in solid understandings of the inner psychic processes as well as the social and cultural contexts of large-scale violence and trauma (Mays *et al.* 1998; see also De Vos and Suárez-Orozco 1990).

In the next section, we examine the ways in which trauma and violence have been conceptual meeting grounds for earlier generations of anthropologists and psychoanalysts. This is not intended to be an exhaustive review of interdisciplinary approaches to large-scale violence and massive trauma. Rather, it serves to place the chapters in this book in a genealogical conceptual history.

The historical development of the concept of massive trauma from 'shell shock' to 'post-traumatic stress disorder' reveals remarkable periods of cross-fertilization between the disciplines of anthropology and psychoanalysis. There have also been moments of considerable distancing, mutual neglect, and basic distrust.

We hope to demonstrate how several path-breaking concepts such as those emerging from studies of the Holocaust can be applied to the interpretation of large-scale violence and massive trauma in other societies. The work on second-generation Holocaust survivors is particularly important for a theoretical understanding of one of the fundamental problems in the study of trauma: its transgenerational transmission from parents to children to grandchildren. We highlight the social practices and cultural models that are relevant to the understanding of such transgenerational processes.

After examining some of the critical contributions to the study of trauma, we turn to the study of large-scale violence. Our point of departure is Freud's complex, multi-faceted, and often contradictory explanations of human aggression and violence. The Freud of *Civilization and Its Discontents* presents a somewhat different hypothesis on human aggression and violence than the Freud of *Beyond the Pleasure Principle*. Much of his work of course has been superseded by more sophisticated psychoanalytic interpretations and falsified by superior ethnographic knowledge. Nevertheless, Freud's ideas deserve attention because they have inspired many students of violence and trauma. We then proceed with a critical appraisal of various disparate psychoanalytic interpretations of aggression and violence – from Melanie Klein's innate theories of aggression to Erich Fromm's interdisciplinary approach to human destructiveness. We critique these works on empirical and theoretical grounds. Next, we discuss some more recent psychoanalytic ideas about the 'reactive' nature of human aggression. These ideas require still further theoretical development in the area of violence and trauma, but are promising new avenues of inquiry which find an implicit resonance in anthropological studies.

The chapters in this volume are organized into two parts. Part I addresses *the management of collective trauma.* Part II discusses *cultural responses to collective trauma.* The chapters in this book suggest that social violence continues to pursue its victims long after the slaughter ends and the peace treaties are signed. The work of Robben, Gampel, Apfel and Simon, Luhrmann, de Levita, and Volkan and Itzkowitz examine the various ways violence continues to shape the inner, interpersonal, and socio-cultural worlds of victims and their children. And because social violence always aims at a multiplicity of fields it, in turn, generates multiple sequelae. On the physical and psychic level, the work of healing most often includes some effort to restore some semblance of basic trust. The data in this book suggest that this work is quite complex, open-ended, and far from always successful. While the work of de Levita and Apfel and Simon suggest that massively traumatized children may, under certain conditions, make significant progress, the transgenerational data (see Gampel) suggest a cautious interpretation of long-term outcomes.

Luhrmann, Ewing, and C. Suárez-Orozco suggest that, on the socio-cultural level, the work of healing also involves the issue of 'basic trust' – this time reconstructing trust in the social institutions and cultural practices that structure experience and give meaning to human lives. Large-scale violence and massive trauma disintegrate trust in the social structures that make human life possible. Institutional acknowledgment – in the form of 'truth' commissions and reparations (monetary and symbolic) – and justice – in the form of trials of perpetrators – can begin partially to restore the symbolic order that is another casualty of the work of violence.

This volume does not draw a firm line between what might be called 'hard' violence (physical) and 'soft' violence (symbolic or psychological). Like the lines in many maps, such division would be artificial, arbitrary, and even dangerous. Physical violence may be easier to identify, name, and quantify than psychic or symbolic violence. We can always do a body count, discern patterns in the amputation of limbs, or explore a torturer's agenda by the marks he leaves in his victim's body. On the other hand, the workings of psychic and symbolic violence are often more elusive but may be equally devastating in the long run.

Towards an interdisciplinary dialogue on violence and trauma

Why have entire nations collapsed and consumed themselves with hatred and destructiveness? How are we, at the start of the twenty-first century, to think about the recurrence of rape camps, torture camps, and ethnic camps? Just what *is* the answer to Einstein's famous question: 'Is there a way to liberate mankind from the doom of war?' (Einstein 1978:1)? In the last decades of the twentieth century we have witnessed the resurgence of systematized torture, forced disappearances, group rapes, and ethnic massacres and 'cleansings' as organized practices for dealing with historical and cultural *chagrins*, political dissent, ideological orthodoxy, and ethnic and gender difference.[3] Interdisciplinary explora-

[3] Systems of organized violence are anchored in various ideological structures. We use the term 'ideology' to refer to the 'doctrines, opinions, or ways of thinking of an individual or class' (Webster 1983:902). Ideologies of hatred and terror may include pseudoscientific notions of biological inferiority and fear of pollution (Nazism).

Some recent ideologies of hatred have developed intertwining pseudo-sociological notions of 'cultural inferiority' (the new anti-immigration and racist movements in Europe and the US), or ethnic incompatibility and hatred (such as in the former Yugoslavia and in the Hutu–Tutsi case). Neo-nazi anti-immigrant groups in Europe share a cultural narcissism: there is a fear that somehow the foreigners will pollute and injure Europe's 'culture' (language, mores, way of life). The logic of pollution remains but no longer based on pseudo-biological arguments. Ideologies of hatred leading to massive social violence have fixated on historical fictions of lost privilege, or cultural narcissistic injuries (Germany after Versailles; the Greek–Turkish disputes explored by Volkan and Itzkowitz; the suicide bombers described by Apfel and Simon). A great deal of ideological hatred has been grounded on deadly political obsessions over orthodoxy (Stalinism, Pol Pot, and various recent anti-Communist regimes in Latin America). Religious scripts have fed ideologies of hatred (the Jews as Christ-killers). If rage in loss, endangerment, and mourning offers the psychological framework to systematized violence, ideology offers it an intellectual and moral framework.

Organized systems of terror always are guided by an intellectual framework. The Nazis operated with European fantasies of biological superiority by claiming a link to the Aryans, the upper caste conquerors of the Indic subcontinent. They updated and refined ancient European hatred of the Jews ('the Christ-killers': Fromm 1973:305) with pseudo-scientific claims of superiority. Biological purity had to be guarded by eliminating biologically inferior groups.

In the recent Argentine 'dirty war' (see Robben, in this volume), the so-called 'Doctrine of National Security' gave the Generals an intellectual framework for their actions. The anti-communist ideology of the Cold War offered the theoretical framework that led to the creation of a state-operated Dantesque machinery of illegal kidnappings and torture, and the deaths of thousands of innocent non-combatants.

Ideological frameworks may be laced with messianic fantasies and harsh moralistic dictates: the end of our way of life is near, everything must be done to prevent this. Sagan's (1988) notion of the 'corrupt superego' is particularly relevant here: in a terrorist system it is the corrupt superego that dictates that a group must be eliminated in the name of a grand cause.

During the Cold War, communism and anti-communism served as powerful ideologies for the organization of hatred and for structuring violence. Paradoxically, the terror of a nuclear holocaust served as an effective force to keep in check hatreds based

tions of psychological, social, and cultural frameworks can generate important answers to such unsettling questions.

How can we do analytical justice to collective violence and trauma, without unduly distorting the shattering experiences of the victims? Is Elie Wiesel right when he argues: 'The truth of Auschwitz remains hidden in its ashes. Only those who lived it in their flesh and in their minds can possibly transform their experience into knowledge. Others, despite their best intentions, can never do so' (Wiesel 1990:166)? Are we condemned to succumb to the executioner's victory over truth, understanding, and imagination? Is, paraphrasing Adorno's famous words, to write social science after Auschwitz barbaric? How can we create a space where the urgency for action and the necessity to inscribe and understand do not overwhelm each other?

While Adorno's warning does not preclude the scientific analysis of genocide, mass extermination, and large-scale violence, it does highlight the unbridgeable gap between the theoretical models at our disposal and the unfathomable depths of human suffering. On the other hand, Raul Hilberg, in his monumental three-volume *The Destruction of the European Jews*, has argued that, although the suffering is unique to each individual, the testimonies of many survivors are indeed remarkably similar. Hilberg's claim – a claim we share – is that the professional duty of the social scientist is to analyze those patterns and attempt to (re)construct the past, without pretending to have grasped the horror in its myriad manifestations (Hilberg 1988). Furthermore, victims, perpetrators, eyewitnesses, writers, and scientists alike are all condemned to the restrictions of representation. Understanding surely depends on which events are remembered, how these memories are given form, and through which perspective they are analyzed (Young 1988:1–3).

Perhaps the most serious paradox we face is an awareness that massive trauma is in important ways inherently incomprehensible. Cathy Caruth (1995, 1996) has wisely argued that traumatic events are by definition incomprehensible because partial forgetting is a defining characteristic of trauma. This inability of the traumatized to recover fully the traumatic event, and the failure to integrate the 'uncanny' experiences into consciousness (see also Gampel, in this volume), may be logically extended into literature and science. The refusal to force the inexplicable into interpretational schemata and, instead, to bear witness, to listen, and to allow testimony to unfold itself with all its contra-

on religious and ethnic differences. With the demise of the Soviet Union as a viable political project, and with the collapse of the Soviet Union as a broker in the balance of nuclear terror, ideologies of hatred are once again thriving along cultural, religious, and ethnic lines.

dictions and enigmas, is an alternative way of communicating massive trauma to the world.[4]

The essays included in this volume share a vision that the complexities of large-scale violence and trauma – their origins, structures, and consequences – are best approached from interdisciplinary and multi-layered perspectives. Although psychodynamic variables, such as narcissistic injury and pathological mourning, may be critical for understanding violence, it is unwise to underestimate the role of social, economic, and institutional factors in organizing the human capacity for destructiveness into powerful cultural forms.[5] Reducing organized violence to the 'death instinct', or to group frustration leading to

---

[4] See Felman and Laub (1992) on the affective and epistemological difficulties of bearing witness to testimonies of massive trauma.

[5] We must keep in mind the economic foundations of violence. Economic forces may be a powerful instigator of social violence. Certainly, terror often yields significant wealth. The lavish lifestyle of the Nazis and the shady dealings of Swiss World War Two bankers come to mind.

A number of scholars have been interested in outlining the economic motives behind systems of violence. Chomsky, for example, has pointed out the extraordinary gains often associated with social violence and domination. Chomsky has claimed that a principal mission of US diplomacy has been to guarantee a steady flow of natural resources and a favourable business and investment climate in the Third World. Preferably, these goals are achieved in a democratic climate. However, if state terror and dictatorial rule are needed to secure US interests, then so be it (1993:30). Chomsky argues that: 'In the post-World War II era, the US has been the global enforcer, guaranteeing the interests of privilege. It has, therefore, compiled an impressive record of aggression, international terrorism, slaughter, torture, chemical and bacteriological warfare, [and] human rights abuses of every imaginable variety' (Chomsky 1993:31). For Chomsky economic greed is a most powerful force for human destructiveness.

Taussig (1987) has likewise highlighted some of the economic foundations of violence. Taussig explored the terror which flourished in the Anglo-Peruvian rubber plantations in the Putumayo districts of southwestern Colombia at the turn of the century. Taussig relates terror to the political economy of the colonial 'encounter' (crush might be a more appropriate word) between 'capitalism' and what Taussig calls (others reject his claims) 'pre-capitalist' forms of production. Terror, Taussig argues, was employed to 'recruit' the Indians through debt, into an economic system of commodity fetishism which they resisted as foreign to their hearts. According to Taussig, the capitalist process of ever expanding commodification is so destructive and inhuman that a 'culture of terror' emerged where torture and other obscene rituals of depreciation became the idiom mediating the clash of two worlds in the colonial enterprise. The violence in the Putumayo was, according to Taussig, only a local version of a global movement. Terror is inevitable in the 'global stage of development of the commodity fetish; think also of the Congo with its rubber and ivory, of the enslavement of the Yaquis for the sisal plantations of the Yucatan in Mexico, of the genocidal bloodletting in tragic Patagonia – all around the same time' (Taussig 1987:129).

There are, of course, some limitations to an economic approach to social violence. Reducing organized violence to economic motive tends to ignore the vastly irrational and counter-productive (from a cost–benefit perspective) aspects of terror. It has been noted, for example, that the energy and resources the Germans devoted to the Holocaust may have indeed fatally weakened their war effort against the allies.

aggression, simply neglects the axiomatic fact that *it is only in the context of over-determined socio-cultural climates* that violence becomes organized and evolves into death camps, rape camps, and torture camps.[6] The questions we ask in our conversations avoid 'silver bullets', single origins, and mechanistic causation. None of the authors involved in this volume believes in a single explanation or a single origin of human

---

6 As Apfel and Simon explore in their chapter, social institutions provide the tools, the know-how, and the psychological support for the conduction of systematic atrocities. There is a 'bureaucracy of terror' required to build and operate concentration camps, rape camps, and torture camps. Such institutions might be special units like the SS, death squads such as in El Salvador and South Africa, military schools such as the ESMA in Argentina (see Robben, in this volume; CONADEP 1984; Timerman 1981), and so forth. The Nazis counted on the efficient participation of talented German engineers to construct their monstrous death apparatus. These were men who were 'concerned with improving the performance of the equipment they modified for the purpose demanded by their Government: rapid and efficient cremation of human beings killed in gas chambers' (Fleming 1993:19).

Professional torturers, camp guards, and suicide bombers are not born but made (see Apfel and Simon, in this volume; see also Waller 1993:34–7). Social psychologists have made significant contributions to the psychology of the implementation of terror. Studies by Milgram (1974) on 'obedience to authority', by Zimbardo (1972) on imprisonment, and by Staub (1989) on 'learned disinhibition', reveal how under certain conditions of institutional authority and rigid hierarchy it seems frightfully easy to order individuals to commit atrocious acts.

Torturers, death squad members, and suicide bombers typically work in teams. They go to instruction camps where they learn who the enemy is and how to destroy it. Many US observers were shocked that 'almost three quarters of the Salvadorean officers accused in seven other massacres [in addition to the massacre of the six Jesuit priests at the Central American University] were trained by the Fort Benning school' (Waller 1993:34). Also known as the 'School for Dictators', the School of the Americas at Fort Benning in Georgia has 'trained more than 56,000 Latin soldiers in combat and counterinsurgency skills' (Waller 1993:34). Some of the School's most notorious graduates include Manuel Noriega (class of '65 and '67), the Panamanian general-turned-drug-trafficker; Leopoldo Galtieri (class of '46), an Argentine 'dirty warrior', and architect of the disastrous invasion of the Malvinas/Falklands Islands; and Roberto D'Aubuisson, the reported intellectual father of the Salvadorean death squads (Waller 1993:34).

Institutions of terror provide not only the technical support but also the *psychological support* required to conduct organized terror. Members of such institutions must develop a sense of righteousness about their cause. There is a sense of brotherhood sealed by the blood spilled together. New members may be sent for special assignments (tortures, massacres, etc.) to gain entry into the group. These groups may be sealed off from other groups with less brutal tasks. There is a sense of common purpose and destiny. Non-group members may be seen as inferior, weak, or lacking the courage required to accomplish the momentous crusade.

According to some scholars, institutions of terror play an essential role in generating forms of power (see Scarry 1985; Taussig 1992). Elaine Scarry (1985) in her book on torture and war has argued that the terror manufactured in state-operated torture rooms is critical to creating forms of state power. The electricity discharged through cattle-prods in the torture chambers 'generates' much of the power in highly unstable regimes. The Salvadorean death squads and torture chambers working under the control of the armed forces (see Waller 1993) seemed to be busiest when the regime was being critically challenged by the insurgency.

violence. Nor do we believe that collective violence can be explained in a mechanistic paradigm. No hydraulic models are offered in this volume (Lorenz 1966).

Our specific questions are grounded on experience-near 'thick descriptions' of violence and trauma in a variety of social settings. We ask: How do cultural formations mediate violence and the work of mourning (Robben)? How do institutional contexts affect the psychocultural mechanisms children deploy when facing terror and violence (Apfel and Simon; and de Levita)? How is gender implicated in the experience of violence and trauma (de Levita; and Ewing)? How are identities, specifically ethnic and cultural identities, involved in the incubation of hostility and conflict leading to violence and trauma (Volkan and Itzkowitz)? How are cultural identities shaped and reshaped by the experience of trauma (C. Suárez-Orozco; and Luhrmann)? How does 'memory' – personal, historical, and cultural – relate to the intergenerational forces that perpetuate trauma (Gampel)?

The papers rely on a variety of data sets, including interview materials, the psychoanalytic encounter, the ethnographic encounter, and historical, archival, and media sources. The materials have been gathered, in all cases first hand, in a variety of settings, including Slovenia, Cyprus, Greece, Israel, Turkey, the United States, India, and Argentina.

All papers engage issues of violence and trauma on a scale that involves large social groups. While a number of psychoanalysts have examined the individual and familial dynamics in violence and trauma (see for example Klein and Riviere 1964; Kohut 1972; Kernberg 1992; and Mitchell 1993), only a few have explored violence and trauma as large-scale socio-cultural formations involving groups of peoples – communities, ethnicities, or nations. Large-scale violence engenders dynamics that are unique and in some ways incommensurable with individual violence.[7]

Large-scale violence targets social bonds and cultural practices as much as it targets the body and the psyche. It is often carefully scripted to destroy elemental culturally constituted expectations and functions.

---

[7] Psychoanalysts have had much more to say about *some* forms of violence – including family violence – than about other forms of violence. An important theoretical issue in our conversation is whether the tools of the psychoanalytic project, best deployed to approach conscious and unconscious processes on an individual and small-group level, serve us as well to explore larger formations such as in ethnic, national, or post-national violence. And, if they do apply, and all of the authors involved in this project seem to agree that they do, what are the special problems of moving the psychoanalytic scalpel away from the consulting room to the refugee camp? The essays by Gampel, and Apfel and Simon in this volume explore these and other questions.

The mass and public rapings organized in the recent violence in the Balkans (Serbian soldiers raping Bosnian women) and Rwanda (Hutu soldiers raping Tutsi women) highlight the *socio-cultural* uses of violence. It was aimed, *inter alia*, at destroying fundamental cultural norms and kinship ties. In both Bosnia and Rwanda, fathers and mothers were made to witness the repeated brutal sexual assault of their daughters – destroying the most basic culturally constituted parental function: protect the children. In the words of human rights expert Ken Franzblau, such public rapings had:

> devastating effects on communities, particularly in traditional communities or very religious communities where virginity and the fidelity of women can be central to the make up of that society. Rape is a psychological grenade thrown into the middle of daily life to provoke maximum terror. That is why you see a fair number of these rapes committed in front of family members of the girls or women involved. (quoted in Crossette 1998:6)

Although the essays included in this book share a number of basic tenets, it is important to keep in mind that anthropologists and psychoanalysts belong to quite different intellectual traditions and professional cultures. They therefore approach violence and trauma from very different vantage points. That makes this conversation more difficult but ultimately, we think, more rewarding.

Psychoanalysts are trained to pay attention to the intrapsychic mechanisms mediating violence and trauma. What defence mechanisms are mobilized by extreme violence (Apfel and Simon; and de Levita)? How does the work of mourning relate to healing or, conversely, to new cycles of violence (Volkan and Itzkowitz)? What are the unconscious processes which come to dominate the treatment of victims of extreme violence and terror (Gampel)?

Anthropologists and cultural psychologists, on the other hand, work on interpersonal and socio-cultural formations around violence and terror. How are social institutions and structures involved in the reproduction of violence (Ewing)? How are deep social attachments (ab)used as weapons in the construction of a culture of terror (Robben)? How is trauma implicated in the forming of cultural identities (C. Suárez-Orozco; and Luhrmann)?

Beyond differences in theoretical and empirical style, anthropologists and psychoanalysts have quite different entry points into the problem of large-scale violence. All of the psychoanalysts involved in this volume became enwrapped in problems of large-scale violence in their 'therapeutic role'. For them, the therapeutic role became a causeway into complex theoretical and empirical questions.

The anthropologist's role is, under the best of circumstances, impossibly ambiguous.[8] This is perhaps why anthropologists (with precious few exceptions) have altogether avoided problems of large-scale violence and trauma – and when they found themselves in such contexts, for the most part, they chose not to work with the materials.[9] Unlike psychoanalysts, most anthropologists are not trained to offer therapeutic assistance to victims of massive violence. What, then, should be their role? Should the role of the anthropologist be limited to political activism and moral condemnation of violence? If anthropologists choose

[8] There may be another reason why anthropologists have tended to neglect the study of large-scale violence. There is now an unsettling convergence of fashionable postmodern thought and the manipulation of memory in the service of hatred. The postmodern notion that ethnographic representations are to be treated as arbitrary 'texts' or 'fictions' simply privileging certain capricious positions has a certain rhetorical appeal, particularly when treating quaint folkloristic phenomena like the cockfight or folk poetry. It opens up possibilities for playing certain linguistic games that were not possible before the postmodern moment. Issues of authorship, authority, and the construction of ethnographies can be playfully entertained.

 When turning to death camps, rape camps, and torture camps, the idea of treating events – and their representations – as 'fictions' becomes instantly repulsive. Fictions, be they literary, historical, or ethnographic, are, by definition, unreal fantasies, 'stories'. As cultural anthropology continues its affair with 'subjectivity' (see Suárez-Orozco 1994:8–59) and righteously renounces any 'scientific' pretensions, it is becoming a storyteller's craft.

 According to this new wave, an ethnographic 'story' is just one 'story', no better and perhaps no worse than countless other 'stories' in a sea of infinite capricious, arbitrary, and egoistic fictions. What, then, does a storyteller's anthropology have to offer the troubling *fin de siècle*? How can such an anthropology be of use to our understanding – and dismantling – of ethnic cleansings, rape camps, concentration camps, and torture camps (see Lipstadt 1993)?

 Psychoanalysis has taught us that one of the most important first steps in treating victims of systems of massive trauma is to acknowledge unequivocally the *reality* of the events they endured. As Grubrich-Simitis (1984) and Robben (1996) have noted, victims see in the analyst's emotional response to their harrowing accounts a confirmation of the reality of those traumatic experiences.

 Those who have known a world organized to terrorize and destroy them need, first and foremost, empathy and *acknowledgment* (Weschler 1990). The survivor needs confirmation of the reality of the unreal world that attempted systematically to destroy the ego and, with it, the 'reality principle'. They need acknowledgment of a world nobody is ready to believe could possibly exist (Suárez-Orozco 1992).

 Those advocating a storyteller's anthropology, surely unwittingly, are lending scholarly authority to the sinister attempts to deny the Holocaust, the Latin American 'dirty wars', and other recent episodes of organized destructiveness. Through a postmodern lens, they become just 'stories' or 'fictions'. This is repulsive in intellectual and in moral terms. In intellectual terms, it does violence to a historical period in which the cultivation of organized hatred took new and unparalleled dimensions. In moral terms, it does violence, albeit in another idiom, to the unspeakable suffering of millions. It subverts the mourning process – 'healthy' mourning requires acknowledging the trauma and loss.

[9] Incredibly there is no index entry under 'aggression' or 'violence' in Marvin Harris' (1968) well regarded book *The Rise of Anthropological Theory*. Likewise, Clifford Geertz, someone whose anthropological perspective is quite different from Harris', has until very recently (Geertz 1995:5–11) remained silent on the Balinese massacres.

to take this role, how is their work different from the work of human rights organizations such Amnesty International? The anthropologists involved in this volume, implicitly or explicitly, share a conviction that their task is to deploy the tools of their craft to document, inscribe, and help understand the socio-cultural processes and sequelae of violence and trauma.

Interdisciplinary explorations of massive trauma

Massive trauma inflicted deliberately on large groups of people by other human beings became a major psychiatric concern only during the First World War. Traumatic neuroses, the so-called fright neuroses (*Schreckneurosen*), had been studied at the beginning of the twentieth century but they concerned only small numbers of survivors of mining accidents, and natural disasters such as earthquakes and volcanic eruptions (Kolb 1993:294). The First World War brought millions of dead as well as millions of psychological casualties. The symptoms of combat trauma – crying fits, anxiety attacks, tremors, exhaustion, irritability, jumpiness, loss of appetite, apathy, depression – were at first diagnosed as a physical affliction of the nervous system caused by the concussive effects of exploding shells. However, battle fatigue or shell shock was also found among soldiers without any physical injuries. The symptoms were re-evaluated as a psychological trauma, and now were attributed to prolonged combat duty and the exposure to violent death. Puzzled by this unusual psychopathology, psychiatrists began to develop explanations that were reminiscent of late-nineteenth-century theories about female hysteria, the very hysteria which had drawn Freud to the French neurologist Jean-Martin Charcot at Salpêtrière hospital. Men suffering from shell shock were regarded as cowards and, very much as hysterical women, morally corrupt. The experience of war was believed to build a strong character and make men eager to sacrifice themselves for the fatherland (see Mosse 1990). This myth had to be sustained to replenish the ranks with enthusiastic volunteers who were willing to die in the rat-infested trenches – in search of honour and glory. Men with combat neurosis were court-martialled and discharged. Medical treatment – not to say torture – ranged from electric shocks to psychological intimidation.[10]

---

[10] For instance, the British neurologist Lewis Yealland applied hour-long electric shocks to the throat of a mute patient strapped to a chair. He also recommended the use of threats and inducing shame among traumatized patients.

Interdisciplinary beginnings: Rivers and Kardiner

The physician, psychologist, and anthropologist William H. R. Rivers contributed to a dramatic turn in the treatment of combat neurosis. Rivers had been a member of the famous Haddon expedition to the Torres Straits, and had a great interest in psychoanalysis. Like his fellow Melanesianist Bronislaw Malinowski, he was not convinced of the universality of the Oedipus complex or the sex drive, but he drew freely on psychoanalytic techniques when he became a captain in the Royal Army Medical Corps in 1916. Rivers was soon joined by Charles Seligman, another anthropologist from the Haddon expedition who had an interest in psychoanalysis (Stocking 1986:31).

The medical corps favoured two therapeutic regimes for the treatment of combat trauma. The 'disciplinary method' was based on animal training and tried to force patients into abandoning their symptoms by the infliction of pain. On the other hand, the 'analytic method' was based on the assumption that not repression of the symptoms but remembering the traumatic experiences was beneficial (Young 1995:67–71). Rivers did not use punishment and humiliation to cow the servicemen into combat readiness: rather he openly empathized with his patients, and favoured the 'talking cure' and dream analysis pioneered by Breuer and Freud. In particular, his successful treatment of the war hero and poet Siegfried Sassoon at Craiglockhart Hospital in Edinburgh drew much public interest at the time.[11]

Sassoon had returned with shell shock to Great Britain and had become an anti-war advocate. Rivers took Sassoon under his care and, after treatment, the young officer recanted his pacifist statements and departed again for the front in France. Rivers had demonstrated that even the brave could be paralyzed by fear, and that this fear could be surmounted, not by patriotism, but by the emotional attachment to the fighting comrades. Not moral character, but the severe stresses and group processes to which servicemen were exposed influenced the likelihood of combat trauma. Rivers' approach became the preferred treatment of combat neurosis and was adopted as standard practice by British and American psychiatrists until the Second World War (Herman 1992:22; Langham 1981:52–3; Slobodin 1978:59–65).[12]

Abram Kardiner, who had been influenced by Columbia anthropologist Franz Boas and the psychoanalyst Horace Frink, gave a new

---

[11] This work has recently been given new attention by Pat Barker's acclaimed novel *Regeneration* (1992).

[12] Young (1995:81–4) writes that the figure of Rivers has been misrepresented by Herman (1992), and disputes that Rivers was greatly influenced by Freud.

impetus to the study and treatment of combat trauma. In 1922, shortly after returning from his analysis with Freud in Vienna, Kardiner began to work in the New York Veterans Hospital. He was profoundly moved by the incurable distress of the First World War veterans, and tried to formulate a psychoanalytic theory of war trauma (Manson 1986:76). Unsuccessful, he returned to his private practice, and developed an interest in anthropology. His collaboration with Ralph Linton, a First World War veteran from the Rainbow Division, resulted in *The Individual and His Society* (1939). According to Judith Lewis Herman (1992:24): 'It was only then, after writing this book, that he was able to return to the subject of war trauma, this time having in anthropology a conceptual framework that recognized the impact of social reality and enabled him to understand psychological trauma.' For Kardiner, combat trauma did not arise from the stimulation of infantile conflicts but from the extreme duress of the violent environment.

Kardiner published in 1941 *The Traumatic Neuroses of War*, which was entirely based on his clinical work with First World War veterans. The revised edition of 1947 was co-authored by Herbert Spiegel who contributed his battlefield experiences from the Second World War. Kardiner's clinical description and treatment of combat trauma have remained important to this day, and represent his most enduring scientific contribution. Kardiner emphasized that camaraderie, morale, and strength of the officer–soldier tie were crucial in overcoming fear and preventing an emotional collapse. If the soldier suffered from combat trauma, then he had to relive his traumatic experiences through hypnosis, debriefing (a crash talking cure), or the use of drugs that provoked a catharsis, and then returned to his unit as soon as possible. Kardiner warned that these vehement catharses had to be consolidated into conscious awareness to prevent a relapse. However, the expediency of the war machine was more important than the lasting mental welfare of individual soldiers. The astonishing recovery rate of combat trauma patients (80 per cent were again on duty within one week, including 30 per cent who returned to combat missions) made military psychiatrists neglect their long-term care (Herman 1992:23–6; Kardiner and Spiegel 1947:360–5).

Human-made massive trauma was seen as an exclusive military affair until the Second World War because most casualties had always been inflicted on military personnel. The number of civilian casualties went from 5 per cent in the First World War, and 50 per cent in the Second World War to over 80 per cent in the Vietnam War (Summerfield 1995:17). Civilians were never, of course, immune to the deleterious effects of warfare. They were driven from their homes, suffered the loss of their sons, brothers, and husbands at distant fronts, and carried the economic burden of all-consuming wars. Still, their suffering was regarded as an unfortunate vicissitude of war, but not recognized as a traumatic experience in need of psychiatric care.

Disciplinary divergence: civilian trauma and the Second World War

The interwar years brought about massive trauma. Yet there was little professional attention to the survivors of the massacre of over 1 million Armenians in Turkey, the traumatized victims of the Russian and German pogroms, the civil war in Spain, the state-organized famines in the Ukraine, or the tens of millions of political prisoners rotting in Stalin's Gulag.

The Second World War would eventually bring about the treatment of massive trauma among large civilian populations. The unfathomable traumas inflicted in Japanese and Nazi Germany concentration camps demanded urgent professional attention. However, governments, health professionals, and also the survivors themselves were initially more ready to forget than recall the traumatic memories of the past. Many victims of violence seemed to recover rather well upon liberation, and seemed eager to get on with their lives. Psychic and psychosomatic disorders were dismissed as temporary problems of adjustment, and were thus described as refugee or repatriation neuroses. It was only years, and sometimes even decades, later that psychopathologies appeared.

The term 'concentration camp syndrome' was first coined in 1954, and would influence the direction of scientific investigation as much as the term 'post-traumatic stress disorder' would become a standard concept in the 1980s. Psychoanalysis stood at the forefront of understanding and treating patients suffering from the concentration camp syndrome. A number of European survivors were practising psychiatrists, physicians, or psychoanalysts when they were deported to the camps, while others drew upon their personal experiences when they became analytically trained after the war.

The terror and torture inflicted on political prisoners in German concentration camps became first known in an official report by the British government in 1939. The first psychoanalytic study appeared in 1943. It was written by Bruno Bettelheim who had been incarcerated for one year (1938–9) in Dachau and Buchenwald. Bettelheim (1980) documents the deliberate psychological shocks inflicted on new arrivals, the different responses and adjustments of various social groups, and the nightmares, regressions, and defences of the inmates. In his analyses of human behaviour in Dachau and Buchenwald, Bettelheim developed his notions of 'survivor's guilt' and 'identification with the aggressor', arguing that 'practically all prisoners who had spent a long time in the camp took over the attitude of the SS toward the so-called unfit prisoners' (Bettelheim 1980:78). Bettelheim has been criticized for making generalizations on the basis of camp experiences that are not representative of the extermination camps that were typical of the Holocaust. More important is the criticism that it was not the mimesis of the camp guards that increased the chances of survival, as Bettelheim seems to suggest, but passive subordination, self-respect, the cultivation of friendships, and sometimes even denial of the grim reality (Eitinger 1994:474–6; Wind 1995:32). Notwithstanding this justified criticism of Bettelheim's work, its wider importance lies in his focus on the complex social dynamics between perpetrators and victims of violence, instead of restricting explanations of psychopathologies to intra-psychic processes.[13]

The diagnosis of collective trauma became of acute significance during the post-Second World War decade when increasing numbers of concentration camp survivors, resistance fighters, veterans, and sailors of the merchant marine, and their children began to suffer from the aftereffects of their war experiences. The poor understanding of the stressors that cause trauma, and the failure to distinguish between acute trauma and its post-traumatic effects, not only resulted in inadequate psychiatric care, but was also played out with calculating callousness to withhold the payment of reparative damages.

Psychoanalytic etiology was abused by psychiatrists who had to assess whether or not the restitution claims against the German government made by concentration camp survivors living in the United States were justified. Several of the specialists contracted by the German consulate in New York contended that the physical and psychic damages were not caused by the continued degradation, malnutrition, mistreatment, and assassination of spouse, children, and parents during the years spent in the camps, but were due to pre-internment ailments and dispositions (Eissler 1963, 1967).[14] These psychiatrists supported their prejudiced

---

[13] Paul Friedman was the first analyst who drew attention to persistent psychic problems among concentration camp survivors. He diagnosed Jewish survivors in Cyprus en route to Palestine in 1946, and described their serious mental and physical health problems. Anna Freud was also among the first to work with camp survivors. In 1945 she treated six orphaned children from Theresienstadt at the Hamstead clinic (Grubrich-Simitis 1981:417–18).

[14] Eissler attributes the denial of the concentration camp syndrome by these psychiatrists to an emotional rejection (if not outright prejudice), guilt feelings, and even a repressed contempt for the victims of Nazi persecution. Eissler explains how the anxiety of listening to such traumatic accounts may have resulted in the withdrawal of empathy.

diagnoses with a traditional psychoanalytic explanation of symptom formation, namely that adult neuroses were preceded and determined by early-childhood conflicts.[15]

First, the realization that not only physical but also psychic damage can be inflicted on people is terrifying. The awareness that we may be robbed of our identity, that our personality and self may be damaged irreparably, is one of our greatest fears because our self is the last abode to which we can retreat in moments of threat. The violation of its integrity is a paralyzing thought. Secondly, a survivor represents for psychiatrists and physicians the frightening possibility of their own fate. They could have also been victims of persecution. This thought may lead to the guilt feeling that the survivor's torment somehow saved them from such fate; as if he or she had stood in their place (Eissler 1963:283, 291). The third reason for the insensitivity and even hostility by psychiatrists towards concentration camp survivors is a deep-seated and repressed contempt for victims of persecution. The hatred towards the survivor has to do with incredulity that he or she withstood so much humiliation, and the unconscious awareness that they themselves would have broken under such suffering (Eissler 1967:572–4).

[15] This general model had been first formulated by Otto Fenichel. Fenichel (1945) argued that frustrations during adulthood can provoke regressions which trigger defences that are manifested as psychopathological disorders. For instance, in the case of traumatized victims from Nazi concentration camps, not the mistreatment but the early-childhood neuroses were responsible for the psychic and psychosomatic symptoms.

Two other principal explanations of symptoms have arisen in the history of psychoanalytic thought, both of which were formulated by Freud. Freud's stimulus-barrier hypothesis states that a trauma occurs when the ego's protective barrier, which screens incoming stimuli, is assaulted by uncontrollable stress factors. This hypothesis implies that the weaker the defence barrier, the greater the chance of traumatic disrupture. Freud's experience with First World War veterans who suffered from recurrent nightmares made him formulate the repetition compulsion principle. This third explanation of trauma implies that the barrage of incoming stimuli revives an early-childhood defence which recreates and incessantly repeats the disturbing event in order to be able to handle it. The repetition shores up the ego's defences and allows the sufferer to re-experience the event with greater mastery (Brett 1993:62).

The clinical experiences with traumatized concentration camp survivors revealed the shortcomings of these three traditional formulations of symptom formation. The singular emphases on early-childhood conflicts and on individual psychic processes both became untenable when large numbers of people displayed symptoms of traumas that had obviously been suffered during adulthood and had been inflicted in group situations. Furthermore, the two psychoanalytic explanations of the delayed appearance of the symptoms of massive trauma, namely Fenichel's regression model and Freud's repetition-compulsion model, focused again only on the individual instead of the social, cultural and historical circumstances (Brett 1993:64–5). The understanding of massive trauma asked for a new explanation. Combat trauma proved an unlikely source for inspiration.

Kardiner and Spiegel had already demonstrated the importance of environmental stresses as opposed to early-childhood conflicts, and Bettelheim had shown the relevance of group processes. Henry Krystal's work (1968a, 1978) with traumatized concentration camp survivors made him conclude that the meaning of the event determines whether or not its experience becomes traumatic. The exposure to the event is the primary cause of trauma, while the individual interpretation and reaction constitute the dependent factor. Krystal also distinguished infantile trauma from adult trauma, and differentiated catastrophic trauma from other forms. The term 'cata-strophic trauma' refers only to those situations in which there is a surrender to helplessness because of extreme external stress (Brett 1993:63–4). The existential work

Unfortunately, the paths of anthropology and psychoanalysis did not meet in the study of massive civilian trauma as they had in Rivers' and Kardiner's work on combat trauma. This is somewhat surprising because many anthropologists and psychoanalysts cooperated during the Second World War in the field of 'culture and personality' studies. Margaret Mead and Gregory Bateson made a psychological profile of Adolf Hitler, and tried in 1939 to convince the Roosevelts of an anthropologically informed appeasement strategy to prevent the German dictator from going to war. They also worked in the Committee for National Morale to boost public support for the war effort with insights from anthropology and psychology. The anthropologists Eliot Chapple and Theodore Lockhart, the psychologists Gordon Allport, Gardner Murphy, and Robert Yerkes, and the psychiatrists Ernest Kris and Lawrence Frank were other notable committee members.

In 1940, Mead and Bateson began to develop 'the study of culture at a distance' by examining national documents and interviewing many expatriates of countries that could not be studied through direct observation because of the Second War World. Geoffrey Gorer and Clyde Kluckhohn wrote studies about Japanese 'national character'. In 1946, Ruth Benedict published her classic study of Japanese culture-at-a-distance, *The Chrysanthemum and the Sword*. A few years later, Gorer and Rickman (1950) developed the controversial 'swaddling hypothesis' to explain the national character of the Russian people. All of these studies faced severe criticism on empirical and theoretical grounds (Suárez-Orozco 1994:10–59).

Erich Fromm (1941) contributed a study about the authoritarian national character of the Germans, while Walter Langer (1973) and Erik Erikson (1951:284–315) wrote psychoanalytic reports on Hitler's personality (Bock 1988:80–5; Yans-McLaughlin 1986:194–7). After the national character studies of the two principal enemies, Japan and Germany, psychological assessments were made of over half a dozen occupied countries. Their national characters were compared with respects to 'attitudes toward victory and defeat, relative strength and weakness, standards of truth and falsehood, dominance and submission,

---

of Viktor Frankl (1959) which prioritizes the human need for meaning over survival is of related interest.

   Kardiner's and Krystal's emphasis on the traumatic event as the pathogenic force and the contributing importance of the individual's personal history and subjective interpretation give a heightened relevance to anthropology's concern for the socio-cultural context of massive trauma. As Summerfield (1995:20) points out, the social, political, and cultural context generates the meanings which are the building blocks for the victim's reaction to violence. Massive trauma and the sequelae should therefore be understood within the wider socio-cultural context.

success and failure, under- and over-statement, expectations of death or survival in battle, etc.' (Mead 1979:149).[16] Neither the United States government nor the anthropological community showed any interest in employing anthropological skills to the Korean War, while the persecutory investigations of the McCarthy era placed a further brake on any professional involvement. The Vietnam War also failed to enlist many anthropologists, as only few were willing to perform the counter-intelligence tasks asked for by the Department of Defense (Mead 1979:147).

It seems that the lessons learned by military psychiatrists during and after the Second World War had been forgotten by the time the US became involved in the Vietnam War. In Vietnam combat units were deployed for over-extended times, and combat soldiers and officers who suffered mental breakdowns were returned to the front lines as soon as possible, supposedly to speed up their recovery (Kolb 1993:296). The emotional hardships suffered in Vietnam, the unelaborated mourning over dead comrades, the military defeat, the humiliating reception at home in a society torn by the war, and the overall indifference from the military establishment resulted in more than 35 per cent of the Vietnam veterans being diagnosed as suffering from post-traumatic stress disorder (PTSD) (Shay 1995:168). Shay (1995:169–80) argues that the official criteria used to diagnose PTSD fail to address the profound personality changes caused by severe trauma. Combat trauma shatters the meaningfulness of the self and the world, and makes its sufferers put their bodies and minds on constant alert for any possible attack. They become distrustful of others, their own memories, and visual perceptions.

'Post-traumatic stress disorder' became a term adopted in 1980 by the American Psychiatric Association in its diagnostic manual (Young 1995:107–14). The PTSD construct has resulted in important clinical advances. It has also medicalized trauma into a unilinear and decontextualized disorder. PTSD has become a blanket term for a wide array of conditions. Current uses of PTSD generally fail to take into account key aspects such as the context of the traumatic experience, whether the trauma was inflicted on an individual or a group, through natural

---

[16] Once the war had ended, these scholars did not pursue their interdisciplinary studies into the populations they had studied at a distance. They also failed to become involved in government programmes dedicated to rebuilding the societies ravaged by the war. Their faith in humanity had been profoundly shaken by the atomic attack on Japan, and many were troubled about their use of psychology and anthropology to defeat the people they had studied. Disillusioned and remorseful about this violation of trust, 'The social scientists took their marbles and went home' (Mead cited in Yans-McLaughlin 1986:214).

disaster, conventional warfare, state terror, or interpersonal acts of violence.

The hegemony of the PTSD concept has been so great, and the psychotherapeutic treatment of *individuals* such a large and important professional practice, that *collective* manifestations of massive trauma and their impact on the surrounding society continue to be neglected areas of scientific inquiry. Young's cultural analysis of the PTSD construct and his ethnographic fieldwork in a US Veterans Administration psychiatric facility represent an important anthropological contribution to the study of massive trauma (Young 1995).

Anthropology and the social injuries of massive trauma

The anthropological contribution to an interdisciplinary study of massive trauma has considerable potential. This work can delineate the dynamic relation between society and trauma because, on the one hand, the social context influences the self-perception and recovery of the traumatized and, on the other, the victims themselves, as a social group, have an influence on the society at large.

The importance of the social context was evident in the contrast between the homecoming of Vietnam War veterans and Gulf War veterans. A segment of each group had been traumatized by the war experiences in southeast Asia and the Middle East, but whereas the Gulf War veterans were received with a ticker tape parade on New York's Broadway Avenue, the Vietnam veterans had to sneak home amidst nation-wide protests. The Gulf War veterans were made to feel that they were patriotic heroes, while the Vietnam War veterans were ridden with guilt feelings by a hostile environment. Such different circumstances cannot but have an effect on the recovery of the traumatized war veterans.

Likewise, Nicaraguan soldiers who were maimed in their fight against the US-backed Contras drew moral and emotional strength from the conviction that they had sacrificed themselves for a just cause. The ensuing economic crisis, and the political defeat of the Sandinistas, left these men deeply disappointed and resuscitated the trauma of their permanent disability (Summerfield 1995:20–1).

The affliction of large social groups with massive trauma also has an effect on society. These effects range from social restoration to disintegration. Societies generate cultural systems of support that lessen the impact of massive disruptions. However critical one may be of the psychiatric treatment of trauma in Europe and the US, this approach was a unique cultural response to the millions of military and civilian victims of the savage wars of the twentieth century. In fact, the medicalization of Vietnam veterans with the PTSD concept helped their reintegration into a society which had been unreceptive to their plight until the beginning of the 1980s (Young 1995:108–14).

Many non-Western societies have also been affected by massive trauma but procured other ways of coping. Traditional, non-industrial societies have often sought to collectivize the social injuries of massive trauma. They have created healing rituals, religious ceremonies, communal dances, and revitalization movements, and have restored symbolic places, such as religious centres, community centres, and special places for women and children, as cultural responses to massive trauma (deVries 1996).

Laura Bohannan, under the *nom de plume* Elenore Smith Bowen, wrote in 1954 a novel about her fieldwork experiences among the Tiv of Nigeria. She described how people coped with a smallpox epidemic that spread through the countryside by making witchcraft accusations against political rivals, ostracizing the infected, and ultimately by restoring society in laughter. This laughter 'is the laugh under the mask of tragedy, and also the laughter that masks tears. They are the same. It is the laughter of people who value love and friendship and plenty, who have lived with terror and death and hate' (Bowen 1964:297). Bohannan demonstrated the resiliency of a society under severe stress and the reparative value of storytelling, singing, forgetting, sharing a fireplace, and giving a warm welcome to those who had deserted their sick relatives as they fled to safety.

Michael Taussig, an anthropologist with a background in the medical field, has also examined responses to massive trauma in South America. In his experimental ethnography, Taussig (1987) described how Colombian shamans served as healers of the enduring trauma of the savage exploitation of Indian labour in the extraction of rubber at the beginning of the twentieth century. The shaman in trance appropriated and undermined the hegemonic discourse, and thus came to grips with the collective trauma, without ever arriving at a closure.

Some massive traumas are so disruptive that the forces of disintegration may overwhelm society's restorative capacity. Colin Turnbull has described the social and emotional effects of starvation among the Ik of northern Uganda. His controversial ethnography revealed the total disintegration of family and community under extreme famine, where every individual fended for him or herself, and empathy, love, and compassion were withheld to survive. Turnbull never saw the end of the famine. However, we can imagine the traumatizing memories of children who pried open the mouths of the very old to steal their food before they could swallow it, and the guilt feelings of mothers who put their young children out of the home to survive on their own, while hoping that predators would carry off their infants so that they would no longer have to provide care (Turnbull 1972:136, and 261).[17]

Vamik Volkan (see Volkan and Itzkowitz, in this volume) has made an important contribution to our conceptual understanding of the relation between trauma and society. Volkan has developed the term 'chosen trauma' to describe what happens when social groups are unable to mourn past losses. A given social or ethnic group may develop a collective representation of itself as victim of a past loss or humiliation. In some such cases, an important aspect of the group's social identity is structured around historical humiliations and a need to right past wrongs. While the group does not consciously choose to feel victimized, it does choose to psychologize losses, and to transform them into powerful cultural narratives which become an integral part of the social identity.

There are important transgenerational implications in the theory of chosen trauma. Past humiliations may be passed on from parent to child, and from one generation to the next. Feelings of shame, help-lessness, and loss of self-worth are borne by each generation in the belief that the next generation will undo the past harm and humiliation. Thus, the chosen trauma may threaten a society by burdening future genera-tions with the self-righteous exercise of violence.

Volkan (1996) has examined how the centuries-long hostility of the Christian Serbs towards Bosnian Muslims originated in the chosen trauma of the loss of the Serbian empire to Ottoman domination. The Serbs had conflated their defeat at the Battle of Kosovo in 1389 with the fall of the Serbian empire seventy years later. These separate historic events became fused into one powerful myth of loss and humiliation. The myth was kept alive for more than six centuries in songs, folk stories, and paintings, and in the education of Serbian children. Presi-dent Milosevic stirred up this myth during the political disintegration of Yugoslavia in the early 1990s, and awakened among the Serbs a sense of entitlement for revenge which would undo the chosen trauma, and purify Greater Serbia from the contaminating Ottoman Turks/Bosnian Muslims.

Western psychology and psychiatry have placed such an emphasis on the manifestation of trauma in *individual* psychopathologies that the term 'massive trauma' to date is little more than a quantitative concept.

---

[17] Frederik Barth (1974) criticized Turnbull harshly. He accused him of unethical conduct, insensitivity, lack of compassion, a superiority complex, and of being harmful and irresponsible towards the Ik.

Is a massive or collective trauma more than the sum total of the individual suffering? The term 'massive trauma' applies to any society, ethnic group, social category or class which has been exposed to extreme circumstances of traumatization, such as natural disasters, technological catastrophes, and social, political, cultural, gender, ethnic or religious persecution, that leave them with life-long problems (Krystal 1968).

Kai Erikson (1995:185–8) has argued that the social tissue of a community can be damaged in ways similar to the tissues of mind and body. Massive trauma ruptures social bonds, undermines communality, destroys previous sources of support, and may even traumatize those members of a community, society or group who were absent when the catastrophe or persecution took place.

The social implications of massive trauma can give rise to a collective traumatic memory in which historical remembrance, psychiatric treatment, and intergenerational processes play important roles. Populations subjected to massive trauma are affected as groups, rather than as individuals, even though each person works in a particular way through the effects (see Luhrmann, in this volume). In the words of Maurice Halbwachs: '[I]t is individuals as group members who remember. While these remembrances are mutually supportive of each other and common to all, individual members still vary in the intensity with which they experience them' (Halbwachs quoted in Young 1995:129). These collective traumatic remembrances are reproduced through ritual commemorations, monuments, testimonial narratives, historical studies and even bodily practices (Connerton 1989).

The development of the psychiatric treatment of trauma has also contributed to a collectivization of massive trauma. Individual symptoms can be generalized into common patterns. For example, survivors of Nazi persecution and survivors of the Hiroshima bombing showed some identical psychic problems (Krystal 1968b). The collective recognition of Nazi concentration camp survivors and Vietnam War veterans has led psychotherapists to look for shared symptoms in each group, thus tending towards a homogeneous treatment that creates a collective memory. Young (1995:129) has described this creation as a three-stage process. First, there is an aggregation of people who are interviewed, evaluated, and diagnosed. Next, there is a disaggregation of information in which individual cases are decontextualized, stripped of autobiographical particulars, and standardized. Finally, the data are reaggregated and situated in a medical context. This process will in time, for good or for bad, homogenize the personal coping of individual sufferers and lead to a shared recognition of the massive trauma.

The intergenerational transmission of trauma is another manifestation of the collective impact of massive trauma on society. Even though the study of second-generation traumatization has focused almost exclusively on the Holocaust, its findings provide points of departure for a better understanding of other social and historical settings.[18] Children of Holocaust survivors have tended to become over-achievers who restrain their normal aggression and rebellion in an attempt to compensate for the losses of their parents and magically undo the harm done to them. Survivor-parents show an over-protectiveness towards their children which is interpreted by psychiatrists as a combination of a re-emergence of object feelings suppressed during the Holocaust and a defensive anxiety about new losses (Bergmann and Jucovy 1982:19–23). A number of children of survivors have developed severe psychic problems, such as extreme anxiety, low self-esteem, social withdrawal, impaired reality testing, and persecutory dreams, that can be characterized as a cumulative trauma (Barocas and Barocas 1979; Grubrich-Simitis 1981).

Wardi (1992:26–32) has argued that the intentional destruction of the European Jews made survivors eager to have children as a symbolic victory over the Nazis. One child in each family serves as a link to the perished relatives of the past and is given the obligation to secure their extension into future generations, recreate the broken extended families, restore the vanished communities, and preserve the Jewish cultural tradition. Fortunately, it seems that third-generation children succeed in liberating themselves from the emotional burdens of parents and grandparents, have a renewed trust in their family's continuity, and look with hope towards the future, but without forgetting the fears of the past (Bar-On 1995:347).

The importance of the social context and temporal dimension of the intergenerational transmission of trauma has prompted Bar-On (1995:26) to favour a narrative analysis over psychoanalysis as an interpretive tool. This approach offers great potential for a closer interdisciplinary cooperation of anthropology and psychoanalysis because, on the one hand, anthropologists have a long empirical experience with narrative analysis and, on the other hand, psychoanalysts will in the near future only be able to study Holocaust survivors through narrative testimonies. In turn, psychoanalysts can make anthropologists aware of the importance of the study of massive trauma for an understanding of society and culture because, with the exception of the few ethnographies mentioned so far, there has been a general anthropolo-

---

[18] See Harkness (1993) for a study of children of Vietnam War veterans suffering from PTSD.

gical neglect of the human cost and traumatic aftermath of war and collective violence.

The ethnographic attention had always been directed more at the constitutive than the destructive dimensions of human societies. The extermination of native American and Amazonian tribes by disease and military expeditions, and the abuses by colonial governments during national wars of liberation are strikingly absent from most ethnographies. The case of Evans-Pritchard is illustrative. He was developing his functionalist segmentary lineage system of Nuer political organization in 1930, soon after the British Royal Air Force had bombed southern Sudan to quell unruly tribesmen and their prophet leaders (Johnson 1994:192–5).[19]

Interdisciplinary explorations of collective violence

Of the two disciplines, psychoanalysis has a more systematic history of involvement with the topic of violence via the study of aggression. Although anthropologists have studied war and aggression (for recent examples see the work of Edgerton 1997; Ingham 1996:196–221; Robben 1994, 1996; Aretxaga 1995; Nordstrom and Robben 1995; Edgerton 1992; Nordstrom and Martin 1992; Scheper-Hughes 1992; Feldman 1991; Suárez-Orozco 1990; Manz 1988; Zulaika 1988; Taussig 1987; Tambiah 1986; Knauft 1985; Rosaldo 1980; and Spiro 1978) theorizing violence has been closer to the core of the psychoanalytic project. How have psychoanalysts theorized aggression and violence and what parts of this work are most useful for an interdisciplinary conversation?

The two Dr Freuds

Freud himself initiated an elaborate psychoanalytic discourse on the problem of human aggression, violence, and destructiveness (see, *inter alia*, Freud 1922, 1930, 1933). Freud saw aggression as a fundamental and enduring aspect of human nature:

men are not gentle creatures who want to be loved and who at the most can defend themselves if they are attacked; they are, on the contrary, creatures

---

[19] Evans-Pritchard even witnessed the taking of hostages at his research site by government troops in search of rebel leaders (Evans-Pritchard 1976:11). It would be highly unfair to criticize this formidable scholar, and so many others, for not pursuing research questions which are of our present-day concern. However, the case of Evans-Pritchard serves to demonstrate that anthropologists come far more often into contact with people who might possibly be suffering from traumatic stress than is reflected in their empirical work.

among whose instinctual endowment is to be reckoned a powerful share of aggressiveness. As a result, their neighbor is for them not only a potential helper or sexual object, but also someone who tempts them to satisfy their aggresiveness on him, to cause him pain, to torture and kill him. (Freud 1930:58)

Freud's theoretical thinking on aggression is complicated and contradictory. In parts of his corpus he links human destructiveness to his changing theory of drive. In his latter writings Freud links aggression, violence, and destructiveness to the so-called 'death instinct' (*Todestrieb*). In his 1932 letter to Albert Einstein, Freud wrote,

[T]his instinct works within each living being, eventually trying to destroy it and thus to reduce life to the condition of lifeless matter. It indeed deserves the name of death instinct, while the erotic drive represents the effort towards life. The death instinct becomes the destructive instinct when, with the help of special organs, it turns outward, against objects. The living organism so to speak spares its own life by destroying the alien one. But part of the death instinct remains busy inside the living organism, and we have tried to deduce a great number of normal and pathological phenomena for this internalization of the destructive instinct. (Freud 1978:9)

Freud related the 'death instinct' to the principle of 'tension reduction' and to the idea that all matter strives towards an inert state. The death instinct, 'the instinct to dissolve those units [of life] and to bring them back to their primeval, inorganic state' (Freud 1930:69) is at the root of self-and-other destruction. In the *New Introductory Lectures*, Freud again makes the point: 'It really seems as though it is necessary for us to destroy some other thing or person in order not to destroy ourselves, in order to guard against the impulsion to self-destruction. A sad disclosure for the moralist!' (Freud 1933:11).

Yet in other portions of his work Freud articulates a slightly different view of aggression and violence – a view that does not carry the dubious theoretical baggage of the 'death instinct'.[20] In such writings, Freud places the recurring eruption of violence in human societies in the context of unresolved tensions between social constrictions and unconscious impulses. In several passages of *Civilization and Its Discontents*

---

[20] Erich Fromm has made the case that the principle of tension reduction underlining the idea of the death instinct, derives from old fashioned German mechanistic materialism which erroneously applied the laws of non-living matter to living organisms (Fromm 1973:526–8). According to Fromm, the principle of reduction may apply to the world of inanimate matter but not to living organisms. Fromm quotes René Dubos:
According to one of the most fundamental laws of physics, the universal tendency in the world of matter is for everything to run downhill, to fall to the lowest possible level of tension, with constant loss of potential energy and of organization. In contrast, life constantly creates and maintains order out of the randomness of matter. To apprehend the deep significance of this fact one need only think what happens to any living organism – the very smallest as well as the largest and most evolved – when finally it dies. (Quoted in Fromm 1973:526)

Freud directly links aggression to socio-cultural formations and frustrations. These passages suggest an uncoupling of violence and destructiveness from the 'death drive' and serve as the inkling to what eventually became the various 'reactive' psychoanalytic theories of aggression. Most contemporary psychoanalytic thinkers reject the idea that Freud's concept of the 'death instinct' is the best way to think about aggression and violence (Nemiroff 1993).

A great deal of the early debate in psychoanalysis was focused on the search for the origins of human aggression and violence. Soon, two psychoanalytic camps emerged: those who theorized aggression as an innate drive, not unlike the libido, and those who came to view aggression not as innate but as 'reactive' – a response to frustration (Dollard et al. 1939), narcissistic injury (Kohut 1972), humiliation and meaninglessness (Fromm 1973), and endangerment (Mitchell 1993).

Innate aggression

Four decades after her death in 1960 Melanie Klein remains an influential psychoanalytic thinker. Her theoretical work on early 'internal object relations', 'envy', and 'splitting' has been important to two generations of psychoanalytic theorists in Europe, Latin America, and to a lesser extent the United States. Unlike Freud and the early psychoanalytic thinkers, Klein made no effort systematically to relate her work to the ethnographic record. Like Freud, she related aggression and destructiveness to the idea of the death instinct. Indeed, Klein came to argue that the instinctual basis of aggression represented the greatest impediment to human peace. 'The repeated attempts that have been made to improve humanity – in particular to make it more peaceable – have failed, because nobody has understood the full depth and vigour of the instincts of aggression innate in each individual' (Klein 1975:257).

Klein, a leading child analyst, argued that the 'death instinct' was inborn and expressed itself very early on. She wrote: 'when the baby is hungry and his desires are not gratified, or when he is feeling bodily pain or discomfort . . . hatred and aggressive feelings are aroused' (Klein and Riviere 1964:58).[21] Klein claimed that rage makes the infant 'become dominated by the impulses to destroy the very person who is the object of all his desires and who is linked up with everything he experiences – good and bad alike' (Klein and Riviere 1964:58). In Kleinian terms the

---

[21] Note that Klein in some ways anticipates the popular 'frustration-aggression hypothesis' linked to US social learning theory. Of course, whereas Klein saw aggression as instinctual and inborn, the social learning theorists emphasized the 'learned', i.e. non-instinctual, non-inborn aspects of aggression (see Dollard et al. 1939).

baby's rage is structured by destructive feelings of envy – first aimed at the most important 'object' in the child's life, the breast.[22]

According to Klein, the experience of inner rage becomes unbearable. It must be 'projected' out to be 'contained' by some object. It is via the mechanism of 'splitting' that psychic representations are fractured into the 'good object' and the 'bad object'. The object selected to contain inner rage becomes powerfully charged with 'badness'. This 'bad object' then becomes the target of further rage. She argued: 'Original aggression is expelled as a danger and established elsewhere as something bad, and then the object invested with dangerousness becomes a target at which aggression arising subsequently can be discharged' (Klein and Riviere 1964:13). The 'bad object', in turn, becomes persecutorial and its destruction becomes justifiable. In the Kleinian model, aggression is a defence against unbearable inner rage and destructiveness.

In recent years the psychohistorian Lloyd deMause has attempted to link some of these Kleinian principles to historical and ethnographic materials. Although deMause (1982) uses Kleinian ideas such as projection and splitting, he rejects the instinctual aspects of hatred and destructiveness in Klein's model. Instead, deMause has linked the idea of projection with historical and ethnographic materials relating destructiveness and child abuse.

DeMause argues that human beings often use enemies as 'poison containers' for the unbearable inner feelings of rage resulting from widespread childhood trauma. He has attempted to document how shared feelings of terror and rage inevitably precede episodes of mass destructiveness. DeMause has further argued that large-scale violence, particularly bloodletting, is psychologically experienced as 'cleansing' unbearable inner states of rage and guilt.

Anthropologists – with a few exceptions such as Born (1998) and Bowman (1994) – have neglected Kleinian theory.[23] While it is understandable that her defence of the death instinct is unpalatable to most cultural and psychological anthropologists a number of her theoretical constructions have obvious relevance to the study of large-scale

---

[22] The good breast, the 'reservoir of food, warmth, and comfort', is spoiled 'through fantasized oral and anal-sadistic attacks. The infant's envious psychic attacks on the breast transform it into a denigrated and worthless object, thereby obviating the need for gratitude and dependence' (Moore and Fine 1990:108).

[23] Born argues that the processes described by Klein, such as projection, introjection, splitting, and fragmentation, are highly suitable for the study of group dynamics. 'Group psychic dynamics will profoundly affect the internal states of individuals through a process of introjection of the "social defense system" by members' (Born 1998:373). She warns, however, that such an analytic frame will be too restrictive if not placed within a wider social, political, economic, historic, and cultural context.

violence. For example, Klein's theoretical work on 'projection' and 'splitting' is quite useful to explore recent explosions of ethnic and religious hatred and violence (see Kakar 1996). Many have asked how is it 'humanly possible' that social groups, in an astonishing number of diverse settings, come to impute emotionally charged malevolent traits to a disparaged 'Other' group and then proceed to use these ascribed traits as justification to inflict unspeakable savageries upon them. The Kleinian corpus provides relevant tools to approach such questions.

As the historical and ethnographic records amply suggest, large-scale violence aimed at a particular group can only be sustained in the context of powerful psychological and ideological work. The construction of the enemy, whether structured along ethnic, religious, or political lines, proceeds from a deep sense of badness imputed to the Other. The recent genocide in Rwanda provides ample evidence. In the words of Human Rights Watch spokesperson Widney Brown: 'part of the preliminary campaign that created the atmosphere that allowed the genocide to happen was the demonization of Tutsi women as oversexualized creatures who were seductresses. It is not surprising that during the conflict they were subjected to rape and a lot of sexual humiliation' (quoted in Crossette 1998:6; see also Smith 1998:750).

The mechanisms of 'projection' and 'splitting' come to dominate social practices and cultural models in such contexts. The in-group may come to be collectively represented as inherently 'good' and 'clean' – and indeed embarked on a sacred crusade. The metaphors of purity which saturated Nazi Germany have been quite common in other contexts of collective violence – from the recent episodes of 'ethnic cleansing' in the former Yugoslavia, to the 'dirty war' waged in Argentina to 'cleanse' the fatherland of subversion (Feitlowitz 1998). The envied enemy is powerful – and all bad. In many cases, metaphors of pollution – 'spoiling', in Klein's terminology – come to dominate the social representation of the Other. In perhaps the most monstrous elaboration of this metaphoric logic, Nazi Germany cleansed the fatherland by turning 'dirty' Jews into 'clean' soap (see Dundes 1981).

There are other interesting but under-elaborated vincula between Klein and anthropology. Klein's work on envy is an obvious example. Envy is a powerful destructive wish to do away with what someone possesses and we desire. Various ethnographic accounts have examined how envy is expressed in elaborate cultural forms. The 'evil eye' complex may be said to be a folk theory of unconscious destructiveness: simply by looking at a desired object, according to this folk belief, one can destroy it without being conscious of it (see Dundes 1980). Cultural elaborations of group envy are de rigueur in the organization of large-scale violence.[24] In the context of the recent African genocide, Hutu leaders deployed a carefully scripted narrative of Tutsi malevolent power – in sex, finances, and even magic.

Reactive aggression

Erich Fromm attempted to move the study of aggression away from the early Freudian preoccupation with the 'death instinct'. For Fromm aggression and destructiveness are not innate but 'reactive' to the basic problem of meaning and meaninglessness in the human condition. Fromm's neglected study of human destructiveness represents an early effort to generate a dialogue between anthropology and psychoanalysis on the topic of collective violence. While conceptually ambitious, the book is quite uneven. Fromm's ideological affectations are revealed in the naiveté with which he deals with ethnographic materials on violence in hunting and gathering and early agricultural societies.

Fromm's most useful contribution is perhaps his conceptual approach to aggression. He comes to view aggression along two distinct analytic vectors. First, he claims, there is 'biologically adaptive aggression which serves life' (1973:246) and which humans share with all other animals. Secondly there is 'malignant aggression', which is rooted in *character* and *society*, and is unique to humans. Malignant aggression, according to Fromm, is not 'derived from animal instinct. It does not serve the physiological survival of man' (1973:255). He writes:

[W]hat is unique in man is that he can be driven by impulses to kill and torture, and that he feels lust in doing so; he is the only animal that can be a killer and destroyer of his own species without any rational gain, either biological or economic. (Fromm 1973:246)

'Malignant aggression', Fromm claims, is one of the 'possible answers to psychic needs' that are rooted in the unique existential conflicts common to all humans such as the 'horror of separateness, of powerlessness, and of lostness' that comes with self-awareness (Fromm 1973:246). Fromm made a plea to explore the problem of malignant aggression in the context of an understanding of social institutions and cultural practices. A harsh critic of capitalist bourgeois culture, Fromm argued that the rampant loneliness, anomie, alienation, and boredom –

---

24 George Foster (1972) has examined other psycho-cultural aspects of envy in a brilliant symbolic analysis of the 'anatomy of envy' in a Mexican peasant society. He argues that envy and suspicion thrive in societies dominated by a world-view in which everything good is believed to exist in 'limited' amounts. Foster calls this 'the image of limited good'. In such societies, my gain (be it in terms of economy, prestige, or interpersonal relations) is interpreted as being only possible in the context of someone else's loss. Hence, envy thrives: my gain is your loss.

which he viewed as characteristic of modern societies – are at the root of human destructiveness and pointless violence.

On the other hand, Fromm claimed that face-to-face 'simpler' societies, such as hunting-gathering groups, 'show less destructiveness than more-developed ones' (Fromm 1973:204). Fromm's analysis of the ethnographic data is dated and it smacks of European fantasies of Noble Savages where violence is overlooked, denied, or glossed over in the name of some clever dialectics (see Spiro 1979:5–13) or romantic political visions.

The ethnographic record makes it clear that neither bourgeois capitalism nor 'simpler societies' have a monopoly on malignant destructiveness. Although it is very difficult to make meaningful comparisons (and if we take homicide as an index of human destructiveness), once demographic factors are taken into consideration it has been shown, *contra* Fromm, that homicide rates in some 'simpler' societies are indeed extremely high (Edgerton 1992:172).

Fromm's ideas reverse the concept that 'moderns' are by definition instrumental and rational in the discharge of violence while 'primitive' groups use violence in expressive and irrational ways. According to this view, the violence that modernity generates is carefully and rationally exercised in the name of some instrumental end. State violence comes to mind as an example of a highly rationalized, highly codified, and sanitized use of violence. During the Gulf War, interviews with US pilots returning from the very first wave of bombings were reportedly censored by the military to remove the pilots' (expressive) 'high' in participating in the destructiveness.[25]

On the other hand 'primitive' destructiveness has been depicted as 'expressive' and 'irrational'. The September 1993 brutal murder of Amy Beals, a white American woman in South Africa, was reported by the Western media along these lines. The acts by the South African mob that beat her to death were portrayed as 'irrational' and 'mad', especially given the fact that Ms Beals was actively working to end apartheid in South Africa.[26]

[25] Likewise, during the Argentine 'dirty war' it was said that torturers who took too much expressive interests in their tasks, i.e. they enjoyed torturing too much, were reportedly removed from such duties. The idea in these cases is to erase the pleasure from the destructiveness – to drive a decisive wedge between the 'instrumental' and 'expressive' aspects of destructiveness.

[26] The ethnographic record suggests that organized destructiveness in 'simpler' societies, far from instrumental and in the 'service of life', often led to ongoing cycles of pointless destruction of extraordinary proportion. Edgerton writes:

> The ethnographic record shows that most ('simpler') societies engaged in warfare prior to their pacification. For some the decision to go to war led to tangible gains in arable land, livestock, hunting territory, captives, and other resources. But for most

In the end, Klein and Fromm fall into opposite ends of the same reductionist trap of the nature–nurture dichotomy – as either those who claim that human beings are genetically predisposed to be efficient malignant killers or those who argue that culture is the root of all evil. While Klein was not interested in the social dimension in human aggression, Fromm harks back to Freud's frustration hypothesis by attributing violence to the constrictions of civilized society. Simple, egalitarian societies are postulated as harmonious and close to nature, while complex, stratified societies (bourgeois capitalism being its supreme evil) pay the price of culture with alienating exploitation and social disintegration. Both Klein and Fromm define aggression and violence as either 'natural' or 'cultural', and thus sidestep the vast middle ground of complex, intertwined manifestations of violence in which the authors of this volume have set foot.

Recent psychoanalytic contributions to the study of injury and loss (Kohut 1972), endangerment (Mitchell 1993), and pathological mourning (Volkan and Itzkowitz, in this volume) open up interesting avenues for interdisciplinary dialogue on collective violence. These various authors – each with a somewhat idiosyncratic touch – locate aggression and violence in the *process* of injury, loss, humiliation, and mourning.

Kohut, for example, in a classic study related what he termed 'narcissistic rage' to the problem of 'narcissistic injury' (Kohut 1972). Kohut – not unlike Fromm but within a different theoretical framework – comes to see human aggression as structured along two different axes: normal aggression and pathological aggression. In Kohut's theoretical work both types of aggression are reactive – not instinctive – in nature. Normal aggression is said 'to develop from optimal frustration' and is hypothesized to motivate human beings in a variety of ways (Moore and Fine 1990:175). Pathological aggression, on the other hand, is a reaction to 'less than optimal frustration [resulting in] narcissistic injury that

societies these gains were ephemeral and outweighed by the costs of retaliation and irresolvable violence. For example, the Mae Enga of highland Papua New Guinea fought incessantly to gain and hold arable land, but the price they paid for that meager advantage was high. Twenty-five percent of all male deaths were the result of warfare, and anxiety was endemic. Elsewhere in highland Papua New Guinea the percentage of male deaths due to warfare was even higher. For a modern state to have, year after year, 25 or 30 percent of its male deaths result from warfare would almost be unthinkable. For some societies in highland Papua New Guinea and for others in Amazonia, warfare with terrible casualties was virtually unending. (1992:70–1)
Likewise, Bruce Knauft reports that, among the Gebusi of New Guinea, the homicide rate was one of the highest ever recorded. According to Knauft, homicide rates were so high that the Gebusi population is 'dying out at an exceedingly rapid rate' (1985:457), hardly an indication of biologically adaptive aggression in the service of furthering life.

suffuses the individual with unforgiving hatred, cruelty, and the need to hurt – in contrast to ordinary aggression, which is mobilized to eliminate an obstacle to a goal' (Moore and Fine 1990:175). Kohut related narcissistic rage to injury, loss, and humiliation.[27]

Renato Rosaldo's classic ethnographic work on Ilongot headhunting, while not psychoanalytic in orientation, is an interesting case study of the complex psychocultural dynamics of rage in loss and humilation. According to Rosaldo (1980), Ilongot headhunters are driven to their rageful hacking off of another human being's head in a *culturally mediated* response to grief over loss of a family member or loss of face: 'The point of Ilongot headhunting . . . [is] not to capture a trophy, but to "throw away" a body part, which by principle of sympathetic magic represents the cathartic throwing away of certain burdens of life – the grudge an insult created, or the grief over the death in the family, or the increasing "weight" of remaining a novice when one's peers have left that status' (Rosaldo 1980:139).

Historical narratives of past humiliations have been powerful motivators of group violence. According to some interpretations, the seeds of the Second War World were planted at the Versailles peace treaty: 'a large number of Germans were motivated by the wish for revenge because of the loss of the war in 1914–1918, or more specifically because of the injustice of the Versailles peace treaty in its material conditions, particularly in its demand that the German government should accept sole responsibility for the outbreak of the war' (Fromm 1973:305).[28]

[27] More recently, the psychoanalytic theorist Stephen Mitchell has explored pathological aggression in the context of his theory of self and endangerment (1993). This line of work approaches violence as a process of reacting to highly destructuring identity-threats. This line of work is limited, however, by a failure to examine fully how cultural and social practices are implicated in the construction of what Gampel (see this volume) calls a 'background of safety' and its opposite, a terrorizing background of 'the uncanny'. Indeed, the recent episodes of unspeakable ethnic hatred and violence – *inter alia*, the Hutu–Tutsi blood-bath and the conflict in the former Yugoslavia – were patterned around powerful identity-threats. The work of Sudhir Kakar (1996) on identity and religious conflict in the modern world is quite relevant to the effort to relate psychoanalytic understandings of loss, humiliation, and endangerment to collective violence.

[28] A sense of injury is often a prerequisite to mobilizing group hatred into violence. In some cases, when there are pressing economic or political objectives, it may be strategically necessary to create a sense of outrage to provide the psychological background for the organization of violence. There are reports, for example, that the Argentine intelligence services actively planted bombs and otherwise created some of the terror imputed to leftist insurgents, to mobilize the rage necessary to conduct their 'dirty war' (Anderson 1993). Likewise, on the eve of the US invasion of Panama, it was widely reported in the media that Panamanian security forces had savagely beaten up a US military officer and attempted to rape his wife. The sense of outrage created by these reports was strategically important to mobilize public support for the operation.

New generations may inherit the rage of their ancestors (see Volkan and Itzkowitz, in this volume). The Serbian architects of rape camps and European-style cannibalism – Serbian soldiers have been accused of making Bosnian captives eat parts of dead Bosnian corpses – remain obsessed with the 'grievous wrongs done to previous generations' (Kinzer 1993:1). Consider the following report:

One evening recently (May 1993) the nightly television newscast carried a graphic report that Croatian forces in Bosnia had attacked a Serbian village and systematically killed every man, woman and child there, using not firearms but implements of torture. Inquiries revealed that the report was substantially true, but that the reporter had omitted a detail. The massacre took place more than 50 years ago, during World War II. (Kinzer 1993:5)[29]

References

Anderson, Martin, 1993, *Dossier Secreto: Argentina's Desaparecidos and the Myth of the 'Dirty War'*. Boulder, CO: Westview Press

Aretxaga, Begoña, 1995, Dirty Protest: Symbolic Overdetermination and Gender in Northern Ireland Ethnic Violence. *Ethos* 23(2):123–48

Barker, Pat, 1992, *Regeneration*. London: Penguin Books

Barocas, H. and C. Barocas, 1979, Wounds of the Fathers: The Next Generation of Holocaust Victims. *International Review of Psychoanalysis* 6:331–41

Bar-On, Dan, 1995, *Fear and Hope: Three Generations of the Holocaust*. Cambridge, MA: Harvard University Press

Barth, Frederik, 1974, On Responsibility and Humanity: Calling a Colleague to Account. *Current Anthropology* 15(1):99–102

Benedict, Ruth, 1946, *The Chrysanthemum and the Sword: Patterns of Japanese Culture*. Boston: Houghton Mifflin

Bergmann, Martin S. and Milton E. Jucovy, 1982, Prelude. In *Generations of the Holocaust*. Martin S. Bergmann and Milton E. Jucovy, eds. New York: Basic Books, 3–29

Bettelheim, Bruno, 1980. Individual and Mass Behavior in Extreme Situations. In *Surviving and Other Essays*. New York: Vintage Books, 48–83

---

[29] A number of important theoretical considerations emerge from the comparative record on aggression. First, non-human animals by and large (though there are exceptions) seem less prone to destroy life pointlessly. Secondly, some human beings seem to find pleasure in aggression and violence (Katz 1988). Thirdly, some human aggression appears, from a cost–benefit analysis, to be pointless and in some cases indeed, suicidal: nothing is gained and much can be lost (Edgerton 1992).

Another basic finding emerging from the comparative study of human destructiveness is that technological advancement has brought about ever more efficient ways to be destructive. Increasing technological complexity and control over resources have made the organization of mass destructiveness much more effective than it has ever been before. It took the industrial era and German engineering to create monstrous factories of death complete with technically complex gas ovens and the like (see Fleming 1993).

Bock, Philip K., 1988, *Rethinking Psychological Anthropology: Continuity and Change in the Study of Human Action*. New York: W. H. Freeman and Company

Born, Georgina, 1998, Anthropology, Kleinian Psychoanalysis, and the Subject in Culture. *American Anthropologist* 100(2):373–86

Bowen, Elenore Smith, 1964, *Return to Laughter*. Garden City, NY: Anchor Books

Bowman, Glen, 1994, Xenophobia, Fantasy and the Nation: The Logic of Ethnic Violence in Former Yugoslavia. In *The Anthropology of Europe: Identity and Boundaries in Conflict*. Victoria Goddard, Joseph Llobera and Cris Shore, eds. London: Berg, 143–71

Brett, Elizabeth A., 1993, Psychoanalytic Contributions to a Theory of Traumatic Stress. In *International Handbook of Traumatic Stress Syndromes*. John P. Wilson and Beverley Raphael, eds. New York: Plenum Press, 61–8

Caruth, Cathy, 1995, Introduction. In *Trauma: Explorations in Memory*. Cathy Caruth, ed. Baltimore: Johns Hopkins University Press, 151–7

1996, *Unclaimed Experience: Trauma, Narrative, and History*. Baltimore: Johns Hopkins University Press

Chomsky, Noam, 1993, *Year 501: The Conquest Continues*. Boston: South End Press

CONADEP (Comisión Nacional Sobre la Desaparición de Personas), 1984, *Nunca Más: Informe de la Comisión Nacional Sobre la Desaparición de Personas*. Buenos Aires: Editorial Universitaria de Buenos Aires

Connerton, Paul, 1989, *How Societies Remember*. Cambridge: Cambridge University Press

Crossette, Barbara, 1998, Violation: An Old Scourge of War Becomes Its Latest Crime. *New York Times*, 14 June

deMause, Lloyd, 1982, *Foundations of Psychohistory*. New York: Psychohistory Press

De Vos, George and Marcelo M. Suárez-Orozco, 1990, *Status Inequality: The Self in Culture*. Newbury Park: Sage Publications

DeVries, Marten W., 1996, Trauma in Cultural Perspective. In *Traumatic Stress: The Effects of Overwhelming Experience on Mind, Body, and Society*. Bessel A. van der Kolk, Alexander C. McFarlane and Lars Weisaeth, eds. New York: The Guilford Press, 398–413

Dollard, J., L. Doob, N. Miller, O. Mower and R. Sears, 1939, *Frustration and Aggression*. New Haven: Yale University Press

Dundes, Alan, 1980, *Interpreting Folklore*. Bloomington: Indiana University Press

1981, Life is Like a Chicken Coop Ladder: A Study of German National Character through Folklore. *Journal of Psychoanalytic Anthropology* 4:265–364

Edgerton, Robert, 1992, *Sick Societies: Challenging the Myth of Primitive Harmony*. New York: The Free Press

1997, *Warriors of the Rising Sun: A History of the Japanese Military*. New York: W. W. Norton

Einstein, Albert, 1978, *Why War? The Correspondence between Albert Einstein and Sigmund Freud*. Chicago: Chicago Psychoanalytic Institute

Eissler, K. R., 1963, Die Ermordung von wievielen seiner Kinder muss ein Mensch symptomfrei ertragen können, um eine normale Konstitution zu haben? *Psyche* 17:241–91

1967, Pervertierte Psychiatrie? *Psyche* 21:553–75

Eitinger, Leo, 1994, Auschwitz – A Psychological Perspective. In *Anatomy of the Auschwitz Death Camp*. Yisrael Gutman and Michael Berenbaum, eds. Bloomington: Indiana University Press, 469–82

Erikson, Eric H., 1951, *Childhood and Society*. London: Imago Publishing Co.

Erikson, Kai, 1995, Notes on Trauma and Community. In *Trauma: Explorations in Memory*. Cathy Caruth, ed. Baltimore: John Hopkins University Press, 183–99

Evans-Pritchard, 1976, *The Nuer*. New York: Oxford University Press

Feitlowitz, Marguerite, 1998, *A Lexicon of Terror: Argentina and the Legacies of Torture*. New York: Oxford University Press

Feldman, Allen, 1991, *Formations of Violence: The Narrative of the Body and Political Terror in Northern Ireland*. Chicago: University of Chicago Press

Felman, Shoshana and Dori Laub, 1992, *Testimony: Crises of Witnessing in Literature, Psychoanalysis, and History*. New York: Routledge

Fenichel, Otto, 1945, *The Psychoanalytic Theory of Neurosis*. New York: W. W. Norton

Fleming, Gerald, 1993, Engineers of Death. *The New York Times*, 18 July, 19

Foster, George, 1972, The Anatomy of Envy: A Study in Symbolic Behavior. *Current Anthropology* 13:165–202

Frankl, Viktor, 1959, *Man's Search for Meaning*. New York: Simon and Schuster

Freud, Sigmund, 1922, *Beyond the Pleasure Principle*. Translated by James Strachey. New York: Liveright Publishing

1930, Civilization and Its Discontents. *Standard Edition of the Complete Psychological Works of Sigmund Freud*. Vol. XXI. Ed. J. Strachey. London: Hogarth Press

1933, New Introductory Lectures. *Standard Edition of the Complete Psychological Works of Sigmund Freud*. Vol. XIX. Ed. J. Strachey. London: Hogarth Press

1978, *Why War? The Correspondence between Albert Einstein and Sigmund Freud*. Chicago: Chicago Psychoanalytic Institute

Fromm, Erich, 1941, *Escape from Freedom*. New York: Farrar and Rinehart

1973, *The Anatomy of Human Destructiveness*. New York: Henry Holt

Geertz, Clifford, 1995, *After the Fact: Two Countries, Four Decades, One Anthropologist*. Cambridge, MA: Harvard University Press

Goldhagen, Daniel, 1996, *Hitler's Willing Executioners: Ordinary Germans and the Holocaust*. New York: Alfred A. Knopf

1998, Europe's Success Story. *Newsweek*, 15 June

Gorer, Geoffrey and John Rickman, 1950, *The People of Great Russia*. New York: Chanticleer Press

Grubrich-Simitis, Ilse, 1981, Extreme Traumatization as Cumulative Trauma: Psychoanalytic Investigations of the Effects of Concentration Camp Experiences on Survivors and Their Children. *Psychoanalytic Study of the Child* 36:415–50

1984, From Concretism to Metaphor: Thoughts on Some Theoretical and

Technical Aspects of the Psychoanalytic Work with Children of Holocaust Survivors *Psychoanalytic Study of the Child* 39:301–19

Hallowell, A. Irving, 1940, Aggression in Salteaux Society. *Psychiatry* 3:395–407

Harkness, Laurie Leydic, 1993, Transgenerational Transmission of War-Related Trauma. In *International Handbook of Traumatic Stress Syndromes*. John P. Wilson and Beverley Raphael, eds. New York: Plenum Press, 635–43

Harris, Marvin, 1968, *The Rise of Anthropological Theory*. New York: Thomas Y. Crowell Company

Havemann, Joel, 1993, A Dark Side of Europe's Cultural Hub. *Los Angeles Times*, 9 April, 1–7

Herman, Judith Lewis, 1992, *Trauma and Recovery*. New York: Basic Books

Hilberg, Raul, 1988, I Was Not There. In *Writing and the Holocaust*. Berel Lang, ed. New York: Holmes and Meier, 17–25

Ingham, John, 1996, *Psychological Anthropology Reconsidered*. New York: Cambridge University Press

Johnson, Douglas H., 1994, *Nuer Prophets: A History of Prophecy from the Upper Nile in the Nineteenth and Twentieth Centuries*. Oxford: Clarendon Press

Kakar, Sudhir, 1996, *The Colors of Violence: Cultural Identities, Religion and Conflict*. Chicago: University of Chicago Press

Kardiner, Abram, 1939, *The Individual and His Society: The Psychodynamics of Primitive Social Organization*. New York: Columbia University Press

1941, *The Traumatic Neuroses of War*. New York: Paul H. Hoeber

Kardiner, Abram and Herbert Spiegel, 1947, *War Stress and Neurotic Illness*. New York: Paul B. Hoeber

Katz, Jack, 1988, *Seductions of Crime*. New York: Basic Books

Kernberg, Otto, 1992, *Aggression in Personality Disorders and Perversions*. New Haven: Yale University Press

Kinzer, Stephen, 1993, The Nightmare's Roots: The Dream World Called Serbia. *New York Times*, 16 May, 1–5

Klein, Melanie, 1975, *Envy and Gratitude, and Other Works, 1946–1963*. London: Hogarth Press

Klein, Melanie and Joan Riviere, 1964, *Love, Hate and Reparation*. New York: Norton

Kluckhohn, Clyde, 1962, *Navaho Witchcraft*. Boston: Beacon Press

Knauft, Bruce M., 1985, Reconsidering Violence in Simple Human Societies: Homicide Among the Gebusi of New Guinea. *Current Anthropology* 28:457–500

Kohut, Heinz, 1972, Thoughts on Narcissism and Narcissistic Rage. *Psychoanalytic Study of the Child* 27:360–400

Kolb, Lawrence C., 1993, The Psychobiology of PTSD: Perspectives and Reflections on the Past, Present, and Future. *Journal of Traumatic Stress* 6(3):293–304

Krystal, Henry, 1968a, Studies of Concentration-Camp Survivors. In *Massive Psychic Trauma*. Henry Krystal, ed. New York: International Universities Press, 23–46

1968b, Patterns of Psychological Damage. In *Massive Psychic Trauma*. Henry Krystal, ed. New York: International Universities Press, 1–7

1978, Trauma and Affects. *Psychoanalytic Study of the Child* 33:81–116

Langer, Walter C., 1973, *The Mind of Adolf Hitler.* New York: Signet

Langham, Ian, 1981, *The Building of British Social Anthropology: W. H. R. Rivers and his Cambridge Disciples in the Development of Kinship Studies, 1989–1931.* Dordrecht, Netherlands: D. Reidel Publishing Company

Lipstadt, Deborah E., 1993, *Denying the Holocaust: The Growing Assault on Truth and Memory.* New York: The Free Press

Lorenz, Konrad, 1966, *On Aggression.* New York: Harcourt Brace Jovanovich

Manson, William C., 1986, Abram Kardiner and the Neo-Freudian Alternative in Culture and Personality. In *Malinowski, Rivers, Benedict and Others: Essays on Culture and Personality.* George W. Stocking, Jr, ed. Madison: University of Wisconsin Press, 72–94

Manz, Beatriz, 1988, *Refugees of a Hidden War: The Aftermath of Counterinsurgency in Guatemala.* Albany: State University of New York Press

Mays, Vickie M., Merry Bullock, Mark T. Rosenzweig and Michael Wessells, 1998, Ethnic Conflict: Global Challenges and Psychological Perspectives. *American Psychologist* 53(7):737–42

Mead, Margaret, 1979, Anthropological Contributions to National Policies During and Immediately After World War II. In *The Uses of Anthropology.* Walter Goldschmidt, ed. Washington, DC: American Anthropological Association, 145–57

Milgram, Stanley, 1974, *Obedience to Authority.* New York: Harper & Row

Mitchell, Stephen, 1993, Aggression and the Endangered Self. *Psychoanalytic Quarterly* 62(2):351–82

Moore, Burness and Bernard D. Fine, eds., 1990, *Psychoanalytic Terms and Concepts.* New Haven: The American Psychoanalytic Association and Yale University Press

Mosse, George L., 1990, *Fallen Soldiers: Reshaping the Memory of the World Wars.* Oxford: Oxford University Press

Nemiroff, Robert, 1993, Introductory Remarks. *The University of California Interdisciplinary Psychoanalytic Consortium.* Lake Arrowhead Conference, 7 May

Nordstrom, Carolyn and JoAnn Martin, eds., 1992, *The Paths to Domination, Resistance and Terror.* Berkeley: University of California Press

Nordstrom, Carolyn and Antonius C. G. M. Robben, eds., 1995, *Fieldwork Under Fire: Contemporary Studies of Violence and Survival.* Berkeley: University of California Press

Robben, Antonius C. G. M., 1994, Deadly Alliance: Leaders and Followings in Transactionalism and Mass Psychology. In *Transactions: Essays in Honor of Jeremy F. Boissevain.* Jojada Verrips, ed. Amsterdam: Het Spinhuis, 229–50

1996, Ethnographic Seduction, Transference, and Resistance in Dialogues about Terror and Violence in Argentina. *Ethos* 24(1):71–106

Rosaldo, Renato, 1980, *Ilongot Headhunting.* Stanford: Stanford University Press

Sagan, Eli, 1988, *Freud, Women, and Morality: The Psychology of Good and Evil.* New York: Basic Books

Scarry, Elaine, 1985, *The Body in Pain: The Making and Unmaking of the World.* New York: Oxford University Press

Scheper-Hughes, Nancy, 1992, *Death Without Weeping: The Violence of Everyday Life in Brazil.* Berkeley: University of California Press

Shay, Jonathan, 1995, *Achilles in Vietnam: Combat Trauma and the Undoing of Character.* New York: Simon & Schuster

Slobodin, Richard, 1978, *W. H. R. Rivers.* New York: Columbia University Press

Smith, David Norman, 1998, The Psychocultural Roots of Genocide: Legitimacy and Crisis in Rwanda. *American Psychologist* 53(7):743–53

Spiro, Melford, 1978, Culture and Human Nature. In *The Making of Psychological Anthropology.* George Spindler, ed. Berkeley: University of California Press, 330–60

1979, Whatever Happened to the Id? *American Anthropologist* 81:5–13

Staub, Ervin, 1989, *The Roots of Evil: The Origins of Genocide and Other Group Violence.* New York: Cambridge University Press

Stocking, Jr George W., 1986, Anthropology and the Science of the Irrational: Malinowski's Encounter with Freudian Psychoanalysis. In *Malinowski, Rivers, Benedict and Others: Essays on Culture and Personality.* George W. Stocking, Jr, ed. Madison: University of Wisconsin Press, 13–49

Suárez-Orozco, Marcelo, 1990, Speaking of the Unspeakable: Toward a Psychosocial Understanding of Responses to Terror. *Ethos* 18(3):353–79

1992, A Grammar of Terror: Psychocultural Responses to State Terrorism in 'Dirty War' and Post-'Dirty War' Argentina. In *The Paths to Domination, Resistance and Terror.* Carolyn Nordstrom and JoAnn Martin, eds. Berkeley: University of California Press, 219–59

1994, Remaking Psychological Anthropology. In *The Making of Psychological Anthropology II.* Marcelo M. Suárez-Orozco, George Spindler and Louise Spindler, eds. Fort Worth, TX: Harcourt Brace, 8–59

ed., 1998, *Crossings: Mexican Immigration in Interdisciplinary Perspectives.* Cambridge, MA: DRCLAS/Harvard University Press

Summerfield, Derek, 1995, Addressing Human Response to War and Atrocity: Major Challenges in Research and Practices and the Limitations of Western Psychiatric Models. In *Beyond Trauma: Cultural and Societal Dynamics.* Rolf J. Kleber, Charles R. Figley and Berthold P. R. Gersons, eds. New York: Plenum Press, 17–29

Tambiah, Stanley, 1986, *Sri Lanka: Ethnic Fratricide and the Dismantling of Democracy.* Chicago: University of Chicago Press

Taussig, Michael, 1987, *Shamanism, Colonialism and the Wild Man: A Study of Terror and Healing.* Chicago: University of Chicago Press

1992, *The Nervous System.* New York: Routledge

Timerman, Jacobo, 1981, *Prisoner Without a Name, Cell Without a Number.* New York: Alfred A. Knopf

Turnbull, Colin M., 1972, *The Mountain People.* New York: Simon & Schuster

Volkan, Vamik, 1979, *Cyprus – War and Adaptation: A Psychoanalytic History of Two Ethnic Groups in Conflict.* Charlottesville: University of Virginia Press

1996, Bosnia-Herzegovina: Ancient Fuel of a Modern Inferno. *Mind and Human Interaction* 7(3):110–27

Waller, Douglas, 1993, Running a 'School for Dictators'. *Newsweek,* 9 August, 34–7

Wardi, Dina, 1992, *Memorial Candles: Children of the Holocaust*. London: Routledge

Webster, Noah, 1983, *Webster's New Universal Unabridged Dictionary*. Second Edition. New York: Simon & Schuster

Weschler, Lawrence, 1990, *A Miracle, A Universe: Settling Accounts with Torturers*. New York: Pantheon Books

Wiesel, Elie, 1990, *From the Kingdom of Memory: Reminiscences*. New York: Summit Books

Wind, Eddy de, 1995, Encounter with Death. *Dutch Annual of Psychoanalysis* 2:25–39

Yans-McLaughlin, Virginia, 1986, Science, Democracy, and Ethics: Mobilizing Culture and Personality for World War II. In *Malinowski, Rivers, Benedict and Others: Essays on Culture and Personality*. George W. Stocking, Jr, ed. Madison: University of Wisconsin Press, 184–217

Young, Allan, 1995, *The Harmony of Illusions: Inventing Post-Traumatic Stress Disorder*. Princeton: Princeton University Press

Young, James E., 1988, *Writing and Rewriting the Holocaust: Narrative and the Consequences of Interpretation*. Bloomington: Indiana University Press

Zimbardo, P., 1972, The Pathology of Imprisonment. *Trans-Action* 9:4–8

Zulaika, Joseba, 1988, *Basque Violence: Metaphor and Sacrament*. Reno: University of Nevada Press.

Part I

The management of collective trauma

Antonius C. G. M. Robben and
Marcelo M. Suárez-Orozco

The papers by Gampel, Robben, Apfel and Simon, and de Levita evolve around the traumatic aftermath of large-scale physical, psychic, and symbolic violence. These chapters examine the effects of massive trauma on physical, mental, social, and cultural levels. They also explore how traumatic experiences may be transmitted from one generation to the next.

Yolanda Gampel demonstrates how social violence does not just affect the intra-psychic inner world but also the coexisting psychic spaces which relate a person to the outer world. Victims of extreme social violence often have difficulties relating to family members and to the community at large because they cannot come to terms with their suffering. On the basis of her work with Holocaust survivors and their children in Israel, Gampel concludes that a trauma of such magnitude is 'indigestible'. The inner world, she claims, collapses under the strain of a threatening outer world of violence and terror, and can never recover fully.

During childhood the work of culture includes achieving a psychic 'background of safety' through the constitution of 'basic trust' (see Robben, in this volume) by nurturing parents and other culturally appointed care-takers. Extreme violence 'un-makes' the internalized culturally constituted webs of trust, based on social norms, world-views, and moral conventions. The topsy-turvy world of social violence – a world in which everything is incommensurable with the safety of the familiar everyday world – produces overwhelming feelings of terror and anxiety.

Gampel argues that the 'background of safety' – inner representations of trust and safety shaped during childhood – cannot be reconciled with a monstrous outer reality which is unspeakable, unthinkable, and indigestible (in Gampel's terms 'the background of the uncanny'). The Holocaust survivors in Gampel's study try to keep the 'background of safety' and the 'background of the uncanny' separate because the two realities cannot be psychically integrated. At times, the world of the uncanny with its repressed traumatic experiences comes to the fore, overwhelms the 'background of safety', and manifests itself in nightmares, somatization, and psychotic behaviour.

Massive traumas do not just nestle themselves in the victim's inner world: they are transmitted within the family and across generations. Gampel introduces the concept of 'radioactivity' in her reflections on social violence to describe how traumatic experiences can continue to do emotional damage to future generations. A 'radioactive' leakage occurs when parents' debilitating traumatic memories affect their children. The children of survivors often internalize incomprehensible fears and anxieties which undermine a healthy separation of inner and outer reality. The 'radioactivity' of trauma also spills into the intimacy and safety zone of the analyst's consulting room. A powerful countertransference makes the analyst share the patient's uncanny background and may provoke intense feelings of guilt and shame-ridden resentment in the analyst.

This intrusion can be magnified further when both patient and analyst are living in a society contemporaneously troubled by social violence – as in the case of Israel during the Gulf War. Gampel analyses how the political violence in Israel invades the safety of the analytic setting and becomes confused with the inner world of the patient's anguish.

Antonius Robben's chapter elaborates on the psychocultural aspects of guilt in the parental generation associated with failure to protect the children from the ravages of political terror. The chapter is a contribution to our understanding of the psychosocial sequelae of systematic political terror in Argentina – including the very special problems embedded in mourning the 'disappearance' of a son or daughter.

Robben's work highlights how large-scale violence always works on various levels: physical, psychological, and symbolic (socio-cultural). The physical assault was obvious – torturing the body. The psychological assault, Robben claims, was aimed at destroying 'basic trust'. The socio-cultural assault relates to the obscene manipulation of social relations in the manufacturing of terror, as well as the symbolic attacks – including 'disappearing' the corpses, 'remodelling' homes of victims, stealing children of the disappeared to give to sterile military families, and so forth.

The assault on the psychological and symbolic levels – the devastation of libidinal attachments, the onslaught on culturally elaborated role expectations including the parental authority and protective functions – was the preamble of many key subsequent developments in the Argentine terror. The birth of the Mothers of Plaza de Mayo – mothers of the disappeared – as a powerful social movement can be traced to the psychological and symbolic devastation of a 'dirty' war.

Robben argues that in 'dirty war' Argentina: 'The corpses of the disappeared came to mark the transition from war to victory, and the anguished search of their relatives as the means to paralyze political opposition.' This statement captures some of the more uncanny formations generated during the years of repression. The 'anguished search of their relatives' itself became a supreme aspect of the political opposition. The mothers of the disappeared brilliantly appropriated and deployed culturally constructed imagery – such as wearing cloth diapers as headscarves – to forge a powerful political project of resistance to the military during the years of terror and afterwards.

Roberta Apfel and Bennett Simon explore the intergenerational dynamics of violence and trauma in the war-torn Middle East. They share with us a project which is in some ways very different from standard psychoanalytic projects. This effort is based on an interdisciplinary borrowing of tools and techniques from ethnographic and sociological approaches (interviews, participant observations, and the like) rather than resting solely on traditional psychoanalytic techniques. What began as a transnational project 'carrying' and 'containing' anxieties from Boston to Jerusalem and back, slowly evolved into a long-term inquiry on children in war.

Apfel and Simon examine the trauma of war in relation to two kinds of institutions: schools where adults create spaces of safety, where war-traumatized children are protected and can begin the work of healing; and 'schools' that recruit youth to carry out murderous acts of violence, where they graduate to become suicide bombers. Their work theorizes a fundamental problem in the transgenerational workings of violence: how 'adults may deal with their own traumatic histories by using their children to enact their own troubled past'. Their section on suicide bombers includes a chilling portrait of the 'institutional' supports required for the propagation of terror.

Apfel and Simon argue that Israeli boys cope with the terror and violence in their lives in part by identifying with their heroic male ancestors – particularly in their roles as powerful warriors. They claim that these familiar and cultural narratives 'protect' the children from feelings of impotence and helplessness inherent in war. This scenario presents a very different set of psychodynamic and cultural factors from the issues confronting many Palestinian boys whose fathers – as exiles – are often unable to discharge some of the critical culturally constructed paternal functions.

Three themes surface as critical to an understanding of the 'happy death' among Palestinian suicide bombers. First, the authors point out the psychosocial aspects of alienation, despair, and humiliation. This suggests that there is a great deal of free-floating 'narcissistic rage' in the youth who become suicide bombers. Secondly, the authors describe what we might call 'narcissistic propping up' done via culturally powerful 'mythohistorical' narratives. These narratives, saturated with past glory and grandiosity, seem to betray a massive sense of social inferiority and helplessness. The third critical axis in the making of a suicide bomber has to do with the institutional-social supports that are psychologically required to carry out these murderous attacks.

David de Levita explores how children cope with the ravages of war and how the social environment may assuage their suffering. In the context of the violent disintegration of the former Yugoslavia, hundreds of thousands of children were expelled from their homes, forced into exile, and made unwilling witnesses of rape and murder. De Levita diagnoses the psychopathological behaviour of refugee children in Slovenia examining their impaired functioning in the home, the school, and in public places. His psychotherapeutic experiences suggest that child-rearing practices affect the behaviour of war-traumatized children in culturally specific ways and that therapists need to acquire a cultural sensibility to be able to distinguish normal developmental problems from post-traumatic afflictions.

Children acquire different cultural practices on how to conduct themselves under threatening circumstances, and how to express feelings of fear and sorrow. Gender and culture intersect to mediate responses to violence in distinct ways. Serbian refugee boys never admitted to be suffering from anxiety or grief because, de Levita claims, they had been reared with culturally idealized male warrior images of heroism and sacrifice. Boys in the Slovenian refugee camps played at being soldiers, while their mothers actively encouraged them to avenge one day the injustices of the past. Serbian girls, on the other hand, would weep openly and search out the company of relatives for comfort. Boys and girls come to deal with the traumatic events differently as a function of culturally constituted childhood socialization and gender identities.

Taking into consideration the horrifying war-related traumas, the refugee children treated by de Levita's team have shown a remarkable capacity for recovery. Even though the long-term prospects for improvement are uncertain, it seems that adequate treatment, improved social conditions, and healthy functional trust are crucial in healing. The presence of loving and understanding teachers, the relative safety of the

refugee camp, and the signing of peace treaties are of particular importance in coping with traumatic experiences.

It would be important to find out if, over time, boys and girls show
divergent outcomes as a function of their different coping styles. Despite
the positive response to treatment, de Levita hints at possible long-term
transgenerational problems. Indigestible humiliating experiences may
incubate and generate feelings of revenge that are reinforced with
powerful cultural and historical scripts – becoming a transgenerational
'chosen trauma', in the words of Vamik Volkan.

2 Reflections on the prevalence of the uncanny in social violence

Yolanda Gampel

In this reflection on war and other forms of extreme social violence, I would like to put forward some thoughts related to the articulation between internal and external worlds, utilizing 'the uncanny' as the basis of my exposition. The uncanny will guide me to read the phenomena that occur in the inner world of individuals facing situations of real crisis in their external world. The sudden transformation of an individual's external world, at a moment of violence and terror, can cause that individual to crumble due to internal and/or external alienation, or even to disappear (metaphorically or realistically).

The reflections and conceptualization presented herein represent a synthesis of my thoughts on the theme of social violence over the past several years. These thoughts have formed themselves into concepts which may enable us to enter the zone of the unthinkable and the unspeakable, in order to help victims of social violence overcome the effects of their past traumas and begin to live instead of merely to survive. They are based on my work with child and adolescent Holocaust survivors[1] and their children and with South Americans who have suffered torture and imprisonment, as well as on discussions with Palestinian psychologists and psychiatrists.

My understanding of social violence and its affects and aftereffects has also been deepened by psychoanalytic work with survivors and their children, from consultations with children and adults undergoing traumatic situations in Israel, South America, and the former Yugoslavia, as

---

[1] My work with Holocaust survivors over the past fifteen years began with a series of in-depth interviews in which the survivors were asked to try to describe the traumatic experiences of their past for the purpose of documentation. The material uncovered in these interviews disclosed variations, modes, and other dimensions of coping in the present lives of survivors which led us to form an ongoing open group comprised of a non-clinical population. The aim of this group is to reflect on the traumatic events of the past and their influence on the present, as well as to conduct empirical studies. Since the participants had all been interviewed previously, the meetings allowed for longitudinal observations on both individual and group levels. This group, of between forty and fifty people, has been meeting once a month for the past seven years (Gampel 1998)

well as from studies on the ways in which people cope with traumatic memories in their present lives.

These insights eventually led me to conceptualize three strata of processing the effects of social violence:

1. the uncanny as a feeling and alarm signal;
2. the backgrounds of the uncanny and of safety, which allow us to see the splitting and ambiguity that result when people are unable to confront the feelings connected with their unbearable suffering; and
3. the 'radioactive effect' of social violence that penetrates its victims and is unconsciously transmitted by them to the next generation.

The uncanny

Freud first became aware of and concerned with the effects of war during the First World War. In 1919 he introduced the term *unheimlich*, or 'uncanny', in an attempt to conceptualize qualities of feeling that arouse dread and horror. While he recognized the undubitable connection of the *unheimlich* with that which excites fear, he endeavoured to distinguish the special core feeling of uncanniness from within the field of what is frightening.

Freud speaks of the uncanny as a normative human experience that represents something primary, already experienced, which has been repressed. In this regard, the experience of the uncanny represents a form of dialectic between reminiscence and forgetting. I suggest expanding the meaning of the uncanny to include frightening experiences that cannot be expressed in words, and not to restrict the concept merely to primary infant experiences that have been repressed. For, in the social historical context, the uncanny – the dread and horror of social violence – is itself primary, as it has been repeatedly experienced in the history of our century. As such, although it belongs to the familiar, it is hidden and dangerous (Gampel 1996).

In my search for a way to give a name to the emotions aroused in human beings by traumatic experiences like the Holocaust, I have found the term 'uncanny' to be helpful despite its built-in paradoxes. For the Shoah and other forms of social violence bring to light the unthinkable and the unrepresentable or unspeakable, that return continuously as *erfülung*.

These formulations can be applied to a discussion of the Holocaust, the 'disappeared' in Latin America, and the genocide and 'ethnic cleansing' still being carried out in places as diverse as Africa and central Europe, resulting in experiences that could not and cannot in any way be assimilated into the individual's range of inner representations, or, as Volkan (in this volume) has termed them, 'mental images'. These experiences stand as 'deep memories of a buried self' (Langer 1991). Those who experience such traumas are faced with an unbelievable and unreal reality that is incompatible with anything they knew previously. As a result, they can no longer fully believe what they see with their own eyes; they have difficulty in distinguishing between the unreal reality they have survived and the fears that spring from their own imagination. This is particularly true of children: they lack previous experiences which might serve as preparation for the 'situation in extremity'.

Freud considers the uncanny as a return of what has been repressed. This repression effaces thoughts at the same time that it preserves them. It makes them known and recognizable through fragmentary obsessional manifestations or incomprehensible impulsive acts that kill thought, leading to a feeling of uncanniness. Repressed material sometimes appears in the form of a metaphor, as an attempt to recover and denounce this material. When one experiences the uncanny or the *unheimlich*, what has been hidden becomes visible, what is familiar becomes strange and frightening.

For Bleger (1967), the uncanny is not merely a simple return of the repressed and does not comprise only something familiar and known which has become ambiguous, but refers also to the sudden appearance of the ambiguous which exists in all that is familiar. We move within a familiar environment comprised of discriminated objects, situations and individuals. However, within this familiar and discriminated environment, there are always ambiguous aspects that must remain hidden and secret. Bleger further argues that the uncanny is not a state of doubt or uncertainty, but one of disorganization or reorganization suffered by the ego, in which the integrated ego is broken down and a new ego structure of an ambiguous nature is formed. Bleger speaks of a break, a cleavage between the 'me' and the 'not-me', which can become an unstoppable wellspring of uncanniness.

This sensation of the *unheimlich* or uncanny corresponds to an emotional state in which an individual experiences terror when facing an object or a situation that turns what is known and familiar upside down. The German term *heimlich* relates to all that is familiar and soothing. The *heimlich*ness of the exterior world affords the ego a security that permits evolution, one that corresponds to the continuity of the original containment by the parents. The *unheimlich*, on the other hand, is related to losing what is perceived as familiar. An object becomes *unheimlich* when it contains some characteristics of the familiar object, but with a twist that is threatening. Feeling uncanny is a special form of anxiety, a warning sent by the ego facing a situation that threatens it. When this combination of the familiar (soothing) and the unfamiliar (dangerous) confronts the ego with a paradox that it cannot solve, the experience becomes traumatic, obstructing the ego's ability to function.

In situations of socio-political crisis, where terrorism transforms all that is real into total ambiguity (Bleger 1973), the ego feels threatened by a very different form of destruction than that caused by, say, anxiety. Whereas anxiety evinces a state of alertness, terror brings the ego to the verge of shattering. The experience of the uncanny lies somewhere between anxiety and terror. As such, it can become the model for a defence that leads to a state of confusion and ambiguity (Amati 1988, 1992).

When traumatic events suffered in the Shoah are repressed, they often reappear as uncanny feelings experienced as madness. The following clinical example illustrates the experience of one aspect of the uncanny in a child survivor who came to me for therapy at the age of forty-one.

In her fourth session, T said she had to tell me something which embarrassed her greatly. She wanted to tell me despite her embarrassment because she had entered therapy to tell the 'whole truth'. T explained:

When I left here last time, all of a sudden I saw my father in the car behind mine. I felt uncomfortable, as I always do when I see my parents unexpectedly and out of the familiar context in which I am prepared to meet them. So I did everything possible to turn left at the first opportunity. Whenever this happens, I feel like some crazy person. Isn't that totally crazy? It is such a strong feeling that all my rational thinking cannot help me overcome it.

I asked T if her feeling was similar to the *unheimlich* (she knows German, and this word expresses the feeling better than the Hebrew or the English). 'Yes', she said. 'That may be the exact word.' For her, this experience is always accompanied by an unbearable feeling of panic, horror and desperation. 'But it is only with my parents!'

We can attain an understanding of T's feeling by addressing her past. She was born in 1943, in a concentration camp in Europe. It was a camp for people of 'status', who thought their money and position might help save them. But T's parents soon learned that this was not to be the case. They managed to escape from the camp after T was born and to find refuge in the homes of non-Jews. 'Wanted' by the Germans, it was too dangerous to move from place to place as a family. Thus, when T was two months old, her parents left her with a childless non-Jewish couple who were delighted to receive her, and then went into hiding separately.

T's parents came to take her back a year and a half later, when the war ended. From the stories T was told after that, she knows that she cried terribly when she was taken from her 'adopted' parents. They had become her parents, and she loved them deeply. T's mother related that, no matter what she did to try and induce T to adjust to her, T would not look at her face. So she decided to force T to spend hours looking at her face in an effort to get the child to become accustomed to her. This would cause T to burst into tears, turn her head away and close her eyes.

T added that her parents had spoiled her after the war, doing everything possible to prove that she was emotionally healthy and successful despite her separation from them at such an early age. Although T had wanted to seek therapy for many years, she dared not do so because it would have shattered her parents' illusion that she had not been hurt by this separation. Seeking treatment for T with a professional care-taker would make them feel that they had again failed to take care of her themselves. Indeed, she now keeps her therapy with me a secret from her parents. She also says that she feels 'at home' with me, as she did with the family that hid her.

We hypothesized that, when T sees her parents outside the expected framework, it might return her – either in thought or language – to a situation she already experienced. Although her parents are very *heimlich*, whenever she sees them unexpectedly they quickly become something 'uncanny'. We related this to the strange faces that had arrived to take her away from them when she was less than two years old. T could not escape from this situation as a child. But she can today. So, when she runs from unexpected meetings with her parents, she is running from something that is very secret as well as very frightening. Her ability to understand her present experience through this historical material helped her to stop thinking of her reaction and herself as 'crazy' (Gampel 1996:88–9).

This clinical example illustrates Freud's discovery and Bleger's insight that the familiar may suddenly disclose a primary ambiguity, and provoke a nearly paralyzing state of uncanniness.

The three psychic spaces of the traumatized

In 1915, Freud (1915a:65) wrote that war:

tramples in blind fury on all that comes in its way, as though there were to be no future and no peace among men after it is over. It cuts all the common bonds between the contending peoples, and threatens to leave behind a legacy of embitterment that will make any renewal of those bonds impossible for a long time to come.

The fury and embitterment that Freud wrote about have continued and deepened over the past eighty years, the power of the destructive forces he described appearing repeatedly and in an unequivocal manner in both the individual and society.

Today, more than ever before, we find ourselves treating an increasing number of disorders, both on the individual and on the societal level, that are revealed to be linked with trauma due to social violence (Gampel 1992b). The question of how the social violence that affects our lives enters the clinical material is particularly relevant in countries where war and its attendant horrors bring individuals to seek treatment. The questions that arise from this situation include: How does social violence affect the psychic reality of those who experience it? Do the same theories of personality development worked out for the population in general apply to those who underwent the trauma of social violence in childhood or adolescence? How should psychoanalysis be practised with such people? And, finally, is there a relationship to the attempts to cope with the effects of social violence, moral judgment, and the reconciliation process?

The differentiation, integration, and dynamic interplay of the internal and external realities has long preoccupied students of the human experience. Whereas sociologists, social psychologists and anthropologists tend to concentrate on external reality, psychoanalysts focus mainly on inner psychic reality or on the world that unconsciously influences individuals.

Psychoanalysts come into contact with this internal world in the context of a transferential relationship, that is, in the presence of another. Freud (1921:66) points out:

In the individual's mental life someone else is invariably involved, as a model, as an object, as a helper, as an opponent; and so from the very first individual psychology, in this extended but entirely justifiable sense of the words, is at the same time social psychology as well.

In this context, Melanie Klein's elaboration on the theory of internal reality and internal objects has contributed greatly to our understanding of how we can relate to both realities and still remain within the realm of psychoanalysis. According to Klein's model of the mind, we live in two worlds, not one, and our internal world is as real to us as the outside world.

Puget (1989) and Berenstein (1990) have broadened the context by postulating the existence of three different yet coexistent psychic spaces, which mediate the encounter between the two realities. They propose a model of the psychic apparatus which is organized in separate zones, or psychic spaces. These spaces constitute a metaphor for a type of mental representation and link that the ego establishes with the body and with one or various others in the environment. This idea of space suggests certain borders, a sort of organization, as well as interstitial zones, which allow the differentiation between the distinct spaces. The authors offer an additional metaphor, according to which the subject takes root and lives in separate worlds simultaneously. Each of these worlds appears successively in a scene, dependent upon the stimulus perceived from within the mind or from the outside. The internal world consists of the subject's representations, images, dreams, and fantasies. In this realm we find the body representations and the mental functions. In the interpersonal world the ego joins others in privileged, intimate relations. An interchange of love, tenderness, irritation, aggression, hatred, etc., takes place between the subject and the others in this space. In this world the different interchanges, such as sexual, economic, or linguistic relationships, leave their specific marks. Furthermore, these inter-changes allow for the construction of the subject's sexual identity, as well as for his insertion into a genealogy. The basic interpersonal structures are the couple, the family, the circle of friends, in which emotional states of a primary type are created. Yet another world is the sociocultural world, where relations with different representations of society are established: values, beliefs, ideologies, moral principles, and histories. Each one of the aforementioned three spaces has a life of its own, and all constitute the pillars of the feeling of belonging (Berenstein and Puget 1997:22).

We can learn how the uncanny enters into each one of these spaces and affects, to a certain extent, due to its ambiguity, the sense of belonging.

The above conceptualization has particular relevance to the under-standing of the legacy of embitterment we have inherited from ongoing wars and other forms of social violence. With regard to this conceptua-lization, I should like to expand on it as it relates to my clinical experience with the victims of these upheavals. The theoretical model I suggest, which has been verified empirically through clinical work, posits the existence of two polar backgrounds within individuals whose lives are lived in the context of social violence: the 'background of safety' and the 'background of the uncanny' (Gampel 1999).

When Joseph Sandler introduced the concept of 'the background of safety' (Sandler 1960), he emphasized the notion of safety as a feeling or state quite distinct from the feeling of sensual pleasure. In citing perception as one example of an activity that can generate feelings of safety, Sandler stated that 'the successful act of perception is an act of integration that is accompanied by a definite feeling of safety – a feeling so much a part of us that we take it for granted as a background to our everyday experience' (Sandler 1960:2).

The background of safety originates from the sense of safety developed in primary relationships. The infant is helpless. It is mainly the adult who provides the context of its experiences. Normal development is determined when the external world, initially represented by the parents, neutralizes what is aggressive, fearful and anxiety-producing. This external world reveals to the child the giving, accepting, and peaceful behaviour, that is consolidated in organized families and social contexts, whose norms, ethical and moral customs, traditions, and rules are transmitted clearly and experienced as such. Robben (in this volume) describes this as the constitution of 'basic trust'.

What happens when the background of safety given by the social context is lost, when horror, violence, and torture force distortions of reality on those confronted with perceptions that in fact belong to the background of the uncanny? The pain and terror of war and social violence often overwhelm and sometimes destroy our apparatus for perception and its representations because their terrible spectacles often paralyze our capacity for symbolization. We feel safe when we exist in a constantly affective background, in a constant social context. The feeling of uncanniness overwhelms us when we are thrust into a fragmented, violent social context, one without any continuity and which transmits extremely paradoxical messages. The two backgrounds – of safety and of the uncanny – exist within all people. They work in the three separate psychic spaces, on different levels, at different moments. When one is in the foreground the other lies in the background, and *vice versa*.

At this point it is important to distinguish between those who have lived or are living in the context of social violence, where terrible perceptions of anger, death, torture, and destruction bring the background of the uncanny to the fore, and those who are living in such a context without being directly involved in the violence around them. There is a difference between those who know of torture as a result of having experienced it with their own bodies, in concentration camps, in hiding, in ghettos, and those who witnessed it intermediately, such as by being exposed to the televised coverage of it. In the case of survivors of traumatic social violence, people who were children or adolescents in the Holocaust, the uncanny background cannot be assimilated or integrated into pre-existing structures or present life experiences. This uncanny background, side by side with the safety background, results in a world of estrangement.

The following is an excerpt from a meeting in the third year of the group of survivors with whom I work. It illustrates how incidents are 'forgotten' or discarded when their effects are so violent that they exceed the ego's capacity to regulate them. B was in the Lodz Ghetto until age eighteen and in Auschwitz from eighteen to nineteen. He said:

I've been wanting to say something. At the last meeting, actually at the last few meetings, a lot of things were said, there was a lot of talk, about how it's possible to go through life after the Shoah experience. I have children and grandchildren, and I'd like something to remain, because in another generation or two it'll all be history. The Shoah time exists for me in all sorts of things, throughout the day. And it somehow always takes me back to there without my being aware of it.

I don't want anyone to think that that's all I think about all day. I work, I've got children, I've got grandchildren. There's the radio, there's television, there are books. I'm not short of things to do. But it's still there in my thoughts. And it doesn't go away. I have the feeling that every year it gets stronger and stronger. I mean deeper. Of course it's farther away, but in terms of depth and strength it seems to me that it's much stronger.

Yesterday at lunchtime, as I took a piece of bread from a package of pre-sliced bread, I suddenly remembered the Lodz Ghetto, what a slice of bread meant there. It was life! Or ladling soup, for example. What's a ladle of soup? Nothing. Nothing at all. And then you remember what soup meant in the Lodz Ghetto. It was life. It was more than life. It was a dream.

When I read *The King of the Jews*, the chronicle of the Lodz Ghetto, I experienced a personality split. For a minute, while I was reading it, I was there, but I was here at the same time. I was there with the soup, with Roskowsky, with the Germans, with the decrees. And I was here with my wife, my children, the stock market and the radio. It's a sort of personality split all the time . . . all the time in two places.

Y, another participant in the group, was eight years old when he was taken to Terezienstadt with his mother. He said:

About the subject that's just been raised . . . it's interesting. I've been thinking about it at home. We're talking here about all sorts of things, but where is the everyday? Where is the always? Where is the all the time? I want to tell you that I'm a lot younger than you are – anyway, it looks that way – and I still work full time, and I haven't read any Shoah literature recently. Let's say, too, there's always a TV program on the Shoah. Well, I haven't been watching any of them recently. But these feelings you just told us about . . . it's as though it was me talking, because that's exactly how it is. You don't know where it comes from. Suddenly, it's there. It can be with anything at all.

I've got a story from childhood. From my childhood, that is. I was maybe fifteen then, in a kibbutz, in a 'mobilization' where everybody is organized to work together in the fields. We were gathering sugar beets. Farmers. A tractor was moving along digging out the sugar beets. I went along after it and piled them into stacks. As I was going along, I picked up one sugar beet and threw it onto the stack of beets, and it went 'pphht', and I just stood there. That's it.

With that stack of sugar beets I saw pictures of white smoke stacks, going 'kchch.' Another one comes and goes 'kchch.' And I stood there. And, listen, that picture, let me tell you, it was the first of my flashbacks – of these things that keep coming back all the time now. One time I said to my wife: 'I'd describe it as a library, a filing cabinet. There's some sort of cabinet of drawers there, and all of a sudden a drawer opens, something pops out of it, and it closes.' (Gampel 1992b:46–7, 1998, 1999)

The above illustrates how the backgrounds of safety and of the uncanny are often separated by survivors, who place the uncanny in a filing cabinet and try to keep the drawers locked so that nothing pops out suddenly (in their intra- and intersubjective spaces). For they are aware that, if a drawer does open up, they will have to confront the concrete memories that come through sensory impressions, memories that cannot be transformed in dreams or thought since they come from having lived through such a terrible reality. These memories represent a concrete metaphor for the horrors, and will affect the intersubjective space. For survivors, the lived reality and the transformation of their emotions occurred simultaneously, and this has saturated their psyches to the point where it hinders the stimulus of current perceptions.

Since both backgrounds exist in the preconscious, they are suppressed rather than repressed. Freud views suppression as a conscious mechanism working on the level of 'second censorship', which he places between the conscious and the unconscious. According to him, suppression involves an exclusion from the field of consciousness and not a translation from the preconscious to the unconscious system (Freud 1915b:153; 1915c:178).

From my clinical experience with child survivors of the Shoah, it appears that the backgrounds of safety and of the uncanny are not always present side by side. A part of the uncanny background seems to infuse into the background of safety, creating an area of ambiguity characterized by confusion, nightmares, somatization, discomfort, and disbelief. When the uncanny covers too large a part of the background of safety, more serious symptomatology results. In the most extreme situation, where the uncanny covers the background of safety almost completely, the result is psychosis (Gampel 1999).

In psychoanalytic practice we see many cases where the uncanny background seems to have engulfed a large part of the background of safety, and may affect the intra- and intersubjective space. This often results in these survivors finding it difficult to accept any hatred, cruelty, violence or aggression within themselves and instead directing these toward themselves and the people they love. When this becomes evident during a session, it is extremely difficult for survivors to take responsibility for this side of their nature, which they view as undermining their capacity to love and be constructive. It is also extremely difficult for the analyst to point out these emotions to survivors, who connect any form of aggression, hatred or sadism with out-and-out Nazism.

The issue of different backgrounds and the link or dissociation between them is relevant not only to our feelings of affiliation to a community or to conflicts between or within nations, but may also provoke reactions among others. For example, what Palestinians take as a background of safety represents an uncanny background to Israelis, and *vice versa*. Moreover, what provides a background of safety for left-wing Israelis and Palestinians represents the uncanny to nationalists on both sides. The roles that these backgrounds play are relevant to the impact of social violence on psychic reality and their manifestations in clinical psychoanalytical work (Moses and Hrushovski 1986; Berenstein 1987; Puget 1988; Jimenez 1989).

And here, again, I differ from Freud as to the sources of the uncanny. For, while every individual harbours a silent and hidden legacy of aggression within him- or herself, those who have been the victims of violent social trauma have been forced into acquaintance with extreme aggression by a brutal external world and not by their own hidden aggression. This will affect and will differentiate between the type of mental representations and the link that the ego has established with the environment, the body, and the others. In relation to the three psychic spaces, we know that each of these spaces has an unconscious component, and the discovery of an imperfection or defect in any of the spaces is transformed into narcissistic injury. All of this is relevant in clinical practice when faced with the task of differentiating between inner human aggression, related to the drives and to the intrasubjective space, the aggression that derives from the intersubjective space, and the aggression provoked by social violence, that violates the boundaries of the mental spaces; the individual can take responsibility only for his intra- and intersubjective aggression and violence.

Radioactive identification

The different modes of coping with 'knowing' and 'not knowing' about massive trauma have been recorded at length. People who have experienced a trauma – the most unthinkable nightmarish occurrence – deal with the return of a perception of horror unconsciously, through such defence mechanisms as 'affective anesthesia' (Minkovski 1946) and 'psychic numbing' (Lifton 1967), or consciously, through refusing to perform the act of perceiving violence by choosing to not read, to not listen to or to not watch anything related to their trauma. What is less well known is how such traumatic experiences penetrate people's psychic constitution and continue to cause damage there, even into the next generation. I have used the term 'radioactivity' (Gampel 1993a) to describe how the perception of violence makes its way into people's psyches, touching Puget's (1989) and Berenstein's (1990) three psychic spaces and their representations.

In my view, radioactivity takes place when an external reality enters the psychic apparatus without the individual having any control over its entry, implantation or effects. I use the term 'radioactive identification' to provide a conceptual and metaphoric representation of the penetrations of the terrible, violent, and destructive aspects of external reality against which the individual is defenceless. This 'radioactive identification' or 'radioactive nucleus' (Gampel 1993b, 1994, 1996) comprises non-representable remnants of the radioactive influence which cannot be spoken about or described in words but instead reveal themselves through images, nightmares, and symptoms. These unconscious remnants are internalized so that the individual identifies with them and their dehumanizing aspects. As time goes by, such individuals act out these identifications, which are alien to them, and/or transmit them to their children, who may act them out and even transmit them to the third generation. Robben (1997) suggests that we label this process 'transgenerational indigestible trauma'.

There are several psychoanalytic models of the zone in which words do not exist. Freud (1915c) speaks of 'thing representations', Lacan of 'the real'; Bion (1962, 1967) has presented a model of preconceptions, Aulagnier (1975) of the 'pictogram', Rosalato (1985) of 'demarcation signifiers', and Anzieu (1987) of 'formal signifiers'. All these refer to an inherent potential of human nature that is part of the individual's development to what may be termed the 'ineffable' or that which cannot be described or expressed.

'Ineffable' also refers, however, to the unspeakable. Taking social violence into account, Puget (1988) broadens this concept to include the unthought and the unthinkable. She understands the effects of social violence to be 'the eruption of contents and meanings that cannot be approached or understood by the mind because of their traumatic character (direct attacks), and because of the paradoxical nature of their messages' (1988:100). According to her, people whose lives are dominated by the unthinkable and the unthought tolerate 'the existence of an unknowable mental space [because its] transformation into words would produce madness and death. It also means tolerating the existence of a world outside the ego, in which the subject is immersed but without being able to know that this is so. It also suggests recognition of the unknowable – unshareable, of sensorial knowledge' (Puget 1988:123).

Although many of those who experience the unthinkable and unspeakable nightmares of social violence utilize a variety of defence mechanisms to deal with their conscious and unconscious perceptions of the horror, or cut themselves off from anything that might remind them of their trauma, like radioactivity, the perception of violence has entered and contaminated the three spaces of their psyches. Each space will accept or reject this radioactivity in conjunction with its own rules of functioning. Since the drive cannot be seen in the intrasubjective space, we can only hypothesize the process in that space. I believe that the radioactivity penetrates without any representation, destroying some parts of this space and perhaps joining the drive and its representations in the unconscious. In such instances, people utilize repression in an effort to keep the combination of this terrible radioactivity and the drive from emerging.

When the repressed succeeds in emerging through a nightmare or a symptom, we can perceive the drive itself as well as the destructive radioactive elements that lie behind it. The following example illustrates how radioactive infiltration can enter the unconscious directly and bind itself to the sexual drive.

The father of one of my patients, who had been forced to gather the naked corpses in the concentration camp where he was incarcerated and bury them in mass graves, would lie around in the family living room wearing nothing but a baggy pair of underpants that exposed his sex organs. Although my patient and her family were so ashamed of this 'exhibitionist' behaviour that they refrained from inviting friends home, it is clear that this man was not a sexual exhibitionist, and that his appearing dressed – or undressed – in this manner was a form of identification with the dead bodies of long ago.

When such material is revealed in the transferential context of treatment, the psychoanalyst must enter the intrasubjective space and differentiate what belongs to the drive from that which belongs to the penetration of social violence. This can take place through the reconstruction and reintroduction of material that the patient has brought to previous sessions. Such reconstruction and reintroduction is sometimes aroused through counter-transferential urgency, when patients ask the therapist to fill the role of historical memory and help them think about the unthinkable, the unspeakable and the heretofore unspoken (Gampel 1993b).

The radioactivity that has infiltrated the parent's intrasubjective space and exists in his or her unconscious is deposited by way of the parent's intersubjective space into the child through transgenerational transmission. Traumatic transmission occurs when a mother is unable to contain and transform her child's death anxiety. Bion (1962) states that young infants are unable to organize feelings and depend upon the mother's capacity for reverie to organize their experiences. When the mother cannot perform this function, the death anxiety remains meaningless and is internalized by the child as a nebulous and nameless fear that impels the infant, in its very primary awareness, to take this function upon itself.

The child's intrasubjective space can be endangered by radioactive identification when parents have not worked through their mourning – as in the case of the man forced to bury the bodies of his murdered brothers – and remain unaware that they may transmit the traumatic social violence they suffered in the past to their own children. Such individuals may also place unconscious pressures on their children to assume the burden of their suffering, thereby forcing them to enter their own nightmarish world.

Auschwitz and Hiroshima have shown us that death and violence belong to the most intimate and concealed parts of our identity. The monstrous and painful memories they have left behind overload or destroy the perceptual and representational systems of their victims, leaving behind a heritage that gives rise to cruel and violent forms of identification in themselves and their children. While the children of survivors do not have personal memories of the Shoah, the internal reality of their family's past loss, suffering, and humiliation has been deposited in them by intergenerational transmission. The aim of analysis is to help such children work through these deposits so they will be able to distinguish between internal and external reality and gain a secure identity that will allow them to gain a measure of control over their lives (Kestenberg 1982; Gampel 1986, 1992b).

During certain periods of history, individual and collective experiences can be undermined, as though forgotten and suppressed, while at others these experiences can gradually 'reappear' to form an existing source of knowledge within which both individuals and the collective can assimilate earlier experiences of estrangement (Lifton 1979; Langer 1991; Segev 1991; Herman 1992). Volkan refers to it as a 'chosen' trauma (Volkan 1996:92–6).

Nietzsche (1980) writes: 'Modern man drags an immense amount of indigestible knowledge stones around with him which on occasion rattle around in his belly.' We would add that at the end of the twentieth century, post-modern man drags an immense amount of destruction, of horror, that belong to man-made disasters. These are similar to indigestible stones, that rattle around the belly of the world.

As has already been noted above, it is important to provide people who have experienced situations of social violence the space, be it psychoanalytical or anthropological, to talk. Alluding to Robben's (personal communication) concept of the 'indigestibility of trauma', this opportunity to speak and to be listened to may assist survivors of extreme situations to try and 'digest' the trauma, or at least to render it more 'digestible'. Ironically, the 'undigested' may also be passed on temporarily to the psychoanalyst or anthropologist through the process of radioactive identification.

We all form models in order to contemplate our emotional experiences and thoughts about them. Analysts and anthropologists, too, form models that allow them to derive meaning from their observations, analysts of what they think is going on in the analytical relationship, and anthropologists on their subject, themselves, and the interaction between the two. Thus, Bion (1972, 1995) has examined what goes on in emotional experience with the 'digestion' involved in thinking. In his model, he points out how we often use the same terms for our thinking process that we do for ingesting and digesting food. For example, we 'take in' material for thought, 'chew over' a proposition, 'digest' or 'absorb' an idea, and are sometimes left with 'undigested' thoughts.

Psychoanalysts can facilitate this work without obliterating past or present effects of social violence in either ourselves or our patients. We can do so by helping to reconstruct the social network and thereby facilitate its transformation. However, the uncanniness created by war or social violence raises a series of questions concerning the role and practice of psychoanalysis. Psychoanalytic work simultaneously exposes the analyst to the depths of the internal currents of another's mind and stirs up similar currents within her own internal depths (Gampel 1992a). Thus, when patient and analyst have both been exposed to the same traumatic external circumstances, and share a common external reality, they are faced with the phenomenon of overlapping worlds (Puget and Wender 1982). However, analysts can utilize the analytic setting and their knowledge of transference and counter-transference in an attempt to understand both the eruption and its symbolic value or meaning for the patient. For this process to occur, analysts must maximize their counter-transference readiness, listening to the patient who is 'using them' (Winnicott 1969). It is therefore critical that analysts in this situation locate the experience of extreme violence within the temporal and spatial context of the patient's present life, and not confuse the past infantile unconscious with the present unconscious (Sandler and Sandler 1983).

Anthropologists also try to come to grips with the emotional effects of social violence on themselves and their interlocutors. Devereux (1967) used the term 'seduction' in his discussion on counter-transference among anthropologists, referring only to an unconscious emotional attraction, whereas Robben (1996:73) extended this 'concept to the conscious utilization of the complex social, emotional, dialogic, and transferential dynamic between ethnographer and informant'. This notion of 'ethnographic seduction' is used by Robben to describe the anthropologist's personal working-through process when working with people who have suffered from social violence.

We who live in countries exposed to social violence (Moses 1983), even if we are not ourselves directly touched, are affected by infiltration through our senses and our perceptions, as well as by representations of that violence in the media. The feelings of uncanniness thereby aroused cast a shadow of uncanniness on our background of safety.

In the current reality of Israel, the safety background of sessions and treatments are constantly being threatened by the background of violence, of the uncanny, and it is very difficult for psychoanalysts to close the window on this external violence. Since this violence infiltrates both analyst and patient, we analysts have to tread a very difficult path, like someone walking on a tightrope, as we endeavour to attune ourselves to the unconscious internal world of the patient while taking into account the infiltration of the social violence into the clinical material. Freud (1937) says that interpreting only the inner world, as it reveals itself in the transference, ignores and violates personal and external history, as well as the process of history-making that ensures the continuity of life. By relating to the shared external reality, the analyst can slowly help transform the impersonal external event into an experience with a quality specific to the patient. Only then can we continue our regular work of the here and now in the transference and maintain a dialogue between internal and external reality.

We can exemplify my conceptualization about the two backgrounds using Kracke, who describes the experience of a man who lived as a Parintintin in an Amazonian society. This man left his background of safety, his house and his family, when his father died, and he began wandering from settlement to settlement. Although this nomadic pattern is characteristic of the Parintintins, it took a much more extreme form than usual in this case, for when Bebe abandoned his house, he also repressed the memory of his childhood language and of the culture he grew up in. He therefore entered an extremely uncanny world: 'To flee the pain he had to flee his childhood' (Kracke 1996:21). It was his nomadic life experiences, together with the traumatic experiences from his childhood, including the death of his father, that formed the background of uncanniness. When he became ill and returned home, the two backgrounds, which had heretofore existed side by side, seeped into one another and led to confusion, nightmares, somatization, discomfort, and disbelief. It was only through his interview with the extremely sensitive and psychoanalytically minded anthropologist that Bebe could begin to confront both these backgrounds and to create a dialogue between them. Kracke, in his study of natives of the Amazonian region, informs us that:

numerous families rooted in the Amazon for generations harbor resentments for grandparents or great-grandparents killed in conflicts with Indians who were defending their territories against the encroachments of growing rubber plantations or farmer colonists . . . these families extend their unforgiving rancor to all native peoples and of all succeeding generations. (Kracje 1996:6)

His detailed exposition and interview illustrate the direct and long-standing effects of external violence in psychic disorder.

Yerushalmi (1982) says that what is labelled forgotten occurs when a human group is unable to transmit through words a historical catastrophe that has violently interrupted the flow of human events. In this sense, the command 'to remember' and 'to not forget' which the Torah directs at the Jewish people has become an effective way of transmission. In the intergenerational associative group chain, missing links are represented by fantasies that tell us about the 'forgotten'. If future generations are to rescue themselves from a heritage of social violence – whether their parents were its victims or its perpetrators – they must confront the radioactive social-historical identification that results from the inexorable penetration of violent and destructive external reality, and this can be achieved.

From the comfortable armchair in my background of safety – my consulting room – T68

I am looking at a patient lying on the couch. I hear his words – the manifest content of his narration – with one ear, I hear the latent content of his discourse with the other. He is talking about a dream, about aggression, about incestuous desires, about his passions and temptations, about his loves and hates, his libidinal and sadistic fantasies. The session ends and I enter the kitchen to make myself some coffee. I have twenty minutes until my next patient.

I open the newspaper and I read about Gaza, about Yugoslavia, about Germany, about Somalia, and I am thrust into contact with the domain of the uncanny in daily life. It is the manifest discourse of violence, of hate, of death. This is reality, not the internal reality I dealt with above. The print spread before me is a symbol of our time, culture and civilization. It is the concrete metaphor. What I heard in the previous hour is related to the internal world and internal vicissitudes, which I think I can deal with through my relatively comfortable and safe technical and theoretical psychoanalytic background. However, the newspaper has forced the external reality of our world upon me. And I feel helpless.

When I open the door to the next patient, these external realities and the feelings and thoughts they arouse in me are filling my mind. I try to rid myself of these intrusions of sadness and helplessness, to put them aside, to suppress them from consciousness so that I may be with my patient without the infiltration of the uncanny. In this instance, I succeed.

Later the same day, however, in a session with E, a six-year old, reality intrudes through the patient. My notes on that session follow.

E charges in and moves around the room restlessly. He says: 'Mother brought me a boxing bag. It's a present from grandmother, and Mother bought it.

Jumping up and down, his hands waving in the air, E tells me that he has two pairs of boxing gloves and how he hits with them.

I say that his 'mother must be very pleased with the present you got. Now you can beat the boxing bag as much as you like and not hit or annoy your brothers.'

He looks at me in surprise!

Then I tell him: 'Mother telephoned me and told me that she had a very difficult time with you and that she wanted to send you away from home' (thereby introducing his external reality into the session).

E says, 'She would never do that, and I am going to keep on doing whatever I want.' I tell him that we should try to look at his need to adopt such a role at home. E doesn't want to talk about this and puts his hands over his ears and closes his eyes. When he takes his hands off, I ask him if this behaviour may be related to his father's now being in Gaza on reserve duty.

'Perhaps you are worried about him?'

'What? Can't I miss Father? I miss him, and that's all!' E collects the cushions from around the room, lies down and goes to sleep for about five minutes. When he gets up, he says: 'I'm going to put on a play for you.' He turns off all the lights, sits in a chair in a corner, puts his finger in his mouth, and cries and cries and cries. Then he gets up: 'The first play is over!'

I ask him: 'Can you tell me about the play?'

'A baby is sleeping, and they left the window open, and his back is cold, and he is crying.'

E then acts out another scene, in which a baby is again crying because it is uncomfortable and nobody comes to help it.

I say, 'You are telling me that, in addition to the E who hits his brothers and is naughty, there is an E who feels like a helpless little baby who is uncomfortable and miserable, and who cries and cries, but there is nobody to make him feel better.'

Calmer, E turns the lights back on. From the game that develops afterward it seems that he had felt held and contained by me in the three psychic spaces.

This session forced me to face a technical problem related to the intrusion of external events into the session. When E's mother called me to tell me that her son had been behaving terribly over the previous two days and that her husband was away in Gaza on reserve duty for the next two weeks, I connected E's bad behaviour to the absence of the father and the whole family's fear that something would happen to him there as the situation in Gaza was, as usual, dangerous.

I believed that this external situation of violence was mixed up with E's oedipal conflicts. But it was necessary to take into account and clarify the external situation before I could analyze his internal conflicts. Here it is interesting that, in his play, the fantasy was of an open window, which allows what is happening in the outside world to seep in, and that there was nobody there to close this window (Gampel 1999:707).

If every real external situation has the potential of being linked symbolically to internalized figures and events of the past, how can we relate to past and present, to the external and the internal, without giving up any of them? With regard to real external and historical events, Freud (1937) says that interpreting only the inner world, as it reveals itself in the transference, ignores and violates personal and external history, as well as the process of history-making that ensures the continuity of life. When a patient confronts an analyst with external events, that analyst is faced with what is known. Thus, patient and analyst share a common external reality, and are faced with the phenomenon of overlapping worlds (Puget and Wender 1982). However, this is where we enter the unknown, as every external reality has specific meanings for specific individuals. By relating to the shared external reality, the analyst can slowly help transform the impersonal external event into an experience with a quality specific to the patient. Thus, the ideal analytical framework maintains a dialectical process between internal and external reality.

References

Amati, S., 1988, Avatars de l'angoisse de separation dans des conditions extremes. In *Communications*. Congrès des psychanalystes de langue française des pays romans. Genéva, May 1988

1992, Ambiguity as the Route to Shame. *International Journal of Psycho-Analysis* 73:329–41

Anzieu, D., 1987, Les significants formels et le moi peau. In *Les enveloppes psychiques*. Paris: Dunod

Aulagnier, P., 1975, *La violence de l'interpretation*. Paris: Presses Universitaire France

Berenstein, I., 1987, Analysis Terminable and Interminable, Fifty Years on. *International Journal of Psycho-Analysis* 68:21–35

1990, *Psicoanalisis de la estructura familiar*. Buenos Aires: Paidos

Berenstein, I. and J. Puget, 1997, *Lo Vincular: Clínica y Técnica*. Buenos Aires: Paidos

Bleger, J., 1967, *Symbiose et Ambiguité*. Paris: Presses Universitaire France

1973, Ambiguity. In *The World Biennal of Psychiatry and Psychotherapy*. Vol. II. S. Arieti, ed. New York: Basic Books

Bion, W. R., 1962, *Learning from Experience*. London: Heinemann Medical

1967, *Second Thoughts*. London: Heinemann

1972, *Attention and Interpretation*

1995, *Cogitations*. London: Karnac Books

Devereux, G., 1967, *From Anxiety to Method in the Behavioral Sciences*. The Hague: Mouton

Freud, S., 1915a, Thoughts for the Times on War and Death. *The Standard Edition of the Complete Psychological Works of Sigmund Freud*. 1968. Ed. James Strachey. Vol. XII. London: The Hogarth Press

1915b, Repression. *Standard Edition* vol. XIV. London: The Hogarth Press

1915c, The Unconscious. *Standard Edition* vol. XIV. London: The Hogarth Press

1919, The Uncanny. *Standard Edition* vol. XVII. London: The Hogarth Press

1921, Group Psychology and the Analysis of Ego. *Standard Edition* Vol. XVIII. London: The Hogarth Press, 65–143

1937, Constructions in Psychoanalysis. *Standard Edition* vol. XXIII. London: The Hogarth Press, 255–69

Gampel, Y., 1986, L'effrayant et le menacant: De la transmission à la repetition. *Psychanalyse a L'université*, 87–102

1992a, Psychoanalysis, Ethics, and Actuality. *Psychoanalytic Inquiry* 12(4):526–50

1992b, Thoughts about the Transmission of Conscious and Unconscious Knowledge to the Generation Born after the Shoah. *Journal of Social Work and Policy in Israel*. Special Issue. 5:43–50

1993a, From the Thing in Itself by Modeling through Transformation by Narration in the Therapeutic Space. *British Journal of Psychotherapy* 19(3):280–190

1993b, 'Prendre Conge' del pasado familiar. *Cuadernos Clínicos. Revista de psicoanalisis con niños y adolescentes* 6:23–34

1994, Abschiednemen von der Familienvergangenheit durch den Geist des Analytikers. *Kinderanalyse* 3:311–33

1996, The Interminable Uncanny. In *Psychoanalysis at the Political Border*. L. Rangell and R. Moses-Hrushovski, eds. Madison: International Universities Press

1998, Some Thoughts about the Dynamics and Process of a Long Term Large Group of Child and Adolescent Survivors of the Shoah. In *Psychoanalyse in Israel: Theoriebildung und therapeutische Praxis*. R. Moses, ed. *Psychologische Blatter* 9:83–104. Gottingen: Vandenhoeck & Ruprecht

1999, Between the Background of Safety and the Background of the Uncanny in the Context of Social Violence. In *Psychoanalytic Theories in Practice: A*

Festschrift to Joseph Sandler. P. Fonagy, A. M. Cooper, and R. Wallerstein, eds. London: The New Library of Psychoanalysis

Herman, J. L., 1992, *Trauma and Recovery.* New York: Basic Books

Jimenez, J. P., 1989, Some Reflections on the Practice of Psychoanalysis in Chile Today. *International Review of Psycho-Analysis* 16:493–504

Kestenberg, J. S., 1982, A Metapsychological Assessment Based on an Analysis of a Survivor's Child. In *Generations of the Holocaust.* M. S. Bergmann and M. E. Jucovy, eds. New York: Basic Books, 145–55

1989, Transposition Revisited: Clinical, Therapeutic and Developmental Considerations. In *Healing Their Wounds: Psychotherapy with Holocaust Survivors and their Families.* P. Marcus and A. Rosenberg, eds., New York: Praeger, 67–82

Kestenberg, J. S., and Y. Gampel, 1983, Growing up in the Holocaust Culture. *Israel Journal of Psychiatry and Related Sciences* 20(1):129–46

Kracke, Waud, 1996, Violence and Oppression: Vicissitudes of a Native Brazilian Society and the Personal Experience of the Dominated. Paper presented at the conference *Civilization and Its Enduring Discontents: Violence and Aggression in Psychoanalytic and Anthropological Perspective.* Bellagio, Italy, 2–6 September

Langer, L. L., 1991, *Holocaust Testimonies: The Ruins of Memory.* New Haven: Yale University Press

Lifton, R. J., 1967, *Death in Life: Survivors of Hiroshima.* New York: Random House

1979, *The Broken Connection.* New York: Simon & Schuster

Mazor, A., Y. Gampel, R. D. Enright and R. Ornstein, 1990, Holocaust Survivors: Coping with Post-Traumatic Memories in Childhood and Forty Years Later. *Journal of Traumatic Stress* 3(1): 1–14

Minkowski, G., 1946, L'anasthesie affective. *Annals Medical Psychologiques* 104:80–8

Moses, R., 1983, Emotional Response to Stress in Israel: A Psychoanalytic Perspective. In *Stress in Israel.* S. Bresnitz, ed. New York: Van Nostrand Rhinehold

Moses, R. and R. Hrushovski, 1986, A Form of Denial at the Hamburg Congress. *Review of Psychoanalysis* 13:175–80

Nietzsche, F., 1980, *On the Advantage and Disadvantage of History for Life.* New York: Hackett

Puget, J., 1988, Social Violence and Psychoanalysis in Argentina: The Unthinkable and the Unthought. *Free Associations* 13:84–140

1989, Un Espace Psychique ou trois espaces? Sont-ils superposes? *Revue de Psychothérapie Psychanalytique de Groupe* 13:5–16

Puget, J. and L. Wender, 1982, Analista y paciente en mundos superpuestos. *Psicoanalisis* 4:502–3

Robben, A. C. G. M., 1995, Seduction and Persuasion: The Politics of Truth and Emotion among Victims and Perpetrators of Violence. In *Fieldwork under Fire: Contemporary Studies of Violence and Survival.* C. Nordstrom and A. C. G. M. Robben, eds. Berkeley: University of California Press, 81–103.

1996, Ethnographic Seduction, Transference, and Resistance in Dialogues about Terror and Violence in Argentina. *Ethos* 24(1):71–106

1997, Personal comment

Rosalato, G., 1985, *Elementes de l'interpretation*. Paris: Gallimard

Sandler, J., 1960, The Background of Safety. In *Safety to Superego*. Sandler, J., 1989. London: Karnac Books, 1–8

Sandler, J. and A. M. Sandler, 1983, The 'Second Censorship', the 'Three Box Model' and Some Technical Implications. *International Journal of Psycho-Analysis* 64:413–42

1987, The Past Unconscious, the Present Unconscious and the Vicissitudes of Guilt. *International Journal of Psycho-Analysis* 68:331–41

Segev, T., 1991, *The Seventh Million: The Israelis and the Holocaust*. Hebrew edition. Jerusalem: Domino Press

Volkan, V. D., 1996, Intergenerational Transmission and 'Chosen' Traumas: A Link Between the Psychology of the Individual and That of the Ethnic Group. In *Psychoanalysis at the Border*. L. Rangell and R. Moses-Hrushovski, eds. Madison: International Universities Press

Volkan, V. D. and M. Harris, 1992, Negotiating a Peaceful Separation: A Psychopolitical Analysis of Current Relationships Between Russia and the Baltic Republics. *Mind and Human Interaction* 4:20–39

Winnicott, D., 1969, The Use of an Object. In *Playing and Reality*, 1971. London: Tavistock.

Yerushalmi, Z., 1982, *Jewish History and Jewish Memory*. New York: University of Washington Press

3   The assault on basic trust: disappearance, protest, and reburial in Argentina

*Antonius C. G. M. Robben**

Often, as I returned to my house late at night, I saw lights burning in your windows and I asked myself who was living there, how the decisions that we had taken that day affected you, to what extent I was fulfilling my obligation to watch over the destiny of my fellow countrymen, and I would have liked to enter each and every house and talk to you, listen to you, and ask you about your joys and disillusions. (Admiral Emilio Massera, member of the three-man junta, on 17 September 1978)

The Argentine dirty war that raged from 1976 to 1983 was a massive assault on the foundation of the social contract.[1] The violence unleashed penetrated deep into the homes of the Argentine people, and disrupted the relations of protection, safety, trust, and love that dwelled there. Nearly two-thirds of all disappeared were abducted at home.[2] These disappearances were so frightening because they were not public but intensely private and personal. The violation of the home by the State, and the invasion of the inner by the outer reality, shattered ego and superego boundaries. Political violence was directed at the cultural and

* Research in Buenos Aires, Argentina, from April 1989 until August 1991 was made possible by grants from the National Science Foundation and the Harry Frank Guggenheim Foundation. I thank Wolfgang Stroebe of Utrecht University, Marcelo Suárez-Orozco, and the members of the Trauma group at the 1996 Bellagio conference for their stimulating comments.

[1] The political violence of the 1970s or, more narrowly, the military rule of Argentina between 1976 and 1983, has been described with a confusing array of names that each betray different imputed causes, conditions, and consequences. The military have used terms such as dirty war, anti-revolutionary war, fight against the subversion, and the Process of National Reorganization. Human rights groups talk about State terror, repression, and military dictatorship. Former revolutionary organizations employ terms used by human rights groups, but also talk about civil war, war of liberation, and anti-imperialist struggle. Whether the violence of the 1970s is described with the term anti-revolutionary war, civil war, or State terror is important because each designation implies a different moral and historical judgment that may turn patriots into oppressors, victims into ideologues, and heroes into subversives. I have chosen to use the term 'dirty war' because of its common association with disappearances and State terror.

[2] To be exact, 62 per cent of the people still missing in 1984 were detained in their home, 24.6 per cent in the street, 7 per cent at work, and 6 per cent in their place of study (CONADEP 1986:11).

70

psychological divisions between public and domestic, family and community, and even at the passage between life and death.

Disappearance was the preferred tactic of the Argentine military to combat the revolutionary movement that had emerged during the early 1970s. The most immediate military objective was to sow terror and confusion among the guerrilla forces, but the repressive method soon spread to civil society as a whole. The disappearance of combatants debilitated the guerrilla organizations because of the fear that under torture they would reveal sensitive information. The operational goal of the disappearances was inextricably tied to the express wish to annihilate the enemy by breaking its will to fight.[3] Wish turned into desire with the obsession to annihilate opponents also physically; not only by killing them but by destroying their remains. The annihilation of the dead became the most concrete measure of success. The corpses of the disappeared came to mark the transition from war to victory, and the anguished search of their relatives the means to paralyze political opposition.

Paradoxically, the attempt to silence the opposition had a reverse effect. Human rights organizations kept demanding information about the whereabouts of the disappeared, a group of mothers held weekly protests in front of the presidential palace, and a clamour was raised abroad. Apparently, the military had underestimated the human need for mourning and the moral obligation to care for the dead. The powerful need of parents to bury their dead children became the driving force behind a political opposition movement that contributed greatly to the eventual downfall of the military regime. The fabric of resistance was woven from highly conflicting feelings of trust and guilt that were evoked by the disappearances.

I shall argue that the disappearances carried out in the intimacy of the home invaded the primary object-relation of parent and child, and provoked intense guilt feelings among the surviving parents about having failed to protect their adult and adolescent children. Most disappeared were killed within days or weeks after their detention by the security forces, and their bodies interred in mass graves. Parents were deliberately left in the dark about the fate of their missing children, and were thus denied the right to properly bury and mourn their dead. It was at this intersection of the political and domestic domain that parental trust and protection became mobilized. I shall conclude that the politicization of the dead by the military led mothers to cope with

---

[3] On 6 October 1975, the Argentine government signed secret decree No. 2772 which authorized the armed forces 'to carry out military and security operations necessary to annihilate the actions of subversive elements in the territory of the entire country'.

their separation anxiety either by a projective search for the human remains or by an introjective vindication of the revolutionary ideals embraced by many disappeared before their abduction.

The constitution of basic trust

Freud has argued consistently that human beings are driven by the desire for pleasure and the avoidance of pain (Freud 1905:217–19, 1920:7–11, 1930:76). Relational psychoanalysts, such as Fairbairn (1962), Bowlby (1981a) and Winnicott (1965), shifted the attention from libido to object by emphasizing that human beings are not endowed with random psychic energy but that the libido is directed at other human beings.[4] Desire is relational. Infants do not seek pleasure but company, because human beings have an evolutionary predisposition towards attachment and sociality. People are social beings first, and psychological beings second. An infant begins its existence in a relationship with another human being, usually the biological mother. The gratification pursued, whether pleasure or pain, is therefore not causative but derivative of the relation with the primary caretaker. The child's ego development depends thus to a great extent on the quality of that relationship.

Erik Erikson considered basic trust as essential to the development of a healthy ego. Basic trust is constituted during the earliest stage of childhood when the baby learns to rely on the primary caretaker. 'The infant's first social achievement, then, is his willingness to let the mother out of sight without undue anxiety or rage, because she has become an inner certainty as well as an outer predictability' (Erikson 1951:219). There are inevitable moments when basic trust is frustrated, for instance when the mother cannot provide relief when the first teeth appear. The pain is relieved by biting; a self-infliction that marks the beginning of the ability to externalize internal discomfort. Erikson argued that the origin of the psychological defence mechanisms of projection and introjection lies in this differentiation of inside and outside. Inner harm is projected on meaningful others as if it were foreign, while outer pleasure is internalized as if it were innate (Erikson 1951:221). Erikson believed that the successful surmounting of the tension between satisfaction and frustration will lead to a healthy transition to the next stage of ego development.[5]

---

[4] For accessible up-to-date reviews of object-relations theory, see Elliott (1994:63–72), Mitchell (1988), and Mitchell and Black (1995:112–38).

[5] Erikson gives an overly harmonious portrayal of the infant's ego development, and fails to acknowledge the fundamental ambiguity of the self. He ignores the Kleinian

The development of basic trust and the ensuing constitution of an inner and outer reality are manifested in the infant's use of a transitional object, such as a blanket or teddy bear. This special object marks 'the infant's transition from a state of being merged with the mother to a state of being in relation to the mother as something outside and separate' (Winnicott 1988:17). The teddy bear functions as a defence in moments of anxiety. The nature of the defence is that the toy bear symbolizes the relationship between mother and infant because the child projects on the bear the feelings associated with the primary care relation (Winnicott 1988:114). The transitional object is thus imbued with the same ambivalence as the mother–infant relation, and can be experienced as both an object and a source of aggression and affection. The teddy bear bridges the worlds of me and not-me, and is abandoned as soon as the differentiation between inner and outer has come to maturity and basic trust is firmly established. In an anthropological sense, the transitional object is the first cultural artifact created by a child (Spain 1994:113), and can thus be used to interpret the cultural mediation of mother–child interaction.

Although basic trust is regarded as a universal stage of ego development, its objectification has personal, social, and cultural dimensions. Each mother shapes in her own unique way her child's ego values by dispensing and withholding care. A mother who attends tenderly to the needs of her baby creates a favourable environment that produces 'in the child a high degree of confidence in the mother' (Winnicott 1986:36) and thus contributes to the development of a strong ego. Winnicott has pioneered the importance of loving primary care with his term 'good-enough mothering' (1986:145). On the group level, the mother, father, and siblings provide a protective shield for the baby against threatening incursions from the outside world (Bowlby 1981a:292; Freud 1920:27; Giddens 1991:40). The particular social dynamics of the nuclear family influences the forms of trust inculcated in the child. Finally, the cultural environment influences the infant's budding self. Parents transmit certain expectations about human gratification and frustration through culture-bound child-rearing practices, and teach their children whom to trust and mistrust (Erikson 1951:221; Caudill and Weinstein 1972; LeVine 1988; LeVine et al. 1994:247–56).

On this foundational trust established in the home, relationships are built with the extended family, neighbours, friends, colleagues, and

---

contribution about projective and introjective identification. Klein (1988) argues that, after the infant projects its inner harm on the mother, this same mother is then introjected in a persecutory fashion as a hated object. This self-destructive introjective identification is resolved by a psychical splitting of the object into a good and a bad part.

society at large (Bowlby 1981a:414). The confidence in one's fellow-beings is at times frustrated but becomes stabilized in reality-testing. Drawing extensively on Erikson and Winnicott, Giddens (1991:36–40) has argued that this basic trust provides an ontological security which allows people to bracket the anxieties of their unpredictable social environment. Daily routines and social conventions keep anxieties at bay and establish patterns of expectations that allow people to interact. These everyday practices serve also to continuously renew basic trust, because persons cannot feed for the rest of their lives on the trust established in early childhood. Basic trust is not an inalienable part of the personal constitution but can disintegrate beyond recovery after undergoing traumatic experiences. The terrifying memories have become indigestible, as Yolanda Gampel shows in this volume, because they cannot be accommodated in an everyday world of safety and trust.

Trust is by definition intersubjective, and the basic trust given needs to be reproduced just as much as the trust received. The protective shield provided by the mother and the father shapes them as much as their infant. Parents will continue to reproduce their good-enough fathering and good-enough mothering for the rest of their lives, wanting to protect the child even when he or she has grown into adulthood. It is the impotence at being unable to give this enduring care to the suffering child that can be so traumatic, as I will continue to demonstrate with an analysis of dirty war disappearances in Argentina between 1976 and 1983.

The transgression of inner and outer boundaries

The abduction of political suspects from their homes and the humiliation of their relatives by the Argentine military led to the deliberate destruction of the parental protective shield, the disintegration of ego boundaries, the disturbing intrusion of a threatening outer world, and lasting damage to the self by the transgression of deep-seated cultural values.[6] The home is where the child inculcates the organization of its physical and moral universe in an inner sanctuary and an outer world (Piaget 1971:331). The home exudes trust and safety because these values are constituted there between child and parents. The forced entry of the home by a military task force is therefore an attack that takes place as much on the physical and psychological as on the social and cultural level. The basic trust of a person is assaulted as much as the

---

[6] Such massive assaults on ego and superego boundaries have been analyzed most extensively in the study of Nazi concentration camps. See, e.g., Grubrich-Simitis (1981), Krystal (1968), Pawelczynska (1979), and Trautman (1971).

integrity of the body, and primary relations are damaged together with the symbolic order of society.

Argentine military assault teams had a preference for arresting people at home (see note 2 above), and especially at night. The analysis of such nightly assaults demonstrates clearly how this violence was always multipronged and multilayered. The bewildered residents were at their most defenceless as a flashlight shone in their face while they were fast asleep. As it is written in an operation manual of the Argentine army: 'The sudden glare shall cause blinding when the eyes are opened . . . Whenever possible the approach must be made from behind the bed's headboard. This will put him in a position from which he will not be able to fire with precision when he awakens' (Ejército Argentino 1972:21). In most cases, however, the assault teams knew they were abducting unarmed civilians. 'They detained me at home', so began Rubén Darío Martinez' typical account of his abduction from his apartment. 'A group of people, seven or eight persons, entered . . . I was asleep. They broke down the door, covered me with a hood, put me against the wall, and began to inspect the entire place. They asked me where the weapons were, turned the mattress over, broke everything, and forced me to the floor. After hitting me at my home, they placed a pistol to my head, and then took me downstairs' (*Diario del Juicio* 15:331).

The socio-cultural violence, added to the physical and psychological violence of these abductions, was particularly intensive because of their occurrence in the home. These assaults transgressed the deep-seated opposition between the public and the domestic domain that is so common in all Latin societies, including Argentina.[7] Latin societies have created many social, material, and symbolic barriers to prevent the two domains from mixing. The public sphere is often seen as a polluted and dangerous place whose harmful influences must be stopped at the doorstep. Thresholds, material demarcations, and open spaces are erected that impede a free interchange and serve to transform people symbolically during their transition from one social sphere to another (Brown 1987; Robben 1989b; Taylor and Brower 1985; Van Gennep 1960:15–25).[8] These socio-spatial divisions reinforce the ego differentiation between inside and outside. A forced entry is thus experienced as

---

[7] The roots of this division lie in ancient Greek and Hebrew culture (Arendt 1958:22–78). A similar dichotomy can be found in contemporary Islamic and Mediterranean cultures. The opposition between public and private is elaborated in cultural values such as honour and shame, modesty and display, and loyalty and betrayal (see Benn and Gauss 1983; DaMatta 1987; Moore 1984; Peristiany 1965; Robben 1989a, 1989b).

[8] See Feldman (1991:88–97) for a Foucaultean analysis of the transgression of the domestic sanctuary by the nightly house arrest of political suspects in Northern Ireland.

an attack on the ego, and violates the emotional, physical, and cultural protection offered by the home. Children sense this infraction on the sanctity of the house immediately. When in November 1976 a nightly task force broke into the house of Marta Lifsica de Chester to abduct her husband Jorge, the twelve-year-old daughter Zulema woke up and entered the living room. The surprised commanding officer asked her: ' "What are you doing here?", to which the girl responded: "I am in my house. What are you doing here?" ' (*Diario del Juicio* 32:594).

The assaults were also extended on the symbolic level to the objects that gave content and meaning to people's existence (see Csikszentmihalyi and Rochberg-Halton 1981). Photographs, paintings, porcelain, toys, and mementos were often broken and even urinated upon. This aggression against the home went in one case even to the extreme of tearing down walls and modifying its socio-spatial organization. This happened to Mrs Garcia Candeloro who, together with her husband, had been abducted in June 1977 from their home in the Andean capital of Neuquén. Her husband died under torture. After her release six months later, Mrs Garcia Candeloro decided to sell her house and move to the coastal town of Mar del Plata. To her surprise she discovered that a group of policemen from the provinces were living in her Neuquén residence: 'My house was completely plundered. They had destroyed the bookcases and even the walls. They had made compartments. The house had four rooms and with those compartments made out of broken bookcases they had created about seven rooms in the dining room' (*Diario del Juicio* 8:175). The restructuring of the dining room into provisional bedrooms turned socio-spatial functions and cultural meanings upside down that had been inculcated during childhood (see Robben 1989b). The semi-public place where guests used to be received had now become confounded with the most intimate retreat of the house. The symbolic separations of body and community, intimacy and sociality, and inner and outer were all thrown together in a disturbing whole into which refuge was no longer possible.

The way Argentine parents responded to such ego assaults reveals how they coped with separation and loss in times of political violence. They demonstrate how they gave expression to universal feelings of trust and protection, and how parents tried to restore the protective shield of their children.

Forced separation and the attack on basic trust

The tacit parental security offered in daily life becomes visible when the primary relation is endangered. The threat of loss makes parents place their children's well-being ahead of their own (Weiss 1993:274–5). Drawing extensively on Bowlby, Weiss argues that the mother and father seek to be physically close to the child so that it can be reassured of their protection by touching or at least hearing and seeing its parents. This attachment behaviour can be recognized in the forced separation of mother and child in Argentina. The empirical material from Argentina suggests that, emotionally, the age of the child matters little under such traumatic circumstances as mothers imagine their adolescent and adult children to be as infants in need of maternal protection. The use of diapers as headscarfs by mothers protesting the disappearance of their adult children is another indication of such protective feelings. Elsa Sánchez de Oesterheld, who lost her husband and four daughters aged between 17 and 23, asked herself eight years later in desperation: 'What happened to those wonderful little girls? I speak of little girls [niñas] while I had women. This is, of course, a generic matter for all mothers who lost their children without knowing what happened to them' (interview, 15 April 1991).

Whenever a task force entered a home during those cruel years between 1976 and 1983, the thoughts of the mother went invariably first to the son or daughter, and only later to her husband and herself. Generally, the mother would run to the child's bedroom and stay at its side. When Margarita Michelini was ordered to come along, 'I told them to kill me right there, but that I was not going to give them the baby' (Diario del Juicio 9:207). The twelve-year-old daughter of Nelida Jauregui was awakened 'with a machine-gun to her head and they wanted to take her away from me, so I embraced her and I told them that this was not going to be possible because she was an infant and I took her to my bedroom' (Diario del Juicio 31:568). The resistance of mothers in such tense moments was so unexpected that in a number of cases the infants were not abducted to be given to childless military couples (see Herrera and Tenembaum 1990; Nosiglia 1985).

The feelings between mother and child were reciprocal in the sense that the protection went out not just from parent to child, as Weiss (1993:275) suggests, but also from child to parent. Twelve-year-old Zulema Lifsica de Chester, who had earlier questioned the intruders' presence in her home, protested again when her blindfolded mother was thrown to the floor: 'My daughter saw this and began to scream that they shouldn't push her mommy. Then they asked her: "Why do you defend your mother?" She told them: "Would you have liked it if someone did something to your mother?", to which she did not receive an answer' (Diario del Juicio 32:594). The girl was taken to her bedroom and interrogated about the hiding place of the political pamphlets. The anguished mother heard the men's questions but not her daughter's replies. 'Then I also begin to scream: "Where is my daughter? What is happening with my daughter?", until they finally throw us together in the hall' (*Diario del Juicio* 32:594). Mother and daughter were separated once more and interrogated in their respective bedrooms. Zulema declared nine years later in court that her interrogation took between thirty and forty-five minutes during which she was beaten and sexually abused. But even under these trying circumstances her attention went out to her parents: 'And I ask him where my parents are; so he tells me that I can go and look for my daddy in a ditch. Then I asked him for my mother and again he tells that my mother is fine, that she is in the other bedroom' (*Diario del Juicio* 32:595). Zulema asked to be taken to her mother but, instead, the men fetched the mother, tied her back to back to her daughter, and left the house taking the father with them.

Throughout the testimonies trails the constant concern between mother and child towards each other rather than to themselves. They clutch in these uncertain and threatening moments to the deeply embedded trust of the primary relation. This need to be close enters even the realm of fantasy. The uncanny creeps into the everyday as mothers imagined themselves to be in telepathic contact with their children. 'I think and think, "Where are you, my son? Are you in some place, maybe closer than I can imagine?" . . . Every day and even more at night, I see you coming or I hear knocks at the door. I open and there is only silence, silence above all . . . What are you thinking, my dear, you who always thought so much? Who now occupies your thoughts? . . . Close your eyes, like I am doing now and think of me. I am certain that in this way everything is going to pass very soon' (Hebe de Bonafini in Sánchez 1985:106–7). Some mothers believed they could give their children strength through telepathic communication. 'Sometimes I seemed to hear Pablo's voice. I lived as if hallucinating. When I was not doing something, some formal procedure or task for Pablo, I maintained even more this mental contact with him and I talked to him in thought. I told him "Hold on, Pablo . . .", "stay alive, Pablo . . ." I didn't know very well what Pablo had to endure but I imagined the horror of being alone, the anguish, the impotence . . . I thought "Pablo must be having faith in us; he knows that we are going to get to him . . .", and . . . we couldn't. This still bothers me so much!'(Graciela Fernández Meijide in Ulla and Echave 1986:37–8).

The need to offer protection endured even under torture, and illustrates Winnicott's notion of good-enough mothering. How can a mother ever betray her children when she raised them with the certainty that they can trust her unconditionally? Iris Etelvina de Avellaneda was asked in 1976 for her last three wishes as her tormentors were preparing her for a mock execution, 'I asked him about my son and he answered that I shouldn't ask anymore because "Your son, we already tore him to pieces"' (*Diario del Juicio* 2:3). Melba de Falcone, who had helped her son move to another house as he had just married, was detained for abetting a subversive and tortured with an electric prod to reveal his location: 'I asked them if they didn't have a mother. I asked them how they could do this to me. I had gone to help a son move, and they screamed at me that the mother in them had been killed by the guerrilleros . . . I really didn't know where he had gone, and if I would have known I would have died for my son, because he was my son' (*Diario del Juicio* 3:67). Maria Elisa Hachmann de Lande was tortured for forty-eight hours to reveal the whereabouts of her son. 'At that time they thought that it would be easier to force the mother to say something, no? Or to say where they were. But if I gave life to my son, would I then bring him death?' (interview, 13 April 1990).

When the torture of parents did not yield the information they wanted, then the torturers exploited parental feelings by torturing infants and even unborn babies (CONADEP 1986:305–10; Suárez-Orozco 1987). This perverse practice demonstrates clearly the complex connections between the various physical, psychological, and socio-cultural levels on which repressive violence is exercised. Norberto Liwski was told that he was soon going to accompany one of his daughters into the torture chamber. The attending physician told the torturer that he could only use the electric prod on children that weighed more than 25 kgs. In a psychological torment, Liwski was shown the soiled underpants of his little girls. 'This went on and on, this torture of using the children in this way. At various opportunities they told me that they had such control over my daughters that they had films of them on which I could ascertain myself – if I cared to see them – the degree of control they had over them' (*Diario de Juicio* 30:549).

The newspaper publisher Jacobo Timerman witnessed the devastation of the Miralles family as they were tortured in each other's presence: 'The entire affective world, constructed over the years with utmost difficulty, collapses with a kick in the father's genitals, a smack on the mother's face, an obscene insult to the sister, or the sexual violation of a daughter. Suddenly an entire culture based on familial love, devotion, the capacity for mutual sacrifice collapses' (Timerman 1981:148). From his cell, Timerman hears the father trying to get an apple to his children, and the children trying to learn about the fate of their parents. He learns of the father's powerlessness, 'that impotence that arises not from one's failure to do something in defense of one's children but from one's inability to extend a tender gesture' (Timerman 1981:148–9).

The protective shield ruptured when adult and adolescent children endangered themselves through their political activism during the turbulent 1970s. While trust and protection coincide during the early stages of dependency, from adolescence onwards they sometimes become opposites. The parental desire to isolate children from outside threats clashes with the need to raise them into independent adults. This made some mothers decide that it was better not to question the political judgment of their children. Matilde Herrera trembled when her children told her that they had decided to join the outlawed People's Revolutionary Army (ERP): 'I knew that it was best not to argue with the children when they took such a decision. What I most wanted was that they wouldn't lose trust in me. One way or the other I was always at their side, and I thought that the worst I could do was to leave them unprotected, that they would feel abandoned by their mother. Society was already hostile enough to them' (Herrera 1987:182). The scales of trust and protection tipped for this mother towards supplying a nurturing emotional environment as a last refuge from a threatening world, even when her fear of separation and political judgment told her that the armed struggle would end in certain death.

Other mothers chose safety over trust. This placed them before a different but equally desperate dilemma. They would have to avoid any further contact with their children and thus abandon them to the uncertain existence of a life in hiding. Elsa Sánchez de Oesterheld disapproved of the leftist political ideals of her husband and four daughters. Although not armed combatants, they performed political tasks for the Montoneros guerrilla organization. They went underground in 1976, and eventually all disappeared. 'Death doesn't make me anxious because I know that my daughters, my husband, were at peace once they died. What worries me, what torments me, what makes me crazy is what happened before their death; this yes, when these thoughts come to me, which is usually at night, when one cannot sleep and begins to think and think. For fifteen years I have been brooding over this drama' (interview, 15 April 1991).

The two dilemmas outlined above are magnified when the child disappears: waiting quietly for the abducted child to reappear is felt as abandonment, while active protest is regarded as endangering. These dilemmas became even more painful during an official media campaign that carried slogans such as: 'How are you raising your child?' 'Do you know what your child is doing at this precise moment?' (Kordon and Edelman 1988:34). Intended to make parents aware of the education of their children and make them responsible for the company they kept, it produced tremendous guilt among those parents whose children had been abducted. Mothers were indirectly blamed for not giving a good-enough education that could have prevented the children from becoming involved with the guerrilla organizations, and were now obliged to ask help from the authorities to locate their missing children.

In September 1977, a group of mothers of abducted sons and daughters decided to stage a weekly protest against the disappearances. They became world-renowned as the Mothers of the Plaza de Mayo (*Madres de Plaza de Mayo*). They identified themselves as mothers by wearing a diaper as a headscarf because 'it is going to make us feel better, closer to the children' (Sánchez 1985:141). This reflexive act marked the beginning of half a decade of heroic resistance and protest against the military junta. The creative cultural strategies devised to draw attention to their plight, and the determination to fight for their children were natural expressions of maternal protection. They socialized their private pain as mothers, while their husbands either resigned to the omnipotence of the military junta or pined away in isolation (Navarro 1989:256; Suárez-Orozco 1991:491).

The military junta was at a loss about how to react to the public protest. They did not conceive of the mothers as political actors. 'Paradoxically . . . the military in these societies preach traditional family values and valorize motherhood in an attempt to strengthen patriarchal rule in the home. This insistence upon the woman's sacrifice for and obedience to the family and to her children has backfired on the military as women have demanded to know what has happened to their sons and daughters' (Schirmer 1988:45; see also Navarro 1989). At first, the Madres were ignored, then belittled as 'the crazy women of Plaza de Mayo' (*las locas de Plaza de Mayo*). Later, the protests were repressed. Numerous women were abducted, tortured or detained, while some leading figures disappeared altogether.

The Madres utilized their role as mothers brilliantly in their resistance strategy. They emphasized that they had no political motives or feminist sympathies, and identified themselves simply as housewives and mothers who wanted to have news about their disappeared children. What was more natural than a mother wanting to know about the fate of her child? What made their demand unusual was that they expressed these maternal feelings in a public domain dominated by a repressive patriarchal State. They traversed the public–domestic divide, so dominant in Latin American culture, in a reverse direction than the one used by the military assault teams which had invaded their homes to abduct their children. In a second transgressive act, they domesticized the public space by introducing symbols of the home. They donned their heads with diapers and displayed photographs of their loved ones (Schirmer 1994:203). The maternal feelings of protection and trust were the principal driving forces behind their quest.

Guilt feelings, although unjustified, also played a role in this incessant search. Some mothers imagined that they had not done their utmost to prevent the abductions. They experienced a form of survivor's guilt, believing that they were responsible for their children's disappearance, were unworthy mothers, and should have disappeared instead (see Bettelheim 1979:26–37).

The struggle of the mothers between 1977 and 1983 has been documented extensively (see Bousquet 1984; Fisher 1989; Guzman Bouvard 1994; Oria 1987; Simpson and Bennett 1985). What is of more concern here is how mothers affiliated with the Madres and other human rights organizations reacted after a government investigative committee concluded in 1984 that the disappeared could be presumed dead. Once again, conflicting maternal feelings of protection and abandonment were stirred up as now the loss had to be mourned but the final rites of death could not be administered in the absence of a corpse.

Desecration of the corpse in Argentine political culture

When Raúl Alfonsín assumed power in December 1983, he installed a national commission (CONADEP) to inquire into the fate of the disappeared. This was a difficult task because the military junta had destroyed all operational evidence of their repression and had gone to great efforts to conceal or annihilate the corpses of their victims. These corpses were regarded as legitimate military targets in an all-out war on the revolutionary guerrilla movement and the progressive sectors of Argentine society. Admiral Massera had not by accident declared at the height of the repression, 'We are not going to fight till death, we are going to fight till victory, whether it will be beyond or before death' (La Nación, 3 November 1976). Not only was victory more important than life, but the battle continued into the land of the dead.

The disappearances responded to at least five objectives. The three tactical goals were to instil fear in Argentine society, spread confusion in the guerrilla organizations, and avoid martyrdom. Unsuspected civilians were abducted without any formal charge, while the sudden disappearance of guerrilla fighters severely hampered insurgency operations. Doubts were raised whether the captured combatants were dead or alive, had defected or deserted, or were being tortured for information.

Some of the detained reappeared after days, weeks or even months as political prisoners, but most were killed, their bodies discarded or obliterated. The physical annihilation of the corpses served to avoid the dead being turned into martyrs. Their remains could become relics, and their graves the object of political pilgrimages. The disappearance of the corpses was also motivated by two strategic concerns about the political future of the armed forces. Eventually the military would have to hand power to a democratic government, and they knew that criminal prosecution would be impossible without any *corpora delicti*. Corpses were therefore cremated, abandoned at roadsides, thrown in rivers, or interred in cemeteries as unidentified bodies.[9] The Navy even had the practice of flinging heavily drugged detainees from planes at sea (García 1995:461–70; Verbitsky 1995). Finally, the military leaders believed that historical judgment could be decisively influenced in their political direction if there were no bodies to mourn, deaths to commemorate, or epitaphs to read. The importance given to this objective, and the means chosen to achieve it, are rooted in long-established practices of Argentine political culture.

The dismemberment and mutilation of enemy corpses have been practices of warfare in Spanish America since the days of the independence war from Spain during the early nineteenth century. All across the continent, royalist and rebel troops quartered the bodies of soldiers and civilians alike, and sent the remains of important commanders as trophies for display to regional capitals (see Mitre 1969; Molas 1985). A proper Catholic burial was impossible as the parts of the body were sent to different locations in the country.[10] This was an extreme humiliation

[9] The military rulers made two official attempts to have the disappeared pronounced dead, even in the absence of a corpse. A law was issued in September 1979 that declared all persons presumed dead who had disappeared between 6 November 1974 and 6 September 1979. They hoped that this decree would end the insistent appeals from human rights organizations. After the 1982 defeat in the Falklands/Malvinas War, the interim government of General Bignone published a final report about the 1976–82 dictatorship and declared once again all disappeared as presumed dead (San Martino de Dromi 1988:343 and 360; *Somos* 1983 346:15).

[10] It is plausible to assume that the desecration of the corpse was also related to the Catholic belief in purgatory and the survival of the soul after death. The mutilated were believed to suffer horribly as they were cleansed of their earthly sins. There was a widespread conviction that the soul survived after death, and that human remains carried a spiritual power that could affect the world of the living. Natalie Zemon Davis comes to the same doctrinal explanation in her interpretation of the mutilation of corpses by Catholic crowds during the sixteenth-century religious wars against the Huguenots in France. Protestant crowds were particularly keen on torturing Catholic priests, but were indifferent to the corpse, possibly because 'the souls of the dead experience immediately Christ's presence or the torments of the damned, and thus the dead body is no longer so dangerous or important an object to the living' (Davis 1975:179). On the other hand, the exhumation, mutilation, and public display of the

that symbolized the political dismemberment of the enemy forces, and the power of the new rulers. The importance of honour, charisma, and clientalism made decapitation the predilected celebration of victory. The flight of a party of defeated soldiers with the putrefying body of General Lavalle in 1841 to prevent it from falling into the hands of his enemies has become legendary. It would take two decades before the remains were repatriated and reburied with national honour (Frias 1884). The defamation of the dead may have been the result of the brutalization of war but it also had considerable political significance. The mutilation of the vanquished was as important to emphasize total subjugation as the stately reburial of slain victors was to advance power and dominant ideology. Dismemberment and reburial were two sides of the same political struggle. The destination of the remains of friend and foe became therefore a matter of great significance.

Many generals and politicians of the civil wars have been reburied at the national Recoleta cemetery, even though a good number of them had died in exile. Their remains were exhumed in places such as Washington, Paris, Montevideo, and Santiago de Chile and brought to Buenos Aires. Mortal enemies were eventually buried next to one another as each new government honoured its own forebears with a stately reburial. In this way, the Recoleta cemetery became the pantheon of the nation. However, the presence of former enemies, such as Dorrego, Lavalle, Sarmiento, and Facundo Quiroga, in the same cemetery may have represented their reconciliation in death, but did not end the animosities among their political heirs. New conflicts were always explained in terms of old scores, and the political obsession with the corpse continued well into the twentieth century, albeit in a different form. Death through torture replaced throat-cutting as the predominant practice of terror on political opponents, while enemy corpses were no longer displayed openly but disappeared secretly. The body of one of the most prominent and charismatic figures in twentieth-century Argentine politics, Eva Duarte de Perón, is paradigmatic of the abuse of the corpse as an object of political contestation.[11]

Evita died in 1952. She was embalmed after nearly 1 million people had passed by the body laying in state. A military coup by General Aramburu against Perón in 1955 ended the official Evita cult. Her name

mummified remains of priests, nuns, and saints during the Spanish civil war was an iconoclastic attack by the republican left on the conservative church and the nationalists (Lincoln 1989:117–27).

[11] The body of Juan Domingo Perón was also disturbed. In July 1987, someone broke into Perón's tomb at Chacarita cemetery and stole the hands from the corpse, the very hands Perón used to raise in his characteristic pose as he received the cheers and chants from the Peronist masses.

was removed from buildings, streets, squares, and public works, and Aramburu ordered the disappearance of Evita's embalmed body. Eloy Martínez captures the political meaning of Evita's corpse acutely in his fictionalized account *Santa Evita* when he imagines the lieutenant colonel entrusted with making the body disappear saying that 'the dead and useless body of Eva Duarte has become confused with the country' (Martínez 1995:34). History was left inside by embalming Evita. The mummified body was removed from Argentina in 1957. In 1970, a commando force of Montoneros kidnapped and executed General Aramburu for overthrowing Perón in 1955 and for defaming Evita's body. In 1971, her body was exhumed at a Milan cemetery and returned in perfect state to Perón living in exile in Madrid. In October 1974, a Montoneros task force kidnapped the body of General Aramburu from the Recoleta national cemetery as ransom for Evita. Evita's body was repatriated in November 1974 and eventually reburied at her family's tomb at Recoleta (Gillespie 1982:183; Page 1983:344 and 424–5, 500; Taylor 1979:69–71; *Somos* 1984:46–9).

Clearly, the body of Evita was a relic for her followers and a source of evil for her opponents. The powers attributed to her by common people gave her a saintly aura. What matters here is not whether Evita's remains had such powers, but the symbolic significance they acquired in the process of disappearance and reburial. To use an observation made by Winnicott (1988:xii), it is 'not so much the object used as the use of the object' that is important here.[12] Evita's body functioned as a transitional object in the incipient civil war between conservative and revolutionary political forces.

Anna Freud (1969:310) was the first to consider the dead as transitional objects. She argued that this unconscious treatment of the dead might facilitate the mourning process, and function as a defence against separation anxiety. Likewise, just as the child's transitional object can be interpreted as a cultural artifact, so the cultural significance of the corpse can be derived from its treatment. However, for corpses to function as transitional objects in political struggles, they need to have significance for victors and vanquished alike; they need to represent a transitional phase for both parties in conflict, and be centred around the anxieties of death. Since the nineteenth-century civil wars in Argentina, the corpse has functioned as a transitional object between war and

---

[12] An analogy can be drawn with the medieval theft of religious relics from an obscure resting place and their display at a more prominent church or religious centre. The theft resembled a rite of passage for the ossified or mummified spirit which passed from neglect and insufficient veneration to a proper place of honour and devotion (Geary 1978:156).

victory on which the parties to the conflict projected the hatred of their political adversaries, and separation anxiety has been used as a weapon by denying the opponents the right to honour and bury their dead. This practice was anxiety-ridden because the violence inflicted on the opponent might rebound with a vengeance. Notwithstanding the risk of retaliation, the corpse became the tally of war, and its eventual destiny a way to gauge its success. The enemy represented the 'not-me', the 'other', whose disappearance and annihilation implied a victory, and the end of war. Just as the bodies of nineteenth-century commanders had been important in the civil wars, so did Evita's embalmed body and the remains of the more than 10,000 people who disappeared between 1976 and 1983 function as transitional objects in a deeply divided society. Political meaning became added to the personal grief of the bereaved.[13]

Anna Freud (1969:313) also drew attention to the ambivalent attitude of the bereaved towards the deceased. Feelings of abandonment, anger, and hurt are displaced on the physical remains. The mourner is torn between abandoning and clinging to the body, representing the transitional phase between denial and detachment.[14] Having borne the child,

[13] The use of human remains as transitional objects must be distinguished from their use as linking objects. Volkan (1972, 1981:101–6) has pioneered the important concept of linking objects to describe a pathological attachment to possessions that stand for the lost person. He has called such possessions 'linking objects' because mourners cannot separate themselves from the deceased and therefore cling to an object that relates them to the dead person. Unlike transitional objects, which are eventually abandoned, linking objects are always kept under tight control, either locked away or, at certain moments, caressed, held or looked at compulsively. Unlike inherited mementos, linking objects provoke great anxiety and ambivalent feelings of attraction and rejection. Consequently, the human remains of the Argentine disappeared are, in most instances, not linking but transitional objects for the following reasons. First, the relatives of the disappeared are conscious of their search for human remains. Secondly, unlike linking objects which are unique, all relatives search for the same type of object. Furthermore, these remains are not ideational but genetic extensions of both bereaved and deceased. Thirdly, the skeletal remains are reburied once they have been found. Fourthly, the bones do not provoke anxiety but relief. They allow people to complete the mourning process instead of prolonging it indefinitely. Fifthly, the search for human remains marks a transitional phase of personal and political significance with a clear beginning and end. Sixthly, the linking object 'is a token of triumph over separation' (Volkan 1981:106). Instead, reburial turns the exhumed skeleton into a token of triumph of separation. Personally, the reburial symbolizes the final reconciliation with the death of the former disappeared. Politically, it represents the liberation from the totalizing grip of the military who were the masters of their dead and their unfinished mourning.

[14] Several attempts have been made to capture the process of mourning in a developmental model. Kübler-Ross (1993:149) discovered that terminally ill patients and their relatives shared five basic defence mechanisms, namely denial, anger, bargaining, depression, and acceptance. Bowlby (1981b:85) has delineated four phases, namely numbing, disbelief, despair, and reorganization. Such stages do not of course represent a universal unilinear development among people. People may skip stages, revert to previous ones, manifest several stages simultaneously, or never come to reconcile themselves with the loss of a son or daughter.

the mother now has to let go. The corpse becomes the transitional object, virtual yet inert, that allows the parents to mourn the loss. Funeral rites are the cultural scenarios that provide parents with a social form in which to manifest their grief and to allow the transition to occur. The function of the corpse as a personal transitional object explains the anguish of disappearance. The importance of its function as a political transitional object explains the meaning of disappearance in the practice of warfare. The absence of a corpse leaves parents suspended between two emotional worlds. They can neither pour their grief into the human remains nor mourn the loss in a politicized public rite of passage.

The Argentine mothers searched for the remains as if these were still their suffering children, while feeling guilty not only about having abandoned them in the hour of death but also about being unable to provide the maternal care of a proper burial. Their wandering spirit reflects the mourner's loss. Eternal rest can only be achieved 'after the survivors have performed the difficult task of dealing with their bereavement and of detaching their hopes, demands, and expectations from the image of the dead' (Freud 1969:316). Identification and projection are therefore likely outlets when the corpse is missing. A mother can turn her grief inward through identification or externalize her anger on those responsible for the loss.

Chronic anxiety and impaired mourning

The mourning process of the parents of the disappeared was severely hampered by the politicization of the corpse as a transitional object in the dirty war on the Left. They had to reconcile themselves with the uncertainty of death, the absence of the corpse, the inability to perform burial rites, and the political repression expressed through the disappearance. Since many of the emotional reactions of the parents resemble grief, I will draw upon the extensive psychoanalytic literature on loss and mourning to analyze their reactions.

Empirical research has demonstrated that the death of a son or daughter is the most painful of all losses, that mothers have more difficulty coping than fathers, and that the emotional recovery is slower with the sudden death of a grown than a young child (Gorer 1965:121; Rubin 1993:299). There is something unnatural about a child dying before its parents, especially when it has grown through the fragile stage of infancy into healthy adulthood. The severing of this relation is experienced as the destruction of self, the world, and the meaning of life (Klass 1989:152; Rosenblatt 1993:103; Rubin 1993:288).

Dennis Klass has observed that parents come to accept the reality of a child's death by learning the full details. 'Autopsy reports, medical examiner's reports, and, where they exist, police reports are read over and over' (Klass 1989:159). The immense grief over the loss of a disappeared child is that such details are seldom available; that there is neither a certainty of death nor a body to mourn. Many of the psychological problems mentioned by Klass, such as crying fits, domestic tensions, emotional emptiness, and profound sadness exist also among parents of missing children. The health problems of bereaved Argentine parents have been multiple. Clinical work has shown that they suffer frequently from insomnia, loss of appetite, anxiety attacks, depression, psychosomatic disorders, and suicide attempts (Edelman and Kordon 1995:103; Sluzki 1990).

Denial is the most common response of people confronted with the death of a loved one. But, as Freud (1917:244) has observed, 'respect for reality gains the day', and the bereaved reconcile themselves with the inevitable loss. In the case of a disappeared person, however, the denial of death is confirmed in reality-testing, as a search in police-stations, military bases, hospitals, and morgues does not provide any conclusive indication of death. Argentine parents who saw their children being abducted alive, but heard stories about the torture and killings in the secret detention centres, agonized about the fate of their loved ones, but hardly ever considered them to be dead.

Bowlby (1981b:28) and Parkes (1970; 1972:39–56) believe that the desire to search for the deceased is innate to mourning. 'Pining is the subjective and emotional component of the urge to search for a lost object' (Parkes 1972:40). This urge has an entirely different meaning in the case of a disappearance than for a demonstrable death. The search is not an echo of the lost relationship but an urge to recover it. The hope that the loved one is still alive makes the disappearance so tantalizing. Mourning disposes people of this hope, and overcoming sadness is experienced as abandoning the child.

The absence of any trace is bewildering. Reality and fantasy are hard to disentangle as the parent is thrown between hope for life and resignation to death. Just as a bereaved person, the relatives of the disappeared imagine seeing or hearing the lost person (Parkes 1972:45–9). These parents composed and frequently readjusted their mental picture of how the lost child might have aged as the years passed. It is revealing that the list of disappeared compiled by the national commission CONADEP did not provide the date of birth but the date of disappearance and the person's age at the time the report was published in late 1984.

The continued search was burdened by the secrecy that surrounded the disappearances during the years of repression. Sharing the loss with others, which is so therapeutic for bereaved parents, could not be done during the first years of the dictatorship when human rights organizations were few and small. A double stigma surrounded parents of the disappeared. First, there was the stigma that envelops all mourners. They are often shunned because their loss is regarded as a weakness (Gorer 1965:131; Parkes 1972:8). Secondly, people feared that their association with the relatives might be politically dangerous. Julio Morresi recalled that 'me and my wife were sowing fear around us with our desperation and anguish, because I realized that there were friends who were even afraid to talk to me. I mean to say that we were like an antibody for them' (interview, 15 May 1990).

The years of uncertainty manifested themselves often in emotional reactions that resembled various forms of anticipatory and pathological grief (see Lindemann 1944; Parkes 1972:106–17; Stroebe and Stroebe 1987:17–21; Volkan 1981:53). Argentine psychoanalysts who have worked extensively with relatives of the disappeared mention impaired mourning as the most common emotional disturbance (Braun de Dunayevich and Pelento 1991; Edelman and Kordon 1995; Kaës 1991:160; Nicoletti 1988). The term 'pathological grief' is problematic in the Argentine context because the belief that the disappeared were still alive was confirmed by the reappearance of small numbers of former disappeared after months or even years in secret detention. Furthermore, the Argentine military kept denying that they had any of the disappeared in custody. Instead, with an uncanny sadism, they said that the persons reported as missing were living in voluntary exile in Europe or Latin America.[15]

Resignation to death was emotionally and socially less acceptable than postponing grief for years until the fate of the disappeared was entirely clear. Julio Morresi never succeeded in pronouncing his son dead: 'you were searching for a loved one without knowing what had happened. You said that he was alive somewhere, because you were not going to kill him with your conscience by saying "my son is dead." I never ever thought that my son was dead, if not it would have given me the feeling that it was me who had killed him' (interview, 29 March 1991). Morresi eventually found his son. He was exhumed in 1989.

Gorer (1965:85–7) has pointed at mummification as a form of chronic grief. Mummification refers to the preservation of the lost

---

[15] Defence lawyers in the trial against the junta members supported this claim by arguing that at least twenty-nine names of missing persons appeared on the official list of Argentine citizens who had survived the 1985 earthquake in Mexico City (*Somos* 1985 474:6–10).

person's room and possessions. However, for many parents, this was a perfectly reasonable expression of impaired mourning. Mummification was only pathological after 1984 when it became clear that the disappeared were dead. I have visited people between 1989 and 1991 who still changed the sheets on their disappeared daughter's bed or prepared every few days their son's favourite pudding so that he could enjoy it as soon as he would appear at the doorstep (see also Suárez-Orozco 1991:495).[16]

Parents were placed before an agonizing dilemma after the fall of the military dictatorship: maintaining hope implied that the search would likely continue indefinitely, while mourning meant giving up hope and accepting the death of the missing children without being able to provide them with a proper resting-place and observe the departure with a culturally prescribed funeral. Parents of the disappeared are painfully aware of this dilemma as Graciela Fernández Meijide reveals: 'And it is a road which I don't know will ever end. It is what psychoanalysts call "unelaborated grief." Because you don't know how to elaborate it. For those who are religious or who want to have a place on earth where they have their dead to take flowers to, to say a prayer, whatever, this is denied to them' (Ulla and Echave 1986:34–5).[17] People dealt with the dilemma in a number of ways. Some displayed pathological grief and continued to believe that the disappeared were alive. Others reconciled themselves with the inevitable and tried to reconstruct their lives. Some were even unwilling to accept the human remains of the disappeared upon exhumation. These reactions were confined entirely to a private coping with death. Others added a political dimension to their personal grief. Political activism and the search for skeletal remains became the predominant ways to solve the paradox of knowing the unknowable.

Contested exhumations and revolutionary protest

The first evidence of the existence of mass graves appeared in late October 1982, only months after the military junta fell after its defeat in the Falklands/Malvinas War. Eighty-eight unmarked graves with an estimated 400 unidentified bodies were found at the park cemetery of Grand Bourg near Buenos Aires (Cohen Salama 1992:60–62; *Somos* 1982 319:11). The effect of the discovery on the Argentine public was

---

[16] See Robben (1995, 1996) on the methodological problems of conducting interviews with victims and perpetrators of violence.
[17] Danieli (1989), Kestenberg (1989), Meerloo (1968), and Trautman (1971) describe similar difficulties by Nazi concentration camp survivors in mourning close relatives without evidence of their death.

devastating. There was both disbelief and anger. Soon, more mass graves were opened and the bullet-ridden skulls exhibited on the edge of their makeshift graves in what was called a 'horror show'. The display of piles of bones and perforated skulls revealed to the stunned Argentines the horrors of the military regime as well as their own mortality and the chance that they could very well have met the same fate. For the surviving relatives, in particular, the psychological impact was great: 'the *desaparecidos* were most often young and healthy when they were taken and they now return in the form of an unrecognizable mass of bones' (Suárez-Orozco 1991:495). Now, at least, the impaired mourning in which many people had been caught could be lifted.

Even though the exhumations provoked mixed reactions, the human rights organizations which had demanded the truth about the disappearances were much in favour. Hebe de Bonafini, the undisputed leader of the Madres de Plaza de Mayo, believed in October 1982 that the exhumations would give the disappeared a name and identity. At last, the hastily interred bodies would be wrested from anonymity and given a proper burial (*Humor* 1982 92:47). As new mass graves continued to be opened to provide evidence of the military repression, but the victims could not be identified, questions were raised about the sense of continuing these exhumations. In January 1984, De Bonafini was convinced that 'there is sufficient proof to send a great number of those guilty of this horror to prison', but she expressed doubts about the political will to prosecute them (*Somos* 1984 382:20). Faith in the justice system declined further when the Alfonsín government decided that the nine commanders of the three 1976–82 juntas were to be tried under military instead of criminal law. By 1985, a fundamental split had developed among the Argentine human rights organizations between those in favour and those against exhumations. The division corresponded to two different responses to the loss suffered by the disappearances. Both groups were aware of the political dimensions of their positions, but the proponents wanted an honourable reburial, while the opponents desired the vindication of the political ideals of the disappeared. These responses to separation anxiety shall be interpreted as respectively projection and introjection (Volkan 1981:70–2), and analyzed as the final enactments of maternal trust and protection.

A growing number of the Madres de Plaza de Mayo were having misgivings in 1984 about the exhumations. It would lead in 1986 to a tragic split within the organization that had most courageously opposed the military dictatorship. The majority followed Hebe de Bonafini in her condemnation that the exhumations were a government scheme to have them accept and psychologically participate in the death of all disappeared. The Madres demanded that first the assassins had to be identified before any further exhumations were to be carried out (*Madres* 1984 1:2). Reflecting on the intense soul-searching that preceded their stance on exhumations, Hebe de Bonafini has said: 'It cost us weeks and weeks of meetings at which there were many tears and much despair, because the profound Catholic formation of our people creates almost a need to have a dead body, a burial, and a Mass' (*Madres* 1987 37:10).[18] Despite the anguish, the De Bonafini group decided to keep their emotional wounds open in order to resist the societal process of forgetting. 'It has been eleven years of suffering, eleven years that have not been relieved in any sense. Many want the wound to dry so that we will forget. We want it to continue bleeding, because this is the only way that one continues to have strength to fight . . . But, above all, it is necessary that this wound bleeds so that the assassins will be condemned, as they deserve to be, and that what has happened will not happen again. This is the commitment in the defence of life which the Madres have taken upon themselves' (*Madres* 1987 29:1). The suffering of the disappeared has been introjected by the mothers, and resulted in their identification with the ideals that caused these wounds to be inflicted.

The leading figures of the Madres were of course well aware of the psychological toll of the enduring uncertainty, and had a team of psychoanalysts at hand to provide assistance. They realized that the recuperation of the remains would allow relatives to mourn their dead, but regarded the deliberate setting in motion of this mourning process as a sinister ploy by the government to achieve resignation and depoliticization among the surviving relatives. Mourning would break the solidarity of the Madres and produce a reconciliatory attitude. Continued political protest weighed more heavily than individual relief because anxiety was the hinge of memory and oblivion. The belief that the son or daughter disappeared for a just and noble political cause made the mourning process resemble war bereavement (see Stroebe and Stroebe 1987:213).

The chronic anxiety, the impaired mourning, and the continued hope that characterized the years between 1976 and 1982, turned to anger and disillusionment in 1983 and 1984 as increasingly more mass graves were discovered. It was followed by a profound identification with lost sons and daughters. Activism helped them cope with their grief (see

[18] Elena Nicoletti, a member of the psychological team of the Madres, has argued that the Madres have rejected all mortuary rituals of Western culture because these rites cannot set in a genuine mourning process without any certainty about the fate of the disappeared (Nicoletti 1988:116).

Maxwell 1995). A majority of the Madres de Plaza de Mayo began to emulate political ideals which many had opposed in the late 1960s and early 1970s. They began to regard themselves as the embodiment of their children's ideals and struggles. 'In many respects it was like this: my children had given birth to me . . . If they are not here, then I have to be them, shout for them, vindicate them with honesty and return if even a small piece of life to them. They are in my rallying cries, in this fatigue that maybe nobody can understand but which always recuperates itself; they are in my head and in my body, in everything I do. I believe that their absence has left me forever pregnant' (Hebe de Bonafini in Sánchez 1985:74–5). Are these sublimated guilt feelings about desertion? Are these mothers resurrecting the disappeared or do they want to demonstrate their unconditional trust in their children?

Impaired grief transformed into introjection and identification as the Madres wanted to keep the disappeared alive by leaving their remains unidentified in mass graves, and divulging their ideals instead. 'If my son is interred in a place with his companions then let him stay there, because a dead son doesn't serve me. I want my son alive. And if my son is not alive then I want the culprit. So, to take my son to a small piece of land to go and cry for his remains doesn't serve me' (Maria del Rosario de Cerruti, interview, 9 April 1990). 'It doesn't matter where they have interred their bodies, but their spirit, their solidarity, and their love for the people can never be buried and forgotten' (Hebe de Bonafini, *Madres* 1989 58:11). Reburial would bury the mothers' pain of separation, instead of assuring their children's presence through the promulgation of their political ideals. The acceptance of death is harder than a defiant denial because such resignation is experienced as the final victory of the military dictatorship; another notch on their tally. The spirit of the disappeared about which the Madres speak does not reflect 'the wandering and searching of the survivor's libidinal strivings which have been rendered aimless, i.e., deprived of their former goal', as Anna Freud (1969:316) has argued, but represents their renewed embodiment and continued presence in the world of politics. Ironically, it is the same belief in the embodiment and resurrection of revolutionary ideas that made the military regime decide upon the disappearances.

By late 1988, the idea arose that the Madres had to 'socialize their maternity' (*Madres* 1988 48:17) and embrace the suffering of all victims of political violence in the world. 'When we understood that our children were not going to appear, we socialized motherhood and felt that we are the mothers of everybody, that all are our children' (Hebe de Bonafini, *Madres* 1989 53:17). Pressing social problems, such as widespread poverty, declining social services, high unemployment, insufficient benefits for the aged, government corruption, police brutality, and the privatization of state companies became a political platform to pursue the revolutionary ideals of their children. Clearly, the Madres wanted to extend the maternal protection they had been unable to provide to their own children at the hour of abduction to all victims of repression, and at the same time be faithful and loyal to their sons and daughters by embracing their radical political ideas. Trust and protection were the unconscious motives of their political position.

Reburial and collective mourning

The radical opposition of the Madres de Plaza de Mayo to the exhumations was not shared by most human rights organizations. They became convinced of the importance of forensic investigations during the 1985 trial against the supreme commanders of the dirty war. Exhumations supplied evidence for legal prosecution, provided historical testimony of the human rights violations committed by the military, gave forensic proof about the birth of children by pregnant disappeared, and allowed surviving relatives to begin a process of mourning. Exhumation has become a recourse for many relatives, as much for their emotional peace as for the political significance of a funeral during the transition from dictatorship to democracy. Reburial reconciles the bereaved with their loss, restores the public honour of the victims, reincorporates them into society as deceased members, and politicizes the recovered skeletal remains. They are able to project their feelings on the bones and end their search.

Julio and Irma Morresi found their son Norberto in 1989 and reburied him in the same grave as the disappeared person who was exhumed together with him. 'The truth, however hard it may be, will in the end bring tranquility. I am no longer searching in that god-knows-where place, as I commented before, to see if it's Norberto, or visit a madhouse to see if he is there. I know, unfortunately we have this little heap of bones at the Flores cemetery, no? It is like a ritual that we go there every Sunday to bring him even if it is only one flower. It is completely useless, but it helps spiritually . . . We go there, we kiss the photo that is hanging on the niche, and it makes us feel good' (interview, 29 March 1991). The importance of finding the remains of a loved one is expressed in a moving way by Juan Gelman and Berta Schubaroff after forensic anthropologists had exhumed and identified their son Marcelo in 1989. 'I felt that I was emotional because I found my son', Marta Schuberoff recalled a few days after the funeral. 'I kissed him again. I kissed all his bones, touched him, caressed him. But the emotion confounded with the pain, because once I found him, he turned out to be dead. So I cried the death of my son, and those thirteen years of search vanished. I can't relate anymore to this period' (quoted in Cohen Salama 1992:249). Juan Gelman confessed to similar sentiments a few weeks later: 'I feel that I have been able to rescue him from the fog' (quoted in Cohen Salama 1992:250). I wonder through which fog Juan Gelman seized his son. The fog that drifts between the land of the living and the land of the dead? Or does he mean to say that he was finally able to deliver his son from the mists of oblivion?

Juan Gelman's sentiments about finally being able to help his son can be understood within the wider social significance of reburials. The French anthropologist Robert Hertz distinguishes three purposes to reburials: 'to give burial to the remains of the deceased, to ensure the soul peace and access to the land of the dead, and finally to free the living from the obligations of mourning' (Hertz 1960:54). Reburial allows parents to express their basic trust to their deceased children by providing them with a proper resting place and observing their departure with a culturally prescribed funeral. The torn fabric of society is restored by funerary rituals, the remains come to share sacred ground, and their souls are reconciled in the society of the dead, only to be recaptured periodically in annual remembrance or collective religious rites. These purposes seem to have been served in Argentina for nearly 200 disappeared who were reburied, were it not that their violent death accords them a special position in society and turns the reburial from a ritual of restoration into a political manifestation. It is therefore precisely the political nature of their death that gives the fate of the body such importance.

The reburial of Marcelo Gelman had not only an emotional but also a deep political significance. Berta Shubaroff decided to bury her son in a Jewish cemetery out of vindication, even though she never practised the Jewish faith. She had become conscious of her Jewish heritage when she learnt that her son's tormentors had treated him as a 'shit jew' (*judío de mierda*), and she therefore wanted to demonstrate her forgotten identity openly through a Jewish reburial (Cohen Salama 1992:250). Furthermore, the wake had taken place at the headquarters of the Buenos Aires press workers' union (UTPBA). Marcelo Gelman was one of ninety disappeared journalists, and his reburial served to draw attention to their plight.

Robert Hertz (1960:83) has observed that: 'It is the action of society on the body that gives full reality to the imagined drama of the soul.' What a society does with its dead determines the place of their souls in society. The disappearance of the body implies that the soul can neither pass from the land of the living to the land of the dead. The wandering spirit continues to haunt the living in the form of the constant anxiety of relatives who cannot mourn the disappeared and keep demanding a reckoning from society.

The two predominant responses of Argentine mothers have been either to search for the remains of their children or to propagate the revolutionary ideals associated with the disappeared. Both reactions arise from the same basic trust and unconditional support which they want to provide to their disappeared children. The public protests against pressing social problems and the reburial of identified remains in a cloak of maternal protection seem to offer the mothers some emotional respite from their tremendous grief. However, the realization that justice was not served, and that those responsible for the disappearances are scot-free, keeps troubling them. Peace cannot return to a society when its members are unable to reconcile themselves with the past. Impaired mourning can affect societies as much as individuals, as Volkan (in this volume) has demonstrated.

The treatment of the dead by the living is thus a reflection of the state of their collective relations. The rite of passage between life and death symbolized in funerals is analogous to the transition between war and peace. Political violence in Argentina was directed in the dirty war at the corpse as a transitional object between war and victory. The deliberate obstruction of funeral rites impedes a return to the normalcy of peace and a repair of the social fabric. The sorrow and rage of the living will continue to trouble the nation as long as the corpses of the dead are not recovered and a process of collective mourning has begun.

The long-term psychosocial consequences of the dirty war are impossible to fathom, but the continued uncertainty about thousands of unrecovered dead and the impunity of their executioners cannot but gnaw at the heart of the nation. The massive trauma of the dirty war has undermined people's trust in the State authorities, their fellow human beings, and maybe even themselves. The traumatic past threatens to become indigestible as the mourning continues impaired because a society that does not assume responsibility for its dead can never entirely trust the living.

References

Arendt, Hannah, 1958, *The Human Condition*. Chicago: University of Chicago Press

Benn, Stanley I. and Gerald F. Gaus, 1983, The Public and the Private: Concepts and Action. In *Public and Private in Social Life*. Stanley I. Benn and Gerald F. Gaus. London: Croon Helm, 3–27

Bettelheim, Bruno, 1979, *Surviving and Other Essays*. New York: Vintage Books

Bousquet, Jean-Pierre, 1984 [1980], *Las Locas de la Plaza de Mayo*. Córdoba: Fundación para la Democracia en Argentina

Bowlby, John, 1981a, *Attachment and Loss*, Vol. I. *Attachment*. Harmondsworth: Penguin Books

1981b, *Attachment and Loss*, Vol. III. *Loss: Sadness and Depression*. Harmondsworth: Penguin Books

Braun de Dunayevich, Julia and María Lucila Pelento, 1991, Las vicisitudes de la pulsión de saber en ciertos duelos especiales. In *Violencia de Estado y Psicoanálisis*. Janine Puget and René Kaës, eds. Buenos Aires: Centro Editor de América Latina, 79–91

Brown, Barbara, 1987, Territoriality. In *Handbook of Environmental Psychology*. Daniel Stokes and Irwin Altman, eds. Vol. I. New York: John Wiley, 505–31

Caudill, William and Helen Weinstein, 1972, Maternal Care and Infant Behavior in Japan and America. In *Readings in Child Behavior and Development*. Celia Stendler Lavatelli, and Faith Stendler, eds. New York: Harcourt Brace Jovanovich, 78–87

Cohen Salama, Mauricio, 1992, *Tumbas anónimas*. Buenos Aires: Catálogos

CONADEP, 1986, *Nunca Más: The Report of the Argentine Commission on the Disappeared*. New York: Farrar, Straus, Giroux

Csikszentmihalyi, Mihaly and Eugene Rochberg-Halton, 1981, *The Meaning of Things: Domestic Symbols and the Self*. Cambridge: Cambridge University Press

DaMatta, Roberto, 1987, *A Casa e a Rua: Espaço, Cidadania, Mulher e Morte no Brasil*. Rio de Janeiro: Editora Guanabara

Danieli, Yael, 1989, Mourning in Survivors and Children of Survivors of the Nazi Holocaust: The Role of Group and Community Modalities. In *The Problem of Loss and Mourning: Psychoanalytic Perspectives*. David R. Dietrich and Peter C. Shabad, eds. Madison: International Universities Press, 427–60

Davis, Natalie Zemon, 1975, *Society and Culture in Early Modern France*. Stanford: Stanford University Press

Ejército Argentino, 1972, *Procedimientos para las operaciones contra la subversión urbana*. Manual M-8-1

Edelman, Lucila and Diana Kordon, 1995, Trauma y duelo. Conflicto y elaboración. In *La Impunidad: Una perspectiva psicosocial y clínica*. Diana Kordon *et al.*, eds. Buenos Aires: Editorial Sudamericana, 101–10

Elliott, Anthony, 1994, *Psychoanalytic Theory: An Introduction*. Oxford: Blackwell

Erikson, Erik H., 1951, *Childhood and Society*. London: Imago Publishing Co.

Fairbairn, W. Ronald D., 1962, *Psychoanalytic Studies of the Personality*. London: Tavistock Publications

Feldman, Allen, 1991, *Formations of Violence: The Narrative of the Body and Political Terror in Northern Ireland*. Chicago: University of Chicago Press

Fisher, Jo, 1989, *Mothers of the Disappeared*. Boston: South End Press

Freud, Anna, 1969, About Losing and Being Lost. In *Indications for Child Analysis and Other Papers, 1945–1956*. Anna Freud, ed. London: The Hogarth Press, 302–16

Freud, Sigmund, 1905, Three Essays on the Theory of Sexuality. *The Standard Edition of the Complete Psychological Works of Sigmund Freud* 1968, ed. James Strachey. Vol. VII. London: The Hogarth Press, 125–245

1917, Mourning and Melancholia. *Standard Edition.* Vol. XIV. London: The Hogarth Press, 243–58

1920, Beyond the Pleasure Principle. *Standard Edition.* Vol. XVIII. London: The Hogarth Press, 7–64

1930, Civilization and Its Discontents. *Standard Edition.* Vol. XXI. London: The Hogarth Press, 59–145

Frias, Félix, 1884, Exéquias fúnebres al General Lavalle. In *Escritos y Discursos.* Félix Frias, ed. Vol. III. Buenos Aires: Imprenta y Libreria de Mayo, 319–25

Garcia, Prudencio, 1995, *El drama de la autonomía militar: Argentina bajo las Juntas Militares.* Madrid: Alianza Editores

Geary, Patrick J., 1978, *Furta Sacra: Thefts of Relics in the Central Middle Ages.* Princeton: Princeton University Press

Giddens, Anthony, 1991, *Modernity and Self-Identity: Self and Society in the Late Modern Age.* Stanford: Stanford University Press

Gillespie, Richard, 1982, *Soldiers of Perón: Argentina's Montoneros.* Oxford: Clarendon Press

Gorer, Geoffrey, 1965, *Death, Grief, and Mourning.* Garden City, NY: Doubleday & Company

Grubrich-Simitis, Ilse, 1981, Extreme Traumatization as Cumulative Trauma: Psychoanalytic Investigations of the Effects of Concentration Camp Experiences on Survivors and Their Children. *Psychoanalytic Study of the Child* 36:415–50

Guzman Bouvard, Marguerite, 1994, *Revolutionizing Motherhood: The Mothers of the Plaza de Mayo.* Wilmington: Scholarly Resources

Herrera, Matilde, 1987, *José.* Buenos Aires: Editorial Contrapunto

Herrera, Matilde and Ernesto Tenembaum, 1990, *Identidad: Despojo y Restitución.* Buenos Aires: Editorial Contrapunto

Hertz, Robert, 1960, *Death and the Right Hand.* Aberdeen: Cohen and West

Kaës, René, 1991, Rupturas catastróficas y trabajo de la memoria. Notas para una investigación. In *Violencia de Estado y Psicoanálisis.* Janine Puget and René Kaës, eds. Buenos Aires: Centro Editor de América Latina, 137–63

Kestenberg, Judith S., 1989, Coping with Losses and Survival. In *The Problem of Loss and Mourning: Psychoanalytic Perspectives.* David R. Dietrich and Peter C. Shabad, eds. Madison: International Universities Press, 381–403

Klass, Dennis, 1989, The Resolution of Parental Bereavement. In *Midlife Loss: Coping Strategies.* Richard A. Kalish, ed. Newbury Park, CA: Sage Publications, 149–78

Klein, Melanie, 1988, Love, Guilt and Reparation. In *Love, Guilt and Reparation and Other Works 1921–1945.* London: Virago Press, 306–43

Kordon, Diana and Lucila I. Edelman, 1988, Observations on the Psychopathological Effects of Social Silencing Concerning the Existence of Missing People. In *Psychological Effects of Political Repression.* Diana Kordon *et al.,* eds. Buenos Aires: Sudamericana/Planeta, 27–39

Krystal, Henry, 1968, Studies of Concentration-Camp Survivors. In *Massive*

Psychic Trauma. Henry Krystal, ed. New York: International Universities Press, 23–46

Kübler-Ross, Elisabeth, 1993 [1969], *On Death and Dying.* New York: Collier Books

LeVine, Robert A., 1988, Human Parental Care: Universal Goals, Cultural Strategies, Individual Behavior. In *Parental Behavior in Diverse Societies.* Robert A. LeVine, Patrice M. Miller, and Mary Maxwell West, eds. San Francisco: Jossey-Bass, 3–12

LeVine, Robert A., Suzanne Dixon *et al.*, 1994, *Child Care and Culture: Lessons from Africa.* Cambridge: Cambridge University Press

Lincoln, Bruce, 1989, *Discourse and the Construction of Society: Comparative Studies of Myth, Ritual, and Classification.* New York: Oxford University Press

Lindemann, E., 1944, Symptomatology and Management of Acute Grief. *American Journal of Psychiatry* 101:141–8

Martínez, Tomás Eloy, 1995, *Santa Evita.* Buenos Aires: Planeta

Maxwell, Carol J., 1995, Coping with Bereavement through Activism: Real Grief, Imagined Death, and Pseudo-Mourning among Pro-Life Direct Activists. *Ethos* 23(4):437–52

Meerloo, Joost A. M., 1968, Delayed Mourning in Victims of Extermination Camps. In *Massive Psychic Trauma.* Henry Krystal, ed. New York: International Universities Press, 72–5

Mitchell, Stephen A., 1988, *Relational Concepts in Psychoanalysis: An Integration.* Cambridge, MA: Harvard University Press

Mitchell, Stephen A. and Margaret J. Black, 1995, *Freud and Beyond: A History of Modern Psychoanalytic Thought.* New York: Basic Books

Mitre, Bartolomé, 1969 [1893], *The Emancipation of South America.* New York: Cooper Square Publishers

Molas, Ricardo Rodríguez, 1985, *Historia de la tortura y el orden represivo en la Argentina.* Buenos Aires: Editorial Universitaria de Buenos Aires

Moore, Barrington, Jr, 1984, *Privacy: Studies in Social and Cultural History.* Armonk, NY: M. E. Sharpe

Navarro, Marysa, 1989, The Personal Is Political: Las Madres de Plaza de Mayo. In *Power and Popular Protest: Latin American Social Movements.* Susan Eckstein, ed. Berkeley: University of California Press, 241–58

Nicoletti, Elena, 1988, Missing People: Defect of Signifying Ritual and Clinical Consequences. In *Psychological Effects of Political Repression.* Diana Kordon *et al.*, eds. Buenos Aires: Sudamericana/Planeta, 113–22

Nosiglia, Julio E., 1985, *Botín de Guerra.* Buenos Aires: Cooperativa Tierra Fertil

Oria, Piera Paola, 1987, *De la Casa a la Plaza.* Buenos Aires: Editorial Nueva America

Page, Joseph A., 1983, *Perón: A Biography.* New York: Random House

Parkes, Colin Murray, 1970, 'Seeking' and 'Finding' a Lost Object: Evidence from Recent Studies of the Reaction to Bereavement. *Social Science and Medicine* 4:187–201

1972, *Bereavement: Studies of Grief in Adult Life.* New York: International Universities Press

Pawelczynska, Anna, 1979, *Values and Violence in Auschwitz: A Sociological Analysis*. Berkeley: University of California Press

Peristiany, J. G., ed., 1965, *Honor and Shame: The Values of Mediterranean Society*. London: Weidenfeld and Nicolson

Piaget, Jean, 1971, *La construction du réel chez l'enfant*. Neuchatel: Delachaux et Niestlé

Robben, Antonius C. G. M., 1989a, *Sons of the Sea Goddess: Economic Practice and Discursive Conflict in Brazil*. New York: Columbia University Press

1989b, Habits of the Home: Spatial Hegemony and the Structuration of House and Society in Brazil. *American Anthropologist* 91(3):570–88

1995, Seduction and Persuasion: The Politics of Truth and Emotion among Victims and Perpetrators of Violence. In *Fieldwork under Fire: Contemporary Studies of Violence and Survival*. Carolyn Nordstrom and Antonius C. G. M. Robben, eds. Berkeley: University of California Press, 81–103

1996, Ethnographic Seduction, Transference, and Resistance in Dialogues about Terror and Violence in Argentina. *Ethos* 24(1):71–106

Rosenblatt, Paul C., 1993, Grief: The Social Context of Private Feelings. In *Handbook of Bereavement: Theory, Research, and Intervention*. Margaret S. Stroebe, Wolfgang Stroebe and Robert O. Hansson, eds. Cambridge: Cambridge University Press, 102–11

Rubin, Simon Shimshon, 1993, The Death of a Child is Forever: The Life Course Impact of Child Loss. In *Handbook of Bereavement: Theory, Research, and Intervention*. Margaret S. Stroebe, Wolfgang Stroebe and Robert O. Hansson, eds. Cambridge: Cambridge University Press, 285–99

Sánchez, Matilde, 1985, *Histórias de Vida: Hebe de Bonafini*. Buenos Aires: Fraterna/Del Nuevo Extremo

San Martino de Dromi, María Laura, 1988, *Historia política argentina (1955–1988)*. Buenos Aires: Editorial Astrea de Alfredo y Ricardo Depalma

Schirmer, Jennifer, 1988, 'Those Who Die for Life Cannot Be Called Dead': Women and Human Rights Protest in Latin America. *Harvard Human Rights Yearbook* 1:41–76

1994, The Claiming of Space and the Body Politic within National-Security States: The Plaza de Mayo Madres and the Greenham Common Women. In *Remapping Memory: The Politics of TimeSpace*. Jonathan Boyarin, ed. Minneapolis: University of Minnesota Press, 185–220

Simpson, John and Jana Bennett, 1985, *The Disappeared and the Mothers of the Plaza: The Story of the 11,000 Argentinians Who Vanished*. New York: St Martin's Press

Sluzki, Carlos E., 1990, Disappeared: Semantic and Somatic Effects of Political Repression in a Family Seeking Therapy. *Family Process* 29:131–43

Spain, David, 1994, Entertaining (Im)possibilities: Chance and Necessity in the Making of a Psychological Anthropologist. In *The Making of Psychological Anthropology II*. Marcelo M. Suárez-Orozco, George Spindler and Louise Spindler, eds. Fort Worth: Harcourt Brace College Publishers, 104–31

Stroebe, Wolfgang and Margaret S. Stroebe, 1987, *Bereavement and Health: The Psychological and Physical Consequences of Partner Loss*. Cambridge: Cambridge University Press

Suárez-Orozco, Marcelo, 1987, The Treatment of Children in the 'Dirty War': Ideology, State Terrorism and the Abuse of Children in Argentina. In *Child Survival: Anthropological Perspectives on the Treatment and Maltreatment of Children*. Nancy Scheper-Hughes, ed. Dordrecht: D. Reidel Publishing Company, 227–56

  1991, The Heritage of Enduring a 'Dirty War': Psychosocial Aspects of Terror in Argentina, 1976–1988. *Journal of Psychohistory* 18(4):469–505

Taylor, Ralph B. and Sidney Brower, 1985, Home and Near-Home Territories. In *Human Behavior and Environment, Advances in Theory and Research*. Vol. VIII: *Home Environments*. Irwin Altman and Carol M. Werner, eds. New York: Plenum Press, 183–212

Taylor, J. M., 1979, *Eva Perón: The Myths of a Woman*. Chicago: University of Chicago Press

Timerman, Jacobo, 1981, *Prisoner Without a Name, Cell Without a Number*. New York: Alfred A. Knopf

Trautman, Edgar C., 1971, Violence and Victims in Nazi Concentration Camps and the Psychopathology of the Survivors. In *Psychic Traumatization: Aftereffects in Individuals and Communities*. Henry Krystal and William G. Niederland, eds. Boston: Little, Brown and Company, 115–33

Ulla, Noemí and Hugo Echave, 1986, *Después de la noche: Diálogo con Graciela Fernández Meijide*. Buenos Aires: Editorial Contrapunto

Van Gennep, Arnold, 1960, *The Rites of Passage*. Chicago: University of Chicago Press

Verbitsky, Horacio, 1995, *El Vuelo*. Buenos Aires: Planeta

Volkan, Vamik D., 1972, The Linking Objects of Pathological Mourners. *Archives of General Psychiatry* 27:215–21

  1981, *Linking Objects and Linking Phenomena: A Study of the Forms, Symptoms, Metapsychology, and Therapy of Complicated Mourning*. New York: International Universities Press

Weiss, Robert S., 1993, Loss and Recovery. In *Handbook of Bereavement: Theory, Research, and Intervention*. Margaret S. Stroebe, Wolfgang Stroebe and Robert O. Hansson, eds. Cambridge: Cambridge University Press, 271–84

Winnicott, D. W., 1965, *The Maturational Process and the Facilitating Environment*. London: The Hogarth Press

  1986, *Home is Where We Start From: Essays by a Psychoanalyst*. London: Penguin

  1988, *Playing and Reality*. London: Penguin

Newspapers and periodicals

El Diario del Juicio
Humor
La Nación
Madres de Plaza de Mayo
Somos

4 Mitigating discontents with children in war: an ongoing psychoanalytic inquiry

Roberta J. Apfel and Bennett Simon

An intergenerational perspective on the transmission of resilience is necessary to understand what mitigates discontents for children in war and what modifies and transforms the traumatic effects of violence and loss. The psychological and institutional structures provided by adults for children during war and in its aftermath play a crucial role in helping children cope with and, at times, transcend the impact of the armed conflict in their lives. Looking at the intergenerational transmission of trauma and resiliency allows an alternative way of conceptualizing 'Civilization and its Discontents'. The pressure for aggression is not civilization versus instinctual expression, but rather the pressure for each generation to transmit the experience of its own trauma to the next generation.

This thesis frames the data in this paper, data derived from interviews with a group of Israeli children and a group of Palestinian children over a period of eight years around issues of war and peace.

The counterpart of transmission of resiliency is the propensity of the traumatized person or group to use hatred and violence as ways of coping with traumatic wounds. Our thinking has been influenced, over a period of years, by the works of Dan Bar-On (1989, 1995, 1996), Yolanda Gampel and Vamik Volkan on the societal transmission of trauma intergenerationally. The papers of Gampel and Volkan in this volume, as well as those of de Levita and Robben, provide additional tools for conceptualizing the pathways of transmission of both trauma and of healing from generation to generation. Our work has also been influenced by studies of the transmission of violence and trauma within families, and studies on the perpetuation and/or interruption of cycles of physical and sexual abuse of children.

Terms such as 'resiliency', 'risk factors', and 'preventive factors', developed over the last three or so decades of research on 'children at risk', help frame the questions we are investigating. At a broad level, there are questions such as 'Why does the majority of people who have been severely abused as children not become abusive and murderous as adults?' (Perhaps only 20 per cent of abused women and 30 per cent of abused men become child abusers (Herman 1992:113–14).) A more refined level of analysis involves studying the majority who do not abuse: what are the psychic strugggles and the psychic tolls for this group? Concomitantly, what about the group that does become abusers? When, how, and with what psychic struggles do they abuse, and what are the vicissitudes of their aggressive patterns over their life course? A further refinement is a detailed study of the interaction between abused child and abusing parent, and the role that familial institutions (such as the presence of helpful intervening relatives) and social institutions (schools, courts, and welfare agencies) play in shaping outcome. Understanding how any individual child deals intrapsychically over the course of a lifetime with abuse requires tools and methods specific to that level of inquiry.

Definitions

The term 'trauma' here refers to events in life generated by forces and agents external to the person and largely external to his or her control, and specifically to events generated in the setting of armed conflict and war. Thus, separation and loss, imprisonment and exile, threats of annihilation, even death and mutilation, are the order of magnitude of what we refer to as trauma in this paper. These are events or processes that can severely shake the child's expectation of parental protection and severely tax the parental expectation of providing such protection.We differentiate these from 'ordinary traumas', 'necessary losses', such as the birth or a sibling, natural death of a parent or sibling, divorce, illnesses, and accidents, whether man-made or natural – an earlier psychoanalytic use of 'trauma.'

'Resiliency', in the social and political context here examined, is the capacity to survive violence and loss, and moreover to have flexibility of response over the course of a life time. The inner experience of such behavioural flexibility includes a sense of agency and a sense of capacity to choose – among courses of action and among conflicting moral values.

A psychoanalytic inquiry

This project, open-ended annual interviewing by two psychoanalysts with ten Israeli and ten Palestinian children since the Gulf War in 1991, is, strictly speaking, not composed of psychoanalytic data, in that the data are not derived from a clinical encounter, from in-depth interviews of individual children, from dream material, or art productions. There-fore, we use Kakar's phrase, 'a psychoanalyst's exploration' (1996:ix) rather than psychoanalytic. What characterizes our approach as psycho-analysts is:

1. Ongoing self-reflection and self-analysis in the course of the inter-views and in the course of processing our experience (including attending to our ambiguous political status *vis-à-vis* each group of children).
2. Close attention to the associative processes both of individuals and of the group in the interviews.
3. Close attention to the affects in the group, affect contagion and particularly to shifts in affect over the course of the interviews.
4. A developmental sensitivity to how children at particular ages process, understand, and misunderstand certain events.
5. A clinically derived willingness to be surprised, to see and hear what neither our hypotheses nor our theories would have led us to predict.
6. While broad psychoanalytic principles and theories inform, shape, and undoubtedly bias our collection and interpretation of data, we rely heavily on a particular aspect of psychoanalytic theory. This is the model of parental transmission of impulses, traumatic effects, defences, and values and ideals to their children, including the transformations of parental experience in the course of parent–child interaction. This particular model also serves as an important bridge between psychoanalytic and anthropological inquiry.

None of these points is unique to psychoanalysis or psychoanalytic research; each of them can be found in other realms of behavioural research, especially anthropology and social psychology. We have not been able to use certain tools of psychoanalytic anthropologists (e.g., Devereux and Spiro (see Spindler 1978; Suarez-Orozco *et al.*, 1994)) that have been developed over the past four or so decades, such as projective tests, recording and analyzing dreams, systematic study of artwork, and spontaneous and traditional tales. We have not been able to study specific transferences and counter-transferences, let alone influence the emergence of new data by clarification and interpretation of transferences. In an annual group interview format we can neither adequately nor responsibly attempt such interpretations. We have been able to achieve a measure of immersion in the local contexts and been able to interact with a larger number of informants other than the children themselves.

This approach, using a psychoanalytic stance to investigate group issues such as political behaviour, touches upon a fundamental tension within psychoanalysis, which is at once a method of raising questions and of answering questions. Posing psychoanalytic questions about group motivation, conflict, and defence opens possibilities for richer and more complex interdisciplinary exploration of the mental life of individual actors and agents in the political process.

Psychoanalysts studying violence

In the course of our own personal movement towards the study of the impact of war and communal violence on children,[1] we came to learn much more about the history of psychoanalysts studying violence. The story, untold in any systematic way, involves some of the pioneers of the field, Sigmund and Anna Freud, Ferenczi, W. R. Rivers (during and after the First World War), and the generation of British and American psychoanalysts involved with armed forces during the Second World War. Some of our esteemed mentors and senior colleagues had been much more politically attuned and active than we had appreciated, several being explicitly devoted to working on problems of children in war.[2]

For a number of reasons, analysts willing to study violence more directly are swimming upstream. Analysts are most experienced in dealing with the milder forms of aggression seen in neurotic patients, and occasionally in patients at the more psychotic end of the spectrum. For one thing, analysts do not usually go to the places where the violence is, whether in their own countries and cities, or in sites of armed violence abroad. Analysts typically stay away from working with people who are victims of violence, let alone perpetrators of violence – this latter group does not come to analysts, though they may occasionally be seen by dynamically oriented professionals in hospitals or forensic settings. Situations where violence is ongoing are dangerous and are scary to enter. Even when it may not be physically dangerous, as in some refugee camps, mental health helpers coming from the outside may be subjected to the anger of highly traumatized victims of war. We are not accustomed to analyzing our political positions and political 'counter-transference'

---

[1] See Apfel and Simon 1996:1–3.
[2] Judith Kestenberg studied adults who had been child survivors of the Holocaust (with Yolanda Gampel in Israel and Judit Mézaros in Hungary); Vamik Volkan studied how hatred between Greek and Turkish Cypriots was inculcated in infancy; the Group for the Advancement of Psychiatry committee studied ethnicity and injured narcissism; John Mack studied children exposed to the threat of nuclear war. Argentinian, Chilean, and Uruguayan analysts studied the impact of the persecutions perpetrated by military dictatorships, working, for example, with the children and parents of the 'disappeared' persons. These analysts, their families, and their children were profoundly affected and traumatized by these same events that they were studying (see Puget et al. 1989).

and may find ourselves uncomfortable confronting political conflict. Outside the office situation we do not control the parameters of the encounter and hence might feel helpless and not know how to operate; we rationalize our insecurities by a kind of phobic avoidance.

Even when victims of violence have been analyzed, they have tended to protect the analyst from the full onslaught of their terrible experiences. Colleagues who, as children, had survived concentration camps and as young adults entered psychoanalytic treatment told us how they spared their analysts from hearing and themselves from telling. Only as they grew much older, in later treatment, were they able to talk more openly about concentration camp horrors.

Going to the sites of violence, whether a few miles or thousands of miles away, takes away time from the routine of seeing patients one by one in the office. We realize our own ongoing tensions in this regard, often feeling guilty at taking time away from patients or students to work with people outside of the office. However, as an outgrowth of our interest in 'children in war', we had been planning annual visits to Israel and the Occupied Territories, and the first such visit coincided with the outbreak of the Gulf War.

A friend and colleague told us that her child and his third grade classmates had many questions about the import of the Scud attacks for children in Israel and the Territories. We thought to collect such questions and send them to colleagues in Israel who might bring them to children there. After the first week or so of the war, when it became clear to us that it was in fact again possible to travel to Israel, we decided to bring the questions directly to Israeli and Palestinian children (see the appendix to this paper for a list of the questions).

The interview study

Interviews based on these questions turned out to be the first of annual visits, continuing over eight years as of this writing.[3] Our selection of children to interview was based on personal contacts – whom could we get to talk to on short notice that would not involve lengthy official clearance and bureaucratic tangles at a time when infrastructure was shutdown (a usual wartime condition). A group of ten Israeli children,

---

[3] We subsequently reported back to the third grade class about the questions they had sent, and in 1994 we reported back to a group of sixth graders in Boston questions that Israeli and Palestinian children had about the life of American children. In 1995 and 1996, we met with a group of high school students in Amman, Jordan (in the American School, an international group of students mostly from Arabic speaking countries), and several groups of high school students in two secular Israeli kibbutzim, and all along had opportunities to speak informally with children of both Israeli and Palestinian friends.

aged eight, were recruited through the auspices of an art teacher at a religious kibbutz. The orginal group of Palestinian children were at a municipally operated school in Jerusalem, but after the first two years, those children were no longer in the same school. We were able to connect with a group of ten year olds at a religiously based English-speaking private school in the West Bank, interviewing them since 1993. In February 1995 we began interviewing families of the Israeli children, and in 1997 families of the Palestinian children. We have been able to maintain some continuity via mail, e-mail, photos and personal messages in between our visits. On a number of occasions, we were also able to see drawings that some of the children had made, and/or made for us.

The group interviews, lasting an hour and a half to two hours (tape-recorded for later review and any necessary translation) were held, for the Israeli children, in the art studio of the kibbutz where they lived, with their familiar and beloved art teacher presiding and translating from Hebrew. In the first Palestinian school, several teachers sat in. In the second Palestinian school, where the children speak English, the principal sat in, more like a visible fly on the wall than presider or translator. The presence of a familiar adult seemed absolutely necessary, especially in our first forays into a school setting, and the interactions with these adults were an important aspect of what we learned in the interviews. These adults – themselves sensitive and experienced teachers and parents – reported surprise at what they heard and learned from the children talking, that they had not fully appreciated the extent of the children's knowledge of situations of war and politics, and definitely had not fully appreciated the extent and nature of their anxieties. The Palestinian adults quite openly conveyed to us their own fears, and especially their fears for their own children. They were also concerned about the moral lessons the children would draw from the violence and conflict around them, which ran so counter to the basic lessons they were being taught at home and school. These private interviews with the adults also provided important background, corroborative and normative information about the children.

Over the years, limitations of our time and energy and our lack of research expertise quickly became apparent. We also encountered substantial logistical difficulties in arranging meetings with both the children and their families, difficulties in part engendered by the unpredictability of events (e.g., closures) and in part undoubtedly due to ambivalences and reluctances about such meetings. At times there was misunderstanding or forgetting of instructions we had provided for meetings, though several of these 'difficulties' turned out to be serendipitous opportunities for new information and insights.

We analyzed the interviews by later listening to the tapes, reviewing our notes, and checking some facts with informed adults. We did not develop a systematic method of analysis or scoring, but rather picked out salient themes and trends, striking examples, and utilized our own emotional reactions to various parts of the interviews. Presenting our findings to knowledgeable colleagues provided valuable ongoing feedback.

Open-ended interviewing

In the first Palestinian school, during the Gulf War, we were greeted by a teacher who said half-jokingly but half-seriously: 'Talk to me first, I'm a child of war!' Later, during the interview with the children, when we asked if anyone is having bad dreams, she playfully-seriously raised her hand and said 'Me'.[4]

Overall, the children exhibited quite a detailed knowledge of various aspects of war and danger and of politics. For the Israeli children, the Gulf War was 'their war' – the war they knew first hand (as opposed to other Israeli wars which they had heard about from their elders or siblings or from study in school) and, when it was over, various aspects, especially the apprehension, seemed to fade. For the Palestinian children, the daily events of the *intifada* constituted the ongoing war, the Gulf War only a brief interlude in that longer and larger 'war' which affected every aspect of their daily lives.

The questions of the American third graders were the jumping-off point for open-ended discussion. Having formed some idea initially as to which questions would elicit which kinds of responses, we encountered important surprises. Overall, these interviews quickly engaged the children and tapped into affective, personal and interpersonal relational aspects of their thinking about war, peace and politics, and conflict resolution. There was a chance to observe the children in interaction with their peers in a school setting, and to be able to pursue affectively charged topics as they emerged. The children clearly welcolmed the chance to talk with us. In the initial meetings during the war anxiety was high and they were warding off being frightened and overwhelmed. They wanted to show off what they knew, in age-appropriate ways, to

---

[4] We ourselves were initially propelled by anxiety, a visceral sense of 'our people' and our friends in danger and a need to help and do something. We later realized that our feelings mirrored those of the people actually in the situation – a certain helplessness and sense of passivity *vis-à-vis* the larger situation. In part, we dealt with our own anxieties and needs by having a project – doing something is better than nothing. Some thirty studies were done during and soon after the Gulf War by Israeli psychologists and psychiatrists – a kind of collective adaptation to trauma.

compete with each other, to exhibit to and communicate with the teachers present, and to teach us things we did not know. Both initially and in subsequent interviews, we heard a lot of jokes, songs, teasing, and banter which intermixed politics and personal relations among the children.[5]

The importance of these meetings for the children has become more apparent with the passage of time. At our 1995 meeting with the Palestinian children, we were delayed by an urban traffic jam (a sign of normalization) and the students were waiting and, on our arrival, saying: 'Where were you? We have so much to tell you!' Over time, we have also been struck with the basic intactness, liveliness, optimism, and affective flexibility of these children. In the February 1996 interview, the children by then well into puberty, we were treated politely, but obviously their minds and hearts and libido were not fully in the interview. In two subsequent interviews, the group gave out mixed signals: their eagerness and need to talk with us, and the sense that we were not too relevant to the main preoccupations of their life.

The group interviews have allowed observation of both sudden shifts in affect, and of affect contagion within the group. In the initial interviews during the war, we asked both Israeli and Palestinian children: 'What do you see on television?' We had expected reports about the military technology, bombing, 'smart bombs' – the stuff most Americans were watching on CNN. Up to that point in the interviews, the children had generally been excited, eager to be the first to tell us something, and even a bit giddy about some of the potential and actual dangers. In both groups, the affect shifted to one of noticeable quiet distress and sadness, as the children said: 'We see the children of Baghdad roaming the streets, looking desolate, hungry, having to wash in the river.' An Israeli boy also expressed his distress with the pictures of the birds covered with oil, and unable to fly, or even to survive.

[5] Much of the joking and jostling was done in Hebrew or Arabic – where we were able to catch the music but not the words, as it were. At our initial meeting with the Israeli group, they gleefully sang for us songs about Saddam Hussein written by one of their teachers, songs making fun of him, but also with very serious undertones. The holiday of Purim was approaching, a holiday of gaiety, rejoicing, joking, and a sense of triumph over the wicked man Haman, to whom Saddam Hussein was liberally compared. The Israeli children spoke Hebrew, gradually speaking more English over the years. Their teacher translated, but we knew enough Hebrew to pick up when she was glossing over something important, and she would respond to our request for fuller translation, and at times later tell us why she had 'censored' something in translation. The first group of Palestinian children spoke in Arabic, and we had translation going on in Hebrew and English. The second group of Palestinian children spoke English and we required only occasional translation. Jokes and more private comments were interspersed in Arabic, and we had to stop and ask the children to 'decode' what was transpiring, which they usually did.

Another sudden shift in affect occurred in our 1994 interview with the Israeli children. They were talking in an excited and elated mood about travelling around the world (as their older brothers and sisters do and have done after finishing their army duty), telling stories about what their older siblings saw in different parts of the world – and alluding to frequent and expectable thievery in different parts of the world. We asked if there were any thefts on the kibbutz, and their affect shifted as they began to tell about two (seemingly unconnected) incidents that did not address the question we thought we were asking: they brought up how a kibbutz girl had almost been kidnapped by a passing Palestinian car, and then brought up a recent incident when the fence at a nearby kibbutz had been broken and the army was called out to help look for infiltrators. Much more anxiety and apprehension appeared in the group as a whole. They soon regrouped and recouped, as several children brought forth the current theory about the fence break – some Israeli hunters were chasing a wild boar, who then crashed through the kibbutz fence. Thus, we saw how they allowed a group anxiety to emerge, and then fairly quickly 'rebuild the fence' with an acceptable, though improbable, group story.

The flow of associations allowed further glimpses in the groups' anxieties. A Palestinian child told about a small scar left on a woman's face by a gas-mask, and this led to escalating tales among the children of bigger and bigger scars. We assumed this was symbolic of 'the scars of war', but what followed were stories about masks, and then about episodes of Palestinians humiliated by Israeli soldiers. It is more likely that the 'scars of war' with which the children were living included issues of 'face' and humiliation.

Developmental observations: shifts over time in the nature of political awareness

The interviews have provided an opportunity for us to see developmental aspects of their thinking, as well an opportunity for the children to reflect on their own past political thinking. In 1995 the Israeli children began to comment on their own growing sophistication about politics and war and peace. One child said: 'Oh, then [during the Gulf War] we were young and didn't know anything. We thought you could just get a pistol and shoot Saddam Hussein and it would be all right. Now we know better.' Discussion ensued about how children form their political opinions, with a group consensus emerging that children up to age eighteen had their family's views, but after that might develop their own opinions.

A major developmental turning point in self-awareness seems to have occurred for a number of the children around age 14–15. In an interview with the Palestinian children in November 1996, several weeks after the terrible and lethal violence precipitated by the Israeli government opening a tunnel under the most sacred mosque, several children spoke with phrases like: '*Now* I realize what has been going on all these years – I mean, I always knew about the occupation and violence – but I never quite realized what was happening and what it meant. Now I know what it is about and what my task is' (see Case 3, p. 122 below). What was striking was that the children did not necessarily agree on what it meant and what they had learned! One girl drew the conclusion that she had to be a political activist, that demonstrating and activism were necessary, and that the Palestinians cannot meekly accept their lot. One boy drew the conclusion that if he really wanted to help his people and their cause, he would accomplish more by staying home and studying chemistry than by going out and throwing stones and shouting slogans at Israeli soldiers.[6]

At every juncture, over the years, the larger political situation and the children's personal situation were continually interwoven. In the 1994 interview with the Palestinian children (age 11), there were some painfully vivid stories about sibling rivalry within families, and conflict between parents and children which were reminders of how much private suffering children can experience within well-functioning families. The stories were particularly upsetting to hear, and surprising to the principal, because of the immediacy of the pain and sorrow these children conveyed. One child told of running away from home and hiding out for several nights while his parents were looking for him. Another told ruefully of how 'my sister really hates me'. By the next year we heard a humorous reversal as this girl cheerfully announced that she no longer had the problem, 'because my sister is now studying in the United States'!

These stories kept overlapping with the children's concerns about violence and conflict among the Palestinians. With the peace accords setting in, and very limited autonomy being put in place for the Palestinians, these children felt the possibilities of their space and their world contracting, and of the even greater dangers of intra-group conflict when the external enemy, Israel, pulled out (a number of these children are from families with many contacts abroad and, for some, close contacts with Israelis). At one point in the discussion of sibling issues, one child brought up the tale of two neighbours in his building

---

[6] A similar 'realization' in adolescence is to be found in autobiographies of political figures.

who have terrible fights, and at times the Israeli soldiers had to be brought in to break up their fights. 'What will happen when the Israelis go home and leave us to ourselves?' There followed a few moments of silence, when one of the children cheerfully volunteered: 'Oh, by then we will have our own policemen. You can call them.' Law and order and political and familial harmony restored! Further, we learned repeatedly from the teachers and principals in the Palestinian school (and some of the parents) of their perception of increased aggression and fighting among the students in the school, especially among the boys.[7]

Gender differences

In the last few years, as these children are pubertal, we have had a chance to see emerging aspects of gender role and gender relations that are more readily available in the group setting than they would be in individual interviews. These gender roles and relations are embedded in the setting of discussions of political issues and issues of violence and conflict resolution. For example, in 1995 the Palestinian girls were quite concerned about Hamas, and other Islamic fundamentalists, regulating their dress code, and being harsh and at times violent in the treatment of young girls violating the religious dress codes. This was at a time when they were asserting their own burgeoning sense of how to be a teenager and how to be a woman, needing to experiment and not just to conform. Three of the girls made a pact not to wear skirts, and a number of the girls intended to wear shorts that summer in the streets and market place. In 1996, when questioned about this problem, the girls sadly detailed how the situation had gotten even worse, and they no longer would risk wearing shorts, 'unless you were two years old or younger'.[8]

The Israeli children anecdotally told how the girls are afraid to take

---

[7] While we did not hear this concern among the parents (and teachers) of the Israeli children we were interviewing, we did encounter this concern among other Israeli teachers and parents. At various points during the *intifada*, Israeli newspapers (echoing reports by mental health professionals) reported increased domestic violence in Israeli homes, dangerous games of 'chicken' – young teenagers risking crossing major highways – and increased aggressiveness in school in children who already had some degree of disturbance. See Serge Schmemann, 'News of the Week in Review', *New York Times*, 16 March 1997, citing the Israeli criminologist, S. Landau. In our 1998 interviews, we learned of a new kind of intra- and inter-group tension in the school, as Americans of Palestinian background were moving back, and their teenage children were enrolled in Palestinian schools. Conflicts between the 'Arabs' and the 'Americans' were of great concern to the students.

[8] Clearly Islamic fundamentalism is affecting the daily lives and the larger vision of these students. A small but increasing number of young women at the school are wearing the traditional headdress. Forms of solidarity between Christian and Moslem students are reflected, for example, by the Christian students not eating in school during Ramadan.

the garbage out at night, since the garbage dump is near the kibbutz protective fence; the boys are not so afraid: 'girl soldiers become teachers, and boy soldiers go into combat.' During this particularly anxiety-provoking discussion about safety from external attack, one little girl is sitting and drawing a wedding band on her finger – perhaps her reaching for a role and relationship that might give her safety. While we can detect gender differences in attitudes about war and violence, these differences do not neatly correspond to boys being more 'hawkish' and girls more 'dovish'. This seemed to be the case in several discussions we had with larger groups of older children, high school classes that we met with only one time. In discussions of the Hebron massacre of February 1994 when an Israeli settler-doctor, Baruch Goldstein, shot and killed over thirty Moslem worshippers in a mosque, we heard both boys and girls condemning or supporting the shooting.[9]

The boys seemed to articulate their feelings more motorically, and the girls more affectively. In the 1995 interview with the Israeli children (then about thirteen), we asked how they were dealing with fears of terrorist attacks. One boy dramatically mimed shooting a machine gun, and a few minutes later, in a related context, mimed driving very fast on the road. The girls looked on a bit amused, but mostly concerned and disapproving, and then – by association – turned to us to ask if we had heard about the massacre in a Hebron mosque, which had taken place a full year before.

Developments in the relations between the genders appear to be on roughly the same timetable as for middle-class children in the United States (assuming some 'average expectable development' here). Dating and pairing off, let alone sexual activity, however, are discouraged in both school settings. There is now flirting mixed in with the arguments between the boys and girls. In a recent interview with the Israeli children, the issue of girls going into combat led to a heated and passionate argument about the relative physical strength of boys and girls. One girl won a temporary victory when she announced: 'Yeah, but who do you think carries the babies for nine months!' In February 1996, the Palestinian girls complained of being harassed by 'the wolves' in the street; the only good guys are the ones in the school. This assertion was

9 Polls conducted in recent years by Professor Galia Golan (Political Science) and others at the Hebrew University in Jerusalem show trends in female–male differences, with the women being somewhat more supportive of an active peace process and the men less so, but there is also a considerable degree of overlap between the genders. Differences in style and in what are the focuses of concern do show up – such as the women talking more about the well-being of their children – but that concern not necessarily correlating with a particular political position

immediately followed by a humorous jab by one girl at one of the boys, 'mishinta' (Arabic for 'except for you'), and all present took it in good fun.

Ways of processing unpleasant realities

In a very general way, the ways of processing painful realities matured with age, but humour was present at every age. All the children, at each annual interview, had a high level of a capacity to make jokes, observed ironies, and poked fun at each other, the adults in their life, their own political leaders, and the enemy. Defences against helplessness were especially related to younger age. The Palestinian children at age eight, during the Gulf War, markedly exaggerated their own capabilities in learning about gas masks and teaching their parents. They were much more dependent on the teachers than they described. This may be related to the young child's reworking the feeling of helplessness (see Pynoos and Nader 1989).

Analogously, the Israeli children could selectively deny unpleasant realities that would increase feelings of helplessness. A year after the Gulf War, when asked about reliable reports from the government auditor that a great many gas masks had been defective and would not have protected their wearers, they simply asserted that the government was to be trusted and its critics were not to be believed.

As the children grew older, they expressed more awareness of moral complexity and evinced greater ability to acknowledge all sides of the contradictory facts of political life. Some children were more able than others consciously to hold on to such complexity around major political events during their teenage years – the assassination of Rabin, Palestinian elections, the withdrawal of Israeli troops, and the terrorist actions and suicide bombings by Hamas. They have also experienced prejudice first-hand and are more reflective about the effects of prejudice. The Israeli children spoke more openly about different opposing positions being held within their own kibbutz and, indeed, within their own families. Sometimes, the conflicts within the group are argued among them, in an impressively open manner. More recently, the children themselves say how confusing it all is, stating positions of their teachers and parents, but simultaneously showing more global interest in teenage music, and American pop culture (e.g., the most popular song: 'I'm full of money, full of drugs, full of pimples on my face and back'). When asked what they worried about, we were told: 'We think about our friends more than about politics, but we think about politics because it's our future and the future of our children.' Then one teenage girl added:

'If there are no *chaverim*, there is no future' (*double entendre* of *chaverim* – boy friends, and friends).

The reactions of the Israeli children to Prime Minister Rabin's assassination included an awareness of the dangers of extremist political rhetoric: 'People say things too easily, that they mean to kill him, but now think more carefully about what they say; people were nicer and quieter for a while, with fewer car collisions.' They assessed the funeral applying some age-appropriate teen-age values – sincerity, excitement, commitment, hypocrisy: Rabin's granddaughter's eulogy was the most compelling; King Hussein especially spoke from the heart; others, like Mubarak, were not sincere; Clinton got credit for mentioning that the scriptural (Torah) portion for the week of the funeral included the story of 'Akedat Yitzchak', the sacrifice of Isaac – Yitzchak, son of Abraham, and Yitzchak Rabin.

Empathy and awareness of the 'other'

Along with development in the direction of more complex moral and political thinking, there was also a clear assertion by the Israelis and Palestinians of their respective partisan interests . 'Peace for peace', instead of 'land for peace', proclaimed one Israeli boy, and the Palestinians certainly were clear about their wishes for a Palestinian state and a place in Jerusalem. The fourteen-year-old Israeli children, asked what they wanted to study, put Arabic on top of list, 'because it will be a world of peace', yet showed no spontaneous curiosity about the other group. Both groups, however, ask eagerly about American teenagers.

The Palestinian group did not mention the Rabin assassination and the Israeli children made little note of the Palestinian elections. Attempts to engage each group in a discussion of a moral dilemma confronting the other group fell flat. Some mixture of anxiety, anger, ignorance, and shyness goes into this attitude. It would be quite difficult, emotionally and logistically to get the groups together. A few of the students in our group have been or will be going to camp settings in Norway or the US, together with Israeli teenagers, experiences which are intense, and painful, but potentially effecting important transformations. A Palestinian girl, angry and upset, after the September 1996 violent confrontations after the tunnel opening, told of how Israeli friends from the Peace Camp called her at once to share her sorrow and anger, and to express their condolences. An interview with her father confirmed that these telephone calls had reinforced a long-standing parental message – keep up personal contacts with Israelis, contacts that can transcend the vicissitudes of conflict.

A poignant tale of empathy with the 'other' and the limits of that empathy came from that same parental interview. An older sister of the girl in our group had for many years been friendly with an Israeli girl, the daughter of Israeli friends of her parents. When this Israeli girl, about to enter the army, was coming with her parents to visit the Palestinian family, the older Palestinian girl said that she could not bear to see her, knowing that soon she would be in the enemy army. Going off to her own friends, at the last moment she changed her mind, came back, walked and talked with the Israeli girl. They cried and embraced, but have never had any contact since.

The role of elders and generational continuity

For the Israeli children there was a clear sense of generational continuity in Jewish history, augmented by the presence in Israel or even in the kibbutz of grandparents and other relatives, even though some children were from families that had suffered enormous losses in the Holocaust.[10] As a religious kibbutz, there is a very strong commitment to teaching about the generational bonds and the generational responsibilities. There are role models for both boys and girls within the kibbutz, as well as within the larger Israeli society. Especially for the boys, the knowledge that their fathers and older brothers had been or were in the army gave a shape to their future – especially a male heroic shape.

For the Palestinians, the continuity, especially for the boys, was disrupted by many of the fathers and older brothers and male relatives being in jail, or in exile. Some fathers were overseas for extended periods of time in order to earn a living, and there were major separations between fathers and children. Both fathers (in prison or otherwise away) and mothers had to work very hard to maintain a sense of paternal presence and paternal caring. The repertory of stories told by elders, such as grandparents, seems crucial in sustaining both a sense of continuity with the past and hope and purpose for the future. Though these children have role models within Palestinian society, their possibilities compared to those in Israeli society are much more restricted. For some of the Palestinian children, the school itself has been a source of generational continuity, as parents, relatives, and older siblings had gone to the same school and the school plays an important community role.

---

[10] An important continuity is provided by the art teacher on the kibbutz, who had been the teacher of the parents of these children, and who keeps records of each child she has taught over the years. She can compare the artistic development of parents and their children.

The role of school in the lives of these children

School for these children has been extraordinarily important, especially for the Palestinian children. Not being able to go to school and see their friends because of frequent closures and curfews was a great deprivation. Also the opportunity to learn and master were very important. Parents and educators, quite concerned about how the *intifada* and school closure have impaired the children's education, are working on how to help make up for some serious educational deficits.

For the Israeli children, school was clearly very important, but the particular setting we saw them in was the art studio of the kibbutz, a place where they can freely draw and paint – a place that is readily and warmly open to them. It is also a place where children can express in art-work their wishes, fears, and traumatic experiences in ways that are relatively comfortable and safe. The teacher will never make comments or interpretations about the content, though she might comment about artistic technique.

For both groups of children, we saw how much the environment in which we interviewed them allowed them rather frank discussion and open disagreement among themselves, expressions of disagreements with their parents, and, indeed, polite but pointed criticism of teachers and schools. The Israeli art teacher proudly exhibited the drawing of a ten-year-old boy, denouncing the art studio – a boy now in his twenties whom the teacher admires and loves.

For both groups, open-ended questions about 'What is most important in the coming year?' or 'What was most important [the best and the worst things] in the past year?' typically elicited comments about school and grades and achievement in school. For example, for Israeli sixth graders, it was a written project, a long essay, that was a demanding and worrisome task. In 1996, in response to the question 'What was the hardest part of this year?', a Palestinian boy put his head between his hands and almost moaned, as he said: 'This year's grades decide my whole future.' And others chimed in with: 'Hardest thing about the year – much more homework.'[11]

We learned much about the school by talking to teachers and principals and by sitting in on classes. A biology class contrasted sharply with a history class. The biology class was a mechanical lecture by an uninspired teacher, with virtually no class participation, with students

---

[11] Compare Anne Frank's description of the students in her Jewish school really 'quaking in their boots' as the net of the Nazi occupation tightens around them – but they are 'quaking in their boots' around the upcoming teachers' meeting which will decide who gets promoted to the next grade and who will be kept back!

bantering quite loudly in Arabic behind the teacher's back. In the history class the teacher devised a participatory exercise that stretched the students' political and historical imagination, an exercise clearly engaging the students. The principal agreed with the students' evaluation but was not then in a position to fire the poorer teacher. There were other occasions where the school authorities granted them the authenticity of their perceptions, but not the confidence that their protests could achieve the goal. Apropos of the Palestinian elections, there is no student government in the school; the children have little experience of voting.

The question of student power and of student rights came to a head with a great upheaval in the school during our visit in February 1997. A group of older children walked out in protest against the inadequate heating in the school. It was indeed cold, but in an advanced physics class, meeting in the coldest room of the school, the students were totally absorbed in the problem sets and discussion led by the teacher. This form of protest, virtually unheard of in this school, confronted the administration, faculty, parents, and students, with what attitudes towards authority are (and will be like) in the new Palestinian society – issues clearly not yet settled either in the school or in the larger society. Characteristically for this school, the punishments for those who had walked out included extra time at community service, with a public health project.

The school setting for both the Israeli and the Palestinian children is one of intense moral education, as well as education in particular subjects and skills. The Israeli art teacher is extremely concerned about the moral development of her children, including learning not to hate the Palestinians. The Palestinian school adults are extremely attentive to issues of aggressiveness among the children, their altruistic development, and quite worried lest in the course of the Israeli occupation the students begin to dehumanize the Israel soldiers, not to see them as eighteen-year-old children of mothers and fathers. Both the kibbutz setting and the Palestinian school setting have a strong emphasis on the responsibility of each member for the welfare of the whole community, and part of their education is the expectation of spending time in unremunerated communal service and/or in raising funds for communal charities.

A willingness to have outsiders come in, look at what is happening, and give feedback on how their children are faring reflects an important characteristic of both settings. There is undoubtedly also a certain kind of political agenda – the wish to have distinguished outsiders better understand and therefore be more sympathetic to their situation and their cause. But, overall, both adults and children allowed us to see a good deal, warts and all.

The role of the *group* of children is extremely important, and we do not know what each child would be like interviewed individually (we have chatted individually or in smaller clusters with the children, but not interviewed them individually). There are anecdotal reports that with groups of severely traumatized children, some of the children functioned quite well until separated from their group and then could dramatically fall apart.[12] These children are neither abandoned nor orphaned, but do rely heavily on group support.

These schools, as the society in which are they are located, present a variety of moral messages, often contradictory. Each school is embedded in a deeply religious context, and Judaism, Christianity, and Islam are certainly not univocal in what they communicate about aggression, revenge, forgiveness, understanding, and the definition of who is the enemy. For these children, not wholly representative of all children in Israeli and Palestinian society, the schools provide better than average resources to live in a morally complex and demanding world.

Illustrative cases

We present the following three vignettes to illustrate the interplay between the historical-political situation, the family's history in relation to that situation, and the attitude and behaviour of individual children over time.[13] They are also vignettes of inter-generational interactions around trauma and resiliency.

Yochai, an Israeli boy

During the Gulf War (February 1991) at age eight, Yochai was one of the children expressing concern over the children of Baghdad, and then added his upset about seeing the birds covered with oil. In the next year's interview (1992), he expressed the opinion that the kibbutz was being visited with many more birds than usual, because, he thought, the smoke from the burning oil in Kuwait was driving them away from Kuwait towards the kibbutz. He was still concerned with the fate of small and helpless creatures. The next year (1993), he had become a

---

12 E.g., the group of Palestinian children in a PLO Tunisian orphanage, some of whom had witnessed their parents being murdered in 1982 in the Sabra and Shatilla refugee camps in Lebanon, and some of whom had literally been rescued as infants from garbage heaps (Vamik Volkan, 1990, personal communication).
13 Names are fictional.

vociferous opponent of any peace plan, arguing demagogically about getting rid of the Arabs. His desk-thumping insistence was clearly upsetting to his peers; even though some might have agreed with his content, they were quite shaken by his vehemence. The following year (1994, age 11), he snubbed us, breezing in and out of the interview room. We assumed that, in the interim, he had become 'socialized' to the dominant right-wing political views of his family, and any evidence of previous empathy for an enemy had gone out the window. The next year (1995), he had a friendly exchange with one us earlier in the day of the interview, showed up for, stayed through, and spoke a bit during the interview, looking subdued and a bit sad. In 1996, most of the boys were away on a hike and we did not see him, but in 1997 (aged 14) he was comfortably engaged in debate with a girl in the group, propounding, but not pounding, the viewpoint that the withdrawal of the Israeli army from Hebron was a good thing, that the rest of the settlers should leave and that the peace process must go on.

In 1995 we met with his family and pieced together the following story. Shortly after the 1992 interview – one year after the Gulf War – his beloved older brother and the brother's girlfriend were in the army together in the Gaza strip. In an attack by Palestinians, the girlfriend's legs were seriously wounded, and it was thought she might need amputation of one or both legs. As she was being transferred by helicopter to a hospital, Yochai's brother promised he would stay with her and marry her no matter what. Over the next one and half years, the brother travelled and stayed with her in hospitals both in Israel and in Canada, for specialized surgery. For Yochai, his beloved older brother was lost to him for that interim. We also learned that, contrary to our assumption about the family's politics, the family was the most dovish on the kibbutz, that on the father's side there were two generations highly committed to peaceful co-existence between Arabs and Jews. Over the previous year, the girlfriend, though severely crippled, did not lose her legs and she and the brother got married, moved back to the kibbutz, and had a baby. Yochai regained his beloved brother, and more.

We subsequently learned that Yochai's extended family was politically quite diverse, and that typically on Friday nights the family would gather at the paternal grandmother's house for dinner and there would often be lively political debate. It seemed to us, in retrospect, that he had now comfortably assimilated the political outlook of his immediate family, was in the process of forming his own set of opinions, was no longer so driven, and was better able to argue and debate, recognizing the viewpoint of the other side(s).

Nomi, an Israeli girl

Nomi was pleasant and hardly spoke over the years of our interviewing. We scarcely knew her and sometimes had difficulty recollecting her face and who she was, for she so rarely put herself forward in any assertive manner. In the 1997 interview, age 14, we got a somewhat better sense of her, as she did speak at times and seemed to play somewhat of a mediating role in the argument between Yochai, presenting a 'left' viewpoint, and a girl who was arguing a 'right' viewpoint. The interview took place the night before this group of children was going on a week's trip to the desert, and she was the first of the group to announce that she had to leave our meeting and go home and pack for the trip.

When we met her parents, we immediately saw the mother–daughter resemblance, and this experience of recognizing her via her mother was perhaps emblematic of her not presenting herself as if she were her own person. The parents were warm, had a sense of humor, and clearly were very involved with and proud of their daughter. We quickly learned from her mother and father that the mother herself is quite a shy and often quiet person (though she spoke quite freely in our meeting) and we somehow all agreed that shyness was probably constitutional, or hereditary. We learned (from her parents) that Nomi was totally unwilling to go away from home and, quite unusual for a kibbutz child, refused to go on overnight hikes and trips with her group of children. We also learned that somehow the other children accepted this about her, and she was definitely not a social outcast, despite her shyness and fearfulness about going away.

As the interview with her parents proceeded, we kept 'incidentally' learning of the mother's history in relation to the various wars she and her family had lived through. When the mother was fourteen, her older brother was taken prisoner in the Yom Kippur war and for a period of time the family was in agony, not knowing if he was alive or dead, and had little information about his well-being even when they learned he was in an Egyptian prison. Nomi herself was born when her mother and father had just moved from the mother's kibbutz to a new kibbutz, and the mother felt a painful separation from her own family. Simultaneously, the Lebanon war (1982) had just started and Nomi's father was called into military service for a period of three months. There was some banter between the parents about how long the father had been away, the father minimizing the length of time he was away, and the mother emphatically remembering how long and how hard it had been. Gradually, we began to realize that whatever role constitutional or hereditary factors may have played in Nomi's shyness, she had undoubtedly repeatedly experienced the mother's pain and anxieties about separations that might lead to loss and death, and this could be an important component of her own behaviour. We were, accordingly, pleasantly surprised (as were her parents!) to realize that now she was agreeing to go away from home for the first time on an extended trip with her group. Our guess is that the fact that the parents were so willing to talk in the interview (especially the mother) was part of a process of their beginning to work through some of their anxieties about danger and separation, and that Nomi was beginning to do her own form of working through. We also learned that Nomi was present at the weekly Friday night family gathering/political debates, and that her 'in the middle' behaviour in the group interview was consonant with her behaviour in the extended family. We surmised that either Nomi had not yet securely formed her own political position, or did not yet feel secure enough to articulate a position that would represent a disagreement (and hence pose the danger of a separation) with one or another beloved family member.

Reem, a Palestinian girl

In a November 1996 group interview (some five or six weeks after the violence ensuing with the Israeli government opening the tunnel underneath the mosque in Jerusalem), with considerable feeling the children were presenting what they had been doing and where they had been on the day that their community (including themselves and the older students) joined in a protest demonstration against the Israeli government. This was a signal event for most of the children, an occasion of crystallization of their political consciousness (though they did not all draw the same conclusions from the event). Most of the children had joined the demonstration, saw the earlier stages of confrontation with Israeli soldiers, but went back to the school (obeying the principal's orders) at a specific time and before the lethal shooting broke out. Reem, a very pleasant, lively and articulate young woman, announced that she had not been in the demonstration, and felt like a coward for not participating. She said that her father was out of the country, and that her mother forbade her to join the demonstration, incidentally mentioning that her father had previously been in jail and that her family did not want her to get into a situation where she could be injured or get into trouble.[14]

---

[14] In informal meetings over the years with Palestinian parents, we learned how painfully conflicted they were about their children participating in demonstrations and/or rock throwing during the *intifada*. They did not want their children to endanger themselves,

Her parents were interested in meeting with us and a few months after this November interview, we met with them in their home. The family was lively and warm, and a very comfortable relationship existed between the parents and the children, including Reem, the oldest. We learned that the father's father had been arrested and jailed under the British Mandate for his political activities and had urged his son not to get into trouble and not to risk arrest. We heard the history of Reem's father's going against his own father and of the several arrests and jail-terms over the years because of his outspoken political activism. We listened to the stories that the older children in the family had heard and in part experienced, stories of the different arrests by the soldiers in their home, the wrenching partings of children and mother from the father, the visits to the father in prison (logistically and emotionally terribly difficult for everyone), and the family's ongoing commitment to the Palestinian cause and to a Palestinian state. The children were greatly admiring of their father.

Subsequently we heard from the father more of his inner conflict around getting arrested again, how this dedicated and outspoken man was experiencing himself with some shame for his not being more outspoken. He detailed more of the history of the relationship between him and his father, and of how the first time he was arrested the army went to the father's house and forced him to go and show them where his son (Reem's father) was hiding out. We can imagine him in conflict as to whether to be faithful to the father's injunctions not to get arrested, or to be faithful to the spirit of protest and political rebellion that his father had transmitted to him.

This history is important background for Reem's statement that she 'felt like a coward' for not joining the demonstration. Out of all of this, however, Reem had decided to take advantage of an opportunity (with the support of her family) to participate in a summer programme with Israeli children in a kind of 'peace camp' where Israeli, Palestinian, and other teenagers would live together, work together, play together, and air their political differences together. We are seeing a flexibility and resilience in both Reem and her family, a transformation of the pain and conflict they had all experienced, with its potential for simply hating Israelis. Conflict and turmoil are not over for either Reem or her family, but we predict that this young woman will continue to demonstrate a flexibility and autonomy, representing loyalty to her family, an apprecia-

but they often could not control the comings and goings of the older children. They were not at all eager to have their children sacrificed for a cause, though they might feel proud of a child who dared to take a risk.

tion of her parents' own divided state, and the development of her own political sensibilities and opinions.

A dramatic contrast: youth who resort to extreme political violence

These vignettes present relatively optimistic scenarios of children in relatively secure and protected families, with caring adults attuned to their children's predicaments. In contrast is a study of youth who turn to extreme violence in the name of a political/ideological cause, namely, the work of Anne-Marie Oliver and Paul Steinberg in Gaza on the making of a suicide bomber.[15] This imaginative and courageous couple has collected the graffiti, pamphlets, posters, audio tapes, and video tapes of the *intifada*, especially in Gaza, and have interviewed many individuals. In the past few years, they have focused more on how fundamentalist groups have recruited older adolescents and young adults to become suicide bombers. Fundamentalist-extremist recruiters find young people in Gaza refugee camps who see little future for themselves beyond being street sweepers in Tel-Aviv. The youth who might become a suicide bomber is then enlisted and inducted into a cell, with a new life of perpetual fear and threat; emergency modes of behaviour become habits of being. He then commits some irreversible act, such as killing an Israeli, or a Palestinian collaborator, so that he is then hunted by Israeli security forces. There appears to be a very intense kind of continuous ideological bombardment of sorts, with a transcendent, literally interpreted, ideology, providing ready-made formulas for thought and action, legitimizing all forms of hatred against the 'other', the enemy. They are exposed to a rich diet of Islamic fundamentalist 'mythohistory' in which they learn about Islamic heroes of yore, such as Salahadin, who drove back the Crusaders, and Qassem, a Palestinian leader of a major revolt against the British and against the Zionists during the 1930s. The clandestine terrorist Hamas group is called the Qassem Brigade.[16] They are also exposed to contemporary Western (American) images of violent, somewhat heroic youth, especially Ninja figures. The group dynamic involves an intense almost eroticized relationship among the cell members, fostered by attachment to a charismatic leader or trainer.

They are promised the immortality of the name 'martyr' on earth, plus substantial material and spiritual rewards for their families (who

[15] This work, extensively presented to political science audiences and mental health audiences, will appear in a book to be published by Oxford University Press.
[16] See Kemmering and Migdal 1995.

often do not know their child is thus involved). Paradise awaits them, with the promise (in this sexually restrictive society) of seventy virgins The leaders foster the drive for glory and heroic identity in relation to the great agony that awaits them, and stimulate feelings of moral superiority over their immediate elders who are seen as passively suffering their victim status.

Crucial to this is the willingness of a group of adults to have young people give up their lives for the cause of an Islamic commonwealth and driving the Israelis into the sea. There is reason to believe that these adults themselves have their own history of the sequelae of violence, of humiliation, and of traumatic separation, and that they create and use the young suicide bombers as a form of acting out their own complex and traumatic history.[17] A current worrisome development is the appearance on 'Children's Club', a television show produced by the Palestinian Authority, of young children singing songs in praise of 'martyrs' and the suicide bombers.

What is resiliency?

The term 'resiliency' arose in the context of studies of children who seemed to be at major risk by virtue of having seriously mentally ill parents, and, in related research, studies of children growing up in very difficult economic circumstances in the United States (e.g, Werner 1977). Researchers in child development, some working both in clinical and in research settings, and some working primarily in research settings, began to catalogue 'risk factors' and 'protective factors' in the attempt to establish a more refined understanding of the phenomena subsumed under the term 'resilience'. Looking at our studies, and many others, we offer the following characteristics which mitigate aggression and contribute to resiliency (for further discussion and references, see Apfel and Simon 1996: chapter 1).

1. *Resourcefulness* including the gift of being able to extract human warmth and loving kindness in the most dire of circumstances, including at times from enemies or persecutors.

---

[17] Cf. Raphael Moses (see Rangell and Moses-Hrushovski 1996), Vamik Volkan (1996) and Hazani (1993) who utilize Kohut's concepts of injured narcissism, to describe how the youth are supposed to repair the injured pride and honour of their elders. Gill Straker and colleagues (1992) have worked with black township youth in South Africa who fought against apartheid, all of them victims of violence and some of them also perpetrators of violent, indeed murderous, deeds. As far as can be told from their material, these youths had not been as overtly instigated to violence by their elders as had the Palestinian suicide bombers, nor had they been instructed in self-destruction. Straker and colleagues are currently conducting follow-up studies of these youth.

2. *Curiosity and intellectual mastery, the ability to conceptualize, and generate knowledge* which provides an important sense of activity, rather than passivity.

3. *Flexibility in emotional experience,* not denying or suppressing major affects as they arise, and the ability to defer or defend against some overwhelming anxiety or depression when emergency resources are needed.

4. *Access to autobiographical memory,* the ability to remember and invoke images of good and sustaining figures, usually parental figures, even if these images might at times be critical and demanding as well as warm, loving, and encouraging.

5. *A goal for which to live,* a *purpose* or task which permits one to find a way to survive. This intertwines with a sense of empowerment and diminished helplessness

6. *Need and ability to help others,* altruism or 'learned helpfulness' which draws upon identification with parents who themselves have instantiated the effectiveness of altruistic acts.

7. *A vision of a moral order* and the possibility and desirability of the restoration of a civilized moral order may be crucial to survival and rebuilding community.

This list constitutes the internal and internally experienced concomitants of complex behaviours that have been shaped interactively. The behaviour of the adults around the child, and of other children, profoundly influence each child. Thus 'resilience' should be viewed as 'resultant' of 'vectors' from within the child and from the child's past and present world. Our interview material illustrates how much the individual child, her or his family, and the institutions surrounding the child all feed into the way each child copes with and perhaps transforms and transcends her or his traumatic burdens.

An opening to an anthropological–psychoanalytic dialogue

It is indeed an irony of Western civilization that its two 'cradles', Greece and Israel, have for millennia been places of violence, war and turmoil – at times epitomizing all that can be called 'primitive', or 'uncivilized'. The current Israeli–Palestinian conflict is indeed a discontented piece of civilization – a fight for political dominance and control of land and water supplies, compounded with demands for justice, dignity, acknowledgment, honour, affirmation of a national identity, and the assertion of the superiority of one religious faith over another. The children we have been interviewing live in complicated and shifting situations, juggling intra-group and inter-group aggression, along with their own developing conscience. They live in families and in communal settings where a high degree of moral integrity and moral maturity is expected of them, along with a pull towards intense loyalty to the group and to religious and national causes.

Freud's model of human aggression in *Civilization and its Discontents* emphasizes the tension between the aggressive and erotic demands of individual human beings and of closely knit human groups and 'an ever-increasing reinforcement of the sense of guilt'. For the purposes of an interdisciplinary dialogue we feel it is more useful to use a model that recognizes the constant temptation of adults to solve their own conflict between aggression and superego by getting children to act out their (adult) aggression. Adults may deal with their own traumatic histories by using their children to enact their own troubled past, in turn traumatizing them. Here the formulation of Vamik Volkan (1996) on 'chosen traumas' becomes particularly useful – historical (or mythohistorical) events (e.g. for Americans, 'Remember the Alamo', 'Remember Pearl Harbor') that loom large as justifications for hatred and for transgenerational hatred of an enemy. 'Chosen traumas' serve to mitigate guilt and responsibility for one's own destructive actions as well as to reduce fear, especially fear of one's own aggressive impulses. They may also deflect from intra-group or intra-familial conflicts, such as aggression towards one's own children. Yolanda Gampel's image of the 'radioactivity' transmitted from adults to children captures much of the unconscious mode of transmission of such hatred and fear, complementing the conscious messages encoded in 'the chosen trauma'.

Parents, driven by their own internal pressures to assimilate or abreact their traumas, are typically torn between how much to protect their children from the knowledge of the traumas in their own lives, and how much to expose the children to that knowledge in order to educate and protect them. We recognize that the universalist view, 'be humane', does not easily or always overlap a view from within the tribe or family as to what is good for one's own children, and therein lies another source of conflict. Clearly conscious and unconscious motivations interact in very complex ways in these transactions including the need to undo traumatic humiliations. A particularly ominous development is when political leaders purposefully create propaganda to increase hatred and dehumanization of the enemy, such as happened conspicuously in recent times in the former Yugoslavia and in Rwanda. Psychoanalytic, anthropological, sociological, and political perspectives are needed to fill out the picture and to generate both testable hypotheses and possible models of intervention.

As for these two groups of children – not necessarily representative of their larger societies – the parents are conflicted, but, relatively speaking, they are not using their children to act out. While we have only a limited glimpse of the parents, we have a fuller picture of the school settings (clearly which are endorsed by the parents). One can witness the flexibility, resourcefulness, and integrity of the adults in trying to help these children in their navigation through the morally and politically complex world into which they were born, a world marked currently by a good deal of actual violence and yet some potential for peace and mutual security. Our cautious prediction is that they will have increasing internal flexibility in their ability to transcend and transmute the multiple chronic violent traumas of their lives. We hope that these children will also be given the opportunity to struggle with the problems faced by so many American children – what will happen to Israeli and Palestinian children if and when some sort of durable peace and mutual accommodation does emerge, and they are no longer mobilized around life-and-death political issues and the entailed commitments? They have asked us: 'Aren't American children bored?' That question reminds us of another value of these interviews – as a mirror for how we regard and take care of, or fail to take care of, children in our own country.

Finally, there is a practical conclusion emerging from these interviews and the attendant theoretical frame. Interventions to help children traumatized by violence, acute and chronic, must build upon the strengths of families and schools, giving the necessary material and spiritual support to the adults who will nurture the children. Our task as anthropologists and psychoanalysts is to use our knowledge, skills, and commitment to strengthen those intergenerational bonds that ultimately make for the welfare of children.

Appendix

Questions from US third graders to their peers during the Gulf War in Israel:

1. What do you think of Saddam Hussein?
2. Have you had Scud missile drills?
3. Is it scary? How scary on a scale of 1 to 10?
4. Are some of your relatives or friends fighting in the war?
5. How does it feel to be in a country in the middle of a war area?
6. How did you feel when you heard the first air raid sirens?
7. What do you do when you are out of school?
8. How did you feel when you first heard there would be a war?
9. Are many shops open?

10. Has a Scud missile hit your neighbourhood?
11. Is it hard to concentrate on your work during this time?
12. How long do you think the war will last?
13. How does it feel to have a gas mask on?
14. Are you worried about coming home one day and finding your house wrecked?
15. Do you worry about something happening to your parents while you are in school?
16. If shops are not open how can you get food?
17. Is your sleep interrupted?
18. Are you getting enough sleep?
19. Have you ever been separated from your parents during an air raid?
20. If so, what was it like?
21. Is your gas mask next to your bed?
22. Do you ever forget about the war?
23. How long does a gas mask last?
24. Are you nervous as you walk along the street?
25. If a gas mask breaks, do you have a replacement?
26. Do you have lots of questions about the war? What are they?
27. What games do you play? Are you having fun at all while you are out of school?
28. Do you play war games?
29. What are your dreams?

References

Apfel, Roberta J. and Simon Bennett, eds., 1996, *Minefields in their Hearts: The Mental Health of Children in War and Communal Violence*. New Haven: Yale University Press

Bar-On, Dan, 1989, *Legacy of Silence: Encounters with Children of the Third Reich*. Cambridge, MA: Harvard University Press

1995, *Between Fear and Hope: Three Generations of Five Israeli Families of Holocaust Survivors*. Cambridge, MA: Harvard University Press

1996, Intergenerational Transmission of Trauma: An Overview and Case Study of a Dialogue between Descendants of Victims and Descendants of Perpetrators. In *Minefields in Their Hearts: The Mental Health of Children in War and Communal Violence*. Roberta J. Apfel, and Simon Bennett, eds. New Haven: Yale University Press

Hazani, Moshe, 1993, Sacrificial Immortality: Toward a Theory of Suicidal Terrorism and Related Phenomena. *Psychoanalytic Study of Society* 18:415–42

Herman, Judith L., 1992, *Trauma and Recovery*. New York: Basic Books

Kakar, Sudhir, 1996, *The Colors of Violence: Cultural Identities, Religion, and Conflict*. Chicago: University of Chicago Press

Kemmering, Baruch and Joel Migdal, 1995, *The Palestinians*. Cambridge, MA: Harvard University Press

Kestenberg, J.S. and E. Fogelman, eds., 1994, *Children During the Nazi Reign: Psychological perspectives on the Interview Process*. Westport, CT: Paeger Press

Puget, Janine *et al.*, 1989, *Violence d'état et psychanalyse*. Paris: Dunod

Pynoos, Robert S. and Katherine Nader, 1989, Children's Memory and Proximity to Violence. *Journal of the American Academy of Child and Adolescent Psychiatry* 27:236–41

Rangell, Leo and Rena Moses-Hrushovski, eds., 1996, *Psychoanalysis at the Political Border: Essays in Honor of Rafael Moses*. Madison: International Universities Press

Spindler, George D., ed., 1978, *The Making of Psychological Anthropology*. Berkeley: University of California Press

Straker, Gill with Faima Moosa, Risé Becker and Madiyoyo Nkwale, 1992, *Faces in the Revolution: The Psychological Effects of Violence on Township Youth in South Africa*. Athens, OH: Ohio State University Press

Suárez-Orozco, Marcelo, George D. Spindler and Louise Spindler, eds., 1994, *The Making of Psychoanalytic Anthropology II*. Fort Worth: Harcourt Brace College Publishers

Volkan, Vamik D., 1996, Intergenerational Transmission and 'Chosen' Traumas: A Link Between the Psychology of the Individual and that of the Ethnic Group. In *Psychoanalysis at the Political Border: Essays in Honor of Rafael Moses*. Leo Rangell and Rena Moses-Hrushovski, eds. Madison: International Universities Press, 257–82

Werner, E. E. and R. S. Smith, 1977, *Kauai's Children Come of Age*. Honolulu: University Press of Hawaii

5 Child psychotherapy as an instrument in cultural research: treating war-traumatized children in the former Yugoslavia

David de Levita

The civil war that disintegrated the former Yugoslavia in the 1990s left thousands upon thousands of traumatized refugee children in its wake. By October 1992 there were already 700,000 officially registered refugees in Croatia, to which we must add a further 150,000 non-registered refugees. Sixty per cent of them were younger than 18 years old. There were fewer refugees in Slovenia (about 70,000 in 1993), but their situation was just as desperate. The number of refugees in Bosnia-Hercegovina is unknown but passes the 1 million figure.

Many of these displaced persons, and in particular the children, need psychotherapeutic treatment. The proper treatment of children is considerably complicated by the large number of children afflicted by the war and the difficulties of making a correct diagnosis. How can a psychotherapist determine the influence of cultural and developmental factors on their behaviour? Which forms of behaviour can be attributed to general developmental processes, which to cultural influences, and which to traumatic experiences? The trauma suffered by these refugee children intermeshes in complex ways with their cultural background and the particular stage of their psychological development. Here, psychotherapy and anthropology find a common ground for interdisciplinary cooperation because the psychological development of a child is forged by the culture of his or her caretakers. Psychotherapists who treat war-traumatized children must therefore be keenly aware of the cultural context in which their young clients have been raised, and understand the social environment in which they try to help them.

Human nature and parental culture find one another in the miraculous happenings of the child's first years of life. Following the natural path of child rearing and in accordance with the traditions of their culture, the parents set processes in motion which will develop the child's social skills. Erik Erikson (1950) made it clear, half a century ago, that there is no such thing as a child waiting for his turn to enter society, but that society is present from the very first day. Jewish babies, who were handed to rescuers during the Second World War to find them a safe haven among non-Jewish families, already underwent the pressures of society: their natural crying often had to be suppressed in order not to betray their presence in the house. A whole range of possible interpretations of such a phenomenon displays itself in this example:

1. an individual interpretation, for in normal life there is an enormous difference as to the degree in which mothers tolerate the crying of their babies;
2. a cultural difference in handling this problem (in some regions of the Netherlands, at the end of the nineteenth century, babies were given dollops soaked in brandy to soothe their crying); and
3. a psychopathological interpretation: is it traumatic to suppress the crying of a baby, i.e. is there a chance that it damages the developing central nervous system?

Under less tragic circumstances it would be best to conduct research on the immediate effect of suppressing the baby's crying, but the methodology is far from simple. Although direct baby observation in this branch of research is advancing quickly, it remains very difficult to attribute a pathological development in a certain baby to a trauma that occurred in the past since nobody knows what his development would have been without the trauma. This is easier in adults because their psychic functioning may display a kink from the time the trauma occurred.

Even in babies, however, the traumatic past is never forgotten. When older, the child and subsequently the adult display behaviour in which the traumatic past may be read by one who understands the language. Dori Laub and Nanette Auerhahn (1993) mentioned the following forms of remembering a trauma without being aware of it:

- not knowing
- fugue states
- fragments
- transference phenomena
- overpowering narratives
- life themes
- witnessed narratives
- metaphors

This list makes clear that psychotherapy and, in this case, child psychotherapy could act as a research instrument for the detection and location of psychotrauma. A life theme for instance, 'I must revenge what has been done to my parents', may be consciously present (as we found in many Yugoslavian children) but in other cases it may reveal itself only during psychotherapy when the question is tackled of why the child is behaving so aggressively. In this paper, I will further explore how to use child psychotherapy as a detector of child psychotrauma.

This paper will begin with an exposé of the general developmental process common for young children and demonstrates how certain behavioural patterns may be diagnosed as psychopathological in one culture and regarded as completely normal in another. Next, I will describe some of the problems we encountered in diagnosing Bosnian refugee children and explain the Respicon-Desensitization method with which we chose to relieve some of their suffering. I will briefly present and analyze three therapeutic cases to illustrate the relations between trauma, culture, and psychological development. Finally, I will draw some tentative conclusions about the transgenerational transmission of the Bosnian war-trauma. This paper is based on my experiences as a member of a psychotherapeutic team which held workshops and treated some seventy refugee children in Ljubljana, Slovenia between 1991 and 1997.

The psychological development of children

The baby requires in the beginning only the satisfaction of basic needs, such as nutrition, body care, contact, stimulation, and protection, but in the second half of the first year his interest shifts from these provisions to *the person who provides them*. The mother, who is usually the protagonist in supplying those needs, is then wanted to be present and it is she who must be there for no other sake than her physical presence. Imagine you have to attend an important conference but cannot take your three-months-old baby with you. So, you decide to bring the baby to your mother with a few instructions about the child's habits and preferences. At your return you will find a happy child who only through a few uneasy nights revealed that your absence did not pass by unnoticed. But when the baby is no longer quite a baby but is fourteen months old, you might have to face a furious child who – it is true – has been too polite to give hell to his innocent host and hostess, but now is determined to let you know that your professional absence had been a grave mistake that needs to be revenged. His sense of *security* has been shaken. He has discovered that his mother, apart from being the source of all good, can also be the source of evil.

This kind of evolution is mirrored in many developmental issues. One example is the development of the baby's *smile*. Already a few weeks after birth it can be 'triggered off by certain primitive stimuli, with no foresight involved on the part of the infant as to the likely consequences of his actions' (Schaffer 1971:79). Then, for some time, the smile will appear to any eye-like configuration, then to what is face-like provided it is moved up and down, then only to three-dimensional objects which have a face-like quality, and then again some time later (about ten months) to a real human face only. This is evidently a *learning experience*: 'born to respond to certain limited stimuli, the infant learns that these stimuli generally appear in a particular context and in time the context is also required as part of the eliciting stimulus' (Schaffer 1971:79). This particular context in which stimuli generally appear is, however, nothing other than *culture*. It is *the totality of child-rearing practices, customary in a certain culture, modified by the individual qualities of the mother.*

A psychotherapist is in constant touch with and in need of the qualities which the client acquired as a young child when his mother succeeded in conveying to him a sense of security. This sense of security can be seen as part of the outcome of a favourable first year and has been labelled by different authors with different terms, for instance as basic trust (Erikson 1950; see also Robben, in this volume) and is prominently present in Kohut's self-object theory (Kohut 1971). The security originally connected to the bodily presence of the mother becomes so firmly internalized, that it lasts also *when the mother has left*. It can be and has been meticulously observed, how the time span of the child's well-being, after his mother has left, increases little by little in time. Be this as it may, this sense of security can later be shattered by traumatization. A psychotherapist who sets out to treat the consequences of trauma will have to face the insecurity of his client brought about by the therapy he administers.

The mother as a source of security is, however, not only effective by her physical presence. A good deal of behaviours and parts of the non-human environment assume symbolically mother-like traits. The culture in which one has been raised, adopts in its totality the meaning of a mother, or, in the terminology of Winnicott, assumes *transitional traits*, i.e. that it is at the same time mother and not-mother, or self and non-self. In many adopted children I have treated as a psychotherapist, this longing for the *lost world of the mother* was not less painful than her bodily absence. It seems, especially in children who were adopted at an early age, that their body preserves somewhere the reminiscences of that early world, its sounds and smells, whereas the image of the mother as a person cannot any longer be recalled. 'The common use of words such as *motherland, mother tongue and fatherland* to refer to a person's country of origin or native tongue suggests a powerful symbolic association between one's country of origin and cultural context and one's relationship to his or her primary caretakers', says Antokoletz (1993). He has recognized that the transition from one culture to another means for a child a developmental crisis. The loss of the familiar (space, language, social and non-human environment) that should further support the still fragile internalizations, may cause a regression to previous stages of development. Many authors agree (e.g. Grinberg and Grinberg 1984) that adults usually have more trouble coping with the loss of their country of origin than children, especially when the children have their parents with them in the new environment. This, however, can be due to the completely different course mourning takes in children (Furman 1974).

Grinberg and Grinberg (1984) distinguish between what they call 'two large categories with regard to the migratory tendency: those who always need to be in contact with familiar people and places, and those who enjoy being able to go to unfamiliar places and begin new relationships'. They add that neither one of these categories by itself constitutes a sign of mental health, and that it would be desirable to achieve a good integration of both in order to be able to react appropriately to changing life circumstances. But they also lend an ear to the many forms of pathology that can be caused by migration, especially in people who are unable to mobilize their resources in order to stand up to its mental inconveniences. They stress the significance of parts of the non-human environment of the native country to support the person in his fight with the unknown and the unfamiliar. One of their clinical examples was the following:

The radical change in a patient who had emigrated, produced by the arrival of her furniture, which had taken longer to reach its destination than she had, was striking. 'Since my arrival, my dreams had been totally crazy; they didn't seem to belong to me; I didn't recognize them. I had never had dreams like these. I wasn't like myself . . . But a few days ago, my dreams have again become the way they always used to be. I think this happened the day I received my furniture: I felt that I was surrounded by "my" things; it was thrilling to find myself with them again. Each object brought the memory of a situation, a moment, a past. I feel more like myself.' (Grinberg and Grinberg 1984:24)

In psychotherapy, particularly in psychoanalysis, this balance between a person's inclination towards the familiar and towards the unfamiliar is constantly put to the test. In the transference the therapist appears as the mother who sometimes acts as a protective shield in whose company one is safe, and at other times as the stimulator of dangerous insights and confrontations. In his own balancing between these roles the therapist needs an intuitive insight into his client's moods and situation. He must have empathy for what his client is able to endure. But what he equally needs is *insight into the culture* in which his client has grown up, because one of his tasks with regard to his client is that he *represents reality for him.* When one has to deal with a client's rage – and which therapist has not? – towards his mother because she neglected some of his most intensive needs, it makes all the difference if one can explain to the client, that his mother did exactly what *all mothers did at that time and in that place,* and that the attention must shift to the personal fantasies the client developed about her behaviour (e.g., that she treated him in this respect worse than his siblings).

The cultural development of Bosnian children

Child-rearing practices involve more than the handling of the baby. A psychological evaluation of the quality of her care comes down to determining to what extent the mother indulges in the baby's needs, and to what extent she imposes frustrations to benefit higher educational objectives. A simple example of a properly balanced care is that she feeds the baby when he asks for it, but does not overfeed him although he asks for it. A host of factors concerning the personality of the mother come into play here (can she stand the baby's crying when he does not get what he wants? etc.). We are confronted with the problem that the personal variations in the mother in our eyes can be of minor significance, seen against the background of cultural practices which – again in our eyes – differ considerably from what we, in our own culture, are used to. In former Yugoslavia where we were involved in a project that treated war-traumatized children, the situation has been described by Puhar. She mentions the *zadruga* as the basic family unit:

these communal families characteristic throughout all of former-Yugoslavia, except Slovenia, differ significantly from the conjugal families which we are familiar with in most of Europe; they involved several biological families living and working together, with men never leaving their native homes and with the eldest man functioning as the leading authority. Predominant features of this type of family were therefore enormous resistant to change and innovation. (Puhar 1994:133)

Children born in these families were subjected to harsh treatment even before they were born . . . the babies were ritually and repeatedly cleansed in cold water . . . swaddled, subjected to various protective treatments against evil spirits, mostly harmful, and severely punished throughout babyhood and childhood. In short, it was a crowded life of neglect, battering, terror and the absence of almost all signs of affection. It was also a life of widespread and routine sexual abuse. Psychohistorically speaking, it was a combination of *infanticidal and ambivalent modes of childrearing.* (Puhar 1994:134)

The author calls this 'the nightmare of childhood'. The present situation – in what we encountered – seemed to be better. It is an open question whether the war, dominated by flight and migration, has had as a side-effect that children became precious to their parents and were therefore more cherished.

One phase is of central importance in the multitude of practices which present themselves in the upbringing of children: *the oedipal complex*. In the course of this stage of life of a 4–5 year old it is determined whether a person will be able to cope for the rest of his life with the problem that he or she is what he is – no less and no more – and must try to find himself a life unhampered by the fact that in his fantasies he is so much more. The fantasy of the toddler, that he is able to take his father's place as his mother's partner, should remain a fantasy. He must understand and accept, in the course of time, the irreality of this fantasy without losing his self-esteem. Parents in this developmental stage of their child have to contribute less than when their child was still a baby. They must provide less in terms of *actions* and more in terms of affections. It is of central importance that they react soundly. The mother must be respectful towards the unfolding masculinity of her son, without provoking him too much. She must show him reality in that he cannot act, as yet, as an adult, but at the same time sweeten the pill by showing her respect for him. The same, with small differences, is valid for a father towards his daughter.

What about the cultural differences as to the way in which parents behave with regard to the oedipal stage of their children? Gaby Garcinovic of the University of Ljubljana, Slovenia, found in recent research that in the *Serbian world* a mother may tell her son that he is 'the light in her eyes', while in Croatia, much more down to earth, a mother will first of all check upon the correctness of her son's behaviour. In the first case, a boy is suggested already at an age of four, five or six years that great deeds are expected of him, that in order to reach a point where women can love him, he has to exceed his present state and attain a much more grandiose state. In the second instance, the boy is much more led to feeling that what he does in the present is important, that on the one hand he is only a child who has to learn much, but that on the other hand he can reach satisfaction just by fulfilling the tasks assigned to him. Just as the first style of education may lack a *sense of reality*, so the second style may fail to transmit *inspiration*. Our scarce material is too little to arrive at firm conclusions, but we were nevertheless struck by the intensity of oedipal ties, as for instance will be seen in the case of Marja.

The consequences of these differences in childhood practices between Serbian and Croatian mothers were tremendous. From our research into what people thought to be the background of the cruelties and atrocities of the civil war, we learned that the older Serbian family members seemed to stir up youngsters rather than calming them down, 'pressing them into virtual competitions to shock and out-shock one another' (Puhar 1994:139). The author calls this a quest of heroism and cites Cvijic who already noted: 'the moment a child leaves the cradle he begins to run after glory and fame, and their great desire is to belong to a heroic family.'

When we try to assess the mental state of children we have to turn to the progress of their development. Adults also develop but, unlike children, they generally cannot be assessed by their acquisition of new *functions*. Psychopathology in adults can be measured by the mental functions that have been impaired, but in children we encounter this very subtle flowering of new abilities and competencies. The most common problem in the assessment of the mental health of children is to ascertain whether a certain function has been impaired or has not yet developed.

Also in the case of children it is their *psychotherapy* that may clarify what exactly is happening. For example, the question of whether a certain young child does not speak either because *he cannot* or because for some reason *he does not want to* (and this at an age when he should) can generally not be answered by psychological testing. If one is lucky, psychotherapeutical means can bring to light *fear of speaking* or *revolt against speaking* or whatever may be found as a plausible explanation. Here the proof of the pudding is in the eating: the only proof that the explanation was valid is produced when the child begins to speak (or begins to function when functioning was hitherto absent) as a result of the therapy.

Returning to the role culture plays in the psychopathology of children, it seems to me that the meaning of cultural practices can be further analyzed by psychotherapy of persons involved in these practices, with benefits for both psychotherapy and cultural anthropology. Especially for the study of psychotrauma, it seems important to identify the role of cultural factors, a task that goes far beyond the range of classification systems. A formula could be used in which (for this special purpose) *culture is defined as the sum total of cultural practices geared to avert universal human fears such as incest, castration, and return of the dead.*

Two small vignettes which originate from the author's own experience as a child psychiatrist are presented here as an illustration of what the editors of the book *Cultural Practices as Contexts for Development* had in mind when in their introduction to Shweder, Jensen, and Goldstein's paper they warned their readers that 'there is not likely to be any neat one-to-one correspondence: one practice, one principle' and that 'a variety of practices may meet the same principle, and practices that appear similar at the behaviour level may stem from different principles'.

John

John, who is nine years old, is referred to the child psychiatric clinic because his school achievements have lately deteriorated, and he is hardly able to learn anything new at school. The parents tell the following story. John's grandfather has recently died. His grandmother came to see her daughter – John's mother – and said: 'As you know I cannot sleep alone. Give me one of your children to live with me for some time.' John had been selected to keep his grandmother company, he stayed with her and slept in her bed.

One is reminded of a section of anthropological research called 'who sleeps by whom' (Shweder, Jensen and Goldstein 1995). The authors cite a research report by Caudill and Plath (1966) in 323 suburban Japanese families during the first sixty years of this century. They found that 'a typical Japanese person, in a life-time, *seldom slept alone'*. In their own research the authors have compared families in Orissa, India, with Anglo-American middle-class families in the US. They have made an inventory of all 'sleeping formulas' they encountered in the two cultures and conclude that in the Orissa community 'there is a single, fixed sleeping pattern'. They have mapped out sleeping combinations of fathers, mothers, daughters, and sons, but mention grandparents only in a note: ' in our data, which were based on reports from children and adults, the co-sleeping network for a child almost never included that child's aunts, uncles, cousins or father's father, although children did sometimes co-sleep with their father's mother. The father's father rarely co-slept with a child and most often slept alone, separated from his wife.'

We may conclude that when co-sleeping with a grandmother is already unusual in Orissa culture, with its so much greater flexibility in co-sleeping than exists in our culture, co-sleeping with a grandmother in our Western culture, as in John's case, might be still more unusual, to the point of being traumatic. How, however, can we find out if this is true with John, i.e. if he indeed has been traumatized? His sudden separation from his family certainly implied much more than the co-sleeping with the grandmother, and definitely resulted from a very complex background with in its centre the relationship between John's mother and grandmother. To identify the pathogenic element in this little story might, however, be important because it could perhaps show where a certain cultural practice, although unusual, still belongs to the normal variations, or is so remote from the normal that it, so to speak, *oversteps the limits.*

In John's psychotherapy (or rather the first interviews with him, conducted by a psychotherapeutic technique) he reported a dream: 'He was at home, an old woman sneaked in, he felt as if she was going to eat him, he fled to the roof, he heard her coming up, a neighbour came to help him, he awoke.' This dream produces no proof that the persecution by the grandmother was felt by John as being more dangerous to him than his separation from home, but it makes it plausible. We told the parents that a child belonged to his family and that they should find other ways to accommodate the grandmother; John returned home and his school achievements returned to normal.

Peter

Peter, eight years old, does not present any symptoms and was not referred to the clinic. His story emerged in a different way. He is, because of certain circumstances, brought up by his maternal grandmother and her sister. In this little household a peculiar habit has developed: when Peter goes to the toilet and is ready, he opens the door and shouts: 'Ready!' At this sign, both ladies get moving and whoever is the first to arrive, wipes his bottom. One day, Peter stays for one night at the house of his mother's sister who herself has children. When at a certain moment he shouts 'ready!', his amazed hostess asks: 'What do you mean by "Ready"?' Peter explains. His aunt tells him that a boy of his age should be able to do that all by himself and teaches him, and from that moment on, he did. The 'habit' has come to an end, also at home.

This may illustrate that bizarre practices which are at variance with current cultural practices need not be traumatic. Peter's psychic health was showing through the fact that he accepted his aunt's guidance and at once reached an age-adequate level in toilet training. Disturbances in toilet training are quite often expressions of serious problems between parents and child. Obstipation and encopresis can frequently be interpreted as a rebellion of the child against parental attitudes and deficiencies. Peter's basic needs were clearly met with; in John there was a beginning of a deficiency that could have done much harm if the parents had not sought professional help immediately. The mother's concern for John reflects her basically warm attitude towards him and explains why John's disturbance disappeared so soon.

As to the character of his reaction, failure at school and in learning is part of the DSM (Diagnostic and Statistics Manual) description of the

PTSD syndrome (D3: difficulty in concentrating) and was present in nearly all traumatized Bosnian children we saw, as will be discussed later in this chapter.

The diagnosis and treatment of Bosnian refugee children

The literature describes several methods for the treatment of PTSD. Apart from techniques of behaviour therapy such as desensitization one also finds psychodynamic psychotherapy (Terr 1985), hypnosis (Spiegel and Gardena 1990), group psychotherapy, family therapy, and pharmacotherapy (Southwick and Yehuda 1993; Kolk and Fisler 1993). As I have already stated, our purpose was to investigate how successful desensitization could be in alleviating symptoms in traumatized children.

We started in 1991 to give workshops, first in Zagreb, later in Ljubljana in Slovenia. The purpose of our workshops in Slovenia was to train volunteers in the treatment of war traumas both in adults and children. Central to this was the method of desensitization developed by Defares (Brom, Kleber, and Defares 1986), a variation of Wolpe's (1969) method of systematic desensitization which he originally designed for the treatment of phobias. Systematic desensitization is aimed at the active re-experience of anxiety under conditions of maximal relaxation, based on the idea that the organism may be in a state of anxiety or of relaxation but not in both at the same time.

Our principal objective was to discover whether or not, and to what extent, this method would also be suitable to treat war traumas. If this were to be the case, then we would have a method available to help large groups of war-traumatized people who, by their sheer number, could not be sufficiently helped with more traditional and time-consuming psychotherapeutic techniques.

The desensitization method induces relaxation by submitting the client to breathing through biofeedback. A small electronical device, called the 'Respicon', is fixed on the client's chest. It measures the breathing rhythm on the basis of the client's initial breathing rate. The device then works out a different rhythm. This rhythm is converted into a rising or descending sound which is fed to the client by an earpiece. The session begins once the client is breathing regularly. The therapist invites the client to re-experience the painful event by evoking the traumatic images. Seeing the images, hearing the sounds, allowing the associated feelings to rise to the surface, the client begins to verbalize this troubling whole of experiences. The therapist then suggests that the client should distance himself from what happened by saying: 'It is over, I am letting it go.' If the re-experienced contents were very traumatic, then the therapist will sometimes suggest that the client should think of something pleasant. The breathing rhythm is measured, and often it will have come closer to the norm. After a short interval, the client is invited to re-experience the traumatic scene again and the process is repeated. Hereafter, I shall refer to this method as 'Respicon-desensitization' (RD).

To prepare the first group of participants (those who eventually would have to be responsible for further applying and teaching of the method) for the task of selection, we started a workshop entitled 'Basic Help for Children'. In this seminar we discussed the general principles of diagnostics with traumatized children. Once again we observed how difficult it was for untrained people to assess the severity of a psychopathological situation. With children it is very helpful to divide their functioning into three areas: the family (primary environment), the school (secondary environment), and friends, hobbies, and leisure time (tertiary environment). The number of areas in which their functioning has been impaired is a useful indicator of the severity of the disturbance. Whereas lay people are inclined to judge the situation according to the presence of *bizarre* symptoms (e.g., Peter's wish to have his bottom wiped by the first arriving old lady in his home, see above) serious psychopathology manifests itself by the loss of important mental functions.

In the refugee camps the children present their symptoms more often at school than in their families because they make great efforts to protect their families from their own disturbed behaviour (Apfel and Simon describe a very similar situation elsewhere in this volume: in their case, the children protected their therapists in a similar way). We were therefore very fortunate that most of the participants in our workshops were Bosnian teachers. They had come from many areas of academic life in Bosnia, but now worked as teachers in the elementary schools of the camps. We were extremely impressed by their importance for the mental health system for the camp children, again very similar to what Apfel and Simon found for Palestinian children.

The Bosnian teachers turned out to play a vital role in recognizing psychopathology in the children under their care. In the later training workshop, the participating teachers themselves selected the children who, they judged, were in the worst condition. We discussed that 'being in the worst condition' is not necessarily the same as 'having experienced the worst atrocities' but that impaired functioning is the central issue when selecting those children who are most in need of treatment.

The situation we encountered was as follows: Bosnian refugees in

Slovenia live either in refugee camps or with relatives. We thought at first, having the camps of the Second World War in mind, that those in the camps would be worst off. This turned out not to be true. A great many refugees live with relatives – according to some people many more than are living in the camps. There is great concern about their situation. Usually their hosts and hostesses are people who came – sometimes many years ago – as *guest labourers* from southern Yugoslavia to the relatively richer Slovenia. Then war broke out and all of a sudden they were saddled with ten or twenty relatives who moved into their impoverished homes without any financial support. One can imagine what situations this produces. Children have to put up with all kinds of snubs, and are not allowed to protest because it might put the shelter of the family at risk. Conditions are so primitive, and even primary needs so badly catered for, that mental health care sounds like a fairy tale. In the camps – of which there are about fifty in Slovenia – there is at least the prospect that one day they will be able to offer mental health facilities, though at present this is not possible. The refugees who live with their relatives, however, have not been registered and cannot be traced.

Nevertheless, there is a ray of hope for the children: *the school.* The importance of this institution for the mental health of the child refugees cannot be overestimated. In all parts of the world there is a great discrepancy between the number of children who require professional treatment and the number of those for whom help is actually sought; the second group of children is less than half of the first. The ratio seems to be even worse among the refugees because there are no facilities and the mothers (the fathers are usually absent) are too depressed anyway to take any initiative. The only nurturing environment available in the camps is the schools. They have been properly set up by UNICEF and the Slovenian government and are praised by the mothers as hospitable places for their children to spend time. The most important ingredient is *the teachers.* They are mostly Bosnian teachers and lecturers from various disciplines who are unemployed and work as volunteers – generally unpaid. They themselves are refugees and know from their own experience what the children have been through. They are in a position to observe the children the entire day and note post-traumatic learning disturbances. This knowledge is crucial for the proper treatment of post-traumatic stress disorders. In my own workshop I regularly saw a group of these teachers – the ones who assessed the children and selected them for treatment.

In addition to the training of volunteers, we taught the Respicon-Desensitization method in workshops for a group of local professionals

(Slovenian as well as Bosnian psychiatrists, physicians, and psychologists). The workshops were organized by the Svetovalní Centre (a mental health centre) in Ljubljana which was under the care of Dr Anica Kos, a wonderful psychiatrist who gives a good deal of her time to working with refugees. Without the support of the Svetovalní Centre our work would not have been possible. The choice of Respicon-Desensitization had been made, it is true, on numerical grounds but it was not our intention to treat great numbers of patients ourselves. Our objective was rather to test the usefulness of the method. This required that contact with the treated children should be continued after we had left; the Centre took care of this.

The procedure was as follows: the teachers from the first workshop selected from their school class the children who they believed were worst off and brought them to the Centre. Treatment was carried out under my supervision (thanks to a translator) by one of the professionals in the workshop.[1]

We were able to see each child three times during the week these workshops were held. The following three cases demonstrate the modest therapeutic success of the RD treatment, and indicate the importance of understanding the psychological development of war-traumatized children, the attachment to their parents, and the influence of their cultural background.

The war traumas of three Bosnian refugee children

When we started the project, the sessions were attended by the child, the therapist (a member of the working group), and myself; a construction customary in psychotherapy. Then we found out by accident that the mother's presence at the session did a lot of good. We had in certain cases allowed the mother to be present because the child seemed scared without her. Mothers and children had gone through so much together and had to such a great extent shared the same fate, that it seemed increasingly odd to leave the mother out. In many cases, such as in the case of Marja, we observed a kind of symbiosis, brought about by fate, which implied that not only the child, but also the mother gained by the session. The feeling of security, irradiating from the *familiar*, was almost tangible in the room. From that time on, we took to inviting *all family members present* to the session, including the siblings and the relatives with whom the family was staying as refugees. The success of this was so convincing that we extended the gathering to the teacher who had made

---

[1] Miss Maja de Graaf, Doctor of Slavic Languages, to whom I am grateful for her devoted and excellent help.

the link between the child and the team, and to the whole group of participants of the working group instead of only to the member who performed the therapy.

As to my own role in the sessions, I felt from the outset a strong transference in my direction. Several sessions which I had not been able to attend fell flat. It was clearly indispensable that someone *from the outside was present who represented the non-familiar element*. This reminded me of what Abelin (1975) has stated about the role of the father with regard to the mother–child symbiosis:

the most definite turning towards the father occurs at the beginning of the practicing subphase. A special quality of excitement is linked with him by the child, who seems by this time to take the mother for granted as a 'home base', for occasional refueling.

In Margaret Mahler's group of co-workers this idea has been elaborated upon, arriving at the concept of the father acting as a kind of hero coming from the outside to free the child from an all to close symbiosis with the mother.

It was striking to observe how in our sessions with the refugee children the meaning of the mother and the other family members *who all shared the same cultural background* represented the *familiar*, whereas I, coming from a completely different background, represented the *unfamiliar* which was quite obviously loaded with excitement.

Marja

The following information was given to us by the teacher. Marja, who is ten years old, saw how her house was set on fire, and her father was murdered. She is very intelligent but gives confused answers, and is unable to do simple sums. When he asks her why she cannot do the sums she starts crying. She writes strange essays, containing beautiful phrases but the whole is incoherent. Every night she has terrible nightmares.

First session

Encouraged to describe what happened to her on that horrible day, Marja says: 'At six o'clock in the morning we heard noises outside, mother thought it was the dog but it was soldiers. The neighbour called to my father and my uncle, there was a shooting. Mother saw . . . we had to go to the neighbour's house . . . after that we went to another place by truck.'

The therapist (a woman paediatrician) asks her what she saw but Marja is unable to speak. Therapist: 'Tell us what you dreamt of.' Marja:

'I dreamt that they came to fetch my father.' She says that her father should not have left without taking her with him. She starts crying.

Second session (afternoon of the same day)

'At six we heard noises outdoors. I felt safe there, and I still felt safe when I went to lie down under the bed . . . then bullets flew through the windows . . . I saw fire everywhere . . . we fled to the neighbour . . . when the shooting was over we wanted to return home but the Chetniks wouldn't let us . . . they threatened my mother.'

Therapist: 'You were afraid that they would do something to your mother?' Marja does not answer but speaks again about how she feared for her own life when the house started burning.

Next day

The teacher tells us that Marja's mother who is with her and was also present at the previous sessions, felt relieved during the evening and slept well, although she had not dared to take her pills for fear that she would oversleep the next day. Marja has not had a nightmare for the first time in many months.

Third session

Marja has dreamt of some shoes her father once gave her and of a doll on batteries which could talk. Her mother disapproved of the second present, which she thought too beautiful a present to be given when it was not a special occasion. Marja therefore never wore the shoes but her mother did not understand, and reproached her for not wearing them. She went on dreaming that she and her mother went with father when he was taken away. The most painful thing is *that she feels she would have been willing to sacrifice everybody if she could have saved her father.* She can now say what she was unable to say in the first session: that when they walked over to the neighbour's house and saw her father's body lying there, her mother had wanted to put on a white veil (the Muslim sign of mourning) but that she, Marja, did not want her to do so. She says she is unable to do anything, now that her father is dead. The therapist says: 'I am sure that your father wanted you to live on.' Marja embraces her.

Three months later

The teacher reports that Marja has developed into a serious girl. According to him a kind of rebirth has occurred. She now writes poems one of which I quote:

I am looking into the distance
and have been thinking
if the war had not existed
they would not have carried you away, daddy
daddy, why have they carried you away
why have they not left you for me
they have injured my heart
wounded my mother
when the war is over
I will think of you, daddy
I will think, keep you in my heart
daddy, my dear daddy
never shall I forget you

gledam v daljinu
i dugo tako mislim
da samo nije bilo rata
ne bi te odveli tata
tata zasto te odvedose
zasto mi te ne ostavise
mo je srce povrijedise
majku moju unistise
i kad ne bude rata
ja cu misliti na tebe, tata
misliti cu cuvati te u srdce
dragi moj tata
nikada zavorit te necu

The therapist at the Centre who continued with the treatment after the workshop was over reports that Marja became forgetful again when treatment was interrupted during the Christmas holidays. Her memory is better now. She is sleeping well.

In the case of Marja, a paediatrician who had never practised psychotherapy intuitively found the right thing to say. The child felt at once freed from an unbearable burden. It was a moving moment which none of us who were present will ever forget. Still, we continue to be concerned about Marja. Her tie to her father was excessively strong, and we wonder if his sudden death will unconsciously reduce his power in her eyes, or will become a fixation since he is no longer there to contribute to the change of his powerful image in Marja's eyes.

This case also illustrates how essential cultural information is to this kind of treatment. We knew that children's deepest anxiety may be the fear that the mother is raped by soldiers in front of their eyes. There is a strong taboo on sexual matters and an issue like this can hardly be discussed by a stranger. The therapist was very wise in not insisting, after she had given a hint in that direction. The point was later taken up when Marja was in regular therapy at the Centre.

Zoran

The following information was given to us by the teacher. Zoran, who is nine years old, has always been a cheerful boy, but now he is depressed. He is alone, his parents have been wounded and are in a hospital in Zagreb. His previous history is unknown. He lives with an aunt. At school he is very quiet, a little lost. He cannot catch a ball. He can write, but only by copying from the blackboard, not by himself. Like the others he has sleeping disorders.

First session

Zoran is unable to say anything, in spite of his therapist's suggestions. He withdraws and tries to express what is going on in his mind by drawing.

In the group we agree that there is a painful lack of information. We understand that Zoran's caretakers have not tried to get information from the Zagreb hospital (which could have been done easily) because they feared it would be bad. The group is afraid that Zoran's parents have died but is convinced that Zoran has to know. We decide that we must try to get information.

At the end of the workshop Zoran feels ashamed that he has not participated. We arrange a special session for him during which it strikes us that his memories are less sharp than those of the other children. He remembers that the family fled, that his mother was grazed by a bullet, that his father carried her but got wounded himself. Zoran feels relieved that he, too, has participated in a session. He sleeps well that night.

Three months later

When we return three months later we learn that Zoran has made remarkable progress at school. He joins in games, aspiring to the role of leader. However, things are going badly just at present. He is angry and restless. The background to this is that news has been sought about his parents, who turn out to be alive but badly wounded. They telephoned and father has even visited on crutches. Zoran was in high spirits. But father promised two months ago that he would soon come to collect Zoran – and he has not yet arrived. We agree that Zoran should be given support and that we should anticipate a much longer wait because his parents obviously are not in a position to take him home: there is no home and they are invalids.

The vignette illustrates a very common problem we encountered. Since the war is still going on one never knows whether a child is suffering from a traumatic event that happened in the past, or whether he is depressed because of the current situation which may be very traumatic too: no information, bereavements, loss of one's own house, village, community, friends, possessions and much more. Here we note a significant difference with what is found commonly in the literature about child trauma. The literature usually describes instances in which the trauma was an incident that ended (accidents, sexual abuse, etc.).

Zoran's shame is brought about at first by his inability to participate in the workshop, and to do what the others do. This is of course a common feeling among children. Zoran, we think, takes this very seriously because as a boy he is under the spell of the cultural obligations that rest upon him: to become some day the revenger of his father.

Ahmo

The following information was given to us by the teacher: Ahmo, who is nine years old, went to a Serbian school, where he learned Cyrillic script. He has finished the first grade. He is a very intelligent boy but the most traumatized of all. His father was murdered along with the other men of his village. The corpses were buried with a bulldozer. They had all been hiding in the woods for months, when Chetniks ambushed them and held them up. Ahmo escaped and returned to the village with the woman next door who hid him under her bed. Later they fled again and ended up in a refugee camp.

At the camp's school he cannot concentrate for longer than ten minutes, after which he starts scratching. He lives with his mother and an aunt, while a brother lives somewhere else. He does not want his mother to be at the session but likes his teacher to be there.

First session

'It is early in the morning. His father who is an early riser is already up . . . he starts climbing the hill . . . his mother prepares breakfast but his father does not return . . . a day later the neighbour says: 'Your father is dead, I'd go and fetch him before he starts stinking' . . . His mother asks the Serbian guard [becomes unclear] . . . she is told that women in the village have been raped . . . his mother and brother were in a room where they did this [becomes inaudible] . . . people fled on tractors . . . in the next village people were killed with knives . . . a bullet narrowly missed his head . . . somebody in the village had revealed where the weapons were hidden . . . the corpses were dug up so that they could be identified . . . the Serbians had drawn stockings over their heads.'

Second session

'He had been so frightened himself . . . the village had had to surrender . . . they had uncovered the weapons . . . he was frightened when his father went away [becomes emotional] . . . he had wanted to go with his father . . . his mother was at home when the notification came [that the father was dead] . . . she said that his father had needed so much gauze for his badly bleeding wound.'

The teacher says that the mother had previously had two unhappy marriages and had been happy with this husband for the first time in her life.

Since there is clearly tension between Ahmo and his mother we decided to arrange a session for her too. It is very emotional. She remembers how they hid for months in the woods: 'They were looking for my husband . . . in the village there were rapes by neighbours . . . but I was too old . . . I saw it all . . . neighbours hauled her from a burning house . . . [asked what was the worst she had seen] people who refused to say where they had hidden their gold and money had their arms and legs chopped off . . . a neighbour was ripped open with nails . . .' She cannot continue.

Next day the mother returns to the Centre of her own accord to tell us that she feels better than she has felt for a long time. Asked whether she is not worried about Ahmo, she replies: 'He'll manage. He is more intelligent than I am.'

Three months later

Ahmo is much better, he is living in another town now where he is receiving treatment. The problem is his mother who is very depressed and should really be admitted to hospital.

A common problem is illustrated in this vignette. The effect of the trauma on the child is determined not only by the child's own personality, but depends also on the reactions of his environment. Sometimes the parent's sorrow about what happened is more important to the child than his own grief. When we had the impression that this was the case, we always tried to treat the parent too if he or she was available. We discussed this with the child because, particularlly in boys, they feel that they must replace the absent father and play the role of the man. It is most important to praise the boy for his effort and to be very careful in how to tell him that he cannot be supposed to act as an adult yet. The pride of the boys is immense and very fragile.

An evaluation of the psychotherapeutic treatment

From these and other examples it appears that desensitization is not suitable for every child: some are too young or too withdrawn. The child who was able to use the method started to talk but skipped the most atrocious details. In the following sessions he or she gradually confronted the worst with the help of the relaxation exercises. Sometimes things developed in quite another direction and the child began to talk about family conflicts which had existed long before the trauma. In some cases so much feeling was aroused that the child began pouring his heart out session after session. This is one of the most intriguing aspects of the method: the sessions with each client are *quite different and develop in unexpected directions* which needs further study. Marja's case illustrates the theory that behaviour therapy activates unconscious conflicts (Marmor and Woods 1980; Fonagy 1989). In a sense this is a relief, since it might seem unlikely that war-traumatized children in the former Yugoslavia are suitable subjects for desensitization, because – as it has been said before – the trauma (or rather a whole series of traumas) continues in the present: their fathers are dead or missing, their homes have been destroyed, their places of birth devastated, their material situation is wretched, their prospects for the future are none too bright. Translating these circumstances from an external to an internal reality, one finds that these children accumulate fears and conflicts most of which were already present before the violence erupted in the former Yugoslavia but which are now activated or reinforced. The child who is hit by a trauma is not a *tabula rasa* but, like anybody else, has his personality structure and pre-existing conflicts.

In practically every case, nightmares and sleeping disorders disappeared after the first session. The effects of the treatment on behaviour and learning disturbances can only appear gradually.

Mental health programmes in war-stricken countries require the treatment of psychotrauma. Essential to fulfilling this task is an institute where local professionals can co-operate with foreign experts, co-ordinate the work and evaluate the results. Among the many supplies needed (of which, in the case of children, the school is of central significance) appropriate forms of psychotherapy may serve to alleviate the suffering caused by psychotrauma. If successful, this treatment may help break the malignant chain of generations who have to take revenge upon what happened to the generation of their parents.

Transgenerational aspects of a Bosnian war trauma

Like all other trauma, psychotrauma denotes that the physical integrity has been lost. Freud understood by trauma a damage of the stimulus barrier, i.e. an injury to the information-processing apparatus. This means that in fact a *brain trauma* has occurred. The consequences of this conception for psychoanalytical and psychotherapeutic work have not always been clear. Recently – with the rise of biological psychiatry – a wealth of evidence has become available which demonstrates the correctness of Freud's original ideas. In particular the symptom of intrusive memories, as they are found in the PTSD syndrome, suggests brain damage. The patients react well to the administered medicines as has been shown by van der Kolk and Fisler (1993).

Traumatized parents of the first generation suffer a disturbance of the stimulus-processing apparatus of their ego. They therefore have great trouble in containing (in Bion's sense) their psychic experiences or, rather, *it is impossible for them to contain them*. This seems similar to what Yolanda Gampel had in mind when she coined the term 'radioactivity':

> [I]n my view, radioactivity takes place when an external reality enters the psychic apparatus without the individual having any control over its entry, implantation or effects . . . [T]hese unconscious remnants are internalized so that the individual identifies with them and their dehumanizing aspects. As time goes by, such individuals act out these identifications, which are alien to them, and/or transmit them to their children, who may act them out and even transmit them to the third generation. (Gampel, in this volume)

The transmission of this ideology to the next generation has by now been going on for centuries in the former Yugoslavia. It has a specific form: *vengeance*, executed by young men. Its structure is an issue crying out for further research. One of its ugliest manifestations is that the *atrocities* committed by the young men in carrying out this vengeance are provoked and encouraged by older family members and a mutual competitiveness among these young men.

All inhabitants of the former-Yugoslavia belong to the second, the third, the umpteenth generation. Avineri (1993) states in a survey:

> [T]he historical background goes further back than the events of the Second World War. For over a century the Serbs have drawn their neighbours and sometimes the whole of Europe into a series of complicated conflicts. It started with the Serbian War of Liberation against Ottoman domination. People in Europe felt a great deal of sympathy for the Serbs, partly because their struggle was also seen as with the battle for Christianity against Islamic domination.

Avineri goes on to describe how each war was, in turn, an effort to avenge the defeats of the preceding generation. This analysis coincides with the observations made above about the way Serbian mothers raise their children.

We have had good evidence of this vengeful state of mind. The school-age boys in our group never admitted having felt anxiety or grief. When asked what plans they had for the future they said unequivocally that they were going to be soldiers and avenge the injustice they had suffered. We encountered this attitude even in the highest circles. This contact – though very possibly unreliable as an indicator of how they really felt, but what other means was there? – gave us a strong sense of alienation where other laws and other psychical processes prevailed. In the stories we heard the emphasis was always on 'what the enemy had done to them' rather than on their own pain and loss. But of course this must be said very cautiously by an outsider who does not speak the language. Destruction, rape, and death seem to mean different things here than in Western Europe. There are indications that these people seem to be imbued with a kind of *warrior ideology*.

References

Abelin, E. L., 1975, Some Further Observations and Comments on the Earliest Role of the Father. *International Journal of Psychoanalysis* 56(3):293–303

Antokoletz, J. C., 1993, A Psychoanalytic View of Cross-Cultural Passages. *American Journal of Psychoanalysis* 53(1):35–55

Avineri, S., 1993, De Balkan lijdt al heel lang onder Servisch nationalisme (The Balkans Have Been Suffering for a Long Time from Serbian Nationalism). *De Volkskrant*, 25 May, 11

Bastiaans, J., 1957, *Psychosomatische gevolgen van onderdrukking en verzet* (Psychiatric Sequelae of Oppression and Resistance). Amsterdam: Noordhollandse Uitgeversmaatschappij

Bion, W. R., 1970, *Attention and Interpretation*. London: Tavistock

Brom, D., R. J. Kleber and P. B. Defares, 1986, *Traumatische ervaringen en psychotherapie*. Lisse: Swets & Zeitlinger, 20–4

Caudill, W. and D. W. Plath, 1966, Who Sleeps by Whom? *Psychiatry* 29:344–66

Erikson, Erik H., 1950, *Childhood and Society*. London: Imago Publishing Co., 219–22

Fonagy, P., 1989, On the Integration of Cognitive Behaviour Therapy with Psychoanalysis. *British Journal of Psychotherapy* 5(4):557–63

Freud, Anna, 1959, Clinical Studies in Psychoanalysis: Research Project of the Hampstead Child-Therapy Clinic. *Psychoanalytic Study of the Child* 14:122–31

Furman, E., 1974, *A Child's Parent Dies. Studies in Childhood Bereavement*. New Haven: Yale University Press

Gampel, Y., 1982, A Daughter of Silence. In: *Generations of the Holocaust*. M. S.

Bergmann, and M. E. Jucovy, eds. New York: Columbia University Press, 120–37

Grinberg, L. and R. Grinberg, 1984, A Psychoanalytic Study of Migration. *Journal of the American Psychoanalytic Association* 32(1):13–39

Keilson, H., 1979, Sequential Traumatisation of Children. *Danish Medical Bulletin* 27(5):235–7

Kohut, H., 1971, *The Analysis of the Self.* New York: International Universities Press

Kolk, B. A. van der and R. E. Fisler, 1993, The Biologic Basis of Posttraumatic Stress. *Prim-Care* 20(2):417–32

Laub, D. and N. Auerhahn, 1993, Knowing and Not Knowing Massive Psychic Trauma: Forms of Traumatic Memory. *International Journal of Psycho-analysis* 74:287–303

Levita, D. J. de, 1989, De identiteit van kinderen (The Identity of Children) In *Eenzaamheid en identiteit* [*Loneliness and Identity*]. Netherlands Instituut van Psychologen, 61–71

Marmor, J. and S. Woods, 1980, *The Interface between the Psychodynamic and Behavioural Therapies.* New York: Plenum Press

Obenchain, Jeanne V. and Steven M. Silver, 1992, Symbolic Recognition: Ceremony in a Treatment of Post-Traumatic Stress Disorder. *Journal of Traumatic Stress* 5(1):37–43

Puhar, Alenka, 1994, Childhood Nightmares and Dreams of Revenge. *Journal of Psychohistory* 22(2):131–70

Schaffer, H. R., 1971, *The Growth of Sociability.* Harmondsworth: Penguin Books, 79

Shweder, R. A., L. A. Jensen, and W. M. Goldstein, 1995, Who Sleeps by Whom Revisited. A Method for Extracting the Moral Goods Implicit in Practice. In *Cultural Practices as Contexts for Development.* Jacqueline J. Goodnow, Peggy J. Miller and F. Kessel, eds. San Francisco: Jossey-Bass Publishers, 21–39

Southwick, S. M. and R. Yehuda, 1993, The Interaction Between Pharma-cotherapy and Psychotherapy in the Treatment of Posttraumatic Stress Disorder. *American Journal of Psychotherapy* 47(3):404–10

Spiegel, D. and E. Gardena, 1990, New Uses of Hypnosis in the Treatment of Posttraumatic Stress Disorder. *Journal of Clinical Psychiatry* 51(10, supple-ment):39–44

Stewart, H., 1992, *Collusion and the Hypnotic State.* London: Tavistock/ Routledge

Terr, L. C., 1985, Psychic Trauma in Children and Adolescents. *Psychiatric Clinics of North America* 8:815–35

Unfinished Peace, 1996, *Report of the International Commission on the Balkans.* Berlin: Aspen Institute

Wolpe, J., 1969, *The Practice of Behavior Therapy.* New York: Pergamon Press

Zivcic, I., 1993, Emotional Reactions of Children to War Stress in Croatia. *Journal of the American Academy of Adolescent Psychiatry* 32:709–14

Part II

Cultural responses to collective trauma

Marcelo M. Suárez-Orozco and
Antonius C. G. M. Robben

The papers by Luhrmann, Carola Suárez-Orozco, Volkan and Itzkowitz, and Ewing describe the cultural ways in which social groups react to dominant or threatening others. They discuss how narcissistic injuries, fears, anxieties, and past and present humiliations affect their social identity and are translated into collective traumas.

The essays by Luhrmann and Carola Suárez-Orozco explore two distinct cases of trauma and the making of cultural identities. The two cases – Parsis in India and immigrants in the US – involve psycho-cultural formations around profound social changes. In one case, among the Bombay Parsis, loss of status seems related to patterns of inner castigation through culturally elaborate forms of self-directed symbolic violence. In the case of immigrants, the trauma of immigration is compounded by the intense anti-immigrant sentiment evident in anti-immigrant legislation and increased violence against immigrants in the United States.

T. M. Luhrmann relates the self-castigation of present day Parsis, a small Indian community in Bombay, to unelaborated feelings of loss and humiliation. The Parsis, who arrived in Bombay from Persia a millennium ago, became the Raj's 'model minority'. During the colonial era the Parsis mimetically imprinted themselves to their British rulers to great profit. In a post-colonial setting where 'the singularity of Parsi eminence has passed', their former identification with the aggressor returns to haunt them. Now, Luhrmann claims, they are a traumatized people, feeling themselves 'marginalized in a post-colonial world, with an aching sense of a loss of status, of cultural genius, of their historical moment'. Luhrmann's analysis of this acute case of post-colonial depression is told as a complex psychoanalytic and cultural story laced with issues of guilt, shame, and the psychic knots of power in colonial situations of extreme inequality.

Carola Suárez-Orozco explores a problem of global dimensions in an American setting. Immigration has become a defining feature of a new transnational order. Today there are well over 100 million immigrants worldwide plus some 30 million refugees. In the last decade of our century there has been an explosion of concern over the economic, cultural, and environmental consequences of large-scale immigration. Carola Suárez-Orozco points out that while nearly all advanced post-industrial economies continue their addiction to foreign workers – both in the high-skilled, high-tech sectors of the economy and in the low-skilled, low-tech jobs – in recent years there have been growing manifestations of anti-immigrant sentiment evident in hostile legislation, public attitudes, and violence against immigrants.

The anxieties activated by global changes have come to be focused on immigrants and have fanned anti-immigrant sentiment. She examines how the losses inherent in immigration are compounded by negative 'social mirroring' with important implications for the cultural identities being forged by immigrant children.

The essay by Volkan and Itzkowitz is a model of how psychodynamic theorizing of loss and pathological mourning can be strategically deployed with cultural and historical sophistication providing at once 'insight' and 'thick description'. Their essay examines Turkish and Greek cultural identities in the context of historical losses, humiliations, and psychodynamic failure to mourn. They claim that the making of modern Turkish and Greek cultural identities is central to an understanding of the ongoing Turkey–Greece conflict. Unelaborated mourning, they argue, has become a powerful force mobilizing group hatred and violence across generations.

Volkan and Itzkowitz examine how traumatic events suffered by large groups are transformed into a 'chosen trauma'. They define 'chosen trauma' as powerful feelings of pride, entitlement, and revenge that are transmitted via culturally mediated forms from one generation to the next. They trace the intermittent border disputes between Turkey and Greece to unelaborated losses surrounding the rise and fall of the Ottoman Empire. Generations of Greeks and Turks, they claim, have incorporated mental representations of past glories and past humiliations – the Greek loss of Constantinople to the Turks in 1453 and the Turkish loss of the Ottoman Empire – into their national identities. Collective narcissistic injuries, never properly mourned, become transformed into feelings of victimization. These transgenerationally transmitted 'chosen traumas' continue to nourish violent outbreaks in current Turkish–Greek relations. They are tied to their respective national identities.

Katherine Ewing's contribution focuses on the symbolic violence and collective injury inflicted by authority figures on Turkish women who insist on wearing Islamic dress in schools, universities, and at work. Worried by the rise of fundamentalism in the surrounding Islamic world, the Turkish government has since the early 1980s clung to the secularist legacy of Atatürk who embarked the former Ottoman Empire on a course of Westernization. Veiling is perceived as a threat to the Turkish aspirations to be part of the Western world and to integrate into the European Union. Is Turkey now at a stage at which Algeria was a decade ago? Are the seeds of future large-scale violence sown by present humiliations in a society that already contains several deep ethnic and political divisions, notably between Turks and Kurds? Are we witnessing the growth of a divide among the Turkish people, a mounting tension which is already visible between secular and Islamist political parties?

Ewing reveals how the tensions in national and gender identities among secularist and Islamic women are being played out at home, in the schools, and at the workplace. Ewing claims that state proscriptions on Islamic dress violate the symbolic construction of self and personhood in the very places important to the women's personal growth and self-realization. Teachers try to break the women's defiance of the prescribed dress codes by treating them as non-persons, as if they were not present. The Muslim women who refused to remove their headscarfs in class and at work were humiliated and attacked. This resulted in a profound identity crisis, social isolation, and self-doubt. Ewing describes in detail how they reasserted themselves as Muslim women by substituting the authority of the state by the authority of Allah. They united into close-knit social groups, and took strength from studying the Koran. Veiling has become an act of resistance in which the symbolic violence rebounds on the state.

6 The traumatized social self: the Parsi predicament in modern Bombay

T. M. Luhrmann

In the world described by modern psychiatry, the word 'trauma' evokes the truly horrific: genocide, war, murder, rape, violence. Those are the kinds of circumstances that typically give rise to the recognized psychiatric disorders of trauma, although it is also typical that not all those who suffer the trauma suffer also the trauma's psychiatric sequelae. Post-traumatic stress disorder develops in people who have witnessed, experienced or been threatened with death, serious injury, or assault, and who felt intense fear and helplessness in that moment. That condition often involves flashbacks, emotional numbing, incomplete conscious memory of the event, and hypervigilance. Dissociative disorders often develop in response to severe childhood abuse – sexual, physical, or, as it is increasingly recognized, emotional – and like post-traumatic stress disorder, these disorders involve flashbacks, numbing, jumbled memory, and sleep and attention difficulties. Trauma of this magnitude deserves serious attention by students of culture and society and, indeed, many of the anthropological studies of trauma have focused on it (Bode 1989, Scheper-Hughes 1992, Daniel 1996, Nordstrom and Robben 1995). But more mundane trauma leaves its mark as clearly, if in a different manner. An executive who has been 'downsized' may not have flashbacks to an assault scene, but his misery is still intense. His shame and anger may still cripple him. If he finds his way into a psychiatrist's office, he will probably look depressed, not dissociative, but the disorder will be as real. The word 'trauma', in common parlance, refers to singular or repeated events which injure. Some injuring events are dramatic and soul-destroying. Some are quiet and humiliating.

This paper describes a quiet trauma and its impact several generations later. Few people were killed. Few people even realized that the trauma took place. But the marks of trauma appear in the model of self in the community involved. An anthropologist can see that there is in this community what one might call a 'traumatized social self', an injury to the self schema which represents what it is to be a good member of this community. This is not to say that individual members of this group are particularly personally distressed. They are, as it happens, a fairly cheerful, upbeat, effective community which became extremely successful during the colonial period and has now adapted to the very different political order of post-colonial independence. But something has gone wrong with their sense of collective self. During colonial rule, they wrote about being effective and worthy in a way which implied an assimilative, Anglophilic way of being. Now, in casual conversation, that account crops up again, but this time it is more often used to capture inadequacy than success. That nineteenth-century model of the good person has became a standard by which many community members are judged morally insufficient. The features of moral selfhood are as they were before, but the expectations of their fulfilment have changed dramatically. The 'good Parsi' has become a model of the ways in which Parsis fail. Why? I attribute this criticism to the quiet trauma that took no prisoners, but daunted this community's otherwise intrepid sense of self.

To make sense of this process, however, requires the kind of re-thinking of the concept of selfhood that has been much discussed in recent years, but has not yet settled down into an accepted paradigm. We think colloquially of the self as person and as identity: as the centre of our individuality and the reference of our 'I'. But what we really mean by those different terms is quite distinct, and to clarify those differences is to sketch the socio-psychological architecture which creates an individual who is truly, recognizably a member of his group, and yet like no one else.

The Parsis

The Parsis are famous for the thoroughness with which their members adopted British ideals, and famous, also, for their brilliant success during the Raj. Bombay is home to the great majority of the 70,000 Parsis in India, and symbolic homeland, perhaps, to another 20,000 who have spread in the diaspora to Britain, Hong Kong, East Africa, Canada, and the United States. They are primarily a middle-class, well-educated community, often involved in the professions: law, medicine, and banking. They are descendants of the Zoroastrians who escaped an Islamicized Persia in the tenth century AD. Those Zoroastrians arrived eventually in Gujarat, where they settled into an agricultural life, with some weaving and trading. When the British arrived, and particularly when the British acquired Bombay in the seventeenth century, the Parsis became involved with them as financiers and mediators. The wealth that made Parsis famous was the opium trade with China. By 1813 there were twenty-nine large Bombay ships in trade with China. Twelve were Parsi owned; seventeen were British owned. They were phenomenally successful. The most famous of the Parsi merchants was Sir Jamsetjee Jeejeebhoy (1783–1859), who was born to humble circumstances but whose prodigious earned wealth he spent in charity, for which he was knighted and then given a baronetcy, the first Indian to receive one. By 1840, Parsis owned 24 per cent of the shares in the Bank of Bombay, next only to Europeans. By 1864 more than half the community was urbanized. In 1869 the Suez Canal was opened and Bombay became India's chief port.[1]

The focal point of modern Parsi identity is the community achievement in the nineteenth century, when Parsis became known as pioneers of modern Indian industry and as the first modern Indian entrepreneurs. The fortunes that Parsis made in eighteenth- and early-nineteenth-century trade were now invested in the emerging Indian industry. Parsis dominated this emerging modern entrepreneurial class for years. When the greatest Parsi industrialist, Jamsetji Nusserwanji Tata, died in 1904, Curzon – then Viceroy – declared that 'no Indian of the present generation had done more for the commerce and industry of India' (Harris 1958:275). And so the Parsis, with Tata and Jeejeebhoy as their exemplars, became remarkably well respected. This respect and approvals runs throughout the English literature of the period.

Parsis achieved this remarkable success at least in part by culturally identifying with the British. In Parsi literature of the period and in at least some British literature, Parsis were consistently presented as the most Westernized community in India. In the best-known nineteenth-century Parsi text, Dosabhai Framjee Karaka's two-volume *History of the Parsis* (1884), the Parsis are rational, progressive, worthily prosperous, and non-Indian (they had been in India for about 1,000 years). Persian ancestry, in Karaka's eyes, spurred Parsis to rise above and beyond a land he almost calls barbaric. But they did so only because they were inspired by the British. Under the British their natural nobility sprang forth and soon, Karaka speculated, they would be indistinguishable from the Europeans. In his closing paragraph he proclaimed: 'to [British power] [the Parsis] owe everything and from it they hope to gain still more' (1884: II:295). At the turn of the century a magazine called *The Parsi: The English Journal of the Parsis and a High Class Illustrated Monthly* is filled with remarks like these: 'The complete Europeanization of the Parsis is now a mere matter of time' (1906:324); 'The Parsis are the one

---

[1] Cf. Luhrmann 1996:96*ff.*

race settled in India . . . that could for a moment be called white' (1906:132); 'The Parsis are so differently constituted from the rest of the Indians that any close union of the two is well nigh impossible' (1906:325); '[Parsi] destiny is bound up with the British in India' (1906:62).

What becomes clear in these publications and in others like them is that the rhetoric of asserting similitude to the European entailed an assertion of distance from other non-Parsi Indian communities. They are 'other': uncivilized, non-rational, dark-skinned, essentially different in their constitution. Some Parsis chastised the community for their separatist sensibility, but it is undeniable in the texts, and in what we know of the practices of at least the Parsi elite.[2] Bombay-based British businessmen remember that the Parsis were 'completely Westernized in their habits' and acted as a kind of bridge between the other Indians and the Europeans (Burns, tape recording). In publications like the 1906 *Men and Women of India* the Parsis are consistently more Western in appearance than members of other communities. Parsis lived in Anglicized houses; they became active as liberal reformists, often attempting to reform 'backward' Hindu customs; they wrote about the 'rational' quality of Zoroastrian religion, its lack of ritual and its compatibility with 'science', a deliberate contrast with 'irrational' Hinduism; by 1901 a quarter of the community spoke English, as compared to less than 1 per cent of the Jains and 0.5 per cent of the Hindus.

It is around this time, in the late nineteenth and early twentieth centuries, at the zenith of Parsi success, that a cluster of attributes of the good Parsi becomes established in the Parsi literature. These attributes transform and extend the fundamental ethical attributes which the Zoroastrian religion has always ascribed to the good person: truthfulness, purity, charity, and progress (see Luhrmann 1996). In the transformation, truthfulness becomes business reliability, purity becomes racial difference from other Indians, charity becomes the sign of business success, and progress becomes the participation in the British project of cultural reform and rationalization. These transformed attributes, in fact, become arguments for the Parsi man's resemblance to an English gentleman and for his status as a worthy economic partner to the British.

The most interesting piece of this clustering of desirable and acquired traits was the sporting manliness of the Parsi man. Turn-of-the-century Parsis represent their men as vigorous and athletic in exactly the sports admired by the middle- and upper-class English. There is a marvellous

---

[2] See for example the speeches of Sorabjee Bengalee, as discussed in Luhrmann 1996:12–13.

early twentieth-century book entitled *Parsis and Sport* (Darukhanawala 1935) whose entirely unsubtle message is that the Parsis are the most physically vigorous men in India. The text reads like a 'believe-it-or-not' encyclopedia of unsurpassed feats, and contains picture after picture of burly young men in scanty clothes: wrestlers, swimmers, weightlifters, cyclists, cricketers, balancing on skates, posed with rapier and helmet, calmly surveying the dead tiger stretched at their feet. The first all-Indian cricket team to visit Britain, in 1886, was an all-Parsi team. There was an annual cricket match in Bombay between a British team and a Parsi team. A British governor of Bombay remarked that there was no sight that testified so eloquently to the success of the colonial administration as this match (Lord Harris 1899 in Karkaria 1915:70); a Parsi commentator on the same match observed: 'In physical matters, too, Parsis are rapidly developing robuster qualities of body, which will in the long run make them the equals of many Western nations, and on which Western supremacy rests' (in Karkaria 1896:50). Repeatedly, the themes were set out: Parsi men are easily more masculine than Hindu and Muslim men, and perhaps even more inherently masculine than the British, who after all are newcomers to the tropical heat – and masculinity is the basis of 'Western supremacy'.

We see here a mimetic mirroring of the British representation of self as transformed in the colonial context. Nandy (1983) points out how profoundly colonialism is a matter of psychological transformation. In the logic of this complex relationship, self-awareness emerges within a hierarchical culture in which colonizers feel themselves superior to and different from the colonized, and the colonized elite desire to have the colonizer's authority through identity with the colonizer. In the late nineteenth and early twentieth centuries, Parsis attempted to see themselves as like the British and as unlike other Indians, and they used their religion to construct the self-representation that shifted the traditional emphasis on truth to a reputation for being more reliable than Hindus, from a ritual purity to a racial difference from Hindus, from religious charity to the Victorian symbol of business success, from the idea of metaphysical progress to the project of British cultural reform of the Hindus. In doing so, Parsis were acting reasonably and appropriately in their setting.

Scholars now argue that the British in India constructed both themselves and their natives as dyadic opposites, particularly around the categories of gender, age, and race. The British were 'hypermasculinized', scientific and progressive, a high step on the evolutionary ladder; the Indians were effeminate, childlike, primitive, and superstitious. This speculative psychology of the colonial relation – Nandy himself depicts it as a myth – is now accepted as a fair portrayal of the British conceptualization of empire and (ultimately) of the colonial elite's identification with the aggressor. (One can find versions of this story in Said 1978, 1993; Ballhatchet 1980; Wurgaft 1983; McClure 1981, 1991; Mani 1987; Das 1986; O'Hanlon 1991, 1992; Stoler 1991, 1992; Callaway 1987; Inden 1990; and others.) Inden takes to its furthest extreme the argument that the India understood in the British civil service, by Western scholars of India, by the ordinary British citizen, and ultimately, by Indians, was an imaginary realm constructed to demonstrate the masculine superiority of its Western imperialist. India's caste system, her spirituality, her ancient little villages, her feminine seduction, were, he argues, essentializing characteristics imposed on her by the colonizers to resist the agency and independence of her Indians. Inden describes the British conception of Hinduism thus: 'Hinduism is a *female* presence who is able, through her very amorphousness and absorptive powers, to baffle and perhaps even threaten Western rationality, clearly a male in this encounter. European reason penetrates the womb of Indian unreason but always at the risk of being engulfed by her' (1990:86). The emphasis here of course is on metaphor, play, resonance – scholars argue that there was a not always conscious, not always intentional, not always consistent but always present undertone in which those in authority were masculine, rational, and progressive and those under authority were not.

To the extent that colonial elites modelled themselves upon the colonizers, they absorbed these peculiar, defensive semiotics. While there are disagreements about the underlying meaning of the metaphor of masculinity – Suleri (1992), for instance, argues that homoeroticism forms the fundamental dynamic of colonial interaction – and complex discussions about the relationship of this trope to the actual interaction of men and women (for example, O'Hanlon 1991 and Stoler 1991), there seems to be general scholarly agreement that, at least in India, there was what Nandy calls a 'language of homology between [the] sexual and political' (1983:6). There was, as Nandy and others argue, a cultural collusion, particularly among the nineteenth-century Indian elite, that saw the British as an agent of change and progress, that accepted a masculinized ethos of aggressive but gentlemanly competition, and that took the existence of British domination as proof of a masculine superiority which they should aim to emulate. Elite Indians, of whom Parsis are only one but a remarkable example, shaped their ideals and sensibilities and the ideals and sensibilities of their children upon the canons of English colonial culture: its literature, its sociability, its competitive athletics, its pianos and lace and fitted suits, but also its dismissal of their countrymen as effeminate, traditional, and lowly. In the attempt to create a monotheistic Hinduism and a martial Indianness, in the hot, unfamiliar suits demanded by the British government which then became the required business dress, in an education replete with Dickens and Wordsworth, nineteenth-century Indian elites replayed this copycat enculturation. Parsis were in many ways the most exemplary example of this process, and while individual Parsis lived lives that were more nuanced and more enmeshed with Hindus than this story suggests, the story's symbolic logic motivated enough Parsi behaviour to make the community famous, then and now, for their entanglement with things British

And then the British left. Parsis led the initial attempts to acquire greater self-rule by Indians. Dadabhai Naoroji was among those who founded the Indian National Congress; he coined the word *swaraj*, home rule. But Naoroji did not actually encourage the British to leave; he wanted to improve the process of British rule until some time in the distant future, when its goal would have been accomplished. In his 1886 address to the Indian National Congress he urged: 'Let us speak out like men and proclaim that we are loyal to the backbone.'[3] When mass politics took over and the message became 'Quit India', the Parsi community for the most part refused to participate. In 1921 the Prince of Wales paid an official visit to India. The nationalists boycotted the occasion, but the Parsis came to greet him. The subsequent riots lasted four days and left fifty-three people dead. At a meeting with some 150 representatives of the Hindu, Muslim, and Parsi communities, Homi Mody – a prominent Parsi politician – was invited by Gandhi to speak. He asserted that the riots were aimed at the Parsis because, as a community, they had failed to join the non-co-operation movement and to join Gandhi's nationalist programme (Mankekar 1968:41–2).

In conversation after conversation, Parsis told me that the majority of Parsis had been unhappy with independence. Older Parsis in particular remembered that the community had been uncomfortable with Gandhi and his 'insults' to the British. The Parsi upper class was more inclined towards Gandhi, and one prominent elite Parsi, Madame Cama, actually unfurled the Indian flag for the first time in 1902, at the Second International Socialist Congress. But the majority of the community seems to have been deeply Anglophilic. A middle-aged Parsi woman told me the following story. A friend of hers was taken by her father to watch the flag-crossing ceremony on 15 August 1947. As the Union Jack descended and the Indian tricolour rose, the father said to his young

---

[3] Kulke 1974:175.

daughter that 'law and order in this country have disappeared'. Nowadays, most Parsis remember their nationalist leaders with pride. At the time, Parsis were far more ambivalent.

In the decade following the Quit India movement, when for the first time it seemed inevitable that the British would be forced to leave, a wave of community criticism appeared. It was different in tone than community criticism from prior decades (as much as I could establish) and strikingly at odds from the common nineteenth-century praise of community success. This new criticism consistently describes the community as having fallen from its peak, and as being essentially decayed. I suggest that this criticism records a profound injury to the sense of being Parsi. 'There seems to be a feeling, however, in certain quarters that the community has reached or passed its zenith' (Markham 1932:xi). This 1932 report to a trust's trustees explains that the Parsi birthrate had declined, that insanity was on the increase, that unemployment had risen, and that even literacy seemed on the decline. The author quotes one Dr Moos on 'the steady fall of the prestige of the community' (Markham 1932:45). In 1935 Bulsara speaks of 'the alarming problem of growing economic misery and the physical, intellectual and spiritual impoverishment of an increasing section of the community' (1935:330). In 1937 Kotwal comments: 'I say, in Education the Parsis were the first and foremost in India. How then came the decay, when and where from, it is necessary to know . . . Ye sons of Rustom, where are those charms of your ancestors that are to this day being boasted of by lovers of Firdoosi?' (1937:13 and 20).

The two most devastating critiques are published just around independence. One is a book entitled *Parsis Ere the Shadows Thicken*, published in 1949 by P. A. Wadia. It remarks that:

a small community like ours can escape the process of decadence and degeneration, if it has the art of rejuvenating itself from within . . . Our community, however, seems to have exhausted by this time the chances of bringing to birth leaders who with courage and understanding can break the ever tightening grip of its dead past. (1949:138–9)

This book presents the community as sinking into poverty and death. Its diagnosis is that Parsis glorify their past and cling to Western values which are maladaptive for modern India. They are maladaptive, the book argues, because the Western lifestyle is very expensive – and yet Parsis refuse to work to maintain that lifestyle. They feel that they can rely on community charity and that this is easier than hard work. They have lost their entrepreneurial spark.

The other critique is *A Community at the Cross Roads*, published in 1948 by S. F. Desai. The foreword asserts:

The broad facts that emerge from any consideration of the problem are that a deterioration in the moral fibre of the community has set in. We have an idle rich class, contributing little to the general well-being of the community beyond indiscriminate charity, and our poor are getting poorer and losing their self-respect. There are many individuals and agencies at work amongst the poorer sections, but their efforts are disjointed and we can see no signs of a definite recovery. (Sir H. P. Mody in Desai 1948:xi)

The work is primarily a treatise on population and the means to increase the number of Parsis; the Parsi reproductive rate is slowing down. The book sets out, however, a fairly comprehensive list of flaws:

Socially, the Parsi of yesterday formed a small unit and lived a more rural than an urban life. Biologically, the Parsi was a healthy, happy being who believed in a settled, married life with an expanding family. Socio-biologically, the Parsi was a product of culture, tradition, civilization, religion, temperance, tolerance and other gainful virtues. Today this coherent life is disintegrating. The Parsi has left his usual expansive rural habitat in favour of an ever circumscribing urban life. The tendency is definitely disruptive and uncongenial to a well-knit social fabric. In such an atmosphere the human mind undergoes a severe strain. The spirit of give and take becomes displaced by dissension and discord; that of mutual accommodation in the interest of the few by the intolerance of a section; that of religious fervor by ridicule; that of cultural preservation by an oblivious disposition; that of inventive ability by an unwitting superimposition of a misfit; that of pleasant relationship by a dislocation of amity; that of virtuous intent by a profanation; that of replacement of the dying genius by a wilful murder of the superior germplasm. A small community can ill afford to indulge in such unprofitable ways of living. Poverty is growing from year to year. A larger number is getting submerged from year to year. A section is growing up in parasitic existence and like every parasite is strangling the host it feeds on. A larger effort than hitherto is now warranted to cement the hiatus and build a superstructure that will endure. (Desai 1948:15)

In bold type the author declares: 'That the decline in numbers is bound to be linked up with a decline in quality also' (Desai 1948:74). The noble, happy, productive past has become an embarrassing, acrimonious present.

This distressing shift to despair in community self-perception is well recognized within the community. As a letter to the *Times of India* remarks in 1944:

Any sane member of the community who observes the present movements and doings of the Parsis will – in spite of all his inborn enthusiasm, affirm that they, as a community, are deteriorating not only physically but also morally, economically, as well as socially and politically . . . *For the last few years this communal depression of the Parsis is being openly admitted.* (Dastoor 1944:28–9; emphasis added)

And in 1977 Dr Lovji Cama, second prize winner in a competition entitled 'The Lost Generation' (the reason for this intriguing name is not clear), remarked in his essay that:

Anyone who reads the *History of the Parsis* [Karaka's 1884 text] cannot but be impressed by the confidence and the sense of identity and direction the community possessed. Yet, only seventy years later, we appear to have ground to a halt, our confidence lost, our numbers diminishing, our commitment to our religion weakened. (1977:32)

Self-confidence has given way to insecurity.

When I arrived in Bombay in 1987, I was not looking for trauma, or at least not trauma in that sense. I was interested in theological debates about suffering and the nature of evil (Zoroastrianism is thought by many scholars to have been a dualistic religion, but most modern Zoroastrians will tell you that it is not; I intended to explore these debates). As a result of my theological interests, I pursued people who talked to me about losing a spouse or a child, about crippling illness, or simply about theology. What I began to hear, however, was something quite different: a litany of complaints about the downturn of the Parsi community and, in particular, their young men. This was hardly the only theme in community discourse, and it was counter-balanced by justifiable pride in an impressive past. But it was a common theme. When I gave a talk on this criticism to a Young Zoroastrian Congress some years ago, the audience laughed uproariously in recognition. Then I linked the criticism to the colonial legacy rather than the actual behaviour of the young men, and they gave me a standing ovation.

To convey a sense of this self-critical discourse, let me turn to a 1982 poem by a Parsi, entitled *Parsi Hell*:

> Standing at the dark house of my dreams . . .
> . . . I hoard my inner fires
> Hoard my semen, brown with inbreeding. Genetic rust?
> Death hums over the wires: what affects the spawn
> is rickets, polio, a drug gone rogue. Daughters
> walk out on the tribe . . .
> A Parsi carries his hell.   (Daruwalla 1982)

The theme that has run through the Parsi literature on Parsis since independence became an inevitability is: 'we are not what we were', 'we have fallen from the top'. Modern Parsi literature seems to circle ceaselessly around a sense of a decaying, sexually devitalized community. There are more positive portraits of the community and modern Indian literature is not sunny in comparison. But I do not find, in the modern Indian writing I have read, such a thread of a deracinated, anomalous culture within the confusion of a bustling post-colonial world. Another Parsi poet wrote a poem entitled *The Ambiguous Fate of*

Gieve Patel, He Being Neither Hindu Nor Muslim in India, in which he asserted that he had no place in the tormented religious crisis in India, that while 'bodies turn ashen and shrivel / I only burn my tail' (Patel 1966). Adil Jussawalla, another one of the major Parsi poets, entitled one book *Missing Person,* because he had (he implied) no more than fragments of an identity: post-independence, post-British, neither Indian nor Western, an intellectual in a country crying out for practical aid, a middle-class citizen in a nation of paupers. In one of his poems, his mirror shouts out to him 'Drop dead colonial ape' and he says:

> 'Wait! You know whose side
> I'm on' he shouts
> 'but the people, their teeth bright as axes
> came after my bride.'
>   (1975:22)

I am part of India, he suggests, but they revile me as a traitor, and (he goes on) I belong neither in India nor in Britain. Cyrus Mistry's *Doongaji House* (1978) is a prize-winning play about the community; the playwright told me that the house is a metaphor for the community as a whole. Doongaji House is a once elegant building in the heart of Bombay. It used to be the tallest building around for miles, and one of the first buildings in Bombay to have electricity. It had been a matter of pride to live in Doongaji House, we are told. But now the electricity has stopped working and the inhabitants fear that the roof will crumble in around their heads.

Parsis spoke to me about the sense of 'something wrong' in many different ways. But, it seemed to me that there was profound ambivalence about being Parsi and about being Indian, and profound ambivalence about the past claims of Parsi superiority. Not every Parsi voiced criticism, and not all the time, and some people were more passionate than others. Nevertheless, these opinions were entrenched enough and common enough to persuade me that they were evidence of a 'cultural model', a commonly available set of ideas and images. I did spend most of my time with the upper half of the community – the same socio-economic group that would have been most responsible for the earlier, confident quotations – but I heard these complaints from Parsis in every tier of community life, although exclamations of community superiority were also common, and, in particular, there was enormous pride in the community's achievements in the past.

On a train from Oxford to London, Yasmin – whom I had met through friends – talked to me about her sense of shame at being Parsi:

It is the feeling you might have if you went to an elite school, and then attended a polytechnic. You feel proud of your school, but you're embarrassed if other people know. You're embarrassed because you think they think you feel superior to them, and you do and know it's wrong. You're also embarrassed because they might think you're no better than they are, and yet you've had these privileges, and that's also wrong. And you are horrified when your community seems to boast at your Hindu friends' expense.

This conflicted attitude was not uncommon, she said: young Parsis who were liberal and sophisticated would be sharply conscious of what non-Parsis might think of them, and would almost insistently attempt to marry out of the community, to dress like Hindus and not like Parsis, to do anything to be different from the Parsi world in which they had grown up:

They don't want to take on the *burden* of being a Parsi. On the one hand, you are immediately thought to be intelligent, far more intelligent than you think you are. On the other, people think of the inbreeding and the Hindi film image of the crazy *bavaji*, and they think you are a fool. You're pigeonholed anytime someone in Bombay hears that you're a Parsi. But you also feel pride. It's a mixture of pride and shame that you feel.

'What happens when you go abroad', she said, 'was that suddenly you talk to people who have never heard of Parsis.' She was not like the Hindus, she said, who want to hang around only with Hindus in Oxford; as a Parsi, she said, she likes mixing. Once she met someone in the New College bar and realized that when she was explaining herself to him, she was talking about the religion and that was the 'essence': it felt good, not the way she had felt ashamed in Bombay. And the English students would get interested, and then she had felt more confident when she went back to Bombay for her sister's wedding, and she found a cassette of traditional songs and played them and loved it. 'In Bombay', she said, 'you're not *supposed* to be interested in being Parsi.' Her parents would think she was out of her mind, she said, if she told them that she thought of doing a doctorate about something to do with Parsis.

You're ashamed, but you'd never want to belong to another community. Every Parsi would admit that. You might even not be ashamed but you'd feel in Bombay that you should act ashamed in front of Hindus. But it's great that there's all this interest in reviving the community.

And the current generation, she said, really is achieving, not like the generation just after independence. 'That's something to be proud of', she said.

The complaints turn each of the salient attributes of the nineteenth-century 'good Parsi' upside down. Parsis are said to be no longer truthful; their genetic purity is said to have turned into genetic corruption through inbreeding; their famous charity is said to have made them lazy; they accuse each other of being unprogressive stick-in-the-mud traditionalists. For example, an elderly women told me that the community had lost its moral integrity. Now, she said, people will lie and steal. 'Before now, truthfulness, honesty, were predominant. But it is not as it used to be before.' Their word, she said, means nothing; the moral fibre of the community has decayed. Most Parsis will tell the anthropologist that in earlier days, the British employed only Parsis as their banktellers because of the renowned Parsi honesty. Along with that story will come the assertion that 'these days, of course, it is not like that, why there was a Parsi bankteller who just the other day . . .'.

Dishonesty is also construed as a symptom of a deeper rot, a consequence but not a cause of decay. Whereas late nineteenth-century Parsis argued proudly that their race was pure from Hindu contamination, late twentieth-century Parsis fret that the commitment to racial purity has produced an insidious, race-rotting inbreeding. They whisper that the Parsi race has been corrupted, its stock gone bad, the strain degenerated. In the passionate debate over intermarriage – whether to allow it, whether the children of mixed marriages should be allowed to enter the fire temples – some Parsis say that inbreeding has reduced Parsi drive, sapped their fertility, and driven them mad. 'We need fresh blood' is a common refrain. For example, I spoke with an upper-middle-class teenager about his cousin's paraplegic child. He pointed out that the cousin had married within the family, and her father before her also within the family, and he vowed bitterly never to marry a Parsi because 'the genes are too close'. It is a weird and telling argument, in India, where endogamy is taken for granted, that in Parsi endogamy the blood of the community should be said to fold in upon itself and implode.

To continue this depressing line, Parsis now often describe their famous charity – Parsis are known throughout India and Britain for their benevolence – in the idiom of corruption-from-within. They explain that charity itself has undermined the community and sapped its strength. The not-so-implicit message is that what is best in the Parsis has contributed directly to their fall. When I visited a Parsi Panchayat (the central administrative unit) in Gujarat, for example, I was told in no uncertain terms that the problem with the community was that the young were lazy. All they wanted to do was to sponge off the charities. Charity, I was told, has ruined them. There is no enterprise in the community, because everything was given free. You can see a Gujarati and a Parsi set up garages next to each other, the trustee told me. The Parsi will be given concessional rent and a grant, and his business will fail while the Gujarati's prospers. Parsis, he told me, were pampered, and did not like to work with their hands. A Parsi woman explained: the fear is that the Parsis have no *dandha*, the money-making, deal-driving ambition to succeed in business. A 1987 detailed thesis on the charities concludes that those who run the charitable trusts were negligent and irresponsible, and that the doles robbed the community of its initiative and its will to work (Mobedji 1987).

With respect to the commitment to the British project of cultural reform, one of the more revealing issues has been the increasing pressure placed, in recent years, on the rather macabre practice of leaving the dead to be eaten by vultures. During the Raj there were many Parsi reformers devoted to tranforming the 'backwards' customs of the Hindus, among them child marriage and the prohibition of widow remarriage. The custom of *dokhmenashini*, as it is called, mostly escaped this reformist attention. Instead, during this period one finds many fervent pamphlets explaining the rational virtues of this practice: it is hygenic, charitable, ecological, and so forth. Even now many Parsis defend the practice on those grounds: once, at a lecture I attended on the practice, a Parsi stood up in the audience and explained in some detail that vultures had a 'scientific' mentality. However, *dokhmenashini* has recently become an example of community backwardness. When a Parsi woman died in a car crash and was refused access to the Towers of Silence, where the bodies are left, the hysterical debate over that perceived injustice focused on the community's refusal to be progressive. The custom was still defended, but many Parsis attacked the community as being mired in traditional ways and not flexible enough to adapt to changing times. In the community paper one read comments like these around the controversy:

As charity begins at home, it is now time to reexamine our customs and jettison them if they clash violently with the demands and aspirations of a changing world.[4]

When customs and traditions become the prime focus towards which the whole religion of the community is directed, when these are allowed to supersede the true religious precepts of the religion, then they become a serious threat to the true religious and spiritual development of the community.[5]

It is horrifying, a wealthy woman remarked to me, that the community can be so backward.

The critique is also sexualized into what one of my colleagues calls 'the New Jersey stereotype': that the men are unambitious, effeminate, impotent and gay. 'I never date Parsi boys', one teenager told me. 'They're so effeminate. Didn't you know that lots of Parsi boys are gay?'

4 Manek Davar, *Jame Jamshed*, 24 August 1990.
5 *Bombay Samachar*, 11 November 1990.

Again, this is only one strain in a complex, heterogeneous discourse, and I wish to emphasize that it is a stereotypical insult, with at best an oblique relationship to male sexual behaviour. In the stereotype, a young Parsi man wants enough money for movies and a motorbike but no more. Yes, an important lawyer sadly nodded in his air-conditioned office, the community is demoralized, the spirit has gone out of the boys. The power they had in the Raj has passed them by, he said, and the entrepreneurial zest has gone out of the community.

I spend some of my second visit to India casually asking Parsis if this criticism of the young men had any truth. I was disconcerted by the frequency with which Parsis confidently affirmed it. Most Parsis, particularly if they were middle-aged or older, said yes, that it was true; there were of course the dynamic boys, they said, but such boys always emigrated to America. A peer of mine said yes, she thought that generally the stereotype held – and yet, she said, somewhat surprised at herself, when she thought of the individuals she knew, the stereotype did not seem to fit them. Sometimes other women made similar remarks: there was so-and-so, he was a real mama's boy, but *their* friends were not like that. Others were quite certain that the stereotype held more often than not. Certainly jokes about Parsi male homosexuality and impotence are common.

Admittedly this is a privately held stereotype, not a publically validated one. In 1990 a young Parsi filmmaker released a film about a Parsi household (*Percy*, based on a story by Cyrus Mistry). Almost to an individual – I met two exceptions – the community hated the film. It portrayed a young, dependent boy, dominated by his mother, too shy to ask out women and too weak to defend himself from the Hindu bully whose dishonesty he reported to his boss. Why film such a story, the Parsis asked? Why not film the Tatas, the Godrejs, Dadabhai Naoroji, the Parsis who helped to give India her greatness? 'There are so few films on the Parsis', a middle-class Parsi mother remarked. 'Yes, there are some mama's boys in the community, but not all the boys are like that. So if you portray the community, why show that? We have had so many great people in the community, it has done such good. They should make a film about them.' Few Parsis seemed to view the film without conceptualizing the community discourse as a judgment on the community for all the world to see. But the film had depicted the entrenched stereotype. The filmmaker told me that Parsis hated his film because it cut too close to the bone. A reviewer exclaimed: 'Pervez Meherwanji had managed to create the perfect Parsi ambience – the house with the four poster bed and round marble table, the good-for-nothing colony *chokras* [boys] hanging out all day, the morning and night *kusti* prayers, the *sukhad-loban* [sandalwood and incense], the character – everything was just right.'[6]

This is an emblematic section of the story which became the basis of the filmscript, as printed in the magazine *Bombay*:

'You'll splash hot oil on yourself, you ninny. Don't even try!' she had brushed him aside, once when he had put the pan on to try and make his own breakfast. 'And how much oil! *Matere mua*, you've finished half my tin! Do you know how much this one tin costs now?' She bullied him too much, she sat on his head. He knew it. Sometimes in his heart, he rebelled against her tyranny, her strict routines. But he never spoke his resentment. It was better to be obedient, if you were a duffer. And Percy had had a long training in servility. Maybe he could manage on his own, better than she thought he could. But he wasn't sure. He had never been without her, and the thought had never occurred to him that he might some day. Half an hour later, Percy was getting dressed to leave for the office, when he discovered that there was not a single button left on the fly of his trouser. His other two pairs were with the dhobi.

'Mumma!' he called out to Banubai in his fluty, quavering voice. 'Mumma, *all* my buttons are gone. Not one left. Stitch me some now, will you? How can I go like this?' 'My eyes don't work so good anymore. Haven't I told you, start doing things with your own hands now. How much can one person do? I have but two hands', Banubai harangued her son. 'If something happens tomorrow and I become supine, God forbid, what will become of you? . . . Give, give . . . Bring the needle and thread. And my specs.' The short, wiry Banubai was 68, and very active still. Holding the needle within an inch of her nose, she threaded it skillfully, at first try. Then, bending over the trousers, she muttered under her breath, softly but audibly, 'Where will I find you a wife? Who will marry you, a chap like you? . . .'

And Percy, who was standing beside her in his shirt and his shoes, with a towel wrapped around his midriff, declared, 'I don't *want* anyone, Mumma, I don't want! I'll stay here with you. You can look after me better than any wife.'

'*Ja, ja gadhera!* Show some sign of brains when you open your mouth', Banubai shouted at him; but it was playful ire, and a half-smile diffused her grouch of concentration.[7]

Few men referred to young Parsi men as impotent, and relatively few women. When I heard the reference I assumed it was a metaphor, a screen memory, as it were, for something else. Sometimes the metaphorical status of the remark was clear. I spent an afternoon with one of the community poets in his beautiful apartment in one of the once most elegant residential areas in Bombay, now still crowded with Parsis. Time, he said, stopped for the Parsis around 1950. Even a few years after independence the community had confidence. Then everything broke down. And he used the term 'impotent': Parsis, he grimaced,

---

6 Review of the film by Prochi Badshah, 'Anyone Heard About Autonomy Lately?', *Afternoon Dispatch and Courier*, 16 April 1990.
7 Cyrus Mistry, 'Percy', 1985:40–56.

were emasculated by their society. Parsis have lost their nerve, they have – he quoted Auden – an ingrown virginity.

The criticism of the young boys is universally affirmed in the area of education, particularly in contrast with the young women. Parsi boys, I was told often, are not as clever as Parsi girls, who earn more and are more highly educated. Parsi girls are hard-working and ambitious. Parsi boys are spineless and undriven. Parsi girls are independent, strong-minded, and determined. Parsi boys are dominated by their mothers until they reach adolescence, when all they want is an easy life. 'Yes, it is very true', a bank clerk insisted. 'The girls work hard. The boys are pampered. Then they reach adolescence, and all they care for is movies and a motorbike. So they fail in school, it does not bother them.' I attended a Youth Congress at which yet another eminent lawyer, in this community of eminent lawyers, addressed the audience of young adults. He urged them to marry inside the community, and then announced that some people said that the boys were not as achieving as the girls. And he said – it was remarkable that he felt the need to say this – 'But I have personally inspected each application to work in my office, and I tell you, the boys are every bit as well-qualified as the girls.'

Yet the account of superior female education and earning power is false. Parsi women do not earn more, work more, and acquire more education than Parsi men, although it is certainly true that young Parsi women work more and are more highly educated than the average urban Indian woman. In a 1982 survey of the community, 44 per cent of the men had gone to college or better, and (admittedly) 45 per cent of the women, but fewer of the women had higher degrees than the men. The average income of all Parsi men was over 1,400 rupees a month, of women over 1,100 rupees; 33 per cent of the men earned more than 2,000 rupees a month, but only 14 per cent of the women (Karkal 1984).

Pushing the inversion even farther, Parsis complain that Parsi men are not as aggressive and as competitive as the Hindus, not as manly as the once-effeminate 'natives'. The Parsi boys, I heard many Parsis say, are used to comfort. The Parsi boys, being used to comfort, will not venture into unknown territory and they will not take risks, like the Hindu boys will. Reciprocally, there seems to be little retaliation from the Hindus for years of British partiality to Parsis, apparently because Parsi charities contributed many hospitals, schools and so forth to Bombay. Parsis have acquired a pan-Indian reputation for generosity and benevolence. And yet, the stock Parsi figure in a Hindu 'masala' film, the guns-and-romance staple of the entertainment industry, is a crazy, old, helpless man, a comic figure who gets stuck in the bus door at the most inconvenient moment. Despite, then, the widespread and (to me) frequently reiterated respect for Parsis by Hindus, there is a hint that Hindus may have resented the successful colonial Parsis, and that the resentment may now reappear as ridicule.

So the Parsi men do not compete and the manly Hindu male is taking their business away, and it is, more or less, the Parsis' fault – so goes the cultural configuration. There is much about this story that is not true: the men earn more than the women; the community is probably on average better off than it was 100 years ago; the community still boasts many powerful professionals; commonsense and observational evidence suggest that the criticism strings together phrases whose purpose is to insult, not to describe social reality.

It is however true that over 20 per cent of all Parsis never marry (the rate for Hindus is under 1 per cent), that reproduction is well below replacement rate, and that the population figures for Parsis in India are falling rapidly, about 10,000 a decade. After the 1981 census, the Bombay Parsi Panchayat initiated a population survey of Greater Bombay. On their behalf the International Institute for Population Studies in Bombay interviewed a random sample of 2,000 households from the seven constituencies in Bombay where most of the Parsis live. Among other interesting facts, the study revealed that one in five Parsis is over sixty-five, making the community among the most aged in the world.[8] And the marriage statistics were striking. The mean age of marriage may now have reached twenty-seven years, one of the world's highest marriage ages.[9] Not only does the community marry late, but the number of women who never marry is stunning. By 1982, more than one in five Parsi women – 21 per cent – never married in their lifetime; for the general population of India in 1971, that figure was 0.58 per

---

[8] Twenty-five per cent of the community is aged between fifty and sixty-four, but only 12 per cent between zero and fourteen, giving the community a very top-heavy appearance: Karkal 1984:38. Other important figures:36 per cent of the men and women between 20 and 39 had graduated from college, a remarkable figure in India; 98 per cent of the community above the age of four was literate; 8.14 per cent of the community described itself as a professional, technical or related worker; 9.35 per cent as administrative, executive, and managerial workers; 8.32 per cent as clerical and related workers; 9.63 per cent as sales workers; 17.35 per cent as students; 28.55 per cent as unemployed or housewives (a remarkably low figure); 9.31 per cent describe themselves as retired. Of those who work, the average income for men was 1,455 rupees a month, and for women, 1,117 rupees per month. This is comfortably within the middle class.

[9] There seems to have been a significant shift in marriage patterns betweeen 1890 and 1930. The mean age at marriage around 1871 was around 14–15 years; between 1891 and 1906 it moved to 18–20 years; by 1932 it reached 25 years. See Patel 1891; see also Axelrod 1974:131; Karkal 1984. There are odd years: 1938, where the average age is 34.9, and 1949, where the average age is 29.2. Karkal's average age for marriage is about 25, but higher ages are cited in Axelrod 1974 and Gould 1987.

cent.[10] When Parsi women did marry, they did not reproduce. Twenty per cent of the married women had no children; another 26.5 per cent had one child. The average number of children per female for all interviewed was 1.62 per female, and for women of completed fertility, 1.85. This figure is well below replacement rate and below the rate for college-educated American women.[11] And yet female Iranis (Iranian Zoroastrians living in Bombay; usually they migrated in the last 100 years) marry at around twenty and only 8 per cent of the female Iranis over 25 had never married.[12] It is important to bear in mind when considering these statistics that the community standards for sexual interaction are fairly strict; while I was aware of some married couples who tolerated infidelity, I encountered little premarital sexual activity. Other anthropologists have also been persuaded that Parsis are not sexually experienced before marriage.[13] These statistics for delayed or rejected marriage indicate a trend towards celibacy and abstinence.

Why on earth would this happen? Parsis often explain that their marital foot-dragging is due to the difficulty of finding appropriate housing for newlyweds. The society highly values a Western lifestyle; it sees neolocal relocation on marriage as intrinsic to that lifestyle; because Parsis refuse to marry until they can live neolocally – so goes the argument – they often refuse to marry at all. It is, realistically, extremely difficult to find housing in Bombay, particularly in the once-colonial areas where the Parsis are concentrated. Stringent rental laws entail that few people rent, and flats are often passed down within the family, left vacant for decades rather than sold and lost forever to the family. The city struggles with ever more people each month, all competing for space. Nevertheless, it seems bold to pin the reproductive failure of an entire community on the paucity of housing, when Hindus in the same dilemma and with the same socio-economic status reproduce with ease (see Axelrod 1974).

The best explanation, to summarize the studies, seems to be that Parsis hold a Western ideal of marriage, prefer to marry 'up', are hesitant to marry non-Parsis, and the women have neither an economic incentive

[10] In 1901 3.33 per cent of the Parsi women between forty and forty-nine had never married.

[11] According to the 1990 US Census, white married women aged eighteen to thirty-four with five or more years of college education – in other words, extremely well-educated women – expect an average of 2.88 lifetime births and had, when interviewed, already produced an average 1.2 children. For married women of all races aged eighteen to thirty-four with five or more years of education, each woman had already produced 2.5 children and had a lifetime expectation of 4.3. Census 1990:43.

[12] Axelrod 1974.

[13] Axelrod 1974:141. Of course, these issues are notoriously difficult to assess in India, even in a Westernized community.

to marry nor a social compulsion to be partnered (Axelrod 1974, Gould 1987, Billimoria 1988, and others). The combination of these factors seems to be sufficient to impede marriage. The problem of maintaining marriage rates in highly educated communities that value a woman's economic freedom and do not demand marriage is, of course, not unique to Parsis. But the added pressure of the Westernized ideal, endogamy, and an obviously shrinking population size makes the problem unusually present for Bombay Parsis. Nevertheless, the pervasive critiques of the community cannot be explained solely by the marriage rates because the critiques emerged prior to the dramatic drop in reproduction rates. If there is any causal connection, it is probably that the critique influences the reproduction rates, and not the other way around.

The more general phenomenon here is that Parsis behave as if they have attacked themselves in response to the loss of their British ideal. The content of the criticism appears to draw directly from the process of the identification with their ideal. During the Raj, Parsis seem to have implicitly accepted the contrast between the British (manly, rational, progressive) and the non-British (effeminate, irrational, traditional) which the British used to undergird their own authority, and they went to lengths to define themselves as on the British side of that opposition; in the contemporary period they are more likely to commend Hindu men as having traits on the British side, and condemn their own sons for traits on the Indian side. It is as if those perceived to be in power are ascribed the traits associated with those in power during the colonial period, and that the markers of identity have not shifted greatly in some respects despite the great shift in political authority since Indian independence.

Discussion

One general framework for understanding this phenomenon is already well established in the psychoanalytic and anthropological literature. In that frame, there is a socio-psychodynamic process here based on what would be called an initial identification with the aggressor. The complex identification of the colonial elite with the colonizers, followed by the loss of the colonial ideal, creates the kind of circumstances in which people experience an ambivalent attachment, are unable to recognize the ambivalence of that attachment adequately, and are unable to mourn the loss of that attachment, which clinically tends to produce self-criticism. The postulated structure of this process, famously recognized by Freud in a paper entitled 'Mourning and Melancholia', is that the person fails to come to grips with a loss, unconsciously fails to acknowledge the loss, and, instead of mourning, becomes intensely self-critical because the person is so disappointed in or enraged at the person or ideal which he still carries emotionally within him.

If one listens patiently to the many and various self-accusations of the melancholic, one cannot in the end avoid the impression that often the most violent of them are hardly at all applicable to the patient himself, but that with insignificant modifications they do fit someone else, some person whom the patient loves, has loved or ought to love. (1975:130)

The early texts that anthropologists read as central to discussions of colonialism and post-colonialism take off from this psychoanalytic argument, and identification with the aggressor is their most consistently theorized theme. For Albert Memmi, for example, in *The Colonizer and the Colonized* (1965), the colonized first models himself on the colonizer, aping his customs and yearning for his appearance. He loses his past; he learns the history of Cromwell but nothing of his own progenitors. He grows embarrassed by his mother tongue. 'The first ambition of the colonized is to become equal to that splendid model [of the colonizer] and to resemble him to the point of disappearing in him' (1965:120). The colonized agrees, in Memmi's words, to destroy himself and become what he is not. But then he learns that in the end the colonizer will reject him anyway, and he is filled with shame and self-hatred (1965:121–2). Ultimately, he has no choice but to recognize the anger in his ambivalence and to rebel. 'Revolt is the only way out of the colonial situation, and the colonized realizes it sooner or later' (1965:127). And yet even if he is successful he remains still tortured, still living in a psyche defined by the colonizer, defined by what he is not. 'So goes the drama of the man who is a product and victim of colonialism. He almost never succeeds in corresponding with himself.'[14] Frantz Fanon, in *Black Skin, White Masks* (1967), wrote even more starkly: 'for the black man there is only one destiny. And it is white'

---

[14] Memmi 1965:140. Nancy Hartsock (1987) uses Memmi's colonized other to set feminism in sharp opposition to a vulgar Foucaultianism. Hartsock takes from Memmi the argument that colonialism destroys both parties to the bargain, and the creation of the colonized through the colonizer's projection of her negative qualities: he is lazy, wicked, backward, and not entirely human. More to the point, to the colonizer all the colonized look alike. 'Feminist readers of de Beauvoir's *Second Sex* cannot avoid a sense of familiarity. We recognize a great deal of this description.' Hartsock's point is that in the construction of theory, *he* theorizes. Both the universalizing and totalizing voice of Enlightenment thinking, and the postmodernism which denounces it, are creations of the dominant power. From this perspective, Foucault is 'a figure who fails to provide an epistemology which is usable for the task of revolutionizing, creating and constructing'. His history is 'parodic, dissociative, and satirical'. It shows how to take things apart, but not how to put them together. He is, she says, in the position of the colonizer who refuses, who by virtue of seeing the exploitation, refusing to exploit, but being himself an exploiter, is rendered impotent.

(1967:10). The terrible cost of colonialism in Fanon's eyes is that in yearning to be like the white colonizer, the black colonized man comes to accept the white man's vision of the black man and so to lose himself. He is alienated from himself when he feels most white, and humiliated when he feels most black. And so, perpetually, the black man is torn, rejecting himself to become white, only then to grasp a more terrible vision of his never-to-be-scrubbed-clean skin. 'A Negro is forever in combat with his own image' (1967:194).

Parsi experience is explicable from this perspective. Because, as a community, Parsis never actually rebelled against their ideal, their ambivalence should be particularly prominent, their unacknowledged anger should be great, and their sense of humiliation keen. They should be strikingly self-critical. Individual Parsis now express a great jumble of varying emotions about their community. But there is no doubt that feelings about British involvement are contradictory and intense. Much about this can be captured by describing them as in a state of humiliation at abandonment, a state of mixed shame and rage, following their identification with, and the loss of, the colonial aggressor.

That explanation is however not satisfying on several fronts. The explanation treats the community as if each individual shares a common private drama, whereas all that is really clear is that many of them make scathing remarks of a certain consistency about each other. Nor does the explanation make sense of the fact that most contemporary Parsis are at least one generation removed from the group which experienced the actual trauma. In fact, the dilemma presented by Parsi self-critical discourse is not unlike the dilemma Charles Berg presented to Edmund Leach (1958). Across the world, as it happens, rituals of hair-cutting accompany sexual abstinence, and rituals of hair cultivation accompany sexual activity, with remarkable frequency. Heads are shaved at clitoridectomy and hair is grown at pregnancy; people who marry comb each other's hair in the public ceremony; they make sexual affairs public by delousing each other in public; women cover their hair after marriage; and so forth. Berg was a psychoanalyst, and argued that this was because hair was a universal sexual symbol. Thus, he continued, when a monk tonsures his head, he feels castrated.

Leach was horrified by this argument. He first tried to discount the empirical association between hair and sexuality and failed miserably. But, he countered, that irrefutable association still gave the anthropologist no right to interpret the private feelings of those participants he observes in public rituals. The new monk may shave his head and by that act indicate his willingness to live by the rules monks accept, but this public communication, using a public symbol of renounced sexuality, tells you nothing of his private conflicts and fantasies. Public symbols communicate information in the public domain, Leach argued, and those symbols are for the actors as emotion-free as a stop sign or a handshake. Private symbols, like a song a married couple heard on the night they first met, are ripe with conscious feeling and unconscious emotion. They resonate inside our heads like music, rather than communicating between us, like language.

Obeyesekere (1981) raised a problem with this contrast (which Leach himself had somewhat qualified). Suppose some public ritual is not required of its participants? All those who enter the monastery must shave their heads, whether they chose monastic life for its free education or for its freedom from marriage. Obeyesekere agreed that the monk's head-shaving told you little of his own sexual anxieties. But suppose, he argued, a woman chooses to become a priestess in a setting where there are many paths to possession, and she chooses out of all the alternatives to acquire lice-ridden, scalp-pulling, supposedly sacred matted locks? Choice may indicate that the public symbol indeed has richly private meaning. The parallel problem in interpreting Parsi self-critical discourse is that even if we accept that the Parsis were quietly traumatized by the departure of the British and that at the time their self-criticism reflected the private pain of those who spoke it, how do we understand that generation's heirs? What is the meaning of the self-critical discourse of Parsis for those who speak it today?

At this point we need to turn to the way we conceptualize the self. To an earlier generation of psychoanalysts and anthropologists, the self was not problematic. That is, it was not, as a concept, puzzling. Self, person, and identity were more or less interchangeable. When Erikson wrote about identity, he described it as a kind of consolidation of self, so that when someone achieved her identity, the way she interacted with the world – her ability to trust, to work and to play – was recognized externally by others in a way that was consonant with her own internal understandings. The Eriksonian self stands facing the world as the private awareness of that person which, when mutually recognized and consciously accepted, becomes her identity.

More complicated psychoanalytic approaches to the self began to emerge with Heinz Kohut's work. In a famous article (1958), he pointed out that the tools of psychoanalysis are introspection and empathy and argued that psychological phenomena like the self thus necessarily include introspection and empathy as essential elements. The 'I-experience', as he called it, captures the way an individual introspects; thus evidence for the self is fundamentally different from evidence for the observable body. Kohut went on to establish his own vocabulary about the 'I-experience', the most useful phrase probably being the 'self-object', the other person that an individual may use to soothe himself and restore inner harmony, as a mother can reassure a child that an imagined dragon is not real and a wife can reassure a husband that his boss is not the incarnation of Satanic vice. His most fundamental contribution, however (at least for the present purpose), was to distinguish between the introspective nature of the self and the differently observable nature of the person.

This is the distinction that Roy Schafer later developed as the distinction between the person, as the agent who acts, and the content of the ideas they have about personhood, the person's understanding of his or her 'I'. He called these 'self-narratives' (but referred to them as selves, a practice I will also follow). Schafer also argued that, from this perspective, there is clearly more than one self, a position that some anthropologists and psychologists also now adopt (Kondo 1990, Gergen 1991). There may be the self who is confident, assertive, and effective and the one who is weak, embarrassed, and reactive (it is that 'second' self which the analysand will present in the analytic hour). There is the self we become when speaking French, freer, more sophisticated, we feel, than our English-speaking self (cf. Kaplan 1993). There is the work self, the play self, the parenting self, the self in different roles, and the self under different circumstances. Schafer quotes a male analysand speaking to his analyst:

I told my friend that whenever I catch myself exaggerating, I bombard myself with reproaches that I never tell the truth about myself, so that I end up feeling rotten inside, and even though I tell myself to cut it out, that there is more to me than that, that it is important to me to be truthful, I keep dumping on myself. (1992:25)

There are, Schafer suggests, eight selves of five types in that remark. The types are: actual self, ideal self, self as place, self as agent or subject, and self as object. The selves are: analysand self, social self (talking to friend), bombarding self, derogated self, exaggerating self, conciliatory adviser self, advisory self, and the defended self with redeeming features. Schafer is perhaps being excessive (it is his exceeding self) but the point is powerful. To call all of what his analysand describes the product of a single self is to lose a good deal of helpful detail.

From this perspective, a self – or more precisely, a self-narrative or self-representation – is a cognitive schema, a bounded collection of conceptions and images that an individual uses to perceive, to categorize, and to experience his world: in short, to think with. This is a more cognized version of the common understanding of the self, as 'the model which underlies virtually all current social science views the self as an entity that a) comprises a unique, bounded configuration of internal attributes (e.g. preferences, traits, abilities, motives, values and rights) and b) behaves primarily as a consequences of those internal attributes' (Markus and Kitayama 1994:569).[15] Markus describes what she calls 'self-schemata': 'self-schemata are cognitive generalizations about the self, derived from past experience, that organize and guide the processing of self-related information contained in the individual's social experiences' (1977:64).

Clearly, people are motivated by more than one simple cognitive packet. We are Americans, professionals, parents, neighbours; we are shy in some settings, assertive in others, skilled and aggressive in some games, cautious and awkward in others. Many theorists conceptualize these 'packets' in terms of roles. Mardi Horowitz (for example, Horowitz *et al.* 1996), more complexly, writes of 'role-relationships.' We establish, he argues, particular ways of relating to people that are driven by our concepts of who they are, who we are in relation to them, and how we are to act in that relationship. He sees these role-relationships as integrated in a sense of personal identity. Claude Steele provides evidence for that integration in an experiment in which women in Salt Lake City were called by a man posing as a pollster. While the call was ostensibly about conducting a future poll on women's issues, some women were told that it was commonly known that they were unco-operative with community projects. Some were told that it was commonly known that they were co-operative. Some were told that they were bad drivers. Two days later, a woman called them back and asked them to help with a community project. Salt Lake City is a heavily Mormon community, with a strong ethic of community co-operation. Perhaps unsurprisingly, those who were insulted as unco-operative were twice as likely to agree to help out as those who were praised, as if to clear their good names to themselves. What was more remarkable, however, is that those who were called bad drivers were also twice as helpful as those who had been praised. Steele went on to argue that people often respond to damage to one self-representation by affirming success in another. I hang back with embarrassment as a lousy athlete when friends at a beach party decide that we should all play volleyball, but I can make myself feel better by reminding myself, when I drop the ball, that I am competent in the classroom. Those of us who drop

---

[15] They go on to argue that in the West, people assume that the major normative task of the self is to maintain its independence, and in other, particularly Asian, settings, the normative task becomes maintaining interdependence with others. They illustrate, however, the cognitive emphasis upon the self as a packet of concepts and images that motivate what I would call the person.

volleyballs can enhance our self-esteem by bringing a terrific homemade pie to the next seaside event.

Still, the self is more complex than even this tale of loosely integrated but shifting roles suggests. The cognitive psychologist Ulric Neisser (1988) argued that there are five kinds of self-knowledge, five ways in which we have knowledge of our 'I'. There is the ecological self, the 'I' perceived with respect to the physical environment; the interpersonal self, experienced in emotional communication, the way 'I' behave in a particular human interchange; the extended self, based on memory and anticipation, the 'I' who has done certain things in the past and will likely engage in certain routines in the future; the private self, experienced as the awareness that other people cannot see your thoughts, that (in some ways) only I can know me; and the conceptual self, the wealth of concepts that I believe comprise my self: my roles (professor, friend, dog-owner), my features (I have a liver, a nose and a mind), and my specific traits (I am tall, short, smart, stupid, brunette, blonde). It is important, Neisser argues, to distinguish between kinds of self-knowledge, because otherwise the self is full of apparent contradictions. It is physical yet mental, public yet private, directly perceived yet incorrectly imagined, universal yet culture-specific. 'Although there is nothing with which we are more familiar, we are often enjoined to know ourselves better than we do' (1988:35). He resolves the contradictions, however, by speaking of different 'selves'. 'They differ in their origins and developmental histories, in what we know about them, in the pathologies to which they are subject, and in the manner in which they contribute to human experience' (1988:35).

The missing element in Neisser's account is emotional attachment, which is the glue that integrates at least our conceptual selves or self-representations, the bundled cognitive packet that underlies a self-narrative or self. We have different kinds of attachments to our various ways of being. Some selves really matter to us. Some don't. Some fill us with shame and loathing. Others make us beam with pride. Luckily, as a lousy volleyball player, my athletic self is far less emotionally significant to me than my classroom self. Nevertheless, because of the way I remember those painful afternoons of schoolyard kickball, my athletic self-representation carries with it more humiliation than someone observing my life (and my active workouts) might suspect. It is far more difficult for an outside observer, or even an introspective observer, to understand the emotional meaning that a set of ideas has for someone than to elicit those ideas as a set in the first place. As a result, a person's emotional attachment to their self-representations is under-theorized because it is hard to capture the way emotions functionally interact with cognitive schemas – although it is true that Steele demonstrates that feeling badly about one self-representation will motivate people towards positive reinforcement in another, and Neisser argues that the extended self (personal memory) interacts with the conceptual self, and Horowitz argues that it is emotion and memory that switch a person's involvement in one role-relationship to another. Self theories tend to be cognitive theories. Nevertheless, they depend upon emotional attachments. The kind of emotional attachment people feel to a self-representation explains how that self is meaningful and begins to explain how it relates to others.

The mark of collective trauma is the sense of distress, humiliation, and self-blame that accompanies a recognition that one belongs to some group. There is a bundle of traits that defines membership in the community, and at a certain point, that bundle comes to be associated cognitively with failure and emotionally with shame and guilt. Vamik Volkan calls this combination a 'chosen trauma', a shared representation of an event that includes realistic information, fantasized expectations, intense feelings, and defences against unacceptable thoughts. He acknowledges that no group chooses to be traumatized. But, he argues, memory is never wholly realistic, and when that memory comes to define collective identity, it becomes a matter of unconscious choice. 'The word chosen fittingly reflects a large group's unconsciously defining its identity by the transgenerational transmission of injured selves infused with the memory of ancestor's trauma' (Volkan 1997:48). I think that the best way to make sense of the Parsi material is to observe that there is a bundle of traits that defines membership in the community, and that at a certain point, that bundle comes to be associated cognitively with failure and emotionally with shame and guilt. That is also the mark of trauma, that the bundle does not change very much in overt composition from its prior, untraumatized state, but the bundle now 'means' inadequacy and humiliation. At the turn of the century, Parsis wrote about and seemed to behave in accord with a particular representation of what a good member of their community should be. The representation included traits of truthfulness, purity, progressiveness, and charitableness, traits which were embedded in the Zoroastrian religion but which had taken on a particular character during the Raj, when the Parsis became involved with the British and in many ways emulated them as a means to achieve success under British rule. More specifically, those traits became an argument for similarity to a British gentleman, in particular a successful English man of business; during this period a new trait emerged specifically associated with this period, which was the trait of sporting masculinity. After independence, the specific bundle of traits remains coherently associated with moral goodness, but now as an indication of failure: that the average Parsi is no longer truthful, that racial purity has led to racial corruption and the decline of the Parsi body, that the average Parsi is not rational and progressive but blindly traditional, that charity has enfeebled the community, that the men are no longer masculine. This bundle becomes a chosen trauma, a self-representation that defines group identity, and carries with it humiliation and self-blame. I call this the 'traumatized social self'.

By 'traumatized social self', then, I mean a self-narrative which is part of the conceptual self, which defines a person's membership in a collective through a collection of traits which are assumed to motivate his or her behaviour, and which are now associated with failure, moral inadequacy, embarrassment, and guilt. This is not the trauma of those devastated by an accidental, natural loss, as in the little town Kai Erikson (1976) described after a dam broke and a river of mining sludge poured down main street, destroying everything in its path. Those people were emotionally sideswiped by the loss of half their tightly knit community, but they did not blame themselves and they did not feel like failures. They felt no complicity in the tragedy. They mourned, seemingly healthily, for their loss. When there is a tornado, or an epidemic, or a flood, there is usually no 'we-ness' to the loss (except, as the old joke has it, for the unlucky Czechs). There is not a sense that 'our people' have let us down, that it is a genetic weakness of our flesh or an inadequacy of the way 'we' live. When a flood wiped out North Dakota farming communities, nobody did it to 'us', although no doubt many rethought their relationship to a caring God (in both directions: one of the great paradoxes of belief is that after tragedy, some people become atheists and others become deeply religious).

A closer comparison can be found within the Jewish-American experience of anti-Semitism. During the Holocaust, and for centuries before, Jews were destroyed because they were Jewish. A Jew would feel unambiguously that it was his 'we-ness', his Jewishness, that led to this trauma. Even in the US, in earlier decades of this century, elite social clubs refused membership to those who were Jewish; a non-Jewish family could (sometimes even now) refuse to allow a child to marry someone Jewish; a Jew could be treated as socially inferior, often in ways that were barely conscious to the non-Jew. For some, not surprisingly, Jewishness came to be associated with being disliked, and the traits which defined them as Jewish became the traits which led to shaming and to failure. These days, American Jews talk about the more recent phenomenon of the 'self-hating Jew'. They point to the emergence, out of centuries of stigmatization, of a kind of character which Woody Allen describes so well: a Jewish man who is obsessed by his Judaism but also apparently revolted by it, a man who feels deeply Jewish and yet associates his Judaism with humiliation, inadequacy, and rightful inferiority. Here there is a self-narrative of membership within a group (Jews) which identifies a set of traits (various ritual and ethnic observances, particular physical traits) assumed to motivate people in the group (they care about their Judaism, they practice their Judaism, they see themselves as Jewish through these traits) and which are nonetheless, to the person with the traumatized social self (but not to others), a source of deep inadequacy.

That there is a moral quality to this traumatized social self should not surprise us. A social self representation models not only what we are, but what we should be: good Americans, truthful, independent people who will fight for the right to democracy, religious freedom, and the liberty of speech. And it is really only a moral representation that can be injured, for it is only a sense of duty and obligation that can be failed. If we are only who we are, our representation shifts simply as we change. If we are whom we aspire to be, we can fail, and then we are ashamed. The Parsi collective self representation under the Raj incorporated a comparative ethical dimension: good like the British, unlike the 'natives'. The injury inflicted during independence (and the period leading up to it) was inflicted on the moral rightness of that comparative dimension. Actual experience of the British before and after 1947 was of course complex: nevertheless, it would have been very difficult for the community collectively to view the British presence with unblemished moral regard. And certainly the fact that the British left India meant that the implied closeness of the self representation was no longer so valid. Those in power were supposed to be strong, good men of a certain sort; and now they were Hindu.

Sometimes Parsis seem to feel deeply affected by and involved with this traumatized social self. It captures something basic about the way they feel themselves to be Parsis. This kind of attachment is best understood through a model of internalization that describes the emotional connection to the schema-in-itself. Melford Spiro presents an account of internalization which distinguishes between degrees of salience for cultural representations. Not all parts of the culture, he points out, are held by people in the same way (Spiro 1987; D'Andrade 1992). At the first level, a person is acquainted with a cultural representation but may be indifferent to it. At the second, the cultural belief is no more than a cliché. Someone may believe that one ought to care for the poor, as Jesus did, but actually have little concern for them. Spiro continues:

It is only when it is acquired by actors as a personal belief system – the third level of acquisition – that a cultural system may be said to be *internalized*. When, for example, the propositions that Jesus died for man's sins, and that one ought to care for the poor, are acquired by the actors at this level, they themselves evince a sense of sin and they are generous in their assistance to the poor. Since, at this level, cultural systems are not only external to the actors (they are not only represented in external symbols or other signs) but are internal to them (they engage their minds and influence their action), they are, as Sapir . . . put it, 'genuine.'

At the fourth (and final) level of acquisition, the cultural system is not only internalized, but it is highly *salient*. That is, the actors hold it with especially strong conviction because it engages not only their minds, but also their emotions. Thus, believing that Jesus died for man's sins, the actors are preoccupied with their own sins; and believing that one ought to care for the poor, their assistance to the poor represents a personal sacrifice. (Spiro in D'Andrade 1992:37)

Roy D'Andrade re-theorizes this analysis as an account of the way cultural models acquired directive force. That a cultural model (attractive women are thin) exists does not make that model relevant to all members of a culture. Only some people put a warning sign – 'a moment on the lips, a lifetime on the hips' – on the refrigerator door. And then only some of those people pay attention to the sign (D'Andrade 1992). Claudia Strauss (1992) interviewed several Rhode Island blue collar men, all of whom in the course of conversation produced some version of the well-worn American phrase, 'hard work breeds success'. She demonstrated with a sophisticated linguistic analysis that only one of them actually seemed to be motivated by the phrase, and he was a marathon competitor. The others simply dropped the phrase into their conversation as if to display their belief in the American dream, despite the notable fact that their jobs did not reward them for hard work.

One could refer to this model as a 'vertical' theory of internalization.[16] The cultural representation – 'we are not what we were' – is always present, and the question for any one person is how deeply it is held emotionally and how much, then, it motivates behaviour. One can ask of any individual whether they have deeply internalized the traumatized social self-representation as a chosen trauma, whether this self-representation truly captures an important dimension of what it is to be Parsi, and whether the traumatized self-representation powerfully motivates their behaviour. One can ask: does this individual Parsi feel embarrassed to be Parsi? Does she mumble the word 'Parsi' in a conversation with

---

[16] I owe this distinction between vertical and horizontal to a conversation with Nancy Chodorow.

Hindus, or wear clothes that are conspicuously non-Parsi in an attempt to pass as Hindu? Or is she more relaxed about her Parsiness: does she chuckle when she is asked about Parsis who displays English royalty on their walls? Different individuals hold their chosen trauma more or less close to their heart.

Another kind of emotional attachment treats the self-representation as a resource, to be used by the individual as his own psychodynamic needs determine. This is an emotional connection to the schema-for-another-purpose. The traumatized social self-representation is after all only one of many self representations that any individual uses to define membership in a (usually ethnic) group. Certainly it is not the only way modern Parsis describe their community. They talk about its great history, its many accomplishments, its glorious Persian past, and its impressive achievements under the Raj. Parsis are immensely proud of their Tatas, their Jeejeebhoys, their charitable generosity and their contributions to modern Indian industry. Sometimes individual Parsis chose to use the traumatized self-representation, rather than these more buoyant forms, in a way which seemed less relevant to being Parsi and more relevant to some other end.

Here, the appropriate model of internalization is 'horizontal' – internalization as a contextual, emergent phenomenon. Sometimes the cultural representation has emotional salience; sometimes it does not. Whether it does depends on the other factors in the context: the specific goals of the speaker, the importance at that time of whatever the representation represents and the specific meaning of that representation for the speaker at that moment. This shifting salience is what Michael Cole seems to have in mind when he talks about situation, practice, activity, and so forth: that people behave in culture relative to a specific context. 'Each situation is idiosyncratic in the mix of resources/constraints brought to bear and hence there is no strict determination of the consequences of action that result' (Cole 1996:143 and 131ff). When the situation calls for it, the traumatized social self-representation becomes a resource. A woman feeling pressed by her parents to marry within the community has different context-specific goals than the same woman explaining the Zoroastrian religion at a bar in New College, Oxford. In Oxford, she feels pride. At home, she needs to dismiss her mother's pleading.

For example, Jean Briggs describes, in an article aptly titled 'Mazes of Meaning', a series of small 'dramas' that an Inuit adult enacts with a small child. Someone threatens to take her home or to take her puppy away. The person who becomes her ally and supporter in that sequence then hits her from behind and then blames the smack on someone else.

The Inuit are often warm and tender with their children. They also tease their children unmercifully, as we would say. 'Why don't you die so I can have your nice new shirt?' 'Your mother's going to die – look, she's cut her finger – do you want to come live with us?' Briggs argues that it is possible to extract core values from a collection of such incidents, but, from the child's perspective, this task is to sort out a maze of meanings – in particular, what the adult's intention is and what would satisfy the adult so as to end the torture. That task, she points out, has to do with figuring out the adult's constantly shifting intentions and implications. 'The "same" value may be psychodynamically different and may play different roles in the psychic economies of different individuals, or of the same individual at different points in the life cycle – or even at different moments in the day – because it is associated with different tangles of experience' (Briggs 1992:48).

When I listen to Parsis criticize themselves, it sometimes sounds as if they use the packet of self-criticisms as a way to accomplish sundry goals of the moment. Parsis are now several generations away from that quiet but significant injury to their sense of being Parsi. Those painful emotional attachments to the traumatized self-representation and its Parsi traits are probably a little less powerful than in earlier decades. Parsis comment, in any event, that the community seems more upbeat and more hopeful than it did in the first two decades after independence. This is not to say that the wound has healed: it hasn't, entirely. But the bundle of self-critical traits crops up nonchalantly in casual conversation. That language of self-criticism catches up, expresses, and is used in service to a complex set of shifting pragmatic and referential needs in the moment: a Parsi woman's casual joke ('he's so typical'), her justification for exogamous marriage ('but papa, I just couldn't find a Parsi man'), a Parsi man's dismay at the difficulty of getting his sons into medical school ('those aggressive Hindus'), his anxiety around the future of his country in a time of political struggle around Hinduism ('what will happen to us?'), his fury at a successful Hindu businessman's willingness to use bribery and tax evasion ('our people became great because we would not stoop so low, and now . . .'). Sometimes the emotional tone seemed closer to irritation or anger at a neighbour or an ex-boyfriend rather than, as in the response to the film *Percy*, genuine and deep collective shame at being Parsi. At these moments, the distress seemed specific and focused on something in particular ('that rat Cyrus') which the self-criticism ('what did I expect, he's Parsi') could justify. The traumatized self-representation serves as a resource the way American feminism becomes a resource for women: often present as a theme, deeply important to some, marginally important to others, or more or less salient depending on the conversation, the attitude and the vent of the moment. A woman can justify her intense drive, seen by others as unfeminine, through feminism; a woman can also hesitate to publish, and blame male bias for her failure to get tenure. Some women live in a near constant state of rage, which they understand as the result of seeing male bias everywhere; some women refuse to see male bias, which they believe the women's movement eradicated; many women pin failures of a variety of kinds on the fact that they live in a male-dominated society. The difference in the way the resource is used results from the specific histories of those particular women – their temperaments, their parental and school environments, their treatment by superiors early in their professional careers. Feminism, and the feminist self-representation, can serve as a traumatized social self-representation for women who felt the impact of the women's movement as a powerful transformation; it can be internalized vertically to a greater or lesser degree. Feminism can also be like a basket of images and concepts from which a woman can take something that serves a more local dynamic need.

For individual Parsis, the narrative of a community that was once great, and now has faltered, will be of varying significance depending on the person's psychodynamic predisposition and the peculiarities of the place and time. Parsis still struggle with the legacy of their previous generations. They struggle as a group, and many of them feel in their hearts a strange mixture of shame, failure, and pride at being Parsi. They seem to have critically internalized the traumatized social self. They share the dilemma of all who have gambled on history, and lost, and must come to terms with the world that fate has presented to them. Probably, as Yolanda Gampel describes in her concept of 'radioactivity', the traumatized social self will diminish in its negative emotional force as the generations continue, if the community lives on. The vertical internalization will increasingly become more shallow. If the community shows signs of dying out, however, the traumatized social self will probably grow in emotional salience for each Parsi, as the sense of collectivity grows more doomed. Meanwhile, that packet of traits remains available for Parsis to use or ignore, depending on context, depending on personal need.

The larger point here is that there is a socio-psychological architecture to our ways of being in the world. No Parsi looks like any other, but many are recognizably Parsi in look and feel, and there is a Parsiness to their robust, confident society with its inroads of self-critical doubt. We can respect their individuality and their collectivity if we understand theoretically that their selves are complex architected structures, built in ways that a fieldworker can understand in part.

References

Album of Men and Women of India. Bombay: Rutnagar. 1906. Special Issue, Vol. II No. 9

Arendt, H., 1964, *Eichmann in Jerusalem*. New York: Viking

Axelrod, P., 1974, *A Social and Demographic Comparison of Parsis, Saraswat Brahmins and Jains in Bombay*. PhD thesis in anthropology. Chapel Hill, NC: University of North Carolina

Ballhatchet, K., 1980, *Race, Sex and Class under the Raj*. London: Weidenfeld and Nicolson

Billimoria, H., 1988, *Attitudes of Parsi Youth (Females) Towards Marriage*. Unpublished typescript (substantial survey). Bombay: Bombay Parsi Panchayat

Bode, B., 1989, *No Bells to Toll*. New York: Scribner

Briggs, J., 1992, Mazes of Meaning. *New Directions for Child Development* 58:1–25

Bulsara, F., 1935, *Parsi Charity Relief and Community Amelioration*. Bombay: Bulsara

Burns, Sir J. C. n.d., Tape recording of a businessman's memories of Bombay before independence. London: India Office Library

Callaway, H., 1987, *Gender, Culture and Empire*. Chicago: University of Illinois Press

Census of Population, 1990, *Education in the United States*. Washington, DC: United States Department of Commerce, Economics and Statistics Administration, Bureau of the Census

Chodorow, N., 1994, 'Identity and the Self': A Contribution to a Symposium on Erik Erikson. Unpublished manuscript

Cole, M., 1996, *Cultural Psychology: The Once and Future Discipline*. Cambridge, MA: Harvard University Press

Dadachanji, F. K., 1941, *Philosophy of Zoroastrianism and Comparative Study of Ethics*. Bombay: Times of India Press

D'Andrade, R., 1992, Schemas and motivation. In *Human Motives and Cultural Models*. R. D'Andrade and C. Strauss, eds. Cambridge: Cambridge University Press, 23–44

Daniel, V., 1996, *Charred Lullabies*. Princeton: Princeton University Press

Darukhanawala, H. D., 1935, *Parsis and Sports*. Bombay: Darukhanawala

Daruwalla, K., 1982, *Keeper of the Dead*. Delhi: Oxford University Press

Das, V., 1986, Gender Studies, Cross-Cultural Comparison and the Colonial Organization of Knowledge. *Berkshire Review* 21:58–79

Dastoor, H. R. H., 1944, *Parsi Problems*. Nagpur: Albert Press

Desai, S. F., 1940, *Parsis and Eugenics*. Bombay: Desai
  1945, *A Changing Social Structure*. Bombay: Parsi Panchayat
  1948, *A Community at the Crossroad*. Bombay: New Book

Erikson, K., 1976, *Everything in its Path: The Destruction of Community in the Buffalo Creek Flood*. New York: Simon & Schuster

Fanon, F., 1967, *Black Skin, White Masks*. New York: Grove

Freud, S., 1975, *A General Selection*. Ed. J. Rickman. New York: Doubleday

Gergen, K., 1991, *The Saturated Self: Dilemmas of Identity in Contemporary Life.* New York: Basic Books

Gould, K., 1987, An Aging, Dwindling Community. *Parsiana* (March): 44–51

Harris, F. 1958 [1925], *Jamsetjee Nusserwanjee Tata.* London: Blackie and Sons

Hartsock, N., 1987, Rethinking Modernism: Minority vs Majority Theories. *Cultural Critique* (Fall) 7:187–206

Horowitz, M., C. Stinson and C. Milbrath, 1996, Role-Relationship Models: A Person-Schematic Method for Inferring Beliefs about Identity and Social Action. In *Ethnography and Human Development.* R. Jessor, A. Colby and R. Shweder, eds. Chicago: University of Chicago Press

Inden, R., 1990, *Imagining India.* Oxford: Blackwell

Ishiguro, K., 1986, *An Artist of the Floating World.* London: Faber and Faber

Jussawalla, A., 1975, *Missing Person.* Bombay: Clearing House

Kaplan, A., 1993, *French Lessons: A Memoir.* Chicago: Chicago University Press

Karaka, D. F., 1884, *History of the Parsis.* Vols. I and II. London: Macmillan

Karkal, M., 1984, *Survey of the Parsi Population of Greater Bombay.* Bombay: Bombay Parsi Panchayat

Karkaria, R. P., 1896, *India: Forty Years of Progress and Reform: A Sketch of the Life and Times of Behramji M. Malabari.* London: Henry Frowde

1915, *The Charm of Bombay.* Bombay: Taraporevala

Kohut, H., 1958, Introspection, Empathy and Psychoanalysis. *Journal of the American Psychoanalytical Association* 7:459–83

Kondo, D., 1990, *Crafting Selves: Power, Gender and Discourses of Identity in a Japanese Workplace.* Chicago: Chicago University Press

Kotwal, N. B. R., 1937, *A Discourse/The Naked Truth/etc.* Bombay: Kotwal

Kulke, E., 1974, *The Parsees in India.* Munich: Weltforum Verlag

Leach, E., 1958, Magical Hair. *Journal of the Royal Anthropological Institute* 88(2):147–64

Luhrmann, T. M., 1996, *The Good Parsi: The Fate of a Colonial Elite in a Postcolonial Society.* Cambridge: Harvard University Press

Mani, L., 1987, Contentious Traditions: The Debate on Sati in Colonial India. *Cultural Critique* (Fall): 119–56

Mankekar, D. R., 1968, *Homi Mody.* Bombay: Popular Prakashan

Markham, S. F., 1932, *A Report to the Sir Ratan Tata Trustees on Problems Affecting the Parsee Community.* Bombay: Sir Ratan Tata Trust

Markus, H., 1977, Self-Schemata and Processing Information about the Self. *Journal of Personality and Social Psychology* 35(2):63–78

Markus, H. and S. Kitayama, 1994. A Collective Fear of the Collective: Implications for Selves and Theories of Selves. *Personality and Social Psychology Bulletin* 20(5):568–79

McLure, J., 1981, *Kipling and Conrad: The Colonial Fiction.* Cambridge, MA: Harvard University Press

1991, Late Imperial Romance. *Raritan* 10(4):111–30

Memmi, A., 1965, *The Colonizer and the Colonized.* Boston: Beacon

Mistry, C., 1978, *Doongaji House.* Unpublished (but performed) manuscript

1985, *Percy.* Bombay, 7–21 March, 40–56

Mobedji, M., 1987, *A Research Study of Charitable Trusts Founded by Parsis in*

Bombay and their Social Welfare Objects, Activities and Administration Process. Master's thesis, Bombay University College of Social Work

Nandy, A., 1983, *The Intimate Enemy.* Delhi: Oxford University Press

Neisser, U., 1988, Five Kinds of Self-Knowledge. *Philosophical Psychology* 1(1):35–59

Nordstrom, C. and A. Robben, eds., 1995 *Fieldwork under Fire: Contemporary Studies of Violence and Survival.* Berkeley: University of California Press

Obeyesekere, G., 1981, *Medusa's Hair: An Essay on Personal Symbols and Religious Experience.* Chicago: University of Chicago Press

O'Hanlon, R., 1991, Issues of Widowhood: Gender and Resistance in Colonial Western India. In *Contesting Power: Resistance and Everyday Social Relations in South Asia.* D. Haynes and G. Prakash, eds., 62–108

O'Hanlon, R. and D. Washbrook, 1992, After Orientalism: Culture, Criticism, and Politics in the Third World. *Comparative Studies of Society and History* 34(1):141–6

The Parsi: The English Journal of the Parsis and a High Class Illustrated Monthly. Vol. I, Nos. 1–12. Bombay: The Parsi

Patel, B. B., 1891, Statistics of Births, Deaths, and Marriages among the Parsis of Bombay During the Last Ten Years. *Journal of the Anthropological Society of Bombay* 2:448–58

Patel, G., 1966, *Poems.* Bombay: Nissim Ezekiel

Said, E., 1978, *Orientalism.* New York: Pantheon

1993, *Culture and Imperialism.* New York: Knopf

Schafer, R., 1992, *Retelling a Life: Narration and Dialogue in Psychoanalysis.* New York: Basic Books

Scheper-Hughes, N., 1992, *Death Without Weeping: The Violence of Everyday Life in Brazil.* Berkeley: University of California Press

Spiro, M., 1987, Collective Representations and Mental Representations in Religious Symbols Systems. In *Culture and Human Nature: Theoretical Papers of Melford E. Spiro.* Ed. B. Kilbourne and L. L. Langness. Chicago: Chicago University Press, 161–84

Stern, D., 1985, *The Interpersonal World of the Infant.* New York: Basic Books

Steele, C., 1988, The Psychology of Self-Affirmation: Sustaining the Integrity of the Self. *Advances in Experimental Social Psychology* 21:261–301

Stoler, A., 1991, Carnal Knowledge and Imperial Power: Gender, Race, and Morality in Colonial Asia. In *Gender at the Crossroads of Knowledge.* Di Leonardo, ed. 51–101

1992, Rethinking Colonial Categories: European Communities and the Boundaries of Rule. In *Colonialism and Culture.* N. Dirks, ed. 319–52

Strauss, C., 1992, 'What Makes Tony Run? Schemas as Motives Reconsidered. In *Human Motives and Cultural Models.* R. D'Andrade and C. Strauss, eds. Cambridge: Cambridge University Press, 191–224

Suleri, S., 1992, *The Rhetoric of English India.* Chicago: University of Chicago Press

Wadia, P. A., 1949, *Parsis Ere the Shadows Thicken.* Bombay: Wadia

Wurgaft, L., 1983, *The Imperial Imagination.* Middletown: Wesleyan

Volkan, V., 1996, Bosnia-Herzegovina: Ancient Fuel of a Modern Inferno. *Mind and Human Interaction* 7(3):110–27

1997, *Bloodlines.* New York: Farrar Straus and Giroux

7 Identities under siege: immigration stress and social mirroring among the children of immigrants

Carola Suárez-Orozco *

Introduction

Immigration is a phenomenon that involves over 130 million people worldwide. In the United States, one out of every five children is the child of an immigrant. In New York City schools today, forty-eight per cent of all students come from immigrant-headed households. This is not only an urban phenomenon – schools across the country are encountering large numbers of children from immigrant families. It is increasingly clear that the adaptations of these children will be an important factor in the remaking of the American economy and society.

For many individuals, migration results in substantial gains. Some escape political, religious, or ethnic persecution while others migrate for economic reasons. Long-separated families may be reunited. Some immigrants are motivated by the opportunity for social mobility while others migrate in the spirit of adventure. Whatever their motives, immigration is considered worthwhile for many. Still, the gains of immigration come at considerable costs which could not have been anticipated at the moment of departure. The costs and pressures of migration are in particular felt by the children of immigrants.

The pressures of migration are profoundly felt by the children of immigrants. These children experience a particular constellation of changes and experiences that are likely to have an impact upon their developing psyches. In this chapter, I examine how the stresses of immigration are complicated by both the structural barriers and the 'social mirroring' of nativist responses and racism that many immigrant children encounter. When the inherent stresses of immigration are

* I would like to thank Marcelo Suárez-Orozco for his helpful comments. I am most grateful to June Erlick, Jennifer Hayes, and Mariela Paez for their careful reading and suggestions regarding an earlier version of the chapter. I would also like to thank the National Science Foundation, the W. T. Grant Foundation, and the Spencer Foundation for their generous support of our Longitudinal Immigrant Student Adaptation Study (jointly with Marcelo Suárez-Orozco).

compounded by patterns of structural and psychological violence, immigration becomes traumatic.

Surprisingly little research has focused on the psychological experiences of immigrant children (Garcia-Coll and Magnuson 1998). Much of the work to date either has emphasized the adult immigrant experience or has examined the physical rather than the psychological health of these children. This chapter is a theoretical contribution to this emerging field based on analyses of the first wave of data from the Longitudinal Immigrant Student Adaptation Study (a large-scale interdisciplinary research project which I co-direct with Marcelo Suárez-Orozco). This project involves five groups of immigrant children coming to the United States from China, Central America, the Dominican Republic, Haiti, and Mexico. We are following 425 recently arrived immigrant children over the course of five years.[1] Using anthropological and psychological techniques, we are assessing the children's adaptation to the new society, with particular emphasis on the schooling context.

Stresses of immigration

Transitions of any kind have long been regarded by social scientists and mental health professionals to be stressful (Schlossberg 1984). Events such as moves, job changes, and ruptures in relationships are known to be highly disruptive, often triggering a variety of reactions including anxiety, anger, depression, somatic complaints, and illness (Dohrenwend 1986). Stress is particularly noxious when the individual is unable to cope in his or her usual manner. The stakes are even higher when (s)he perceives that there are serious consequences to not adapting (House 1974). Both of these conditions are met in the process of immigration.

By any measure, immigration is one of the most stressful events a person can undergo. Most critically, immigration removes individuals from many of their relationships and predictable contexts – extended families and friends, community ties, jobs, living situations, customs, and (often) language. Immigrants are stripped of many of their sustaining social relationships, as well as of their roles which provide them with culturally scripted notions of how they fit into the world. Without a sense of competence, control, and belonging, they may feel marginalized. These changes are highly disorienting and nearly inevitably lead to a keen sense of loss (Ainslie 1998; Grinberg and Grinberg 1989).

[1] The children attend forty-two schools in eight school districts in the Boston and San Francisco area. Ethnographic observations are conducted by twenty-nine highly trained bilingual/bicultural graduate social science students.

At the most dramatic end of the stress spectrum are the stresses that result in post-traumatic symptomatology. Events such as experiencing or witnessing killing, rape, or torture often lead to transient as well as long-term symptomatology. Recent arrivals originating from the former Yugoslavia, Somalia, Indochina, Central America, and Haiti are examples of waves of immigrants who come from regions where they may well have undergone trauma (Somach 1995). Symptom clusters resulting from PTSD include recurrent traumatic memories, and a general numbing of responses, as well as a persistent sense of increased arousal leading to intense anxiety, irritability, and outbursts of anger, difficulty concentrating, and insomnia (Horowitz 1986; Smajkic and Weane 1995). Immigrants who experience trauma will often suffer recurring waves of these symptoms over a period of time; the severity of the symptoms will depend on the extent of the trauma and the psychological, social, and material resources available to the victims. These symptoms add significantly to the stresses of immigration.

Concern with violence is a recurring theme that we have found among many of our informants. An alarming number of immigrant children experience a variety of forms of stress which may lead to post-traumatic symptomatology. In addition to the violence experienced prior to migration (in the cases where families are fleeing war or civil unrest), all too many immigrant children witness a disconcertingly high level of violence in their new neighbourhood and school settings (see below). Furthermore, the actual border crossing is often a traumatic event for adults and children alike.

Scholars and human rights observers of the US–Mexican border – the most heavily trafficked in the world – have noted that undocumented border crossers are subject to a variety of dangers including exposure to environmental extremes (Eschbach et al. 1997) and violence at the hands of border agents, 'coyotes' (paid crossing guides), as well as others (Amnesty International 1998:24). According to a recent Amnesty International report 'women are at particular risk of being physically abused, raped, robbed, or murdered on their journey' (1998:24). The number of women who are raped sometime during their crossing journey is reported to be very high.

Our own interviews with immigrant children reveal that many of them experience the crossing of the border as highly traumatic. Some report actual events that occur to them (such as being detained, deported, humiliated, or beaten). Others report perceptions of potential danger. A nine-year-old Mexican boy with clearly evident fear in his voice told us of his crossing: 'I had to be careful of where I put my feet. My parents told me that the *migra* [slang term for the Immigration and Naturaliza-tion Service] had put pirañas in the river to keep us away.'[2]

A further form of stress specific to immigration has been termed acculturation (or acculturative) stress (Berry 1998; Flaskerud and Uman 1996; Smart and Smart 1995). Acculturation refers to the process whereby individuals learn and come to terms with the new cultural 'rules of engagement'. The individual's place of origin provides her with familiar and predictable contexts; these predictable contexts change in dramatic ways following immigration. As Polish immigrant Eva Hoffmann says in her exquisitely written memoirs, immigration results in falling 'out of the net of meaning into the weightlessness of chaos' (Hoffmann 1989:151). Without a sense of competence, control, and belonging, migrants are often left with a keen sense of loss and marginality. A twenty-three-year-old Mexican informant insightfully summed up the experience: 'I became an infant again. I had to learn all over again to eat, to speak, to dress, and what was expected of me.'

Responses to the stresses of immigration

While anticipating the migration and the initial period following the arrival, many immigrants experience a sense of euphoria (Sluzki, 1979). Expectations are often high as the anticipated possibilities may seem boundless. Energies are focused on attending to the immediate needs of orienting themselves in the new environment, including finding work and a place to live. As the realities of the new situation are confronted, individuals normatively begin to experience a variety of psychological problems (Ainslie 1998; Arrendondo-Dowd 1981; Grinberg and Grin-berg 1989; Rúmbaut 1977; Sluzki 1979; Suárez-Orozco 1998). Most frequently, the cumulative losses of loved ones and familiar contexts lead to feelings along a spectrum of sadness to depression to 'perpetual mourning' (Volkan 1993). The dissonances in cultural expectations and of predictable contexts lead many to experience an anxious disorienta-tion (Grinberg and Grinberg 1989). Disappointed aspirations and dreams, when coupled with a hostile reception in the new environment, may lead to feelings of distrust, suspicion, anger, and even well-founded paranoia (Grinberg and Grinberg 1989).

The repercussions of the responses at the individual level are felt within the family. Sluzki (1979) argues that migration has destabilizing effects on the family. Indeed, migration creates particular pressures on the family system. It is not unusual for there to be an increase in conflict

---

[2] Please note that all quotations from our informants are translations from their native languages.

between family members following migration (particularly if there was pre-existing marital tension). Migration often creates changes within the structure of the family: former family leaders may be 'demoted' (Shuval 1980) and the nature of the gender relationships may shift. Espin argues that 'immigrant families may become entrenched in traditional social and sex role norms as a defense against the strong pressures to acculturate' (1987:493). In other cases, as immigrant women move into the workplace, their new role as family providers may at once provide them with new-found independence and create tensions within their relationships.

Many immigrant families incorporate extended family members and are more interdependent and hierarchical than traditional Anglo-American families (Smart and Smart 1995). Some of these characteristics may be in part culturally determined but others may be secondary to migration. Extended families will often live together to share both the financial and the childcare burdens. In the absence of other social support networks, they may rely on each other considerably more than most non-immigrant families.

Immigrant parents often have to make dramatic sacrifices for what they hope will be a better future for their children. They are frequently fiercely protective of their children with deep-seated concerns about the perceived dangers of the new environment (including the potential of becoming too Americanized). Within the new context, they may set limits that are significantly more stringent than they would have had they stayed in their country of origin. At the same time, immigrant parents are often quite dependent upon their children. The children may develop language skills more quickly than their parents and consequently serve as interpreters and errand-runners for the family. Alternating between 'parentifying' the children and, at the same time, severely constricting their activities and contacts, may create significant tensions within the family.

Many immigrant parents (particularly those coming from poorer families) work in several jobs. These multiple obligations lead them to be relatively unavailable to their children. For example, because their work schedules do not permit much flexibility, immigrant parents are often unable to attend school functions: as a result, educators lament the perceived lack of interest in their children's education. It is a mistake, however, automatically to interpret this as lack of interest or concern. Immigrant parents often tell us that they feel that working hard is the best way they can help their children; yet these long work hours leave the children unattended. This physical absence compounds the psychological unavailability that often accompanies parental anxiety and depression (Athey and Ahearn 1991). These two forms of absence all too frequently leave immigrant children to their own devices long before it is developmentally appropriate. While in some cases this leads to hyper-responsible internalized children, in other cases it leads to depressed children who are drawn to the lure of alternative family structures such as gangs (Vigil 1988).

The time frame for adaptation to the new culture is usually quite different for children than for adults. Children are quickly forced to contend with the host society more intensely than their parents. Schools represent an important first host-culture site encountered by the children. There, they meet teachers (who are usually members of the dominant culture) as well as children from both the majority and other minority backgrounds. Hence, they are forced to contend more quickly and more intensely with the new culture than do their parents who are likely to work in jobs that do not require much in the way of language skills or which may be largely populated by other members of the immigrant community (M. Suárez-Orozco 1998). The relative rapidity of the children's adaptation may create particular tensions. Parents may try to slow down the process by warning children not to act like other children in the new setting. Children may also have feelings ranging from vague to intense embarrassment in regard to aspects of their parents' 'old country' and 'old fashioned' ways.

The potential for miscommunication should not be overlooked or underestimated in immigrant families. As noted earlier, children often learn the new language more quickly than do their parents. Most children long to be like others: many will quickly show a preference for the language of the dominant culture (Portes and Hao 1998). Furthermore, even if the child continues to speak the home language, the level of fluency is likely to be influenced by the fact that after a number of years in the new culture, without a concerted effort, the vocabulary and literacy level of the language of origin usually lags far behind that of the host culture. Hence, while the child may easily communicate about basic needs in her language of origin, she is likely to have more difficulty communicating subtleties of thought and emotion in that language (Wong-Fillmore 1991). By the same token, often the opposite is true with the parents. Hence, one of the parties in the conversation is likely to be at a disadvantage in complicated communication sequences. Furthermore, in complex discussions, subtleties of meanings are likely to be missed and miscommunication may result. It is not uncommon to overhear discussions in which parents and children switch back and forth between languages and completely miss one another's intent. Children are also not above deliberately misleading their parents. A thirteen-year-old Mexican boy admitted to us that he had told his parents that the 'F' on his report card stood for 'fabulous'!

Our new research suggests that tensions between parents and children are particularly heightened in cases where the children have been separated from their parents for long periods of time. A number of the new immigrants are following a pattern whereby one or both parents go ahead to the host country leaving the children with relatives. These separations often last for several years. During this time, the child is likely to attach him or herself to a new caretaker, who may or may not have affectionately attended to their needs. If the child succeeds in attaching to the new caretaker, the separation from this caretaker in order to be reunited with the parent can be quite painful (compounding the mourning and loss that follows the immigration). If the separation was painful and the child was neglected or abused, this too will complicate the adjustment following migration. In any case, there is likely to be some fall-out following these years of separation prior to migration (particularly within the Caribbean immigrant community as well as, increasingly, within the recent Central American community and from some areas in China).

A number of factors may significantly attenuate the severity of response to the transitions and stress of immigration (Garcia-Coll and Magnuson 1997; Laosa 1989; Rúmbaut 1996). These mediating variables can roughly be broken down into two categories: sending factors and receiving factors.

Mediating factors

The sending context

Each individual brings with him characteristics, traits, and experiences which are referred to as sending (or antecedent) factors. The circumstances surrounding the migration can play a key role. Was the individual 'pushed or pulled' out of their country of origin? If the immigrant is lured out of his homeland by the promise of opportunity and adventure, he is likely to be more positively disposed to the experience than if he is 'pushed' out by ethnic, religious, or political conflict, chronic hardship, or famine in the homeland. By the same token, at least initially, the individual initiating the migration is likely to be more enthusiastic about the experience than a reluctant spouse, elderly parent, or child (Shuval 1980). We have found that children in particular often have little understanding of the reasons behind the motivation to migrate. As a result they may not pass through a stage of looking forward in anticipation to the migration and may experience the move as an imposition upon them from which they have little to gain.

Pre-immigration stress and trauma may be critical to the subsequent adaptation of immigrants. Did he experience trauma that was directly linked to the decision to migrate? Individuals and families who flee conflict-torn areas may have witnessed traumatic events and may have been subjected to torture and other forms of physical and psychological violence (Suárez-Orozco 1989). This is almost always true of refugees, a special kind of migrant. In addition, as noted earlier, these traumas may be compounded with further violence during the actual process of migration.

Socio-economic background has been found to be a consistent mediator of the stresses of the migration process (Flaskerud and Uman 1996). Higher levels of education as well as economic resources play a decisive role in minimizing structural impediments (C. Suárez-Orozco 1998). On the whole, upper-middle-class immigrants sustain the least loss. They may be able to retain much of their prestige and may be able to travel back and forth to maintain their social relationships. Individuals and families of middle and lower classes are less likely to have opportunities to visit and may particularly suffer from being cut off from their loved ones.

Immigrants of middle-class backgrounds often experience significant losses in prestige: they frequently find employment in positions far below their training and qualifications because of language difficulties, lack of connections, or lack of certification in certain professions. In addition middle-class immigrants may suffer for the first time the painful experience of prejudice and discrimination in the new country. The poorest immigrants, who are largely members of the lower classes in their country of origin, often suffer tremendous adversity as a result of immigration. In spite of these difficulties – which may include xenophobia, racism, and fierce competition for the least desirable jobs – they often achieve relative improvements in their economic and social circumstances. In addition, while they certainly suffer from discrimination in the new country, social disparagement may not necessarily be a new experience. As members of the lower socio-economic class, they are likely to have suffered such treatment in their country of origin.

Personality and temperamental factors are likely to play a significant role in how the individual will respond to the migration process (Garcia-Coll and Magnuson 1997; Shuval 1980). A healthy response to dramatic change requires the ability to be flexible and adaptable to new circumstances. Individuals who are particularly rigid, or who have a high need for predictability, are likely to suffer more than those who are more comfortable with change and new circumstances (Wheaton 1983). Those who are particularly shy, proud, or sensitive to outside opinions are also at higher risk as are those who are highly suspicious of the motivations of others. An effective arsenal of coping strategies, on the other hand, is a great asset (Lazarus and Folkman 1984; Pearlin and Schooler 1978).

By the same token, psychological and physical health prior to migration will also aid or impede the ease of the response to immigration. Individuals who are suffering from post-traumatic stress (as discussed earlier) are of course highly at risk. So, too, are individuals who suffer from depressive tendencies as well as any of a number of other psychiatric disorders. Physical health may also play a role, particularly if an illness or disability interferes with either maintaining gainful employment or with general quality of life.

A variety of other sending factors can also help to mediate the migration process. Possessing the language skills of the new country, clearly, is an asset. Religiosity and connection with a church may also play a positive role. The rural-to-urban shift (a not uncommon pattern for many immigrants) on the other hand may complicate the ease of transition. Many immigrant children in our study report to us that they find it very difficult to adjust to the *encerramiento* (as many said in Spanish for being 'shut-in'). While they may have had considerable freedom to play and roam their neighbourhoods in their place of origin, they often lose such freedoms when the move to an urban environment.

The receiving context

Just as a number of factors related to the sending situation will ease or impede the adjustment to the new context, conditions in the new host milieu will also play a significant role. At the top of the list is the availability of a social support network. The relative absence of social support has been linked to the etiology of disease, mortality, slowed recovery, and mental illness. By the same token, the presence of a healthy social support network has long been regarded to be a key mediator to stress (Cobb 1988; Cohen and Syme 1985).

Interpersonal relationships provide a number of functions (Wills 1985). Instrumental social support includes the provision of tangible aid (such as running an errand or making a loan); as well as guidance and advice (including information, and job and housing leads) so much needed by disoriented newcomers. Social companionship also serves to maintain and enhance self-esteem and provides much needed acceptance and approval. A well-functioning social support network, quite predictably, is closely linked to better adjustment to the new environment. Of course, in part, the availability of an effective social support structure will be influenced by the individuals' pre-existing social competence. Individuals with highly developed social skills are likely to be better able to establish and draw upon interpersonal relationships (Heller and Swindle 1983).

A number of other factors within the host environment play a role in the adaptation of the immigrants. Whether or not the immigrant is 'documented' or 'undocumented' will obviously impact the opportunity structure in which (s)he is able to participate (Chavez 1992; Smart and Smart 1995) as well as the general quality of life. Feeling 'hunted' by the INS is highly stressful (Padilla *et al.* 1988) and leads to anxiety and (well-founded) paranoia. For adults the availability of jobs will be key. Here, social networks will play a key role as employers often rely on migrant networks to provide them with a constant source of potential new employees (Waldinger 1997; Cornelius 1998). Ability to find work, questions of pay, seasonal availability, safety, and the unpleasantness of the job will also play a role in adjustment.

For children, the quality of their schools will play a key role in the ease of transition. Unfortunately, many immigrant children find themselves in segregated, poverty- stricken, and conflict-ridden schools (Orfield 1998). Fear of violence is a central concern in the lives of many new immigrants. In our sample of schools, a number of administrators have reported high crime rates. In one of our participating middle schools, a student was recently raped and murdered; a high school principal told us of approximately thirty murders within the last year within the immediate neighbourhood; and many other school officials and students complain of significant gang activity within the school environs. A middle school student told us that a security guard, who had supposedly been hired to protect the schools' students, was the main dealer of drugs on campus. During a focus group we conducted with Mexican immigrant students in a San Francisco Bay Area school, students revealed that only a few days earlier, an escaped prisoner had barricaded himself during school hours within the school grounds, leading to an exchange of gunshots between him and the police.

Obviously, neighbourhood safety will do much to influence the quality of life for children and adults alike. Many immigrants move to inner-city areas in search of housing they can afford. Unfortunately, 'affordable' urban housing is often located in areas which may be characterized as 'war zones'. An eleven-year-old Mexican girl told us: 'There is a lot of violence here in the United States. They kill people in the streets.' A thirteen-year-old Mexican girl said: 'There I was freer.'

Here there are bad people who hurt children.' A twelve-year-old Haitian girl recounted: 'I don't like the neighborhood where I live. There is a lot of crime in the neighborhood. One day, we were sleeping and the police came and opened the door. There was a man in the apartment above us who had killed his wife . . . I was scared because he could have come and killed us too.' A ten-year-old Mexican boy reported a frightening incident: 'I saw a man lying out in front of my house with blood on his legs and stomach. I think someone shot him.' Another child, a thirteen-year-old Chinese girl, told us: 'I have seen gang activities near my house . . . I am afraid to go out. I don't feel safe.'

Parents, too, fear for their children's safety. They often require them to stay within the confines of their (often cramped) living spaces, out of harm's way in the streets. Many of our informants lamented the resulting loss of freedom following immigration. A thirteen-year-old Dominican boy said: 'Back home, I had much more freedom. I didn't have to ask permission for every little thing. Here, our parents are much more protective of us. They are always after us telling us to be careful and not to come home late.' When asked about what the most difficult thing about migration was for her, one twelve-year-old Mexican girl replied: 'If you go out in the United States, you are always afraid of everything. In Mexico, you can go out with confidence.' A fourteen-year-old Salvadorean girl said: 'The most difficult thing about immigration is that I am always locked up in the house.' A twelve-year-old girl who recently immigrated from Haiti recounted: 'In Haiti I could go where I wanted. Here I cannot do that because there are bad kids.' A fourteen-year-old Dominican boy said: 'I don't like being closed in. You can't go out.' A thirteen-year-old Chinese girl summed up the feeling of many of our informants: 'It is very lonely in America having nobody to talk to and staying home all day long after school every day.'

The general social climate of reception to the new immigrants plays a critical role in their adaptation. Garcia-Coll and Magnuson (1997:119) argue that 'discrimination against immigrants today, and particularly immigrants of color, is widespread in America'. Prejudice and exclusion are established forms of social traumata. 'Prejudicial exclusion is, even if neglected, a potent psychosocial stressor impinging on the daily lives of many . . . interfering with their mental and social adaptation and adjustment' (Adams 1990:363). The exclusion can take a structural form (when individuals are excluded from the opportunity structure) as well as an attitudinal form (in the form of disparagement and public hostility).

In the following section, I illustrate some of the ways in which both structural and social exclusion are impacting the lives of immigrant children.

The social climate: hostility in the receiving context

Structural violence and exclusion

In recent years, there has been a growing concern about the large influx of new immigrants. A number of public opinion polls reveal negative attitudes towards immigrants. In one recent survey, over two-thirds indicated that they did not want to extend the invitation of the Statue of Liberty to new immigrants (Espenshade and Belanger 1998). In their thorough analysis of recent public opinion polls, Princeton scholars Espanshade and Belanger found that many respondents perceive that immigrants have a negative economic impact, drain the social service system, contribute to crime, and show little prospect of assimilation. These prevailing beliefs and sentiments led to several dramatic anti-immigrant initiatives (see Suárez-Orozco 1996).

California's Proposition 187 illustrates the explosive tensions generated by large-scale immigration in a state which had undergone a severe economic recession. In November 1994, California voters overwhelmingly approved this proposition, known as the 'Save our State' initiative. This initiative was designed to 'prevent illegal aliens in the United States from receiving benefits or public services in the State of California' (Proposition 187 1994:91) including emergency medical services and education for children.

This controversial initiative generated a great deal of legal action including several suits in Federal and State courts. Currently, the law is not being fully implemented. However, if it were to be, it is estimated that some 300,000 undocumented immigrant children in California would be banned from enrolling in public schools. Many observers argue that this proposition would do nothing to prevent further unauthorized immigration to the State of California, and could in the long term cost the tax payers of that state far beyond whatever short-term savings could be realized by not providing public schooling to these immigrant children (Suárez-Orozco and Suárez-Orozco 1995).

The draconian 1996 Illegal Immigration Reform and Responsibility Act is another example of structural exclusion, which some observers have argued will have a harmful effect on large sectors of society (Eschbach *et al.* 1997; Hagan 1998). In addition to a steep intensification of deportations, the internal security provision of this new Act ushered in a nationwide effort at fingerprinting, wiretapping, INS linkages with local and state law enforcement, and other measures supposedly designed to combat links between immigration, the drug trade, and terrorism. The Act has obvious implications for the civil rights of immigrants and citizens alike – particularly those of colour (see Eschbach *et al.* 1997; M. Suárez-Orozco 1998). The new law also changes in significant ways the process by which citizens and permanent residents can bring family members to permanently reside in the United States.

In 1996 President Clinton announced 'the end of the era of big government'. Ironically, that same year, the Immigration and Naturalization Service (INS) experienced an explosive growth. In September 1996 President Clinton signed the Illegal Immigration and Responsibility Act. The Act, *inter alia*, doubled the size of the Border Patrol over five years. Likewise, US military personnel were given a substantial role at the southern border, assisting the INS in various initiatives including surveillance and maintenance and the operation of highly sophisticated military equipment (Andreas 1998). Alarmingly, since the implementation of these policies, there has been a significant increase in human rights violations at the border (see Amnesty International 1998:24; American Friends Service Committee 1992) as well as deaths at the border resulting from exposure and violence as migrants make more dangerous crossings (Hagan 1998). Although the massive new law enforcement effort has made the southern border of the United States harder to cross, scholar Peter Andreas concludes that 'illegal entry is certainly more difficult and dangerous, but there is little evidence to suggest that migrants are giving up and heading home' (Andreas 1998:347).

A side effect of these policies is the increasing criminalization of the border region. Unauthorized crossings went from being mostly acts of self-smuggling to a process structured around widening circles of criminality. Undocumented immigrants must increasingly rely on the work of professional alien smugglers and document forgers – a high-profits growth industry on both sides of the border. Some scholars of immigration have noted that, while the new border control efforts make for dramatic symbolic politics, they largely fail actually to reduce illegal immigration flows through the southern sector (Andreas 1998). While in the past many undocumented migrants would shuttle back and forth across the border in steady transnational flows, increasingly, once they make the crossing into the US, many of them are unlikely to risk a return home. Hence, ironically, they are more likely to stay within the US rather than return to their point of origin. Though these initiatives generate a seductive imagery of state control reinforcing the myth that the problem of illegal immigration is to be found on the border, the problem of unauthorized immigration clearly requires more intelligent, long-term, bi-national responses than we have seen to date (M. Suárez-Orozco 1998).

These exclusionary policies are not limited to the border. In recent years, we have witnessed a range of policies aimed at excluding immigrants (especially undocumented immigrants) from accessing a variety of publicly funded services. Immigration controls have moved slowly over the years from the border to the classroom (Proposition 187), the hospital (see Brown *et al.* 1998) and the welfare agency (see Eschbach *et al.* 1997). Noticeably missing from these initiatives is a systematic attempt to punish or police the businesses that secure significant gains through immigrant labour – whether documented or undocumented. The employer sanction laws have been anaemically enforced due to lack of resources, personnel, and political will. Businesses therefore continue to achieve great gains and risk little sanctioning for widespread use of unauthorized immigrant labor (Cornelius 1998).

These policies and practices are generating a pattern of intense exclusion and segregation between large numbers of immigrants and the larger society. This intense segregation is evident in the work force (see Waldinger 1996), schools (see Orfield 1998), and residential patterns (see M. Suárez-Orozco 1998). Increasingly large numbers of immigrants of colour are settling into highly segregated neighbourhoods where deep poverty, violence, and substandard schools are the norm. In these neighbourhoods, counter-cultural gangs are ever present and eager to recruit and 'socialize' immigrant children into alternative economies where drug-dealing and drug-taking is an important feature of the social scene (Vigil 1988).

These patterns of deep segregation are further intensified by an increasing segmentation in the US economy. While some immigrants, particularly those who are highly educated and highly skilled, are readily moving into the knowledge-intensive sectors of the economy, large numbers of low-skilled immigrants find themselves in low-skilled service sector jobs – a sector of the economy that shows no prospect for status mobility (see Portes and Zhou 1993). Among the children of immigrants, new research suggests another worrisome development. A recent study by Dowell Myers suggests that, while the children of Mexican immigrants have made important gains in terms of school attainment, those gains have not been rewarded proportionally in terms of wages in the marketplace. Particularly for the children of immigrants, there has been a disconcerting pattern of 'declining returns' to education (Myers 1998).

Psychological violence and social exclusion

The structural exclusion suffered by immigrants and their children is detrimental to their ability to participate in the opportunity structure. The attitudinal social exclusion also plays a toxic role. How does a child incorporate the notion that she is 'an alien', 'an illegal', unwanted and not warranting the most basic rights of education and health care? Even if they are not undocumented, the hostility prevalent in the current climate radiates to all children with accents and darker complexions.

A resident of southern California articulated the fears of many: 'You find the huge gangs of illegal aliens that line the streets, shake down our school children, spread diseases like malaria, and roam our neighborhoods looking for work or homes to rob. We are under siege' (quoted in Chavez 1992). One of the leaders in the Proposition 187 effort was propelled to 'do something' after a visit to an Orange County social service agency. She says: 'I walked into this monstrous room full of people, babies, little children all over the place and I realized no one was speaking English . . . I was overwhelmed with this feeling: Where am I? What has happened here?' (quoted in Suro 1994). In Flushing, New York, like in many other communities across the nation, there has been a dramatic increase in its immigrant population in the last ten years. For many long-time residents, the change is 'proving painful, even traumatic' (Dugger 1997). One resident commented: 'Everything is changing' while another said 'It's very discombobulating, very upsetting. We all recognize that change is necessary but it just doesn't sit well.' Though the new immigrants have brought resources to Flushing revitalizing declining neighbourhoods, a Congresswoman said of the new immigrants: '[They are] more like colonizers than immigrants. They sure as hell have lots of money and they sure as hell know how to buy property and jack up rents of retail shops and drive people out' (quoted in Dugger 1997).

Adults are not the only members of American society who share such feelings. Non-immigrant, non-minority students in public high school in northern California had these thoughts to share with educational researcher Laurie Olsen: '[Immigrants] come to take our jobs, and are willing to break their backs for shit pay, and we can't compete.' Another said: 'These Chinese kids come over here and all they do is work and work and work and work, and all you have to do is look in the AP [Advanced Placement] classes and you'll see they are filling them up. No one can compete any more.' Still another summed up a prevailing fear: 'They just want to take over' (quoted in Olsen 1998:68).

These quotes suggest several points. Most obviously, the hostility is undisguised and unambivalent. The immigrants embody the feeling of 'uncanny' (Freud 1968) – the horror of being lost in a changing world that appears to be menacing activates such primitive defences as splitting and projection. In the anti-immigrant talk, 'aliens' appear either as parasites who are siphoning away limited resources (such as jobs and social services) or conversely as powerful and sinister aliens who control vast resources, thus eliciting envy.

Of course, anti-immigrant sentiments are nothing new. During the 1920s a frequent contributor to the *Saturday Evening Post* contrasted the 'old immigrants' (from northern Europe) with the 'new immigrants' (those from southern and eastern Europe): the former, he maintained, were able to blend into the melting pot. The latter he accused of entering the country simply to earn money with the intention of returning to their homelands. Maintaining that many were illiterate, he argued that they would be difficult to assimilate: 'If the United States is the melting pot, something is wrong with the heating system, for an inconveniently large portion of the new immigration floats around in unsightly indigestible lumps. Of recent years, the contents of the melting pot have stood badly in need of straining in order that the refuse might be removed and deposited in the customary receptacle for such things' (Simon 1985:83). Though this was written in the 1920s, the sentiment it expresses is shared by many in the 1990s. The fear (then as now) was that 'America has largely become the dumping ground for the world's human riffraff, who couldn't make a living in their own countries' (Simon 1985:83). The new immigrants of the time were viewed as intellectually inferior, lazy, crime-prone and altogether inassimilable.

Indeed a consideration of the historical record strongly suggests that there is a remarkable consistency in the responses to immigrants. Historian Rita Simon conducted an exhaustive review of media representations of immigrants in the United States over the span of a 100 years (1880 to 1980) examining fifty years of public opinion polls from their beginnings at the end of the 1930s (Simon 1985). Her findings illustrate a classic pattern of response to new arrivals – American citizens have held consistently negative attitudes towards people wishing to enter the United States; the more recent the immigrant group, the more negative the opinion. On the whole, while the people who came in earlier waves are thought to have been 'good folk', new immigrants are viewed as 'pure scum' (Simon 1985:88).

Thomas Espanshade and Maryanne Belanger (1998) of Princeton University undertook a comprehensive study of American public opinion polls on immigration. In their study of national surveys by twenty different organizations over a thirty-year period, they found that, historically, there has been a very strong correlation between anti-immigrant sentiment and economic anxiety, particularly around unemployment rates. Put simply, when unemployment rates are high, anti-immigrant feelings are also high. Likewise, when unemployment rates drop and there is optimism about the economy, negative attitudes towards immigration have tended to level off. It is no accident then, that the high level of anti-immigration sentiment peaked during the economic slump of the late 1980s and early 1990s. In media accounts, in the latter part of the 1990s, concerns with immigration dropped off somewhat though the anti-immigration rhetoric continues to be close to the surface. In general, more educated respondents tend to be more positively disposed towards immigrants than less educated respondents (Espanshade and Belanger 1998). Perhaps, in a world of 'limited good' (Foster 1972), these respondents perceive that they have less to gain and more to lose from immigrants then do members of the more privileged classes. Therefore, although the overall economic situation improved in the latter part of the 1990s, at the lower end of the wage structure native workers already concerned with the segmented hourglass economy, continued to perceive a grave threat from the twin pressures of globalization (jobs leaving for the developing world) and immigration (migrants from the developing world competing for jobs at the bottom of the hourglass).

The fear of the cultural dilution of the country's Anglo-Saxon institutions and values is a enduring preoccupation feeding the anti-immigrant ethos (Espanshade and Belanger 1998). Citizens today feel more positive about immigrants from Europe than they do about immigrants from Latin America and the Caribbean. Immigrants who do not speak English and who 'look' different from the dominant Anglo-European majority make many non-immigrants uncomfortable. The fact that 80 per cent of the 'new immigrants' (post-1965) are of colour (coming from Asia, Latin America, and the Caribbean) is clearly a further complicating factor in our race-polarized society. When it comes to immigration, race and colour indeed matter. Immigration is an enduring concern that lurks just below the surface of public consciousness in the United States. Opportunistic politicians have long found immigrants to be convenient scapegoats onto which to direct righteous anger about all sorts of chagrins (Jones-Correa 1998). At best they are viewed as competitors and at worst they are seen as sinister. As a result, a range of negative attributes can be easily projected onto them.

George DeVos and Marcelo Suárez-Orozco (1990) developed an interdisciplinary, psychocultural framework to explore the experience of self in cultures where patterned inequalities shape social interaction. In addition to the obvious structural inequalities they face, some minorities are also targeted for 'psychological disparagement'. They become the object of symbolic violence which stereotypes them as innately inferior (lazier, prone to crime, and so forth). These attributes make these disparaged minorities, in the eyes of the dominant society, less deserving of sharing in the society's dream and justifies their lot in life.

Identity formation under siege

Social mirroring

How do these charged attitudes and rampant hostilities affect the immigrant child's sense of self? A first point to consider is whether or not children are aware of these hostilities. As part of the data collection for the Longitudinal Immigrant Student Adaptation Study, we asked immigrant children what the hardest thing about immigration was. Discrimination and racism were recurring themes discussed by many of the children. The following statements are representative of the kinds of responses we received. A thirteen-year-old Chinese girl told us: 'Americans discriminate. They treat you badly because you are Chinese or black. I hate this most.' A fourteen-year-old Mexican boy responded: 'The discrimination [is the hardest thing] . . . Here [in the US] Latinos discriminate against African-Americans, African-Americans against Latinos. You see it in the streets, and on TV and you hear it on the radio.' A twelve-year-old Central American girl said: 'One of the most difficult things about immigrating is that people make fun of me here. People from the United States think that they are superior to you.' The perceived discrimination can take a variety of forms. A fourteen-year-old Haitian girl reported: 'I do not like the discrimination. For example, when you go to a store, whites follow you to see if you are going to take something.' A twelve-year-old Haitian boy told us: 'There are many teachers that treat us [the students] well, but there are many who do not. There are teachers who even though they deny it, are racists.' An eleven-year-old Haitian girl recounted that she hated it 'when whites yell at Haitians'. A fourteen-year-old Haitian boy summed it up by saying: 'The racism is here. The Americans believe they are superior to other races.'

We asked all the immigrant children in our study to complete the sentence 'Most Americans think [people from my country] are . . .'. Strikingly, for Latino and Haitian immigrants, the most common response was: 'Most Americans think that we are bad.' Overwhelmingly, the children perceived that Americans had negative perceptions about them. Below are other responses we received:

Most Americans don't think well of us. (fourteen-year-old Central American girl)

Most Americans think that we are poor people. (nine-year-old Chinese girl)

Most Americans think that we are ignorant. (fourteen-year-old Mexican old girl)

Most Americans think that we are stupid. (ten-year-old Haitian girl)

Most Americans think that we are very impolite. (twelve-year-old Chinese girl)

Most Americans think that we don't know anything. (fourteen-year-old Mexican girl)

Most Americans think that we can't do the same things as them in school or at work. (ten-year-old Mexican girl)

Most Americans think that we are good for nothing. (fourteen-year-old Central American boy)

Most Americans think that we are useless. (fourteen-year-old Dominican girl)

Most Americans think that we are garbage. (fourteen-year-old Dominican boy)

Most Americans think that we are members of gangs. (nine-year-old Central American girl)

Most Americans think that we are thieves. (thirteen-year-old Haitian girl)

Most Americans think that we are lazy, gangsters, drug-addicts that only come to take their jobs away. (fourteen-year-old Mexican boy)

Most Americans think that we are bad like all Latinos. (twelve-year-old Central American boy)

Most Americans think that we don't exist. (twelve-year-old Mexican boy)

Clearly then, immigrant children are aware of the prevailing ethos of hostility of the dominant culture. Psychologically, what do children do with this reception? Are the attitudes of the host culture internalized, denied, or resisted? Object relations theorist D. W. Winnicott can provide some insight into the processes at work. Winnicott focused much of his writing on the relationship between the mother and infant adding much to our understanding of the significance of this relationship in the formation of identity and a 'sense of self'. In articulating his concept of 'mirroring', he argued that:

the mother functions as a mirror, providing the infant with a precise reflection of his own experience and gestures, despite their fragmented and formless qualities. 'When I look I am seen, so I exist.' (Winnicott 1971:134)

Imperfections in the reflected rendition mar and inhibit the child's capacity for self-experience and integration and interfere with the process of 'personalization' (Greenberg and Mitchell 1983:192–3).

The infant is highly dependent upon the reflection of the experience she receives from her mothering figure. The mother provides clues about the environment. In determining whether she need be frightened by new stimuli, the infant will first look to her mother's expression and response. An expression of interest or calm will reassure the infant while an expression of concern will alarm her. Even more crucial is the mother's response to the infant's actions. Does the mother show delight when the infant reaches for an object or does she ignore it or show disapproval? No one response (or non-response) is likely to have much effect but the accumulation of experiences is significant in the formation of the child's identities and sense of self-worth. A child whose accomplishments are mirrored favourably is likely to feel more valuable than the child whose accomplishments are either largely ignored or, worse still, denigrated.

Although mirroring (along with a number of his other concepts) is an important contribution to our understanding of the developing child, Winnicott – like many of his psychoanalytic colleagues – overlooks the powerful forces of social systems and culture in shaping self–other relationships. Particularly as the child develops, the mirroring function is by no means the exclusive domain of maternal figures. In fact, with the exception of individuals falling on the autistic spectrum, all human beings are dependent upon the reflection of themselves mirrored back to them by others. 'Others' include non-parental relatives, adult caretakers, siblings, teachers, peers, employers, people on the street, and even the media. When the reflected opinion is generally positive, the individual (adult or child) will be able to feel that she is worthwhile and competent. When the reflection is generally negative, it is extremely difficult to maintain an unblemished sense of self-worth for very long.

These reflections can be accurate or inaccurate. In some cases, the reflection can be a positive distortion or what I call a 'false good': In such a situation the response to the individual may be out of proportion to his actual contribution or achievements. In the most benign case, positive expectations can be an asset. In the classic 'Pygmalion in the Classroom' study (Rosenthal and Jacobson 1968), when teachers believed that certain children were brighter than others (based on the experimenter randomly assigning some children that designation, unsubstantiated in fact) they treated the children more positively and assigned them higher grades. It is possible that some immigrant students, such as Asians, benefit somewhat from positive expectations of their competence as a result of being members of a 'model minority' – though no doubt at a cost (Takaki 1989). In a less benign example of 'false good' mirroring, individuals who are surrounded by those who do not inform them of negative feedback and laud even minimal accomplishments, may develop a distorted view of their own abilities and accomplishments. This would be the case with many political leaders or movie stars as well as others with power and influence. There is also recent evidence that some children are over-praised; the resulting inflated sense of self-worth coupled with low frustration tolerance may be partially linked to violent outbursts (Seligman 1998).

I am more concerned, however, with the negative distortion or 'false bad' case. What happens to children who receive mirroring on the societal level that is predominantly negative and hostile? Such is the case with many immigrant and minority children. When the assumptions about them include expectations of sloth, irresponsibility, low intelligence, and even danger, the outcome can be toxic. When these reflections are received in a number of mirrors, including the media, the classroom, and the street, the outcome is devastating (Adams 1990).

Even when the parents provide positive mirroring, it is often insufficient to compensate for the distorted mirrors that children encounter in their daily lives. In some cases, the immigrant parent is considered out of touch with reality. Even when the parents' opinions are considered valid, they may not be enough to compensate for the intensity and frequency of the distortions of the House of Mirrors immigrant children encounter in their everyday lives. The statements made by the children in our study demonstrate that they are intensely aware of the hostile reception which they are encountering.

What can a child do with these hostilities? There are several possible responses. The most positive possible outcome is to be goaded into 'I'll show you. I'll make it in spite of what you think of me.' This response, while theoretically possible, is relatively infrequent. More likely, the child responds with self-doubt and shame, setting low aspirations in a kind of self-fulfilling prophecy: 'They are probably right. I'll never be able to do it.' Yet another potential response is one of 'You think I'm bad. Let me show you how bad I can be.'

'Segmented assimilation'

A number of theoretical constructs have been developed over the years to explore the immigration experience in American society. Historically, models developed to examine immigration were largely based on the European experience. These studies described patterns of assimilation (Gordon 1964) following various paths on what was depicted as a generally upwardly mobile journey. The argument was quite simple: the longer immigrants were in the United States the better they did in terms of schooling, health, and income.

Most recently, a number of distinguished sociologists such as Gans (1992), Portes and Zhou (1993), Rúmbaut (1996), Waters (1990,

1996), and others have argued that a new 'segmentation' in American society and economy has been shaping new patterns of immigrant insertion into American culture. This research suggests what might be broadly termed a 'trimodal' pattern of adaptation. Some immigrants today are achieving extraordinary patterns of upward mobility – quickly moving into the well remunerated knowledge-intensive sectors of the economy in ways never seen before in the history of US immigration. On the opposite side of our hourglass economy, large numbers of low-skilled immigrants find themselves in increasingly segregated sectors of the economy and society – locked into low-skilled service sector jobs without much promise of status mobility (Portes and Zhou 1997).[3] In between these two patterns are yet other immigrant groups which seem to approximate the norms of the majority population – 'disappearing' into American institutions and culture without much notice.

This trimodal socio-economic pattern seems to be related to how the children of today's immigrants tend to do in school. In the last few years, there have been several studies on the performance of immigrant children in schools. The data suggest a complex picture. In broad strokes, we can say that the immigrant children of today also fit a trimodal pattern of school adaptation (a critical predictor of success in this society). Some immigrant children do extraordinarily well in school, surpassing native-born children in terms of a number of indicators – including grades, performance on standardized tests, and attitudes towards education (De Vos 1983; Kao and Tienda 1995). Other immigrants tend to overlap with native-born children (Rúmbaut 1995; Waters 1996). Yet other immigrants tend to achieve well below their native-born peers (Kao and Tienda 1995; Rúmbaut 1995; Suárez-Orozco and Suárez-Orozco 1995).

In addition to this pattern of variability in overall performance between groups, another disconcerting pattern has consistently emerged from the data. For many immigrant groups, length of residency in the United States is associated with declining health, school achievement, and aspirations (Kao and Tienda 1995; NRC 1998; Rúmbaut 1995; Steinberg 1996; Suárez-Orozco and Suárez-Orozco 1995; Vernez et al. 1996).

A recent large-scale National Research Councils' (NRC) study considered a variety of measures of physical health and risk behaviours among children and adolescents from immigrant families – including general health, learning disabilities, obesity, emotional difficulties, and various risk-taking behaviours. The NRC researchers found that immi-

[3] This was substantiated by the school authorities and news reports.

grant youth were healthier than their counterparts from non-immigrant families. They researchers pointed out that these finding are 'counter-intuitive' in light of the racial or ethnic minority status, overall lower socio-economic status, and higher poverty rates that characterize many immigrant children and families that they studied. They also found that the longer youth were in the United States, the poorer their overall physical and psychological health. Furthermore, the more 'American-ized' they became, the more likely they were to engage in risky beha-viours such as substance abuse, violence, and delinquency (NRC 1998).

In the area of education, Ruben Rúmbaut (1997) surveyed more than 5,000 high school students in San Diego, California and Dade County, Florida. He wrote:

an important finding supporting our earlier reported research, is the negative association of length of residence in the United States with both GPA [grade point average] and aspirations. Time in the United States is, as expected, strongly predictive of improved English reading skills; but despite that seeming advantage, longer residence in the US and second generation status [that is, being born in the United States] are connected to declining academic achievement and aspirations, net of other factors. (Rúmbaut 1997:46–8)

In a different voice, Reverend Virgil Elizondo, rector of the San Fernando Cathedral in San Antonio, Texas articulates this same issue: 'I can tell by looking in their eyes how long they've been here. They come sparkling with hope, and the first generation finds hope rewarded. Their children's eyes no longer sparkle' (quoted in Suro 1998:13).

Negotiating identities

At no time in the lifespan is the urge to define oneself *vis-à-vis* the society at large as great as during adolescence. According to Erickson (1964), the single greatest developmental task of adolescence is to forge a coherent sense of identity. He argued that for optimal development, there needs to be a certain amount of complementarity between the individual's sense of self and the varied social milieus he or she must transverse. This model made a great deal of analytical sense to explain the experiences of individuals living in more homogeneous worlds across their lifespan.

However, in an increasingly fractured, heterogeneous, transnational world, there is much less complementarity between social spaces. Hence, today we are less concerned with theorizing identity as a coherent, monolithic, and enduring construct than in understanding how identities are implicated in the ability to transverse increasingly discontinuous social, symbolic, and political spheres. The children of immigrants must construct identities that will, if successful, enable them to thrive in incommensurable social settings such as home, school, the world of peers, and the world of work.

In this complex world, most children are required to move across discontinuous social spaces. For the children of immigrants, however, these discontinuities can be dramatic. Immigrant children today may have their breakfast conversation in Farsi, listen to African-American rap with their peers on the way to school, and learn in mainstream English about the New Deal from their social studies teacher. Therefore, the experience of the children of immigrants offers us a particularly powerful lens through which to view the workings of identity.

Given the multiple worlds in which immigrant children live, they face particular challenges in their identity formation (Aronowitz 1984; Grinberg and Grinberg 1989; Phinney 1998; Vigil 1988). When there is too much cultural dissonance, negative social mirroring and role confusion, and when the cultural guides are inadequate, an adolescent will find it difficult to develop a flexible and adaptive sense of self. Many are torn between the attachment to the parental culture of origin, the lure of the often more intriguing adolescent peer culture, and aspirations to join the American mainstream culture (which may or may not welcome them).

Optimistic hopes for the future are often tempered by pessimism borne of deprivation and disparagement. While immigrant and second-generation youth may believe that the 'American Dream' should be attainable with sufficient effort, the many limits of this dream become increasingly evident with experience. High school graduation no longer guarantees earnings sufficient to lead a good life, college tuition is prohibitively expensive, and networks and connections – which their parents may not have – do indeed make a difference in the opportunity structure.

To further encumber the process of identity-formation, the children of immigrants are a dissonant combination of precocious worldliness and sheltered naiveté. They are often vested with responsibilities beyond their years. They may be called upon to act as interpreters, to care for siblings, and to attend to chores at home while their parents work. They may be able to manipulate two languages and have insight into two different worlds. At the same time, particularly for girls, forays into the New World are often over-restricted by their anxious parents, which contributes to a relative naiveté. With a limited network of informed individuals to provide adequate information and advice, many immigrant children have difficulty navigating the turbulent waters of adolescence.

Given this multiplicity of factors, it is clear that immigrant adolescents face special struggles in the formation of identity. Each individual forges an identity, finding ways to adapt to the vicissitudes of being a stranger in a new land. In 1937, Stonequist astutely described the experiences of social dislocation. He aptly described cultural transitions, which leave the migrant 'on the margin of each but a member of neither' (Stonequist 1937:4). He emphasized that the common traits of what he termed the 'marginal man' (he wrote in pre-feminist 1937 after all) evolved from the conflict of two cultures rather than from the 'specific content' (Stonequist 1937:9) of any particular culture. Stonequist contended that cultural differences create the most difficulty in circumstances where there are sharp ethnic contrasts and hostile social attitudes. His observations on the psychological costs of marginal status are as useful today as when he first wrote them.

In our work with immigrant children (Suárez-Orozco and Suárez-Orozco 1995) we have noted that youth attempting to transverse discontinuous cultural, political, and economic spaces tended to grav-itate towards one of three dominant styles of adaptation which we have termed 'ethnic flight', 'adversarial', and 'bi-cultural'. A single child, depending upon age at migration, race, and socio-economic back-ground, legal status, and, very importantly, the context of resettlement in the United States, may first gravitate to one style of adaptation. As she matures and develops and as her contexts change, she may develop another style of adaptation. We did not see these styles as fixed or mutually exclusive. We hypothesized that contexts, opportunities, net-works, and social mirroring act as powerful gravitational fields shaping the adaptation of immigrant children.

Youths clustering around the 'ethnic flight' style often struggle to mimic the dominant group and may attempt to join them, leaving their own ethnic group behind. These are the youths who minimize or even deny the negative social mirroring they encounter. An earlier body of social science research examined the related issue of 'passing' among members of some ethnic minority groups (see Tajfel 1978 for example). This line of inquiry argued that individuals who attempted to pass had unresolved issues of what Erickson called 'shame and doubt' (1964:109–12) for which they may struggle to overcompensate. Many immigrant youth who deploy an 'ethnic flight' style may feel more comfortable networking with peers from the dominant culture. For these youths, learning standard English may serve not only instrumental purposes but also often may become an important symbolic act of identification with the dominant culture. Among these youth success in school may be seen as a route for instrumental mobility. It is also a way symbolically and psychologically to dissemble and gain distance from the family and ethnic group. These are immigrants who travel their journey with light affective baggage. The idiom 'making it' for these youth tends to be independence and individualistic self-advancement. Among these youth, typically the culturally constituted patterns of parental authority lose legitimacy. For these youths (as for many of their mainstream American peers) parents are 'out of it' and their ways, moral codes, values, and expectations are rejected as anachronistic. While this style of adaptation might have been consciously and unconsciously deployed by earlier waves of immigrants (especially those from Europe for whom their physical appearance allowed them the option of passing), from the vantage point of the late twentieth century, we are witnessing 'the passing of passing' (De Vos 1992). For many immigrants of colour today, this option is simply not viable.

Youth clustering around 'adversarial styles' of adaptation structure their identities around a process of rejection by the institutions of the dominant culture – including schools and the formal economy. These youths respond to negative social mirroring by developing a defensively-oppositional attitude. As Luis Rodriguez, the child of Mexican immigrants in southern California, recalled in his memoirs:

You were labeled from the start. I'd walk into the counselor's office for whatever reason and looks of disdain greeted me – one meant for a criminal, alien, to be feared. Already a thug. It was harder to defy this expectation than just accept it and fall into the trappings. It was a jacket I could try to take off, but they kept putting it back on. The first hint of trouble and preconceptions proved true. So why not be proud? Why not be an outlaw? Why not make it our own? (1993:84).

These are the children who are pushed out and drop out of school at a time when the US economy is generating virtually no meaningful jobs for those without formal schooling (Orfield 1998). Among these youth, the culturally constituted parental authority functions are typically corroded. These youth, therefore, tend to have serious difficulty with their parents and relatives (see Vigil 1988) and typically gravitate towards those sharing their predicament – their peers. In many cases, the peer group, not the elders, is in charge of the lives of these children. These youths are likely to act out behaviourally (Aronowitz 1984: Garcia-Coll and Magnuson 1997). In these situations, youth often construct spaces of competence in the underground and alternative economies. At the margins of the dominant society, these young people develop an oppositional counter-culture identity from which gangs may emerge. Anthropologist John Ogbu and his colleagues (1998) have argued that in contexts of severe inequality and ethnic antagonism, for many youths learning standard English and classroom success may elicit severe peer group sanctioning when it is viewed as 'acting white' or being a 'coconut', an 'Oreo', or a 'banana'.

Youth clustering around the 'bi-cultural style' deploy what we have termed 'transnational strategies'. These children typically emerge as 'cultural brokers' mediating the often conflicting cultural currents of home culture and host culture. The 'work of culture' (to borrow the term of anthropologist Obeyesekere 1990) for these youths consists of crafting identities in the 'hyphen', linking aspects of the discontinuous, and at times incommensurable, cultural systems they find themselves inhabiting. Some of the youth will achieve bicultural and bilingual competencies, which become an integral part of their identity. These youth respond to negative social mirroring by identifying it, naming it, and resisting it. These are youth for which the culturally constructed social strictures and patterns of social control of immigrant parents and elders maintain a degree of legitimacy. They are able to network with equal ease among members of their own ethnic group as well as with others from different backgrounds. There is considerable evidence that those who develop bi-cultural efficacy (that is to say, social competence in both cultures) are at a significant advantage over those who are alienated with a part of their identity (La Fromboise, Coleman and Gerton 1998).

Among those bicultural youth that 'make it' in the idiom of the dominant society, issues of reparation often become important components of their life trajectories. In some such cases, when one's success appears in the context of the sacrifice of loved ones – which struggled to give them opportunities in the new land – feelings of compensatory guilt are quite common. Among many such youths, success in school will have not only the instrumental meaning (of achieving advancement, better-paying opportunities, and independence) but also the important expressive meaning of making the parental sacrifice worthwhile. To make it for these youth may involve reciprocating and giving back to parents, siblings, peers, and other members of the community (Suárez-Orozco 1989; Suárez-Orozco and Suárez-Orozco 1995).

The majority of immigrant children, coming from a variety of countries and social classes, arrive with extremely positive attitudes towards schooling and education. Three out of four of our 425 recent arrival informants supplied 'education' as the response to an open-ended sentence completion task: 'In life the most important thing is . . .' Yet a number of new studies have shown that the longer the children are in the new environment, the less positive they are about school and the more at risk they are to disengage from academic pursuits. Kohut (1971) theorized that loss, mourning, and the narcissistic injuries of humiliation are linked to destructive tendencies such as aggression and violence. I would argue that the losses and mourning resulting from immigration coupled with the narcissistic injuries of the host culture's reception are a dangerous combination which may in large part account for this disconcerting pattern of decline.

Given that one in five children in the US is a child of immigrants, how these children adapt to their new country should be a crucial societal concern. The pathways they take, and the identities they form are multiply-determined. The resources, experiences, stresses, and trauma, as well as the coping strategies they bring with them play a key role. The structural environment (including neighbourhood, employment opportunities, and schools) within which they find themselves must not be overlooked. I have also argued that the social mirroring which the children encounter is critical. Immigrant children suffer a variety of forms of stress and loss which is only compounded by corrosive social disparagement. We should not underestimate the toll that these experiences and shattered dreams take upon the souls of developing children. The positive attitudes of recent immigrant children are a remarkable resource; as a society we would be best served by harnessing rather than crushing those energies.

References

Adams, P. L., 1990, Prejudice and Exclusion as Social Traumata. In J. D. Noshpitz and R. D. Coddington, eds., *Stressors and the Adjustment Disorders*. New York: John Wiley and Sons.

Ainslie, R. C., 1998, Cultural Mourning, Immigration, and Engagement: Vignettes from the Mexican Experience. In M. Suárez-Orozco ed., *Crossings: Mexican Immigration in Interdisciplinary Perspectives*. Cambridge, MA: Harvard University Press

American Friends Services Committee, 1992, *Sealing Our Borders: The Human Toll. Third Report of the Immigration Law Enforcement Monitoring Project. A Project of the Mexico–US Border Program*. Philadelphia, PA: American Friends Services Committee

Amnesty International, 1998, *From San Diego to Brownsville: Human Rights Violation on the USA–Mexico Border*. News Release, 20 May 1998, http://www.amnesty.org

Andreas, P., 1998, The US Immigration Control Offensive: Constructing an Image of Order on the Southern Border. In M. Suárez-Orozco, ed., *Crossings: Mexican Immigration in Interdisciplinary Perspectives*. Cambridge, MA: Harvard University Press

Aronowitz, M., 1984, The Social and Emotional Adjustment of Immigrant Children: A Review of the Literature. *International Review of Migration* 18:237–57.

Arrendondo-Dowd, P., 1981, Personal Loss and Grief as a Result of Immigration. *Personnel and Guidance Journal*, 59:376–8

Athey, J. L. and Ahearn, F. L, 1991, *Refugee Children: Theory, Research, and Services*. Baltimore, MD: Johns Hopkins University Press

Berry, J., 1998, Acculturative Stress. In P. Organista, K. Chun, and G. Marín, *Readings in Ethnic Psychology*. New York: Routledge

Brown, E. R., R. Wyn, H. Yu, A. Valenzuela, and L. Dong, 1998, Access to Health Insurance and Health Care for Mexican American Children in Immigrant Families. In M. Suárez-Orozco, ed., *Crossings: Mexican Immigration in Interdisciplinary Perspectives*. Cambridge, MA: Harvard University Press

Chavez, L., 1992, *Shadowed Lives: Undocumented Immigrants in American Society*. Fort Worth: Harcourt Brace College Publishers

Cobb, S., 1988, Social Support as Moderator of Life Stress. *Psychosomatic Medicine* 3(5):300–14

Cohen, S. and S. L. Syme, 1985, Issues in the Study and Application of Social Support. In S. Cohen and S. L. Syme, eds., *Social Support and Health*. Orlando: Academic Press

Cornelius, Wayne, 1998, The Strutural Embeddedness of Demand for Mexican Immigrant Labor. In *Crossings: Mexican Immigration in Interdiscipinary Perspectives*. Marcelo M. Suárez-Orozco, ed. Cambridge, MA: David Rockefeller Center for Latin American Studies, Harvard University Press

De Vos, George, 1973, *Socialization for Achievement: Essays on the Cultural Psychology of the Japanese*. Berkeley, CA: University of California Press

1992, *The Passing of Passing in Contemporary Society. Cohesion and Alienation: Minorities in the United States and Japan*. Boulder, CO: Westview Press

De Vos, G. and M. Suárez-Orozco, 1990, *Status Inequality: The Self in Culture*. Newbury Park, CA: Sage Press

Dohrenwend B. P., 1986, Theoretical Formulation of Life Stress Variables. In A. Eichler, M. M. Silverman, and D. M. Pratt, eds., *How to Define and Research Stress*. Washington, DC: American Psychiatric Press

Dugger, C., 1997, Queens Old Timers Uneasy as Asian Influence Grows. *New York Times*. 31 March

Erickson, E., 1964, *Identity, Youth, Crisis*. New York: W. W. Norton

Eschbach, K. J., Hagan, N. Rodriguez, S. Bailey, and R. Hernandez-Leon, 1997, *Death at the Border – June 1997*. www.nnirr.org

Espanshade, T. and M. Belanger, 1998, Immigration and Public Opinion. In M. Suárez-Orozco, ed., *Crossings: Mexican Immigration in Interdisciplinary Perspectives*. Cambridge, MA: Harvard University Press

Espin, O. M., 1987, Psychological Impact of Migration on Latinas. *Psychology of Women Quarterly* 11:489–503

Flaskerud, J. H. and R. Uman, 1996, Acculturation and its Effects on Self-Esteem Among Immigrant Latina Women. *Behavioral Medicine*, 22:123–33

Foster, G., 1972, The Anatomy of Envy: A Study of Symbolic Behavior. *Current Anthropology* 13(2):165–202

Freud, S., 1968 [original 1919], The Uncanny. In *The Standard Edition of the Complete Psychological Works of Sigmund Freud*. Ed. J. Strachey. London: The Hogarth Press

Furnham, A. and S. Bochner, 1986, *Culture Shock*. London: Methuen

Gans, H., 1992, Second-Generation Decline: Scenarios for the Economic and Ethnic Futures of the Post-1965 Immigrants. *Ethnic and Racial Studies* 15 (April):173–92

Garcia-Coll, C. and K. Magnuson, 1997, The Psychological Experience of Immigration: A Developmental Perspective. In A. Booth, A. Crouter, and N. Landale, eds., *Immigration and the Family: Research and Policy on US Immigrants*. Malwah, NJ: Lawrence Erlbaum Associates, Publishers

Gordon, M., 1964, *Assimilation in American Life*. New York: Oxford University Press

Greenberg, J. R. and S. A. Mitchell, 1983, *Object Relations in Psychoanalytic Theory*. Cambridge, MA: Harvard University Press

Grinberg, Leon and Rebecca Grinberg, 1989, *Psychoanalytic Perspectives on Migration and Exile*. New Haven, CT: University Press

Hagan, Jacqueline, 1998, Commentary to the US Immigration Control Offensive. In *Crossings: Mexican Immigration in Interdisciplinary Perspectives*. Marcelo M. Suárez-Orozco, ed. Cambridge, MA: David Rockefeller Center for Latin American Studies, Harvard University Press

Heller, K. and R. W. Swindel, 1983, Social Networks, Perceived Social Support, and Coping with Stress. In R. D. Felner, ed., *Preventative Psychology: Theory, Research, and Practice in Community Intervention*. New York: Penguin Press

Hoffmann, Eva, 1989, *Lost in Translation: A Life in a New Language*. New York: Penguin Books

Horowitz, M., 1986, *Stress Response Syndromes*. 2nd edition. Northvale, NJ: Jason Aronson

House, J. S., 1974, Occupational Stress and Coronary Heart Disease: A Review. *Journal of Health and Social Behavior* 15:12–27

Jones-Correa, M., 1998, Commentary: Immigration and Public Opinion. In M. Suárez-Orozco, eds., *Crossings: Mexican Immigration in Interdisciplinary Perspectives*. Cambridge, MA: Harvard University Press

Kanner, D. A., J. C. Coyne, C. Scaefer, and R. S. Lazarus, 1981, Comparison of Two Models of Stress Measurement: Daily Hassles and Uplifts Versus Major Life Events. *American Journal of Behavioral Medicine* 4:1–39

Kao, G. and M. Tienda, 1995, Optimism and Achievement: The Educational Performance of Immigrant Youth. *Social Science Quarterly*, 76 (1):1–19

Kohut, H., 1971, *The Analysis of Self: A Systematic Approach to the Psychoanalytic Treatment of Personality Disorders*. New York: International Universities Press

La Fromboise, T., H. Coleman, and J. Gerton, 1998, Psychological Impact of Biculturalism. In P. Organista, K. Chun, and G. Marín, eds., *Readings in Ethnic Psychology*. New York: Routledge

Laosa, L., 1989, *Psychological Stress, Coping, and the Development of the Hispanic Immigrant Child*. Princeton, NJ: Educational Testing Service

Lazarus, R. S. and S. Folkman, 1984, *Stress, Appraisal and Coping*. New York: Springer Publishing Company

Myers, D., 1998, Dimensions of Economic Adaptation by Mexican-Origin Men. In M. Suárez-Orozco, ed., *Crossings: Mexican Immigration in Interdisciplinary Perspectives*. Cambridge, MA: Harvard University Press

National Research Council, 1998, *Children of Immigrants: Health Adjustment, and Public Assistance*. Washington, DC: National Research Council

Noshpitz, J. D. and R. D. Coddington, 1990, *Stressors and the Adjustment Disorders*. Wiley and Sons

Obeyesekere, G., 1990, *The Work of Culture: Symbolic Transformation in Psychoanalysis and Anthropology*. Chicago: University of Chicago Press

Ogbu, J. and H. D. Simons, 1998, Voluntary and Involuntary Minorities: A Cultural-Ecological Theory of School Performance with Some Implications for Education. *Anthropology and Education Quarterly* 29(2):1155–88

Olsen, L., 1998, *Made In America: Immigrant Students in Our Public Schools*. New York: The New Press

Orfield, G., 1998, Commentary on the Education of Mexican Immigrant Children. In M. Suárez-Orozco, ed., *Crossings: Mexican Immigration in Interdisciplinary Perspectives*. Cambridge, MA: Harvard University Press

Organista, P., K. Chun, and G. Marín, eds., 1998, *Readings in Ethnic Psychology*. New York: Routledge

Padilla, A., R. Cervantes, M. Maldonado, and R. Garcia, 1988, Coping Responses to Psychosocial Stressors Among Mexican and Central American Immigrants. *Journal of Community Psychology*. 16:418–27

Pearlin, L. I. and C. Schooler, 1978, The Structure of Coping. *Journal of Health and Social Behavior* 19(3):2–21

Phinney, J., 1998, Ethnic Identity in Adolescents and Adults. In P. Organista, K. Chun, and G. Marín, eds., *Readings in Ethnic Psychology*. New York: Routledge

Portes, A. and Rúmbaut, R., 1990, *Immigrant America: A Portrait*. Berkeley, CA: University of California Press

Portes, A. and L. Hao, 1998, English First or English Only?: E Pluribus Unum: Bilingualism and Language Loss in the Second Generation. *Sociology of Education* 71(4):269–94

Portes, A. and M. Zhou, 1993, The New Second Generation: Segmented Assimilation and Its Variants. *Annals of the American Academy* 530, November

Proposition 187, 1994 *Illegal Aliens. Ineligibility for Public Services. Verification and Reporting*. Initiative Statute. Sacramento, CA: State of California

Roberts, R., C. Roberts, and Y. R. Chen, 1998, Ethnocultural Differences in Prevalence of Adolescent Depression. In P. Organista, K. Chun, and G. Marín, eds., *Readings in Ethnic Psychology*. New York: Routledge

Rodriguez, Luis, 1993, *Always Running*. New York: Touchstone Books

Rogler, L., 1998, Research on Mental Health Services for Hispanics: Targets of Convergence. P. Organista, K. Chun, and G. Marín, eds. *Readings in Ethnic Psychology*. New York: Routledge

Rosenthal, R. and L. Jacobson, 1968, *Pygmalion in the Classroom: Teacher Expectations and Pupils' Intellectual Development*. New York: Holt, Rinehart and Winston

Rúmbaut, R. D., 1977, Life Events, Change, Migration, and Depression. In W. E. Fann, I. Karocan, A. D. Pokorny, and R. L. Willimas, eds., *Phenomenology and Treatment of Depression*. New York: Spectrum

1995, The New Californians: Comparative Research Findings on the Educational Progress of Immigrant Children. In R. Rúmbaut, and W. Cornelius, eds., *California's Immigrant Children*. La Jolla, CA: Center for US–Mexican Studies

1996, *Becoming American: Acculturation, Achievement, and Aspirations Among Children of Immigrants*. Paper presented at the Annual Meeting of the American Association for the Advancement of Science, Baltimore, MD, 10 February

1996, Ties That Bind: Immigration and Immigrant Families in the United States. In *Immigration and Family: Research and Policy on US Immigrants*. A. Booth, A. C. Crouter and N. Landale, eds. New Jersey: Lawrence Erlbaum

1997, Achievement and Ambition Among Children of Immigrants in Southern California. Paper presented to the Jerome Levy Economics Institute of Board College, Annandale-on-the-Hudson, NY

Schlossberg, Nancy K., 1984, *Counseling Adults in Transition: Linking Practice with Theory*. New York: Springer

Seligman, M., 1998, The American Way of Blame. *American Psychological Association Monitor* 29(7):2

Shuval, J., 1980, Migration and Stress. In I. L. Kutasshm *et al.*, eds., *Handbook on Stress and Anxiety: Contemporary Knowledge, Theory, and Treatment*. San Francisco: Jossery-Bass

Simon, Rita J., 1985, *Public Opinion and the Immigrant: Print Media Coverage, 1880–1980*. Lexington, MA: Lexington Books

Sluzki, Carlos, 1979, Migration and Family Conflict, *Family Process* 18(4):379–90

Smajkic, Amer and Stevan Weane, 1995, Special Issues of Newly Arrived Refugee Groups. In Susan Somach, ed., *Issues of War Trauma and Working with Refugees: A Compilation of Resources*. Washington DC: Center for Applied Linguistics Refugee Service Center

Smart, J. F. and D. W. Smart, 1995, Acculturation Stress of Hispanics: Loss and Challenge. *Journal of Counseling and Development* 75:390–6

Somach, Susan, ed., 1995, *Issues of War Trauma and Working with Refugees: A Compilation of Resources*. Washington DC: Center for Applied Linguistics Refugee Service Center

Steinberg, S., 1996, *Beyond the Classroom: Why School Reform Has Failed and What Parents Need to Do*. New York: Simon and Schuster

Stonequist, E. V., 1937, *The Marginal Man: A Study in Personality and Cultural Conflict*. New York: Scribners

Suárez-Orozco, Carola, 1998, The Transitions of Immigration: How Do Men and Women Differ? *DRCLAS News*, (Winter): 6–7

Suárez-Orozco, C. and M. Suárez-Orozco, 1995, *Transformations: Migration, Family Life, and Achievement Motivation Among Latino Adolescents*. Palo Alto, CA: Stanford University Press

Suárez-Orozco, Marcelo M., 1989, *Central American Refugees and US High Schools: A Psychosocial Study of Motivation and Achievement*. Stanford, CA: Stanford University Press

1996, California Dreaming: Proposition 187 and the Cultrual Psychology of Ethnic and Racial Exclusion. *Anthropology and Education Quarterly* 27(2):151–67

1998, *Crossings: Mexican Immigration in Interdisciplinary Perspectives*. Cambridge, MA: Harvard University Press

Suro, R., 1994, California's SOS on Immigration. *The Washington Post*, 29 September

1998, *Strangers Among Us: How Latino Immigration is Transforming America*. New York: Alfred Knopf

Tajfel, H., 1978, *The Social Psychology of Minorities*. New York: Minority Rights Group

Takaki, R., 1989, *Strangers from a Different Shore*. New York: Penguin

Vernez, G., A. Abrahamse, and D. Quigley, 1996, *How Immigrants Fare in US Education*. Santa Monica, CA: Rand

Vigil, Diego, 1988, *Barrio Gangs: Street Life and Identity in Southern California*. Austin: University of Texas Press

Volkan, V. D., 1993, Immigrants and Refugees: A Psychodynamic Perspective. *Mind and Human Interaction* 4(2):63–9

Waters, M., 1990, *Ethnic Options: Choosing Identities in America*. Berkeley: University of California Press

1996, *West Indian Family Resources and Adolescent Outcomes: Trajectories of the Second Generation*. Paper presented at the Annual Meeting of the American Association for the Advancement of Science, Baltimore, MD, 10 February

Waldinger R., 1996, *Still the Promised City? African-Americans and New Immigrants in Postindustrial New York*. Cambridge, MA: Harvard University Press

1997, *Social Capital or Social Closure? – Immigrant Networks in the Labor Market*. Los Angeles: Lewis Center for Regional Policy Studies, University of California, Los Angeles, Working Paper Series, No. 26

Wheaton, B., 1983, Stress, Personal Coping Resources, and Psychiatric Symptoms: An Investigation of Interactive Models. *Journal of Health and Social Behavior* 24(9):208–29

Wills, T. A., 1985, Supportive Functions of Interpersonal Relationships. In S. Cohen and S. L. Symee, eds., *Social Support and Health*. Orlando: Academic Press Inc.

Winnicott, D. W., 1971, *Playing and Reality*. Harmondsworth, England: Penguin

Wong-Fillmore, L., 1991, When Learning a Second Language Means Losing the First. *Early Childhood Research Quarterly* 6:323–46

8 Modern Greek and Turkish identities and the psychodynamics of Greek–Turkish relations

Vamik D. Volkan and Norman Itzkowitz

This chapter examines the evolution of the modern Turkish and Greek identities and the psychological forces at work, both consciously and unconsciously, in the conflictual relationship between these two groups. The term 'identity' is relatively new in psychoanalysis. Freud did not mention it often, and, when he did, it was in a colloquial or literal sense. Erik Erikson was the key figure in bringing this concept to the attention of psychoanalysts. Referring to an individual's identity, Erikson (1956) stated that it 'connotes both a persistent sameness within oneself . . . [and] a persistent sharing of some kind of essential character with others' (1956:57). Revising Erikson's statement, we can say that large-group identity, i.e. Turkish or Greek identity, refers to the subjective experience of millions of people who are linked by a persistent sense of sameness while sharing some characteristics with others in foreign groups.

Peter Loewenberg (1995), a historian and psychoanalyst, notes that nations are 'born' differently. Shared realistic or fantasized perceptions of the past and the manner in which a large group's identity was established influence common attitudes and actions within a given society. When a large group interacts with other groups, particularly neighbours, it must protect its identity at all costs, especially when in crises (Volkan 1997, 1999). Historical events cannot be fully understood without an examination of the shared psychological processes which accompanied them or were initiated by them. This chapter examines history through a psychoanalytic lens. It describes how historians and psychoanalysts may collaborate in illustrating how and why identity issues of large groups emerge as a silent, but important factor in international relationships.

Background

In 1071, at Manzigert (today known as Malazgirt), in eastern Anatolia (Asia Minor), a battle took place between Byzantine forces and the

Seljuk Turks. The Byzantine forces were defeated and Turkish tribes, originally from central Asia, began to settle in Anatolia living side by side and intermarrying with existing inhabitants. Even before the Turkish tribes arrived, a variety of ethnic groups lived in Anatolia. These included Greeks who belonged to the Orthodox Church. Since these Greeks had lived for a long time under the rule of the Byzantine (Eastern Roman) Empire, the newcomer Turks called them *Rum* (Roman), as did the Greeks themselves. The more important affiliation for Anatolia's inhabitants at that time, however, was a religious one. As the Turkish tribes had become Muslim during their migration from central Asia, Islam was established in Anatolia alongside other existing religions. Within a century or so, Anatolia was Turkified, though the Byzantine Empire continued to exist, with reduced territory, after the battle of Manzigert. It came to an end some 300 years later when Constantinople (present day Istanbul) fell to the Ottoman Turks on 29 May 1453.

Even before the fall of Constantinople, however, some areas today considered part of Greece proper had already come under the Ottomans' domination. After the fall of Constantinople, the total Greek world became part of the Ottoman Empire. For practical purposes, Greeks and Turks lived in a kind of 'togetherness', under the Ottoman umbrella, for over 375 years, from 1453 until the emergence of an independent (modern) Greece in the 1830s.

The Ottoman Empire was a multi-religious, multi-lingual, and multi-cultural conglomeration with the Sultan as its supreme ruler. Identity in the Ottoman Empire was corporate rather than individual, and one's main identity derived from one's religious affiliation. It surprises many that it was not until the sixteenth century, when the Ottomans conquered the Arab world, that the Ottoman Empire became a society in which Muslims held the majority. However, Christians and Jews, as well as their religions, were protected in the Empire as these peoples were considered people of the Book, and they were included in a system called the *millet* system (Itzkowitz 1972). The word *millet* came to mean nation in the nineteenth century, but it earlier referred to an organized religious community whose head was responsible to the Ottoman government for the good behaviour of its members, payment of the *cizye* (special capitation) tax, and other obligations. There were the Orthodox Millet, the Jewish Millet, and the Armenian Millet. The Muslims constituted the *Ummah*, the community of God or of Muhammad.

The Greeks belonged to the Orthodox Millet or *Millet-i Rum* (the Roman Millet). Also under this category were Serbs, Vlachs, and others, but the Greeks were dominant in the Church's hierarchy. Over time, Turkish words entered the Greek language. The resulting dialect could only be understood by those who had knowledge of both languages. Many Greeks also became *Turcophone*, speaking Turkish, but writing it in Greek letters.

During the Ottoman period, Turks and Greeks cooperated more than they fought (Mango 1987). Many Ottomans of Greek origin (and many more of Greek Orthodox origin, i.e. Serbs and Bosnians) had been levied and educated through the *devşirme* to hold office in the Ottoman establishment (*devşirme* refers to a process through which a Christian youth, taken away from his family, becomes a Muslim and receives education to serve the Sultan). Other Greeks retained their Christian religion while working for the Ottoman State. Some served as translators for the Ottoman government, some even served as governors of Moldavia and Walachia in the eighteenth century. Such Greek family names as Mavrocardatos, Ipsilanti, and Capodistrias are familiar in the annals of Ottoman affairs.

During the last century of the Ottoman Empire, things went badly for the Ottomans, and from the 1850s on the Empire was seen as 'the sick man of Europe'. In 1821, Greeks in the Morea area rebelled. This signalled the beginning of the Greek War of Independence, and it eventually led to the formation of an independent Greek State. Nonetheless, even after a Greek State had been carved out of the Ottoman Empire, many Greeks still remained within Ottoman territory. A few of them would serve as Ottoman ambassadors to Athens, London, and St Petersburg, and another governed what is now southern Bulgaria. Alexander Caratheodry, an Ottoman Greek, represented the Sultan at the Congress of Berlin (1878).

It would be a mistake, however, to consider the Greeks and Turks of the Ottoman Empire congenial 'brothers and sisters'. Although conquerors and conquered had mingled blood throughout four centuries of 'togetherness', differences in large-group identity depend more upon historical processes, belief systems, shared traumas, glories, and myths, than on blood ties and cooperation in administrative matters.

The 'birth' of a modern Greek nation

The mental image of circumstances surrounding the 'birth' of modern Greece in the 1830s affected its identity as a nation. To achieve independence as a nation-state, the Greeks had to accomplish three tasks:

1. fight for independence against the declining Ottoman Empire;
2. reclaim members of their ethnic group in remaining and former territories of the Empire (irredentism); and
3. create a culturally homogenous people.

These three necessities were also applicable to other Christian nation-states born out of the Ottoman Empire. Greece's movement to build a new large-group identity, however, contained a unique element not shared by others: external support, and even pressure, for a specific kind of new identity. The British, French, and Russians (supporters of the Greek War of Independence) demanded that the modern Greek identity be Hellenic and respond to their nostalgia for the restoration of a pre-Christian Hellenic civilization that had been in eclipse for some 2,000 years, long before the Turks and Greeks met at Manzigert. In spite of the ebb and flow of history over such a great span of time (Herzfeld 1986), Europeans confidently expected to see the characteristics of Homer in post-liberation Greeks. The neoclassicism that began in seventeenth- and eighteenth-century Europe as an aesthetic and philosophical idea was to be physically embodied in modern-day Greece and Greeks. This idealistic and hopeful attitude was succinctly expressed in an 1822 speech by American President James Monroe. 'The mention of Greece fills the mind with the utmost exalted sentiments and arouses in our bosoms the best feelings of which our nature is susceptible.' In reality, just before the Greek War of Independence, most Greeks still called themselves 'Romans'. Vlachavas (d. 1809), the priest rebel leader who rose against the Ottomans, declared: 'A Romneos I was born, a Romneos I will die' (Baggally, 1968:84). Interestingly though, a ballad composed a few years later for Diakos, another rebel leader, had him declare: 'I was born a Greek, and a Greek I will die' (Baggally, 1968:92–3). A 'new' large-group identity was in the process of being formed.

The villages in what later became known as Greece had totally Greek ethnic compositions, and the villagers retained their Orthodox Christian religion and customs. Folk traditions characterized their daily lives. Greek women, married at twelve or thirteen years of age, did the farm work, spun and wove, and helped with the harvest. Greek men raised sheep. Those near the sea were sponge divers (Lewis 1971). Some Europeans, and the few Americans who came to help Greece start a new nation-state, were disappointed, even indignant, to discover that among Greece's peasants there were no warrior-heroes like Achilles or Ajax, no statesmen like Pericles, no philosophers like Socrates or Plato, and no poets of the calibre of Aeschylus or Sophocles. There was, in fact, little likeness between nineteenth-century Greeks and the idealized Greeks from ancient history that held such sway on the imaginations of European liberators.

Nevertheless, the idea of a Greek renaissance persisted, perpetuated and embellished by the romantic figure of Lord Byron and his coterie of poets and adventurers. Furthermore, a small group of elite Greeks, educated in Europe, also longed for the revival of a long-forgotten Hellenic identity and rejection of the Romeic one. It was no easy task.

Herzfeld (1986) identifies three major obstacles to the project of re-Hellenizing Greece. First, the people in the new nation-state found it difficult to accept that they should be identical to their land's long-lost inhabitants. Most of the common people had no idea what the founders were asking them to be. Secondly, they could never be 'Hellenic' in the old, pagan sense of the word, since they strongly adhered to the Christian faith and the Orthodox Church. Finally, it was hard to be Hellenic while using a Romeic language, mixed with much Turkish and Arabic.

To deal with these difficulties, Greek intellectuals sought a continuum of Greek life from ancient Greece through the Byzantine period to the nineteenth century. They studied folk tales, dances, poetry, and lifestyles to substantiate this continuum. Thus, Hellenism was embraced, but under the above conditions and pressures, in a special way. They made it 'intimately personal' (Herzfeld 198:32) and identified it as a mystical sensibility that they felt could not be understood even by their Western supporters. George Evlambios in 1843 declared that foreigners should not attempt the impossible by trying to understand the mysteries of Greekness. Greeks still often and openly express such sentiments. It was ironic that the Hellenism thesis, although initially externally directed, would in practice ultimately lead the Greeks to differentiate themselves from the very 'others' who had helped to define them. Differentiation from the Turks would be more rigidified.

A shared and mostly unconscious psychological mechanism was needed for the maintenance of Hellenism: the wholesale externalization and projection of the unwanted aspects of the 'togetherness', which were perceived as oriental (and therefore inferior) by the West. In the Western view, 'oriental' meant being lazy and dirty and not having a very highly civilized background. The Turks provided a handy reservoir for the Greeks' massive externalizations and projections since during their 'togetherness' they had shared some similar characteristics and cross-identifications. Upon 'separating' from the Turks, the Greeks wanted to retain only the 'good' and civilized aspects of their former 'togetherness' which could fit into Hellenism and to dispose of the 'bad' or oriental aspects by externalizing and projecting them onto the closest reservoir.

After embracing the Hellenic identity for most of the first forty years following the Greek War of Independence, Greeks began to weave in elements of the cultural and religious heritage of Byzantium. The urge to retain this aspect of Greek heritage was articulated in the middle and late 1800s by intellectuals, especially through the words of individuals such as Spyridon Zamblios (1856, 1859) and Nikolaos G. Politis (1876, 1882). They took back glorified aspects of Byzantium, and now Greek identity became a *composite* of Hellenic (ancient pre-Christian Greek) and Byzantine (Christian Greek) elements. With this development, a second wave of massive externalizations and projections, of the unwanted aspects (laziness, orientalness) of the Eastern Romeic identity, was heaped upon the Turks. Once made, these externalizations and projections became part of the main support of the modern Greek identity composite. After this, because keeping the new identity in place meant maintaining the externalizations and projections, it became impossible for Greeks to ever feel 'together' with Turks again. Meanwhile, Adamontios Koreas helped develop *katharevousa*, the neoclassical form of the modern Greek language that required the rejection of Turkish words.

The Greeks had to get rid of the Turk *within* themselves, created during the time of 'togetherness'. No one explains this better than the great Greek writer, Nikos Kazantzakis. In his *Report to Greco*, he states:

To gain freedom first of all from the Turks, that was the initial step; after that, later, this new struggle began: to gain freedom from the inner Turk – from ignorance, malice and envy, from fear and laziness, from dazzling false ideas, and finally from idols, all of them, even the most revered and beloved. (Kazantzakis 1965:68)

The reactivation and maintenance of the Greeks' chosen trauma

The term 'chosen trauma' refers to the mental representation (a cohesive image) of an event that caused a large group of people (i.e., an ethnic group) to feel victimized, humiliated by another group, and to suffer losses, especially that of self esteem (Volkan 1991, 1992, 1997, 1999; Volkan and Itzkowitz 1994). While a group does not choose to be victimized, it does 'choose', consciously as well as unconsciously, to psychologize and mythologize what has occurred and define its identity by referring to the event.

Chosen traumas are linked with the inability or difficulty of the large group in question to mourn; for a trauma to be 'chosen', it must be one that cannot be mourned adaptively. It cannot become a 'futureless memory' (Tähkä 1984). Furthermore, the humiliation pertaining to it cannot be reversed. We believe that Gampel's (in this volume; see also Gampel 1996) notion of 'indigestibility of trauma' is applicable here. The adults in a large group and within child–mother (and other caregivers) interactions pass the mental representation of the chosen trauma, along with related feelings of loss, hurt, and shame, and associated defences, to the next generation mostly in non-verbal ways. There is an unconscious expectation that the next generation will complete both the task of mourning and the reversal of humiliation. Each successive generation receives a modified account of the event, but its overall place in the psychology of the group changes very little, and it continues to influence attitudes towards any other threatening group directly or indirectly associated with those responsible for the historic offence.

Once a trauma is 'chosen', the historical truth about it recedes in importance; what matters is its place in the large-group identity formation of the victims and in their establishment of mental representations of the victimizers. It is often the case, too, that the mental representations of other past traumas are condensed with it. While within some generations the chosen trauma may appear to be dormant, it can always be inflamed when the group perceives a threat to its identity or when a leader, for personal or political reasons, unconsciously or consciously, brings it to the group's attention. The influence of a chosen trauma within a society is often expressed by the group's shared political processes. For example, exaggerated entitlement attitudes may be apparent in the prevailing political system, or the subsequent generations may remain infused with a sense of victimhood that influences their political attitudes toward their neighbours.

Let us now examine the Greeks' chosen trauma. Starting around 1868, when Greek Byzantine heritage was condensed with Hellenism, irredentism grew. What made Greek irredentism special was its connection with the political ideology later called the 'Megali Idea' (the Great Idea), which is 'the doctrine . . . whereby all the lands of Classical and Byzantine Hellenism should be reclaimed for the reborn nation' (Herzfeld 1986:119). The Megali Idea did not become mainstream ideology until the middle of the nineteenth century, but its origin actually reached back to the fall of Constantinople. As Young (1969) observed, the seeds of the Megali Idea were sown soon after the Turkish conquest of Constantinople. The Greeks reactivated the collapse of the Byzantine Empire as their chosen trauma.

When the Turks attacked Constantinople in 1453, the Byzantine Empire had already shrunk to little more than the city itself. Thus, one might observe that the ultimate collapse was inevitable, but what matters here is the mental representation of the event and not the historical reality that Byzantium's fall was well under way. The psychological implications of the capture of Constantinople by the Turks created shock waves among European Christians, and its seizure was seen as a reflection of God's judgment upon the sins of Christians everywhere (Schwoebel 1967). Since Constantinople had been taken on a Tuesday, every Tuesday thereafter was regarded as an unpropitious day for Christians. And, in spite of the fact that Rome had refused to provide support to Constantinople against the Turks, word of Byzantium's fall was received there with disbelief. The Turkish victory was seen as a knife plunged into the heart of Christianity. Aeneas Sylvius Piccolomini, a future pope, wrote to Pope Nicholas V on 12 July 1453, that the Turks had killed Homer and Plato for the second time (Schwoebel 1967).

Even after the reality of the Turkish capture of Constantinople became clear, the Western world could not escape the trauma's blow. The desire to undo the sense of loss associated with it expressed itself in rumbling about organizing another Crusade. Nothing came of such talk, but the idea persisted. Christians of the Ottoman territories sang of their lands, 'Again, with years, with time, again they will be ours', a refrain that demonstrates their attempt to deny the changes and undo their loss. Denial also appeared in other ways. For example, some sought a continuous link between the Turks and the Byzantines: this link would lessen the need for Byzantines and other Christians to feel pain. Even Westerners contributed to the project of finding 'good' ancient origins for the Turks. For example, Giovanni Maria Filefo, a humanist, declared that Mehmet II, the Sultan who had seized Constantinople, was a Trojan. Felix Fabri, a German, explored the idea that Turks were descended from Teucer, son of Telemon and friend of Hercules, and the Trojan princess Hesione (Volkan and Itzkowitz 1992).

While these pseudo-historical efforts to find a link between the two sides continued as a way to make loss and change tolerable, a counter-attempt tried to unlink them so that the Byzantines could maintain *their* identity, and this, in turn, led to stereotyping the Turks as the 'aggressive other'. Of course, in the case of the fall of Constantinople, the Turks *were* the aggressors. But to Western Christians, Turkish aggression was different from Western aggression: it was more 'uncivilized' and imbued with sexual symbolism. The epitome of this symbolism was the image of the virile, young Turkish sultan who conquered Constantinople.

Sexual symbolism

Sultan Mehmet II, only 21 when he seized Constantinople, is known as Mehmet the Conqueror, or the Grand Turk. Mehmet's mother is thought to have been a Serbian or Macedonian slave who was brought to the harem of Sultan Murat I and became a Muslim and wife to Murat. When Mehmet was going through his adolescent passage, Murat voluntarily stepped down to allow his twelve-year-old son to reign as sultan, with the assistance of his two mentors and his father's grand vizier, Halil Pasha. Murat had arranged a peace treaty with the Serbs and Hungarians and things were relatively calm when Mehmet became sultan, but military conflicts with the Serbs in the Balkans soon heated up and presented new challenges to the Ottoman leadership. Within two years, Murat retook the throne from then fourteen-year-old Mehmet, a move that was engineered in large part by the Grand Vizier Halil Pasha. Halil's actions humiliated Mehmet, as if saying to the adolescent sultan: 'You are not good enough for a grown-up's job. Your father is better than you and you cannot compete with his power and prestige.' Mehmet's internal response to this affront may later have pushed him to excel and surpass his father by conquering Constantinople, something his ancestors had not been able to do.

During adolescence, a 'second individuation' (Blos 1979) occurs, and a youth internally revisits his Oedipal (as well as pre-Oedipal) issues for review and resolution. Because Sultan Murat remained friendly towards his son and took him with him on various campaigns, it seems likely that to a great extent the boy displaced the 'bad' Oedipal father image (associated with being dethroned and demoted) onto Halil and the Byzantine Emperor. When Mehmet was nineteen, his father died, and he again became sultan. His mother also died between his first and second enthronements.

Young Mehmet addressed the task of defeating the Byzantine Empire with youthful zeal, and the Turks constructed the largest cannons ever made in order to blast a hole in the impenetrable wall protecting Constantinople. The Byzantine Emperor Constantine was killed as the final Ottoman assault surged through the opening in the city wall. His head was cut off and shown to Mehmet. (From a psychological viewpoint, it is also interesting that, soon after the Emperor's death, the triumphant young sultan ordered the arrest of Halil Pasha, the other displaced 'bad' father, and had him put to death.) After Constantine's death, Mehmet declared himself the new chief protector of the Christian Church (the mother), his own mother originally having been a Christian. According to Oedipal fantasy, a son was replacing his father. It was widely believed – as shown in pseudo-historical accounts of the event, in oral histories passed down through generations, and even in modern fictional renditions of the fall of Constantinople – that Mehmet the Conqueror slept with Constantine's daughters. Whatever the truth, such a conjecture echoes an Oedipal theme wherein the father (Constantine in this case) having been killed, the son (young Mehmet) sleeps with his women.

Since detailed information about young Mehmet's internal world is not available, we cannot speak of Mehmet's Oedipus complex with a sense of certainty. Obviously, his preoccupation with Constantinople and seizure of the city should *not* be attributed solely to his unresolved Oedipal strivings. One can assume, however, that his internal motivations might have found some expression in his political and military activities. And, what is important here is *not* the accuracy of Mehmet's Oedipal strivings and his possible wish to surpass his father, but rather the fact that Oedipal fantasies are reflected in the images of this Turkish victory (especially among Greeks) that have been passed down through generations to the present.

The seizure of Constantinople by the youthful and virile sultan through the opening of a hole in the city wall was perceived as a rape, which created an image, especially among the Greeks and other Christians, of Turks as lustful people. What was difficult to assimilate was the fact that the 'rape' was performed not by the father, but by the son, who had achieved an Oedipal triumph. A noted nineteenth-century historian, von Hammer-Purgstall, even wrote that the young sultan lusted after the younger son of Grand Duke Lucas Notaras, who had led the Byzantine fleet in defence of Constantinople (von Hammer-Purgstall 1835–43). Other Christian writers later repeated similar characterizations in 'serious' history books. Thus, a kind of boundless lust was assigned to Mehmet the Conqueror. Historical fact, however, describes Mehmet as a highly educated man who had been taught by special tutors in his youth. He spoke several languages, including Greek, was familiar with Greek mythology, and loved to have discussions on religious and metaphysical topics. He was known as a generous person and after capturing Constantinople worked to restore economic, social, and religious (both Islamic and Orthodox Christian) stability in the city. Nevertheless, the image of Mehmet as lustful prevailed. Over time, Constantinople, later named Istanbul, became symbolized as a fallen or grieving woman, by both Christians and Turks, and was celebrated as such in folk songs and poems throughout many centuries (Volkan and Itzkowitz 1984, 1994; Halman 1992).

The two waves of massive externalizations and projections by the 'new' Greeks onto the Turks led to the perception of Turks as lazy and dirty. These characteristics were adjoined to the projections of lustfulness and aggressiveness that accompanied the chosen trauma of the fall of Constantinople when the Greeks reactivated it in the nineteenth century. Currently, whenever there are political problems between Turkey and Greece, the Greek press, as well as politicians and the military, often refer to the Turks as 'rapists' (Volkan and Itzkowitz 1994).

The absence of an enduring strong leader

The appearance of a strong and enduring leader during and soon after a crisis confers legitimacy on a large group's move from one political or social ideology to another and establishes 'borders' for the transition. For the large group, the function of such a leader is analogous to the role of a 'good' Oedipal father for the developing child. At the Oedipal age, the child (either boy or girl) is drastically transforming his or her self image, and the role of the father (in the traditional family) or parents is essential in providing a 'border' for this transformation. There otherwise remains an ambiguity as to how far this transformation should spread. With this ambiguity comes anxiety of overstepping one's bounds and facing unknown territories and dangers.

During the Greek War of Independence and the formation of the new Greek state, the Greeks had many captains but no single nationally recognized supreme leader. Because the State was not yet formed and they did not have a regular army, the rebellion started with *klephts*, bandits hiding in the mountains who were already engaged in fighting the authorities. As the Greek rebellion became a war of independence, the *klephts* were joined by local merchants and priests, local and diaspora elite, and a handful of European liberals. Thus, the forces used in the Greek War of Independence remained irregular.

Although there were Greek heroes during this war – and foreign ones such as Lord Byron – no long-lasting, strong leadership emerged. President Ionnes Kapodistrias, who was elected in 1827 for a seven-year term, was considered such a leader by some. However, his attempts to turn Greece into a new centralized state won the hostility of most of the population, and, in the end, he became a hated man. Eventually he was assassinated by the Mavro Michili family, important landowners in the Morea, where the Greek War of Independence had begun.

Not having a supreme parent figure to consolidate Greece's new identity and create a definite border to support it, Greeks continued to adhere to irredentism (Megali Idea) as a psychological/political force.

The physical borders of classical Greece and the Byzantine Empire were ambiguous and fluid – so how could modern Greeks decide which lands to reappropriate, and when to stop? Since they had no definite answer to this question, the Greeks tended to press for continual expansion, but with anxiety. They succeeded in expanding against the Ottoman territories until the collapse of the Empire and the birth of modern Turkey. One characteristic of this expansion was that, except for their Asia Minor campaign (1919–22), Greeks generally employed irregulars rather than organized, disciplined troops in almost all expansionist undertakings against the Ottoman Empire, keeping alive the tradition of the Greek War of Independence.

The modern Turkish identity

The psychology of the formation of the modern Turkish identity contrasts with that of the Greeks. The Turkish War of Independence, which occurred about 100 years after the beginning of the Greek War of Independence, followed the Ottoman defeat in the First World War. It resembled nineteenth-century western European revolutions that aimed at removing the monarchy and restricting the scope of religion. For Turks, winning their war of independence resulted in the collapse of the Ottoman Empire which had been rapidly declining for some time.

The Ottoman *millet* system functioned well, for practical purposes, until the nineteenth century, when it was challenged by drastic changes in Europe which led to an increase in nationalistic sentiments and the intrusion of European powers as they championed one or another of the *millets*. The Ottomans' response to this challenge was too little and too late. The last century of the Ottoman Empire was marked by attempts at reforms (such as *Tanzimat*, a process similar to *perestroika*), conflicts and uprisings within the borders, wars with outside enemies, political and social suppression, and human suffering.

During this last and troubled century of the Ottoman Empire, Turks made serious efforts to reconsider their own identity. There were three alternatives. The first was to extend the Ottoman identity to all of its citizens, regardless of their ethnic or religious adherence. This was unsuccessful since, after the French Revolution, investment in ethnicity and nationalism had increased in Europe and within the Ottoman Empire. The second alternative was to put all Muslims in the Empire under the umbrella of Pan-Islamism, but ethnic differences among Muslims of the Empire (Turks and Arabs, for example) precluded the success of Pan-Islamism. The last alternative was to focus on the expansion of the Turkish identity alone. Under this umbrella, Turks, and those who felt like Turks, would be combined (pan-Turanism, *Turan* meaning the land of Turks).

Since there were Turks or Turkic peoples throughout Asia and Europe, the third option, an expanded Turkish identity, might appear to have had the potential to create a powerful political and cultural force. But this idea remained a fantasy due to major and minor differences among the Turkic peoples, to the weakness of the Ottoman Empire at the time, and to the restrictions that an existing government could put on expansionist ideologies. All three alternatives had one aim in common – to keep the sultan in place and in power. A fundamental change which would establish a new Turkish identity apart from the sultan and Ottoman traditions had to await the end of the First World War and the Turkish War of Independence.

The Turkish struggle for independence contrasted greatly with that of the Greeks a century earlier. During the First World War and the Turkish War of Independence, Turks fought major European Christian powers as well as Muslim Arabs in the Middle East. Unlike the Greeks, however, the Turks had an indisputable charismatic leader in Mustafa Kemal (Atatürk, or Father Turk), who provided military cohesion during the struggle and political cohesion after the war was won. The Turkish War of Independence was also fought with a disciplined regular army, and was not burdened by dependence on irregular forces and individualistic adventurers. Accordingly, modern Turkey was able to avoid the general 'lawlessness' that had afflicted the new Greek state.

Atatürk and his associates created a National Pact (*Misak-i Milli*) which drew physical borders (and, in a sense, also psychological ones) indicating the geographical scope of new Turkey (with the exception of the *Hatay* (Alexandretta) which was incorporated by means of a plebiscite in 1938). Turkey would harbour no irredentist aspirations towards former territories of the Ottoman Empire, nor towards territories outside the Empire inhabited by Turks. Thus, modern Turkey did not have the problems that a Hellenistic and Byzantine heritage had raised for Greece. On the contrary, the National Pact contributed greatly to the new Turkish identity by distinctly shaping its borders.

A large part of the population of the new Turkish state consisted of Turks, and those Muslims who considered themselves Turks, who had been forced out of their centuries-old Balkan lands through numerous ethnic purification operations similar to those recently seen in the former Yugoslavia. There was also a forced exchange of population between Turkey and Greece engendered by the 1923 Lausanne Treaty. In effect, there was an attempt to keep a homogeneous population within the borders of modern Turkey.

Although more than 95 per cent of the citizens of the new Turkish Republic were Muslims, homogeneity was based not on religion but on citizenship. This is one of the reasons why ethnic Kurds within the new Turkish Republic, who played an important role in Atatürk's victories during the War of Independence, were put under the Turkish umbrella.

Two splits

The new Turkish nationalism was not to be a continuation of Ottomanism, for secularism sharply differentiated the new Turkish Republic from the Ottoman Empire. Instead, Turkey was to adopt a Westernized identity, this in spite of the fact that during the First World War and the Turkish War of Independence, Turks fought mainly against European powers. Atatürk's interests were in modernizing Turkey, and under his tutelage the country became engaged in a vigorous process of Westernization. After the establishment of the Turkish Republic in 1923, the Turks adopted Western criminal and civil laws, changed the dress code, and adapted the Latin alphabet to the Turkish language, for example.

For the political leaders of modern Turkey, the West was both a 'former enemy' and 'an ideal object'. This paradox was handled by two 'splits', one within individuals and one within the society as a whole. The first 'split' existed within individuals who comprised the Westernized Turkish revolutionary elite and allowed them to perceive Greeks (as well as Europeans) as both enemy and ideal.

Stories, novels, and plays written between 1909 and 1956 by the well-known Turkish writer Yakup Kadri Karaosmanoğlu, a friend of both Atatürk and his successor İsmet İnönü, shed light on the image of the Greek in Turkish literature (Millas 1991) and illustrate a split within individuals who were members of the revolutionary elite. His writings include references to the Greek invasion of Asia Minor and describe irresponsible Greek soldiers who terrorized the citizenry, dishonoured women, and killed children. Paradoxically, he also compares Atatürk to ancient Greek gods and Atatürk's dining room to a gathering of Socrates.

Soon after the Turkish Republic was founded, the Ministry of Culture sponsored translations of Western ideas, novels, and poems, producing massive volumes of books to be read by the new Turks and their children. Included were ancient Greek myths and the works of Homer and others. Jews who fled to Turkey to escape the Nazis in Europe also contributed to Turkey's Westernization; they helped found a Turkish opera and ballet, and many became university professors. Meanwhile, the modern Greeks were stereotyped as 'clamorers', persons who could never be satisfied and who would raise a clamour as they demanded more and more; they were not perceived as dangerous.

The Westernized Turkish revolutionary elite called themselves 'enlightened ones' and separated themselves from the traditional and conservative segments of the population. This was the second 'split', the one within society. Since the 'enlightened ones' were in power and the initial leaders of modern Turkey, Atatürk and İnönü, were heroes, this societal 'split' was obscured, and its political implications were not, immediately, apparent.

The Turkish revolution had come from above and at first it looked as though it would slowly and steadily seep down, especially through the influence of its charismatic leader. As the 'enlightened ones' tried to formulate a new Turkish identity, externalization and projection of unwanted elements were necessary for the cohesion of the new identity. Unlike the Greeks, the Turks did not make wholesale externalizations and projections onto the 'other' with whom they had had a 'togetherness' or onto those with whom they had recently fought. The parent figures (Atatürk and İnönü) promoted identification with the West and therefore prohibited excessive externalizations and projections onto the former enemies. As modern Greeks were perceived as not dangerous, they could be tolerated and externalizations and projections onto them were mild. Instead, the Turkish elite considered Islamic fanaticism the main cause of the demise of the Ottoman Empire, and they thus projected unwanted elements onto the royalty, i.e. the Sultan and the Caliph, the religious leader, who were expelled from the new Turkish Republic, and onto other traditional and conservative segments of the population. In a sense, 'unwanted' elements remained *within* the society, within the Turks themselves.

Difficulty in large-group mourning

When the Ottomans joined the ranks of the losers in the First World War, there was so much loss and grief among the Turks of the Empire it was said that walking through the streets of Istanbul one could hear nothing but the sorrowful voices of mothers who had lost their sons during this and the preceding Balkan Wars. But after the Turkish War of Independence, the Turks' idealization of Atatürk and his vision of modern Turkey kept them from grieving further over the loss of the Empire. They felt adequately compensated for their losses by having gained something good – a charismatic leader. As long as Atatürk's grand image could be maintained, to have lost an empire was nothing. In fact, Atatürk's image emerged as the sacred symbol of new Turkishness.

After the Atatürk and İnönü eras, modern Turkey went through turbulent times and its identity continued to transform. Unsuccessful attempts at shared mourning over the lost Ottoman identity contributed to this turmoil, as did failure to adopt a Western lifestyle, on the part of some citizens, especially those in the countryside. The shared psychological motivations were intertwined with real-world issues. A poor economy helped the continuation of the split within society.

In the 1960s, the conflict between the 'enlightened ones' and the conservatives became more open and spawned an 'identity crisis' for the Turks, which included a bloody, political left–right dichotomy. This in turn would be at the foundation of the Turkish–Kurdish PKK (Kurdish Workers' Party) conflict of the late 1980s and 1990s, since the founder of the PKK, Abdullah Öcalan, or Apo, had switched from being a leftist terrorist to becoming an ethnic terrorist. Captured by special Turkish forces in 1999, Apo is currently awaiting trial.

The Kurdish conflict called attention to such questions as 'What is a Turk?' and 'What does it feel like to be a Turk?' In the 1990s, the Turkish news media and scholarly conferences were full of polls and ideas concerning these questions. The homogeneity issue faced a tough challenge and made its demands on the Turkish identity. The upsurge of Orthodox Islam, especially among the newly urbanized population, was an extension of this problem, intertwined with expectations that equality under the eyes of God in Orthodox Islam could compensate for inequality in economic status.

The Cyprus factor

The problem of Turkey's identity difficulties would have had less to do with modern Turkish–Greek relationships had not events in Cyprus connected the continuing transformation of the modern Turkish identity with Cyprus. An Ottoman island since the early 1570s, Cyprus has been home to both Greeks and Turks for centuries. It was first 'leased' to the British in 1878 and then legally decreed to them after the First World War. When Cyprus became a republic in 1960 (after a period of terrorism carried out by Greek Cypriots against the British rulers), a constitution divided power on the island between Cypriot Greeks and Turks, prescribing, for example, that the president of the new republic would be Greek and the vice-president, Turkish. The Greeks perceived this new development as a step towards *Enosis* (union with Greece) in keeping with the spirit of the Megali Idea (Markides 1977). Within three years of the establishment of the Republic of Cyprus, Cypriot Turks were forced by Cypriot Greeks to live in enclaves under subhuman conditions. While the Turks had previously owned 35 per cent of the island, they were now squeezed onto 3 per cent of the land. The mainland Turkish reaction to the events in Cyprus emotionally, if not legally, challenged the foundation of the *Misak-i Milli* (the National Pact). In 1974, a fight among Cypriot Greeks resulted in a coup. It appeared that *Enosis* would materialize, and Cypriot Turks might be annihilated. The Turkish military intervened and the result was a *de facto* partitioning of the island into northern Turkish and southern Greek sections. The Cypriot Turks later declared their own state, the Turkish Republic of Northern Cyprus, which is officially recognized by Turkey only. Turkish preoccupation with Cyprus resurrected echoes of the Ottoman past, causing a review of the lost Empire, or, psycho-analytically speaking, a group mourning.

It is ironic that mourning the Ottoman Empire was triggered by the 'gaining' of land in Cyprus (although the 37 per cent of the island Turks gained in 1974 was not significantly more than the 35 per cent they had owned in the former British Cyprus). This belated mourning led to a further separation between the heirs of people belonging to a former *millet* system – the Cypriot Greeks – and those of conquerors, the former Ottoman Turks or Cypriot Turks. For Cypriot Turks and Cypriot Greeks, 'togetherness' had not come to an end with the Greek and Turkish Wars of Independence: it continued until the physical and psychological division of Cyprus (Volkan 1979).

The world has been busy attempting to 'reunify' the islanders, an idea that psychologically threatens both parties, albeit on an unconscious level. Large groups who have been 'together' for a long time – for centuries – and then abruptly separated have a tendency to hold more stubbornly onto rituals that maintain and support their separate identities. The history of Cyprus, and international efforts to resolve the so-called Cyprus problem, keep the Turks and the Greeks (both in Cyprus and in their respective motherlands) on their toes. Behind the political statements, so many of which seem contrary to the psychological wish to remain 'separate', there remains a threat of 'togetherness' and identity confusion. The remaining ambiguity of borders (both physical and psychological) between Turks and Greeks in Cyprus as well as in the Aegean Sea is the crucial psychological factor that poisons present Turkish–Greek relationships.

Concluding remarks

The differences between the ways modern Greece and modern Turkey were born and developed created different large-group psychological processes. These processes are still active, silently as well as openly, in the political relationships between the two countries. The two neighbours cannot 'hear' each other's positions with empathic ears because their frames of reference pertaining to large-group identity and nationalism differ. The continuation of Turkish–Greek conflict is psychologically necessary because such conflicts serve to mend each large group's identity demands and difficulties.

There are also similarities: neither Turks nor Greeks have successfully mourned all their past losses or resolved all their past traumas, nor have they modified their negative images of the other group. The Greeks have made *Turkokratia*, their shared perception of the conditions of Greek life under the Ottomans, a marker of their present-day identity. This augments both a sense of victimization and a sense of entitlement. Attempts at genuine friendships with present-day Turks threaten this marker and cause anxiety. Instead, the sense of entitlement embodied in the Megali Idea has to be maintained.

After the Greek defeat during the Turkish War of Independence, Turks perceived the Greeks' maintenance of the Megali Idea as merely clamor – thus not dangerous. This perception drastically changed when the Greeks attempted to take over the island of Cyprus. In addition, the Greeks' wish to expand their territorial seas in the Aegean, thus effectively turning the Aegean Sea into a 'Greek lake', further threatened the Turks. Greek irredentism was answered by the elimination of constrictions provided for the Turks by *Misak-i Milli*. Now each side would see the other as wishing to expand their territories.

For a long time after Atatürk's death in 1938, his image continued to bolster the modern Turkish spirit. He was literally preserved as well: his body was embalmed and was not actually buried for fifteen years. Muslim tradition requires that a dead body be ritually washed, wrapped in white linen, and placed in a coffin from which it should be removed for interment before the next sunset. This tradition was broken for Atatürk whose body was literally needed to help Turks deal with the unfinished psychological business of working through the loss of empire, mourning their losses, transforming their political system, and building a new identity. Atatürk became 'Immortal Atatürk' (Volkan and Itzkowitz 1984), and his immortality was sounded in the writings of Turkish poets and journalists, echoed among politicians and voiced by the common people. By the late 1980s and 1990s, however, the Turkish elite, including former President Turgut Özal, began to indicate that it was time for Atatürk to rejoin the ranks of mortals.

As the people's image of Atatürk became more realistic, he stopped serving as a 'cure' for Turkish loss and injury, and large-group mourning began to take place. Large-group mourning of past losses is usually not experienced as a shared sadness and grief (Volkan 1997). In fact, the average citizen is often not aware that a large-group mourning is in process. It takes its course in societal actions, where its derivatives appear in the review of past affiliations such as emotional attachment to religious institutions of the Ottoman Empire and contemplation of how to integrate them in the modern identity.

Derivatives of Turkish mourning can also be found in the unusual government established in Turkey in 1996. For the first time in its history, the Republic of Turkey inducted a conservative Islamic prime minister, Necmettin Erbakan, who began his tenure by forming a coalition with a secular party led by a Westernized woman, former prime minister Tansu Çiller. This coalition tried to incorporate more Islamic ideas into government activities and was later forced out of power by the staunch Turkish military commanders who perceive themselves as the protector of Atatürk's Westernized ideas. The Turks could no longer find it convenient simply to complain about Greek 'clamoring' and to blame Greeks for Turkey's difficulties in integrating with Europe. They declared that a rift between Islamic traditionalists who oppose Westernization and secular Turks who seek further westernization of Turkish identity, is a grave danger itself.

What Turkey and Greece need are leaders who are psychologically informed enough to be more comfortable with ambiguity. Such leaders would realize that a push toward a new kind of 'togetherness', that is, a political rapprochement between the two countries, may increase anxiety but will not prove fatal. Another way of dealing with the poison in the Turkish–Greek relationship is to secure international help in creating unambiguous borders both in Cyprus and the Aegean Sea.

Bibliography

Baggally, J. W., 1968, *Greek Historical Folksongs*. Chicago: Argonaut

Blos, P., 1979, *The Adolescent Passage*. New York: International Universities Press

Emde, R. N., 1992, Positive Emotions for Psychoanalytic Theory: Surprises from Infancy Research and New Directions. *Journal of American Psychoanalytic Association* (Supplement)39:5–44

Erikson, E. H., 1956, The Problem of Ego Identification. *Journal of the American Psychoanalytic Association*. 4:56–121

Evlambios, G., 1843, *The Amaranth: The Roses of Hellas Reborn: Folk Poems of the Modern Greeks* (in Greek and Russian). St Petersburg: Academy of Sciences (Greek edition: Athens: Notis Karavias, 1973)

Freud, S., 1921 [1961], Group Psychology and the Analysis of the Ego *Standard Edition*. London: Hogarth Press, 65–143

Gampel, Y., 1996, The Interminable Uncanniness. In *Psychoanalysis at the Political Border: Essays in Honor of Rafael Moses*. L. Rangell and R. Moses-Hrushovski, eds., New York: International Universities Press

Halman, T. H., 1992, Istanbul. In *A Last Lullaby*. T. Halman, ed. Merrick, NY: Cross Cultural Communications, 8–9

Herzfeld, M., 1986, *Ours Once More: Folklore, Ideology, and the Making of Modern Greece*. New York: Pella

Itzkowitz, N., 1972, *Ottoman Empire and Islamic Tradition*. New York: Alfred A. Knopf

Jacobson, E., 1964, *The Self and the Object World*. New York: International Universities Press

Kazantzakis, N., 1965, *Report to Greco*. Trans. P. A. Bien. New York: Simon & Schuster

Kernberg, O. D., 1975, *Borderline Conditions and Pathological Narcissism*. New York: Jason Aronson

Lewis, R., 1971, *Everyday Life in Ottoman Turkey*. London: B. T. Batsford

Loewenberg, P., 1995, *Fantasy and Reality in History*. New York: Oxford University Press

Mahler, M. S., 1968, *On Human Symbiosis and the Vicissitudes of Individuation*. New York: International Universities Press

Mango, A., 1987, Greece and Turkey: Unfriendly Allies. In *The World Today* 43:144–7

Markides, K. C., 1977, *The Rise and Fall of the Cyprus Republic* New Haven: Yale University Press

Millas, H., 1991, Türk edebiyatında Yunan imajı: Yakup Kadri Karaosmanoğlu (The Greek Image in the Turkish Literature: Yakup Kadri Karaosmanoğlu). *Toplum ve Bilim* 51 and 52:129–52

Politis, N. G., 1876, The First of March (in Greek). *Estia* 1:142–3

1882, *Introductory Lecture for the Class in Hellenic Mythology* (in Greek). Athens: Aion

Schwoebel, R., 1967, *The Shadow of the Crescent: The Renaissance Image of the Turk (1453–1517)*. New York: St Martin's Press

Tähkä, V., 1984, Dealing with Object Loss. *Scandinavian Psychoanalytic Review* 7:13–33

Volkan, V. D., 1976, *Primitive Internalized Object Relations*. New York: International Universities Press

1979, *Cyprus – War and Adaptation: A Psychoanalytic History of Two Ethnic Groups in Conflict*. Charlottesville, VA: University Press of Virginia

1985, The Need to Have Enemies and Allies: A Developmental Approach. *Political Psychology* 6:219–47

1988, *The Need to Have Enemies and Allies: From Clinical Practice to International Relationships*. Northvale, NJ: Jason Aronson

1991, On Chosen Trauma. *Mind and Human Interaction* 3:13

1992, Ethnonationalistic Rituals: An Introduction *Mind and Human Interaction* 4:3–19

1997, *Bloodlines: From Ethnic Pride to Ethnic Terrorism*. New York: Farrar, Straus and Giroux

1999, *Das Versagen der Diplomatie: Zur Psychoanalyse nationaler, ethnischer und religiöser Konflikte* (The Failure of Diplomacy: The Psychoanalysis of National, Ethnic and Religious Conflicts). Giessen: Psychosozial-Verlag

Volkan, V. D. and N. Itzkowitz, 1984, *The Immortal Atatürk: A Psychobiography*. Chicago: University of Chicago Press

1992, 'Istanbul, Not Constantinople': The Western View of 'the Turk.' *Mind and Human Interaction* 4:129–34

1994, *Turks and Greeks: Neighbours in Conflict*. Cambridgeshire, England: The Eothen Press

von Hammer-Purgstall, R. J., 1835–1843, *Histoire de l'Empire Ottoman*. 18 volumes. Trans. J. J. Hellert. Paris: Ballitarol Barthes

Waelder, R., 1971, Psychoanalysis and History. In *The Psychoanalytic Interpretation of History*. B. B. Wolman, ed. New York: Basic Books, 3–22

Young, K., 1969, *The Greek Passion: A Study in People and Politics*. London: J. M. Dent and Sons

Zamblios, S., 1856, Some Philosophical Researches on the Modern Greek Language (in Greek). *Pandora* 7:369–80 and 484–94

1859, *Whence the Vulgar and Traghoudho? Thoughts Concerning Hellenic Poetry*. Athens: P. Soutsas and A. Ktenas

9 The violence of non-recognition: becoming a 'conscious' Muslim woman in Turkey

Katherine Pratt Ewing

Modernist grand narratives have defined progress in terms of the ability of nations to shape their populations into modern subjects whose most salient identity is a national one. In the wake of challenges to such modernist narratives, the present era is marked by manifold, intense, and violent efforts to negotiate identity in other terms, often within the context of social movements. Social movements are at the centre of global and local politics, and the identities that are crystalized within such movements are often threatening to and threatened by existing institutional arrangements. While there are many ways that such identities become salient for participants, the memory of violence and trauma is a powerful image around which such an identity may crystalize, facilitating the mobilization of individuals, and lifting them out of their everyday practices into a world of collective action. In such cases violence is experienced, remembered, and transmuted into a sign that occupies an important place in the organization of politicized identities.[1] In focusing on such processes, anthropologists have begun to articulate a semiology of violence (Das 1987) to further our understanding of the role of violence in the building and contestation of the modern state.

Yet most researchers with a psychological orientation rightly regard the experience of violence as traumatic and assume that trauma is disruptive of psychological organization and personal identity. Clinical researchers – well represented in this volume – have documented how extreme violence – as in warfare and terrorism – can generate trauma that disrupts personal identity and the ability to maintain relationships in profound ways. As both anthropologists (e.g., Das and Nandy 1985) and psychotherapists working with victims of violence (e.g., Gampel, in this volume) have noted, the immediate experience and aftermath of violence is often surrounded by silence and the breakdown of significa-tion. But even in such cases cultural and personal strategies for creating

[1] David Riches has pointed out that the expressive properties of violence – its visibility and a basic significance that is readily grasped by anyone – make it 'an excellent communicative vehicle' (Riches 1986:12).

meaning in violent situations – the meanings of the violence itself – affect how an individual responds to such violence and is shaped by it. A central aspect of psychological survival and of the healing process is the possibility of putting one's experience into words – the narrativization of the experience of trauma.[2] The process of narrativization can be seen as a recasting of memory and identity so that one's current identity can safely encompass the memory of a past trauma.[3]

Bringing together anthropological concerns with the semiology of violence and psychotherapeutic concerns with trauma and recovery, one may examine how the articulation of a politicized, collective identity may be a form of healing for the individual who has experienced violence, a form of narrativization. But the process also works in the reverse direction: the formation of a political identity within a social movement may also involve the activation and reactivation of traumas that have not been personally experienced but are instead culturally articulated memories of socially distant traumas that take on an important role in mobilizing others within a social movement.[4] The process of narrativization is thus a crucial point at which individual trauma and healing on the one hand and collective action on the other may intersect.

In the literature on violence, a distinction is often made between physical or instrumental violence and expressive or symbolic[5] violence.

[2] While I stress narrativization here, it is important to point out that clinical theories have insufficiently appreciated the role of vivid imagery (mental contents that possess sensory qualities, in contrast to purely verbal activity) in the intrusive re-experiencing of trauma (Brett and Ostroff 1985). By extension, the focus on narrative also underestimates the significance and power of imagery in the healing process.

[3] Freud theorized the importance of mastery in managing what otherwise would be traumatic experiences, a process vividly captured in his description of his grandson's efforts to master his anxiety over separation from his mother by throwing a pull-toy out of sight and uttering '*fort*' (gone), then putting it back and gleefully shouting '*da*' (here) (Freud 1955:14–17). Without such mastery, the imagery associated with the traumatic experience may intrude. In this case verbalization can be seen as an important component of this mastery. Freud contrasts the pleasure of repetition associated with mastery with the intrusive and frightening nature of the repetitive dreams experienced by patients suffering from traumatic war neurosis (Freud 1955:13–14).

[4] See Volkan and Itzkowitz, in this volume, on the concept of 'chosen trauma': 'Once a shared trauma is "chosen", the historical truth about it recedes in importance; what matters is its place in the identity formation of the victims and in their establishment of mental representations of victimizers' (Volkan and Itzkowitz, p. 233 above).

[5] 'Symbolic violence' is perhaps best known from Bourdieu's (1977) very broad use of the term to refer to the inherent but unrecognized violence that is maintained and naturalized within systems of inequality and domination. Though in this paper I address the oppression of a specific social group, I use the term 'expressive violence' to distinguish my usage from Bourdieu's because I am not focusing on hegemonic situations where the authority of the dominant is unchallenged and overt repressive violence is unnecessary, but rather on situations in which there is an overt challenge to established order and the official reactions to the challenge are overt, backed up where

But, as Veena Das has pointed out, a mechanical distinction between the two leads our attention away from the meaning of violence and, hence, from its impact on either the individual or the community. Just as the traumatic effect of violence for the individual is contingent upon the meaning of the experience for that person, at the level of the social meaning of violence, the intensity of the violence or level of trauma for those who actually experienced it first-hand cannot predict how powerful the memory of violence may become when it is used as a sign in the shaping of a social and political identity and in the mobilization of individuals within the context of a social movement.

Expressive violence such as verbal abuse or humiliation may be experienced as immediately as a physical assault and may similarly result in intrusive imagery that is vivid and traumatic. Just as the experience of physical violence overwhelms our abilities to represent or contain it, there are aspects of expressive violence that cannot be encompassed in the narratives that attempt to represent it. Humiliation can be shattering. Fanon, in his effort to capture in words an experience of racial humiliation, hints at the complexity of its effects:

> Then, assailed at various points, the corporeal schema crumbled, its place taken by a racial epidermal schema . . . On that day, completely dislocated, unable to be abroad with the other, the white man, who unmercifully imprisoned me, I took myself far off from my own presence, far indeed, and made myself an object. What else could it be for me but an amputation, an excision, a hemorhage that spattered my whole body with black blood? (Fanon 1967:112)

Fanon's description is, of course, already narrativized, transmuted into a sign, a concept to be used in an argument, a symbol around which an identity may crystalize. This is true of all communicable memories of violence: they are always signs. The stories one tells about an experience of violence are a different order of phenomenon from the violence itself. Whether a story of physical assault or of a 'symbolic' humiliation, it is always a representation, always already narrativized violence, in contrast to the symptoms of trauma. Like the 'fort-da' play of Freud's grandson, the story organizes memory and contains anxiety. It can then form the basis of a relationship with others, and, on a broader scale, the basis for a collective history.

The significant distinction for my purposes, then, is not between physical and expressive violence, both of which can disrupt identity and

necessary with an explicit threat of force. My use of the term 'expressive violence' is also distinct from Scheper-Hughes' (1992) use of the term 'everyday violence' to mean the implicit, legitimate and routine violence of particular social and state formations because neither party to the acts of violence I consider here felt that they were routine or unproblematic. However, the dehumanization process that Scheper-Hughes examines in her work *is* a feature of these interactions.

relationships, but between immediately experienced violence/trauma and the gaps and discontinuities in self-experience it creates on the one hand, and narrativized accounts of violence and trauma, through which an individual may establish new relationships and identity, and through which a social movement may mobilize adherents, on the other hand.

It is this tension between trauma and narrativization in relationship to the construction of a politicized identity that I will examine in this paper. I will do so within the context of struggles over Islamization in Turkey. I focus on Turkish women in their thirties who were high school students in the early 1980s when they decided to adopt the Islamic head scarf.[6] When as students they wore Islamic dress to school, they effectively violated the law by entering a state-run facility in Islamic dress. Remembering the experience fifteen years later, women described how on some days they were physically barred from entering the building. On other days, a young woman would make it into the classroom but once there, she would be utterly ignored, treated as a non-person. On those days, the situation, though it did not involve physical assault or obstruction, was nevertheless a form of expressive violence. In such cases, silence from their teachers was more shattering than a physical blow from a member of a security force might have been.

The violence of non-recognition can be made meaningful and shape identity within a social movement and can actually become a symbol around which people mobilize and become politically active. The expressive violence of non-recognition is remembered not only by the women subjected to such violence, but by those who later join them and take on a collective identity with this memory of violence at its core.

But, as they speak, the women themselves reveal other aspects of their experience that have not been narrativized, such as the rage and conflict they feel about their interrupted career goals and the reactivation of the humiliation they felt at the time. This contrast between narratives and the unspoken relies directly on Freud's observations and his understanding of the therapeutic process. In his discussion of the therapeutic efficacy of psychoanalysis, Freud made a distinction between 'remembering' and 'repeating.'[7] As the analysand develops a transference

[6] Field research for this study was conducted in Istanbul during the summers of 1993 and 1995 and was supported by a summer stipend from the National Endowment for the Humanities and by research grants from Duke University. I would like to thank Kemal Sayar, Ayşe Öncü, Nükhet Sirman, Aynur Ilyasoğlu, Funda Ödemiş, Halide Velioğlu, Esra Özyürek, and the women who generously allowed me to probe their personal lives for their help and advice while I was in Istanbul. Special thanks go to Ayşe Gül Altınay, whose insights, knowledge, and practical help have been invaluable at all stages of this project.
[7] Freud laid this out particularly clearly in the paper 'Remembering, Repeating, and Working Through' (Freud 1958).

during the psychoanalytic process, he or she re-enacts an old conflict or trauma in the presence of the psychoanalyst without being able to remember or acknowledge it, all the while telling stories of other things. The healing narrative, in contrast, emerges only when there is remembrance, so that the experience of trauma and conflict is itself narrativized and incorporated into the conscious experience of self or 'ego'. Among those whom I spoke with in Turkey, there were women, for instance, who could talk to me about the injustice of teachers and administrators in heated terms but were too uncomfortable to describe in any detail their own experiences of distress, which might have triggered a re-experiencing of the stress, humiliation, or depression they felt at the time.

The head scarf as political symbol

The head scarf of the Muslim woman is a vivid symbol of contested identity. Its meaning for women who have recently chosen to adopt it has been constituted in part out of the politics surrounding Islamization and the threat that many secularists and secularist governments feel as Islamization becomes increasingly visible as a social and political force.[8] In Turkey, the debate surrounding Islamization has been highly polarized, and covered women have been a focus of state efforts at suppression. As a result, the politics of Islam and the memory of state-linked expressive violence and humiliation shape and contribute to the crystalization of many Muslim women's identities, however much such women seek to articulate their identities in other terms.

For many modern secularists and feminists transnationally, the head scarf has been a symbol of the oppression of Muslim women, while for politically active Islamists the head scarf as an element of a pan-Islamic ideology signifies rejection of Western domination and secularism and the return to a properly ordered Muslim society. The political significance of the head scarf in public debate and the polarization of positions around it have in large measure been shaped by a discourse that developed within the context of the European colonial project: colonial policy-makers appropriated the language of early feminism to justify their own colonial domination in the name of freeing women from oppression (Ahmed 1992).[9] For the past century, then, gender, in the

---

[8] It should be noted, however, that the politics of Islamization are dramatically different in the various countries where Islamization is occurring.

[9] Ahmed has convincingly argued that colonial administrators, intent on showing evidence for the inferiority of non-European societies, established the association of the veil with oppression, claiming that the Muslim practice of secluding women stood in contrast to a more enlightened European practice (Ahmed 1992). Ahmed also highlighted the self-

form of the dress and position of women, has been a vehicle of political debate concerning the organization of civil society and its relationship to modernity and the West, with the covering of women being regarded as antithetical to the development of a modern population.

As Islamists move into positions of power and vie for control of the state apparatus, the significance of the head scarf has been increasingly linked to the nature of both personal and state authority: who decides what a women will wear? Who has the authority to establish her identity? The answers to these questions have been the focus of worldwide alarm in response to situations such as Iran, where Islamist state authorities harshly control women's street dress, a model that has been reproduced in Afghanistan. In Iran, a woman has no choice but to cover, the alternative being a threat of immediate physical violence from passers-by, a form of violence that is legitimized and reinforced by the state. The question of authority to regulate women's dress has also been the focus of different sorts of controversy in Turkey, in France, and even in the American company J. C. Penney. In each case, secularists have banned the head scarf. The process of taking up an identity through dress is shaped by the specific meanings of citizenship, political participation, and religion in each country. But an important aspect of the debate centres around the control that women should and do have over their own decisions, lives, and bodies, and the terms of the debate are often shaped by specific forms of violence against women.

In Turkey the authority of the state to control women's dress has been a controversial issue, but the discursive relationship between violence and covering is the reverse of the situation in Iran. Women have been a target of expressive violence, but, in this case, it is the women who have insisted on wearing a head scarf who have been subject to the controlling authority of the state.[10] It is also these women who have directly challenged the authority of the state to impose secularism on them. Since the 1920s, women have not been permitted to enter state-controlled schools with a head-covering in place or to practise professions such as medicine or law. Controversy surrounding this prohibition became a visible issue in the 1980s as growing numbers of women explicitly challenged state authority by refusing to remove their head scarves when they attended school (see Olsen 1985).

contradictory aspects of this argument: the men who preached feminist concerns within the context of Muslim societies were often the same men who fought against feminist demands for the vote and equal opportunity at home. For the history of debates over the position of women in Turkey, see Kandiyoti (1989, 1991).

10 Given the current tendency in scholarly circles to focus on women as a symbol of political contestation, it should be noted that the precise cut of a man's moustache is also tightly regulated in secularist Turkey.

The decision to cover as a 'conscious' Muslim was an unusual one in the early 1980s during the head scarf controversy. The women who took on this identity at that time formed a vanguard of the Islamist movement in Turkey. Wearing a head scarf to school at that time was perceived as active political protest, whatever the intentions of the wearer. It could be and was interpreted by many school officials and teachers as an act of expressive violence against the state at a politically unsettled time, when expressive violence readily erupted into physical violence. And certainly the responses that this act generated from school authorities were expressively violent, if not actually involving physical assault. Among the women I met, several had been forced to abandon their educational and professional goals rather than succumbing to the pressure to give up their Islamic dress. Some continue to be bitterly angry more than a decade later. Others have actively pursued careers dedicated to social change. These women continue to represent the vanguard of a movement that seeks to transform the social order, and their experiences colour the discourse of covering even among younger women who have decided to cover at a very different historical moment.

Given the political vicissitudes of Islamization and the head scarf issue, young women who now decide to cover themselves may or may not face active and absolute prohibitions at their high schools and universities and, when they do join the movement, they are likely to become part of a sizeable yet close-knit community of like-minded students at their school or university. For many of these women, covering may not be a difficult act of defiance but rather a way of fitting in with or joining a community they are comfortable with. Nevertheless, they enter a world where the polarization between secular students and Islamist students remains, and they take on a position as 'other' *vis-à-vis* the university social order (see Saktanber 1994). Women who decide to cover while at a university, such as the prestigious Boğaziçic University for example, form a close group that maintains sharp boundaries and interacts little with secularist students.

Vicissitudes in state policy have a direct and immediate impact on the lives of covered women and university students and on their relationships with faculty and other students. In 1988, for instance, the Turkish sociologist Feride Acar began conducting interviews among covered women at Middle East Technical University in Ankara. Her own research was disrupted early in 1989 when a constitutional court decision was passed that made the wearing of a head scarf an offence punishable by the university's disciplinary codes. As a result, relations between these women students and faculty (including Acar) were 'seriously curtailed' (Acar 1995:64 note 2). Young women who chose to cover in 1997, while they still generated intense controversy, had the explicit support of the Islamically oriented government of the Islamist Prime Minister Necmettin Erbakan.

But even when Erbakan was Prime Minister, the secularist threat was ever-present. In early March 1997, for instance, thousands of what newspapers described as anti-Islamist Turkish women staged a demonstration in Istanbul. In an event now known as '28 Şubat Kararlari', the military-dominated National Security Council warned Erbakan's government to take 'no steps away from the contemporary values of the Turkish Republic'. Two of the steps they urged for preserving 'democracy' were 'a ban on propaganda on pro-Islamic television and radio' and 'tighter restrictions on religious dress' (*International Herald Tribune*, 4 March 1997:6). Issues of democracy and authority were still being played out in terms of women's dress.

The situation changed again with the demise of his government and the reassertion of control by secularists. Beginning in January 1998, universities, schools, courts, and State Offices tried to enforce the ban on head scarves with renewed vigour. As the *Christian Science Monitor* put it: 'A government decree last month that bars university students from class for wearing Islamic dress has fanned the conflict between secularism and Islam in Turkey, and once again brought the government and the military to the brink' (Kohen 1998).

Recent newspaper and magazine articles offer anecdotes of the experiences of a new generation of women confronted with this newly enforced ban:

Durdane Deger, a student at Istanbul University, tries to come to campus daily in Islamic dress. But she is refused entry at the gate of the university each time.

'This is inhuman. It is oppression', she says. 'Last year we were allowed to go to class with the turban. Now they want to force us to give up our religious beliefs and traditions.' (Kohen 1998)

For the past $2\frac{1}{2}$ months, Feyza Cicek has not been able to attend her medical-school classes at Istanbul University. There is only one reason: she wears a scarf over her hair. When she tries to enter a lecture, she is turned away. If she refuses to leave, her professors scurry off, wary of losing their jobs for not enforcing a national dress code. (Smucker 1998)

Though the scene as described by these two women could have been a verbatim description of similar events fifteen years ago, its meaning has changed. These images of oppression have been taken up into a highly developed discourse and have become a sign that now plays a central role in challenging the legitimacy of the secular state, as Islamists claim to enact 'freedom' and 'democracy', in contrast to what they regard as the violent and oppressive practices of the secular state, which violates both the freedom of choice and the privacy of women. As the *US News and World Report* put it:

the effort [to ban Islamic dress] has backfired, handing Islamic groups a powerful symbol of state repression and bringing thousands of students – including many moderate Muslims – into the streets in protest. (Smucker 1998)

In response, the secularist Prime Minister caved in and announced that 'girls will not be forced to cover or uncover their heads'.

The debate has thus increasingly become one about the authoritarianism of the secularist State. Islamists in Turkey now claim the moral high ground around issues of freedom and democracy, and the head scarf has become for many a symbol of the right to choose.

While Turkey has not gone as far as Egypt in the move toward popular acceptance of Islamic dress (there are Egyptian women, for instance, who decide to cover because it is 'fashionable' to do so), such events as the show of support against state repression by women who do not cover obviously create a different sort of identity for covered women. Yet the remembered violence – the stories that older women tell about their early efforts to wear Islamic dress – is even for many of the younger women an element of their own identities as besieged yet politically active Muslim women living within a secularist state. With the return of repressive state policies, these memories are renewed for a new generation.

In addition to their publicized stories that serve as models for this political movement, the women who were and are actually subjected to the expressive violence associated with repressive state policies have had reactions that may not so readily be taken up into a political, ideological discourse, particularly those who struggled in the early 1980s, when public perceptions tended to be more generally on the side of the enforcers of state policy. They continue to live with personal reactions of humiliation and anger, ambivalence, and even trauma. Women are not only political symbols: they are also people who must take up personal identities and make life choices in a socio-political field where dressing is, among other things, unavoidably a political act.

Covered women are acutely aware that their style of dress is perceived in political terms and draw a contrast between these perceptions and their own articulations of their motives. This discrepancy emerges as a central aspect of many personal narratives, accompanied by a hypersensitivity to alienating interpellations (see Althusser 1971) by others. Some of these discrepancies are themselves an element of an ideology of resistance, a phenomenon that I will discuss below. Others may not be narrativized but instead appear as gaps and inconsistencies in their personal narratives. In the following sections I will examine the discursive context of this ideological resistance and present portions of a personal narrative of one woman's decision to cover. I will then suggest elements of her experience and of the experiences of other women I interviewed that continue to generate reactions of humiliation and conflict that have not been fully encompassed by the narratives that organize their identities as conscious Muslim women.

An ideology of the conscious self

The concept of 'consciousness' (*şuurluluk*) is central to the articulation of identity among the covered women I met in Istanbul and is associated with what these women see as the proper relationship to God according to Islam.

These women characterize themselves as 'conscious' Muslims who decide to cover as an act of personal choice, drawing a contrast with women who wear a head scarf out of a 'habit' (*adet*) learned in childhood and thus do so 'unconsciously'. As conscious Muslims, they claim self-awareness in a way that creates a tripartite social space: on the one hand, this identity constitutes a Western other as not-self; on the other hand, it constitutes a 'traditional' other as not-self. They thus identify three positions in the debate over women's dress: the secularist position that is seen as carrying the legacy of Atatürk's efforts to make Turkey a modern nation state; the 'traditionalist' position (which like the secularist position can be seen as a product of the Orientalist dichotomy between progressive modernity and that which is static, irrational, and uncivilized); and the 'Islamist' position.[11] The difference between the two categories of covered women is clearly marked by styles of head covering. The 'traditionalist' style is a small scarf that is tied under the chin so that it covers most of the hair but not the throat, while the style worn by conscious women completely covers the hair and throat (after

---

[11] Scholars have made similar distinctions, though they have been at times based on assumptions that can be questioned. As characterized by Kadioğlu, for instance, 'traditionalists' practise an Islam 'confined mostly to the private domain of the believer', while political Islamists have a political mission to transform the secular basis of the nation state (1994:646). This distinction is problematic, however. It suggests that turbaned women have a political agenda that is manifested in the act of covering. But many of these women do not discuss their decisions in terms of a political agenda (though, as I argue, the politicization of women's dress does shape their identities in ways they cannot avoid). Furthermore, it is not really accurate to suggest that Islam was traditionally a 'private' affair and that Islamist activities in the political realm are, therefore, a recent innovation (see Asad 1993). Given these considerations and the unfortunate fact that little research has been done among urban women who have been identified as 'traditional' in their style of dress, I prefer to present the distinction as it is made by the conscious Muslim women I met.

being carefully pinned to do so), usually over a long but colourful and fashionable[12] coat. It closely resembles the dress of Islamist women in other Muslim countries, thereby marking a transnational identification with other Muslims.

Women find models for becoming a conscious Muslim through women's groups such as those who gather to discuss the teachings of Said Nursi[13] and in the wide array of novels, magazine stories, movies, and television programmes that are available through the burgeoning Islamist use of the media. Conscious Muslim women have used the media – such as articles in women's magazines (see Acar 1995; Arat 1995), novels (e.g., Aktaş 1991), television programmes broadcast on the recently established Islamist television stations (see Saktanber 1994), and film (as in the film *Yalnız Değilsiniz*, based on a novel by Üstün Inanç) – to disseminate this cultural model.

A brief, two-page, short story in the women's magazine *Bizim Aile* (*Our Family*),[14] instantiates a typical version of this story (Uçkun 1993:38–3), this one a rather stark and stereotyped model of the experience of becoming conscious. Models such as this potentially create a common foundation for the community of women they address, patterning and narrativizing the experiences of women who may be considering such a step, including the hostility and other difficulties they may encounter at school. In brief summary the story is as follows:

A young girl in her last year of high school finds herself in a state of confusion and crisis, her mind whirling with questions and no answers. She is confused because she no longer enjoys activities she once loved, such as wearing make up, tea parties, and even going to school. She finds answers to her questions when a new (male) teacher at the school gives her a book about Islam. Inspired by the book, the student begins a new life as a young, conscious Muslim girl. She faces difficulties at school because of her decision to cover herself but endures for the sake of Allah.

The story involves a transition from a disturbed inner state to one of peace and satisfaction through a change of identity.[15] The disturbed

---

[12] For example, while I was in Istanbul in 1995, blue denim was a popular fabric for these coats.

[13] Said Nursi explicitly and publicly opposed the secularist reforms of Atatürk and spent a number of years in prison for his activities. Though Nursi's followers in the early years were exclusively men (Mardin 1989:202), women now form separate, parallel groups within the organization.

[14] This magazine is published by the network of women within the Nur movement founded by Said Nursi.

[15] In a survey by Radwan of university women in Cairo, a feeling of peace or centredness is similarly reported as a primary motive for publicly aligning oneself with Islam (Zeinab 'Abdel Mejid Rawdan, *Thahirat al-hijab bayn al-jam'iyyat* (Cairo: Al-markaz al

condition is produced by a spontaneously arising sense of being out of place in the social world in which this young girl found herself. This girl finds herself in a state of confused isolation, with no way to relate to the people around her: she has experienced the stirrings of consciousness. She involuntarily rejects a world of secular, Western-influenced practices – tea parties – and her objectification as a sexual object, represented in the story by her rejection of make up and exposed dress. Through the very spontaneity of the disturbance, which arises in the absence of any role models or other social influences, the story emphasizes that the current social order has disrupted a natural order, creating confusion concerning the organization of gender. The story thus naturalizes a different social order in which women's proper place is separate from men's, making the decision to cover a necessity arising from a growing consciousness of self and one's relationship to God.

This internal source of motivation and the reward of inner peace are the antithesis of an externally based political motivation. This narrative of conversion to true Islam thus serves as an important counter-argument to the accusations of secularists.

Going beyond the story itself to its frame – its appearance in a women's magazine published by followers of Said Nursi – the decision to cover is also understood by at least some readers to occur within a specific social context. The social reconnection offered implicitly in the story to a woman who has lost old social ties because of her decision to adopt Islamic dress is specific to (though undoubtedly not unique to) the Nur group. Among the followers of Said Nursi, women gather regularly to read and interpret Said Nursi's writings together. In the magazine story, reconnection and a reordering of the social world do not come primarily through family or the deepening of social relationships, but through the medium of a book. (It is actually a stranger who offers the young woman the book as a new source of connectedness, and the story does not develop either a personal relationship with the man who gave her the book or his establishment as an authority figure.) The book itself, which can be understood to be the writings of Said Nursi, offers her a relationship with God around which she as an individual con- sciously organizes her new identity.

Within gatherings of Nursi's followers, older, more experienced women act as leaders and interpreters of God's word during readings of Said Nursi's books and serve as role models and a new form of social support for younger women, many of whom do not have family in

qawmi lil-buhuth al-ijtima'yya wa'l-jina'iyya, 1982), cited in Ahmed 1992:223). 'Fifty per cent gave inner peace as the principle effect of adopting Islamic dress' (Ahmed 1992:277 note 35).

Istanbul. In this environment, stories of the experiences of the older women who serve as leaders of these groups that meet to read and interpret Said Nursi's writings play a central role in shaping the meaning of covering and Muslim identity for the younger women. Among the stories that older women tell are those describing the difficulties that many went through to remain covered while getting an education and a good job. For many, these are at one level stories of failure – the failure to achieve their original career goals – that have been transformed into stories of dedication to one's identity as a conscious Muslim woman and stories of new forms of success as they seek to reshape the social order.

The authority of the state

For these conscious Muslim women, the reordering of social and personal space involves a questioning of existing authority relationships. In the *Bizim Aile* story, the new identity of the adolescent girl put her at odds with her other teachers and classmates, and she experienced difficulty at school. This opposition to the covered girl in school is reinforced by the authority of the state, which refuses to recognize the legitimacy of a conscious Muslim identity. A central theme in the story is, then, the subversion of existing state policies and the rejection of the authority of the secular state to dictate dress codes and lifestyles.

The magazine story provides a model for the replacement of the authority of the state in identity formation with a different authority – Allah. As Delaney (1991b) has argued, the Turkish state is organized in terms of a gender-based ideology. The state as 'Father State' (*Devlet Baba*) is a patriarch who protects, administers justice, and demands complete obedience (Delaney 1991b; White 1994:67).[16] In this story, Allah competes with the state as the 'Father' who is to be obeyed. The story offers a model for rejecting the state as the source of morality and codes for proper behaviour. Though this particular story leaves unspecified the image of God that is to replace patriarchal state authority and thus could be interpreted as simply substituting the image of one Father for another, it does, more significantly, alter the position of the subject *vis-à-vis* authority and order. The source of proper order is found within, through a 'consciousness' that allows one to sense God's will, rather than from an external source. Confusion is replaced with inner peace and focused resistance, which takes the form of a struggle against secularism. A social order that has undergone a disruption of gender

---

[16] 'Father' State stands in relationship to 'Mother' land (*Anavatan*), which is felt to give refuge, to serve, and to require emotional loyalty (White 1994:66).

relationships and of gender identity itself is re-established through active resistance against school rules and established authority.

A personal narrative told by one of the vanguard

The disruption of the state as patriarchal authority and the articulation of other models of political order can be seen in the experiences of some of the women who personally resisted the state in the classroom during the 1980s. Rejecting the authority of teachers – who are representatives and employees of the state – is closely associated with rejecting the scope of authority of the state itself. In Turkey secularization had occurred from the top down, with the most dramatic decrees occuring in the 1920s under what many have perceived as the rather heavy-handed authority of Atatürk. The 1980s was a time when notions of state authority – the idea of the patriarchal 'father state' – were themselves undergoing transformation. Many groups across the political spectrum were demanding democratization.

In 1981, when a university student named Sibel decided to cover herself, the overall political situation was highly unstable. The threat of violence had penetrated everyday life as activists challenged the legitimacy of the government. There had been a coup in 1980, and, as she described it, teachers were afraid of any kind of political dissent:

When I started to talk with my teachers about how I did not want to take off my cover while in school, my teachers became afraid. They were very afraid of the political situation in Turkey. It was anarchic – the leftists and rightists were always killing each other. As I remember, there were always bombs going off, and many professors were killed. They were afraid of getting involved in that type of situation. Being political in any way was difficult at that time.

Sibel described a situation in which being 'political' could mean being willing to treat someone on the other side as an enemy, as a symbol of evil or as a target of life-threatening violence, and not as a person. Basic trust in the public sphere had been eroded. In the situation Sibel described, we see a sudden change in the attitude of professors who already knew her as a student and as an individual. They 'became afraid'. When she wore Islamic dress, they no longer saw the same person but perceived her as other, and identified her through the stereotypes of Islamist and political activist – the same types who had already set off bombs and killed other professors. In Turkey, at that time, this meant that she represented the threat of direct violence, of bombs going off in the classroom. Whatever Sibel's personal motivations, her acts of defiance against school rules and state law were immediately perceived in political and ideological terms. Sibel continued:

But my wanting to cover was not an ideology; it was just part of my belief, and I wanted to live in that way. And when I took off the cover, I didn't feel good – I felt psychologically bad, both while covered outside and uncovered in school.

Other women I spoke with alluded to the same discrepancy between their self-characterizations of their motives for refusing to remove their head scarves and others' perceptions of them. A woman interviewed by Feride Acar in 1988 described her own experience of deciding to cover in the following terms:

My aunts reacted negatively. They are both school-teachers. They said that the headscarf is political. They said I was being marked as a political activist. (Acar 1995:57)

Like Sibel, this woman, though obviously part of a socio-cultural trend, refused to accept the characterization of her actions as 'political'. Each sees her actions as divinely inspired and 'natural', in terms very close to those modelled by the *Bizim Aile* story. The gap between such self-perceptions and their experience of faculty who viewed them as a dangerous 'other' created a sense of alienation and humiliation.

Acar, describing trends in her interviewees' responses, reported that students' families were concerned about their wearing the head scarf mainly 'because of the potential problems with public authorities' and alluded in general terms to 'incidental reactions from some faculty members' (Acar 1995:56–7). Several of my own interviewees went on at great length about the intolerance of most faculty and the humiliation they experienced as covered students. The sense of alienation from faculty was further suggested by the difficulty Acar had with her interviewees, which was so intense that she was forced to terminate her research. I, too, found it impossible to speak with any covered students while living and teaching at Boğaziçi University in 1995, despite my close contact with uncovered students who had a covered student as a friend or roommate. One uncovered student, who had assured me that she could arrange a meeting with her covered friend with no difficulty, later reported to me that her friend had responded to her request by saying that the covered women would not talk with secularist researchers after their experiences with another scholar on campus. This professor had, in fact, written a book that was generally regarded as sympathetic toward these women. Communication had clearly broken down,[17] and the covered students refused to accept as legitimate virtually any

---

[17] The fact that the polarization was focused primarily on campuses and did not extend to all social contexts was indicated by the ease with which I was able to contact and communicate with covered women in other situations, particularly situations where

representation of themselves. For instance, people often reported to me how upset various Islamist women were when they saw the published accounts of interviews they had granted to reporters and academics. They could not recognize themselves in these published accounts and were distressed by the narratives others had constructed about them.

Yet the line between secularists and Islamists did not prevent all communication, as Sibel described:

It surprised me that some of my teachers helped me. The ones who helped me were not the ones who I thought were believers [i.e., practising Muslims], but the ones who seemed democratic. One of my teachers – a woman teacher – once said to me that she does not wear any socks although it is written in the rules that women teachers should wear socks. She said, 'if I prefer not to wear them, so you may prefer to wear a cover.' I am still thinking about that, wondering what was wrong about the other teachers that they did not help me, yet the democratic ones helped me.

Sibel, like many Islamists, distinguished secularization and democracy, though both are associated with Western political discourse. Through this personal anecdote, she expressed a basic political argument of Islamist groups: articulating an ideology of democratic Islam, Islamists active in Turkey today claim the banner of democratization for themselves, denouncing the authoritarianism of the secularists. Islamist women like Sibel embrace the idea of democracy and denounce the idea of patriarchal authority, which they associate with both the practice of 'traditional', 'unconscious' Muslims and with advocates of the secularist state who, like the military threatening yet another coup in early 1997, seek to impose bans on a wide range of activities in order to preserve democracy. Sibel, in her struggles against school authorities, identified with the woman who wore no socks, who though herself secularist helped her articulate a justification of Islamic dress. This model of free choice and tolerance pervades Sibel's speech. Like many Islamist women, she has found herself challenging the patriarchal model of authority represented in practices and expectations of the state and its representatives.

Yet she also recognizes that there are Islamists who share their authoritarian model and expect women like her to submit to it. She openly acknowledged that the battle lines in the struggle for social change cannot be drawn in neatly dichotomous terms. Rearticulating the proper organization of gender is not a simple matter, particularly for women who, now in their thirties and married, watched the establishment of an Islamist government by the Welfare party and hoped in vain

they were in control of the environment, such as the meeting place of the followers of Said Nursi and the offices of Islamist women's magazines and a TV station.

for positions within it while they struggled at the same time to maintain their work outside the home, to care for small children, and to maintain viable relationships with their husbands – issues they did not have to contend with when they first became conscious Muslims as students.

Recognition and expressive violence

The struggle over covering has involved a politics of recognition. Is a woman who covers herself to be recognized or even present as a subject? The very act of posing this question is a statement in the Foucaultian sense – a statement that is made possible by an Orientalist discourse that equates the covering of a woman with her degradation, dehumanization, and oppression. In an Orientalist fantasy of veiling, a woman 'disappears' behind the veil and loses all identity. But it would be a mistake to be misled by that fantasy and to assume that by covering women seek to avoid being publicly recognized or acknowledged as a centre of subjective experience.

By calling this view of women an Orientalist fantasy, I do not mean to say that there are not Islamist women who do strive to create for themselves a public non-presence. Yet even the woman who covers herself so completely that her face and hands cannot be seen and thus would seem to be making herself non-present does not construct her identity in terms of non-presence. On the contrary, media evidence suggests that women who cover themselves to this extent are definitely making themselves present. The women's magazine *Mektup*, associated with a radical Nakşibendi group, urges women to cover their faces and to wear gloves yet also contains a more activist discourse about women's public roles than other Islamist women's magazines (Acar 1995:52).[18]

Being a conscious Muslim involves seeking a specific form of social recognition rather than non-recognition. For many women in Turkey, this has involved a struggle in the face of a expressive violence that has challenged their identities as persons – a politics of recognition. Women described how, during their struggle in the 1980s, they were refused any recognition of their very presence by those who wielded authority and

[18] In Fernea's film, *A Veiled Revolution*, a totally covered women allowed herself to be filmed and spoke about her reasons for covering. As I watched and listened, I could not escape what felt like a contradiction between these two channels of communication – between seeking recognition and refusing it. But we must avoid interpretations based on narrow assumptions. It must be remembered that what is hidden is also powerful. In Pakistan, women told me mythical stories of the covered woman who is able to travel incognito to a secret destination, aided by a network of friends who help her repeatedly change from one *burqa* (veil) to another as she moves unrecognized through the city or across a border.

served as role models – teachers. Non-recognition was a psychologically powerful strategy that state-employed teachers used against young women who refused to remove their head scarves and other Islamic coverings in the classroom, a weapon in the struggle against Islamization. Women remembered how it felt to be treated as a non-person – not by fellow Islamists who approved of their dress, but by secularists who ostensibly advocated a Western humanist individualism. These secularists operationalized the Orientalist fantasy that the covered woman has no subjectivity, that she is not present. It is as if such a teacher saw, not a person, but a void.

Refusal to recognize the other as a person is an assault on self-esteem, an act of violence. As Sibel, who was part of this struggle as a university student in 1981 (even before the head scarf controversy had crystalized in public discourse and the media), described her experience of the violence of non-recognition:

When I attended class after I had decided to cover, my teachers treated me as if I were not there. They acted as if I were absent. Once I was asking a question, a very important question, and the teacher would not answer me. My grades started declining even though I did the best on my schoolwork. Being treated as if I were not there was very bad for my personality. I felt too bad during that time. But it helped being hardworking. When I look from here now to those years, I see that I was very hardworking, and this helped me very much.

Even for this young woman, who had had considerable support for her decision to cover and a close network of Islamist friends, non-recognition undercut her self-esteem, at least while she was experiencing it. Sibel persisted and received her university degree, though she was not able to follow her original career goal of becoming a math teacher, because this would have involved continuing an exhausting struggle with school authorities. But she has never given up her position of being at the vanguard of the movement. She has devoted herself to interpreting the writings of Said Nursi so that others might receive the ideological support necessary to establish themselves as conscious Muslim women. She actively addresses the practical tensions that working women face: right now she is involved in setting up a pre-school so that mothers will have a safe place to leave their children while they work that will also provide these children with a properly Islamic education. And, above all, Sibel and women like her seek public recognition. Many write and publish their writings.[19] Another woman I met is an artist who photocopied for me a published article about one of her exhibitions, which

---

[19] When I went to the office of the magazine *Bizim Aile* to interview several of the women involved in its production, I found that their intention was actually to interview me for the magazine, which they did.

included a photograph of herself standing in head scarf and coat beside one of her paintings. Another was a political figure in the Islamist Welfare Party who was taking a leadership role in the struggle to ensure that women did not lose their voice within the party as the party came to power.[20]

Sibel's experience of a refusal of recognition by her teachers altered her relationship to school authorities. If we assume that her teachers represented an ego ideal (becoming a teacher herself was her career goal), Sibel had to make a choice as she constituted her new identity as a covered Muslim. She could either take on the negative self-image and subject position being projected onto her by her teachers, or she could reject her identifications with these people who refused her recognition. Sibel chose the latter course of action. She lost respect for those teachers, refusing their authority. As she put it:

I had been thinking good things about a teacher, that I respected him or her, but when I saw that person in the door telling me I should take it off, it was too bad, and that person lost status. I felt, 'Why should I respect someone like that?'

This refusal was possible for her in part because she knew several young women at another university who were going through the same struggle and served as a support group and role models for her:

After I met those girls, I listened to their stories, how they were struggling against the school authorities. I was just alone in my school, and the teachers would come up to me and tell me I could not. In their school, the other girls' school, even the doorkeepers prevented them, and they were not let into lessons or examinations, and even their identity cards were taken away from them.

Sibel has developed an identity of activism and success, but she also gave up her original career aspiration, to become a mathematics teacher, because she would have faced opposition and struggle every step of the way, and because she had lost respect for the teachers who had served as role models for her. She included in her narrative allusions to her feelings of failure and to the worthlessness that non-recognition in the classroom had induced in her, feelings that have not been eliminated by her transformation of the experience into a public narrative. But Sibel is a very powerful woman, as her leadership position in the Nur group and the dynamics of our own meetings demonstrated. These feelings do not appear to interfere with her ongoing activities and goals. She was able to shift direction and focus her professional energies on writing articles and stories that would help other women to become more conscious Muslims.

Other women confronted with similar acts of expressive violence have

[20] Women's aspirations for public recognition in Turkey would seem to be more closely associated with class position than with religious orientation.

been less successful at narrating their experiences and incorporating them into their present identities in a positive way. I talked with a friend of Sibel, called Nergis, who had been through experiences similar to Sibel's while studying law at Istanbul University. In our conversation about her decision to refuse to remove her head scarf when entering the university, which had occurred in 1984, Nergis focused on the injustices she had experienced when university officials barred her from taking her exams in 1985. According to Nergis, only 100 out of 12,000 students in the university tried to cover at that time, and among the law students she was almost alone. She described the 'punishments' teachers and administrators meted out: posting police at the gates to keep covered students out, sending harsh letters that detailed the 'warnings' they had been given, then issuing one-month suspensions timed to coincide with exams so that they would be forced to fail. She had brought with her to our meeting a collection of carefully organized correspondence with university administrators and government officials detailing the arbitrariness and capriciousness of the ban and its enforcement. Though she was describing events that had occurred several years before, she spoke with barely suppressed rage. Her identity as she presented it to me was organized around the injustice she had experienced. (I hasten to point out, however, that the context was one in which she had been asked to describe that period of her life. Her self-presentation thus did not necessarily reflect how her identity in another context may have been organized.) With me, she seemed to be still waiting for permission to continue her career, frozen in time, and frustrated as a housewife. In this case, the narrative seemed not to heal but to freeze her in the position of victim. She focused, not on her own feelings, but on the unjust acts of those in power. Sibel, in contrast, had drawn her memories of her own feelings into the story, thereby narrativizing them. Simultaneously, Nergis presented me with the outlines of an unarticulated re-enactment of her rage even as she told me her story of the behaviour of state authorities.

I felt a discrepancy between my experience of Nergis in the conversation and Sibel's brief description of Nergis' situation that she had given me before I was to meet her. According to Sibel:

Nergis has lost several years, and it is very difficult for her, because her father is only a village farmer. But those years were not just for nothing because she was able to read more religious books [*risale*s] during those years and become more conscious about everything.

Sibel thus emphasized Nergis's spiritual development arising from her participation in the Nur group and her reading of Said Nursi's books, while I saw the lingering effects of her response to the expressive violence of non-recognition, of being treated like a 'microbe', as she had put it.

Conclusion

Though these examples are drawn from a limited set of interviews and thus do not offer the kind of evidence for a traumatic response to expressive violence that detailed clinical material would be expected to yield, they do illustrate how such experiences are an important element in the organization of an identity that has political as well as psychological components. Sibel's own story of keeping the head scarf on in the face of overt prohibition and humiliation was closely intertwined with the stories she had heard from others going through similar experiences, forming the basis for a common political and social identity. She herself narrativized her experiences in ways that reinforced the ideological position of Islamists who argue that the secularists have less right to claim that they support democracy than the Islamists do. Her humiliation and trauma became part of the narrative, as evidence for the illegitimacy of a repressive government policy. She even drew positively on her lost career, using her math experience as an explanation for why she can now operate so successfully: 'Learning mathematics made me systematic, so I can organize things better.'

Other women use their stories of expressive violence in similar ways, sharing them with other women, but not all are as successful in containing the trauma associated with non-recognition and the inability to continue in their careers in ways that simultaneously foster their own identity as conscious Muslim women within a group of other such women and allow them to transcend the rage and humiliation in a healing narrative. Their reactions are expressed symptomatically in non-verbal ways. In Nergis, these unresolved reactions were manifest in the manner of remembering and the very process of narrating. Others continue to live with stress that cannot be attached to narrative at all.

Ironically, the unnarrativized subtext – the re-enactment of the trauma and the rage associated with it during the act of telling a story – can itself be communicated, often more powerfully than the narrative itself. It is this unarticulated re-enactment (which may detach itself from that story in particular and become attached to another story altogether, a form of displacement) that may produce reactions such as rage in others. This is a kind of social reproduction of memory that may stimulate others to action and even violence. It may also shape the development of the next generation, who must organize their own experiences in terms of the gaps, silences, and sensitivities of a previous generation. Sibel has an explicit agenda for her young son – to make him 'conscious of everything' because 'imitation is very bad'. But he and other children will also be affected by the implicit (unconscious) ways in which their mothers responded to both the empowerment and the humiliations they experienced when they asserted their identities as conscious Muslims.

References

Acar, Feride, 1995, Women and Islam in Turkey. In *Women in Modern Turkish Society, A Reader*. Şirin Tekeli, ed. London: Zed Books, 46–65

Ahmed, Leila, 1992, *Women and Gender in Islam: Historical Roots of a Modern Debate*. New Haven: Yale University Press

Aktaş, Cihan, 1991, *Sistem içinde Kadın*. Istanbul: Beyan Yayinlari

Al-Azmeh, Aziz, 1993, *Islams and Modernities*. London: Verso

Althusser, Louis, 1971, Ideology and Ideological State Apparatuses (Notes Towards an Investigation). In *Lenin and Philosophy and Other Essays*. London: New Left Books, 121–73

Arat, Yeşim, 1995, Feminism and Islam: Considerations on the Journal *Kadın ve Aile*. In *Women in Modern Turkish Society, A Reader*. Şirin Tekeli, ed. London: Zed Books, 66–78

Asad, Talal, 1993, *Genealogies of Religion: Discipline and Reasons of Power in Christianity and Islam*. Baltimore: Johns Hopkins University Press

Benjamin, Jessica, 1988, *The Bonds of Love: Psychoanalysis, Feminism, and the Problem of Domination*. New York: Pantheon Books

Bourdieu, Pierre, 1977, *Outline of a Theory of Practice*. Trans. Richard Nice. Cambridge: Cambridge University Press

Brett, Elizabeth A. and Robert Ostroff, 1985, Imagery and Posttraumatic Stress Disorder: An Overview. *American Journal of Psychiatry* 142:417–24

Çakır, Rusen, 1994, *Ne Şeriat Ne Demokrasi: Refah Partisini Anlamak*. Istanbul: Metis Yayınları

Chodorow, Nancy J., 1989, *Feminism and Psychoanalytic Theory*. New Haven: Yale University Press

Comaroff, Jean and John L. Comaroff, 1991, *Of Revelation and Revolution: Christianity, Colonialism, and Consciousness in South Africa*, Vol. 1. Chicago: University of Chicago Press

Coşar, Fatma Mansur, 1978, Women in Turkish Society. In *Women in the Muslim World*. Lois Beck, and Nikki Keddie, eds. Cambridge: Harvard University Press, 124–40

Das, Veena, 1987, The Anthropology of Violence and the Speech of Victims. *Anthropology Today* 3(4):11–13

Das, Veena and Ashis Nandy, 1985, Violence, Victimhood, and the Language of Silence. *Contributions to Indian Sociology* (n.s.) 19(1):177–95

Delaney, Carol, 1991a, *The Seed and the Soil: Gender and Cosmology in Turkish Village Society*. Berkeley: University of California Press

1991b, Father State (Devlet Baba), Motherland (Anavatan), and the Birth of

270   Cultural responses to collective trauma

Modern Turkey. Paper presented at the Meetings of the American
Ethnological Society
1994, Untangling the Meanings of Hair in Turkish Society. *Anthropological*
Quarterly 67(4):159–72
Deleuze, Gilles and Felix Guattari, 1983, *Anti-Oedipus: Capitalism and Schizo-*
phrenia. Minneapolis: University of Minnesota Press
Erikson, Erik, 1959, Identity and the Life Cycle. *Psychological Issues* 1:1–171
Ewing, Katherine P., 1990, The Dream of Spiritual Initiation and the
Organization of Self Representations Among Pakistani Sufis. *American*
Ethnologist 17:56–74
1991, Can Psychoanalytic Theories Explain the Pakistani Muslim Woman?
Intrapsychic Autonomy and Interpersonal Engagement in the Extended
Family. *Ethos* 19:131–60
Fanon, Frantz, 1967, *Black Skin, White Masks*. New York: Grove Weidenfeld
Fast, Irene, 1984, *Gender Identity: A Differentiation Model*. Hillsdale, NJ: Analytic
Press
Foucault, Michel, 1990, *The History of Sexuality: An Introduction*, 3 vols. New
York: Vintage
Freud, Sigmund, 1955, Beyond the Pleasure Principle. *The Standard Edition of*
the Complete Works of Sigmund Freud. Vol. XVIII. Ed. James Strachey.
London: The Hogarth Press, 3–64
1958, Remembering, Repeating, and Working Through (Further Recommen-
dations on the Technique of Psychoanalysis). *The Standard Edition of the*
Complete Works of Sigmund Freud. Vol. XII. Ed. James Strachey. London:
The Hogarth Press, 145–56
1961, Civilization and its Discontents. *The Standard Edition of the Complete*
Works of Sigmund Freud. Vol. XXI. Ed. James Strachey. London: The
Hogarth Press, 57–145
Gaunt, Marilyn and Elizabeth Fernea, *A Veiled Revolution*. Icarus Films
Gilligan, Carol, 1993, *In a Different Voice: Psychological Theory and Women's*
Development. Cambridge, MA: Harvard University Press
Göçek, Fatma Müge and Shiva Balaghi, eds., 1994, *Reconstructing Gender in the*
Middle East: Tradition, Identity, and Power. New York: Columbia University
Press
Göle, Nilüfer, 1993, *Modern Mahrem: Medeniyet ve Örtünme*. Istanbul: Metis
Yayınları
1996, *The Forbidden Modern: Civilization and Veiling*. Ann Arbor: University
of Michigan Press
Ilyasoğlu, Aynur, 1993, *Örtülü Kimlik*. Istanbul: Metis Yayınları
Kadıoğlu, Ayse, 1994, Women's Subordination in Turkey: Is Islam Really the
Villain? *Middle East Journal* 48:645–60
Kakar, Sudhir, 1978, *The Inner World: A Psycho-analytic Study of Childhood and*
Society in India. Delhi: Oxford University Press
Kandiyoti, Deniz A., 1989, Women and the Turkish State: Political Actors or
Symbolic Pawns? In *Woman – Nation – State*. Nira Yuval-Davis and Floya
Anthias, eds. London: Macmillan, 126–49
1991, End of Empire: Islam, Nationalism, and Women in Turkey. In *Women,*
Islam, and the State. D. A. Kandiyoti, ed. London: Macmillan

Kepel, Gilles, 1985, *Muslim Extremism in Egypt: The Prophet and Pharoah*. Berkeley: University of California Press

Kohen, Sami, 1998, Torn Over Garments, Turkey Hurtles Toward a Showdown. *Christian Science Monitor* 25 March, www.csmonitor.com/durable/1998/03/25/intl/intl.4.html

Lacan, Jacques, 1977, *Écrits: A Selection*. New York: W. W. Norton

Lapidus, Ira, 1984, Knowledge, Virtue, and Action: The Classical Muslim Conception of *Adab* and the Nature of Religious Fulfillment in Islam. In *Moral Conduct and Authority: The Place of Adab in South Asian Islam*. Barbara Daly Metcalf, ed. Berkeley: University of California Press

Macleod, Arlene Elowe, 1991, *Accommodating Protest: Working Women, the New Veiling, and Change in Cairo*. New York: Columbia University Press

Mardin, Şerif, 1989, *Religion and Social Change in Modern Turkey*. Albany: SUNY Press

Mernissi, Fatima, 1987, *Beyond the Veil: Male–Female Dynamics in Modern Muslim Society*. Bloomington: Indiana University Press

Nandy, Ashis, 1983, *The Intimate Enemy: Loss and Recovery of Self under Colonialism*. Delhi: Oxford University Press

Olsen, Emelie, 1985, Muslim Identity and Secularism in Contemporary Turkey: 'The Headscarf Dispute' *Anthropological Quarterly* 58(4):161–9

Peacock, James, 1984, Religion and Life History: An Exploration in Cultural Psychology. In *Text, Play, and Story: The Construction and Reconstruction of Self and Society*. Stuart Plattner and Edward M. Bruner, eds. Washington, DC: American Ethnological Society, 94–116

Radwan, Zeinab 'Abdel Mejid, 1982, *Thahirat al-Hijab bayn al-jamʿiyyat*. Cairo: Al-Markaz al-qawmi lil-buhuth al-ijtimaʿiyya waʾl-jinaʾiyya

Riches, David, 1986, The Phenomenon of Violence. In *The Anthropology of Violence*. David Riches, ed. Oxford: Basil Blackwell

Said, Edward, 1979, *Orientalism*. New York: Vintage Books

Saktanber, Ayşe, 1994, Becoming the 'Other' as a Muslim in Turkey: Turkish Women vs Islamist Women. *New Perspectives on Turkey* 11:99–134

Scheper-Hughes, Nancy, 1992, *Death Without Weeping: The Violence of Everyday Life in Brazil*. Berkeley: University of California Press

Schiffauer, Werner, 1984, Religion und Identität. *Revue Suisse de Sociologie* 2:485–516

Smucker, Philip G., 1998, The Meaning of a Scarf: Turkish Students Fight to Wear Islamic Head Covering. *US News and World Report*, 16 March, www.usnews.com.usnews.issue/980316/16scar.htm ('Room in Turkey for Islam and in Islam for Feminism?', 16 March 1998)

Uçkun, Mümine Müezzinoğlu, 1993, Bir Genç Kızın Dramı. *Bizim Aile* 47(April):38–9

White, Jenny B., 1994, *Money Makes Us Relatives: Women's Labor in Urban Turkey*. Austin: University of Texas Press

Wikan, Unni, 1982, *Behind the Veil in Arabia*. Chicago: University of Chicago Press

Žižek, Slavoj, 1989, *The Sublime Object of Ideology*. London: Verso

Zuhur, Sherifa, 1992, *Revealing Reveiling: Islamist Gender Ideology in Contemporary Egypt* Albany, NY: State University of New York Press

Epilogue

Robert A. LeVine

Our best hope for the future development of psychological anthropology as an instrument of human understanding lies in studies that expand and deepen our awareness of the connections between personal experience, conscious and unconscious, and social and cultural patterns in the contemporary world. This volume gives us access to the connections revealed when the routine activities and processes of social life are violently ruptured, when following the cultural script for social participation no longer provides the expectable sense of security or makes sense at all. These chapters move us into emotional terrain where psychological anthropologists have rarely ventured. Some provide poignant descriptions of children and adults under conditions of terror, traumatic loss, chronic stress and stigma. Others describe the plight of people whose membership in the imagined communities of ethnic, religious, and national groups leads them to experience historical patterns of group conflict or collective decline in their personal lives. The authors feel their way along these dark paths, using conceptual resources from psychoanalysis as well as anthropology as instruments for exploration. The light helps, but there is a long way to go and much more to be done. In the meantime, we have a preliminary picture of these territories and can assess the challenge they present to our models of culture, psychological functioning and development, and our ways of investigating this complex realm.

The contributors to this volume are anthropologists and psychoanalysts, but this is not another search for a generalized common ground between the two fields. With their focus on serious real-world problems instead of theory and method, the authors take as given that unconscious motives and intrapsychic defences as well as cultural ideologies and political conflicts are involved. They vary in how much attention they pay to these two sides of the problems but not in their commitment to the necessity of social and cultural as well as psychological analysis. Most of their studies are frankly exploratory, raising problems without solving them, and are not doctrinaire in their interpretations. The subject matter of their research overwhelms efforts at simple explanation and calls for tentative interpretations, multiple approaches and more detailed investigations. In one of the most intensive studies, Robben shows how interview material combined with detailed historical knowledge can reveal the meanings – cultural and personal – of violent events and their impact on an urban people. The lesson is that in the case of traumatic and disruptive happenings, as in ordinary ethnography and clinical psychoanalysis, extended and microscopic observations, combined with interpretive abstinence and a consistent attention to context, are rewarded with deepening insight. The road to psychological depth begins with the phenomenological account of conscious experience shared by anthropologist and analyst.

Numerous themes in psychological anthropology are common to these chapters, and each reader will find dimensions of significance from a particular perspective. I shall mention two: the intergenerational transmission of stigma and loss, and martyrdom as a cultural representation of psychological significance.

The responses of children to disruptive and threatening conditions are in focus in several of the chapters: children as orphaned by massacres, as affected by ongoing political conflict, as heirs to parents' traumatic experiences, as immigrants in a society that stigmatizes them, and as carrying the burden of group identities inherited from the past that promote hostility to other groups or a generalized sense of failure and decline. Childhood has its vulnerabilities and sensitivities, of which we are perhaps too keenly aware, but children can be resilient, imaginative, and active in creating their own psychological solutions to the stresses and burdens they encounter. We are just beginning to understand and document how children do respond to conditions that seem to us stressful and disheartening and which are collective as well as personal.

The chapters raise many more questions than they answer, but they are unusual questions worth considering and pursuing in future research. On the one hand we see in the chapter by Carola Suárez-Orozco that children born to immigrants in the United States are not psychologically buffered from social stigma and discrimination as their parents were in fulfilling their dream of escaping worse circumstances in the home country; on the other hand, we see in Luhrmann's chapter on the Parsis of India that a pervasive sense of decline from a glorious past can be transmitted from generation to generation and may affect reproductive performance. The chapter by Volkan and Itzkowitz portrays a situation, in Turkey and Greece, in which the grievances of ethnopolitical groups against each other are transmitted to the young in each group over the generations. As with the Parsis, so with the Turks and Greeks, the focus is on the child's acquisition of a social identity that carries with it a sense of being wounded, requiring that the child identify with a symbolic construction several steps away from immediate experience in order to share the feeling of woundedness and the cultural defences against it. All of these chapters, and several of the others, raise questions of how and to what extent particular social and cultural conditions operate to buffer, replicate or intensify the impact of potentially threatening experiences in the parental or grandparental generation. These are questions that will reward further ethnographic and clinical investigation with a more differentiated view of childhood experience. The results are far from predictable, and the evidence as a whole will make it possible to generalize about children and their environments in the management of trauma, stress, and disruption of various kinds.

Another theme that cuts across several of the chapters is martyrdom, that is, the image of death and suffering that has moral meaning and calls for a moral response. Martyrdom may be a universal narrative of undeserved suffering or killing that entails an innocent victim and an evil perpetrator. Around this simple armature are wound amazingly diverse stories that form the core of religion, mythology, and politics in many cultures. In the stories of this volume, one gains insight into the emotional power of martyrdom as a gripping narrative commanding attention, repetition, and compensatory action. Traditional cultural narratives of martyrdom can connect with the psychic needs of individuals for defensive beliefs in the face of loss and injury. But the chapters of this book go beyond a psychodynamic interpretation of traditional narratives to show how, under traumatic conditions, individuals will communicate new accounts of martyrdom that energize collective action.

The creative politics of the mothers of the disappeared in Argentina is a case in point. By dramatizing their own martyrdom as blameless mothers who had lost their children, they were able to mount an appeal so universal among Argentinians that it could not be suppressed even by the dictatorial regime responsible for the disappearances. The repetitive drama of their public demonstrations provided an implicit but unmistakable accusation against the military government. In a different vein, Ewing's account of Muslim girls being excluded and chastised in Turkish schools merely for covering their heads shows how state action against religious zeal can be used to create narratives of martyrdom that propagate and intensify the devotion of the zealous. The Parsis, with their sense of decline and lack of collective action, seem to lack martyrs as well. They may in this sense be the exception that supports the rule, suggesting that heroes alone will not do to inspire renewal in an ethnic community.

Compensatory action for martyrdom can take many forms. Apart from the judicial punishment of murderers and the intensification of religious devotion, the cause of martyrs can give rise to a call for simple retaliation, in which the innocent become vengeful killers or at least rally to the cause of war and aggressive action, as described in this volume by Volkan and Itzkowitz. Thus the image of innocent victim, when publicly communicated as ideology, can give rise to peaceful action and self-control or to warfare and intergroup hostility, or to both, at different levels and across different boundaries of social action. Freud saw these two apparently opposite extremes as dynamically related: the story of Jesus Christ as martyr leaves the world with a message of universal love, but the moral self-policing of Christian guilt creates a need for war and religious persecution as an outlet for the repressed aggression. Freud's view was a pessimistic one in which the achievement of internal order requires a terrible price to be paid, and he would no doubt see the terrors described in this book as examples of that price.

But the world has changed since Freud's time. His pessimism had history on its side in 1929, when he wrote *Civilization and Its Discontents*. We now know an even greater number of terrible events than he did, but we also know societies that have attained what seems to be a permanent state of peace and security. It is because we take these latter societies as our basis for expectations of human social life that we are so shocked by the violence and traumatic experiences of this book. Although we recognize that stories of martyrdom can have a violent ending, we no longer assume that they must. Violence and aggression may reflect our human nature but their expressions and their containment reflect historical contingencies. Thus the diversity displayed in this volume means we need not assume that any of the patterns of violence and trauma described must be passed on to future generations.

Index

Abelin, E. L. 145
Acar, Feride 254, 262
acculturation 197
adoption, and child development 134
affective anesthesia 58
aggression
  Freud on 26–8, 127
  human capacity for 2
  and human nature 26–7
  innate aggression 28–31
  normal 33
  pathological 33–4
  and psychic spaces 58
  and psychoanalysis 26–35
  reactive aggression 31–5
aggressor, identification with 177
Ahmed, Leila 252 n.9
Alfonsin, Raúl 82
Allen, Woody 186
Allport, Gordon 19
ambiguity, and the uncanny 50, 52
American Psychiatric Association 20
Amnesty International 196
analysts, and treatment of victims of
    extreme violence 62, 63
Andreas, Peter 206
anthropologists, emotional effects of social
    violence on 62–3
anthropology
  and psychoanalysis 3
  and study of massive trauma 21–6
  and study of violence 11–12, 12 n.8,
    12–13
anti-Semitism 185–6
Antokoletz, J. C. 134–5
anxiety, and the uncanny 50–1
Anzieu, D. 59
Apo, see Öcalan, Abdullah
Aramburu, General 84, 85
Argentina, dirty war
  assault on the home 74–5

assault on social contract 70–1
'education' 80–1
impunity of executioners 96
intellectual framework for terror 6 n.3
long-term consequences 96
mother–child relations 76–80
objectives of 71, 82–3
operational techniques 75
opposition to 71, 81
symbolic violence 76
torture 79
Argentina, disappeared 71
  commission of enquiry 82
  corpses, obliteration of 83, 86
  discovery of mass graves 90–1
  exhumations 91–2, 94
  political importance of 95
  reburial 94, 95
  secrecy surrounding 88–9
Argentina disappeared, parents of
  and mummification 89–90
  and reburial 94–5
  and unelaborated grief 90
  stigma 89
  impaired mourning 88
  denial of death 88
  psychological problems of 88
  see also Mothers of the Plaza de Mayo
Atatürk see Kemal, Mustafa
attachment, and selves 183–4
Auerhahn, Nanette 132
Aulagnier, P. 59
Auschwitz 7, 56, 61
Avellaneda, Iris Etelvina de 79
Avineri, S. 152–3

babies, and traumatic events 132
Balkans conflict, and chosen trauma 23
Barker, Pat 14
Bar-On, Dan 25, 102
basic trust 55, 134

276